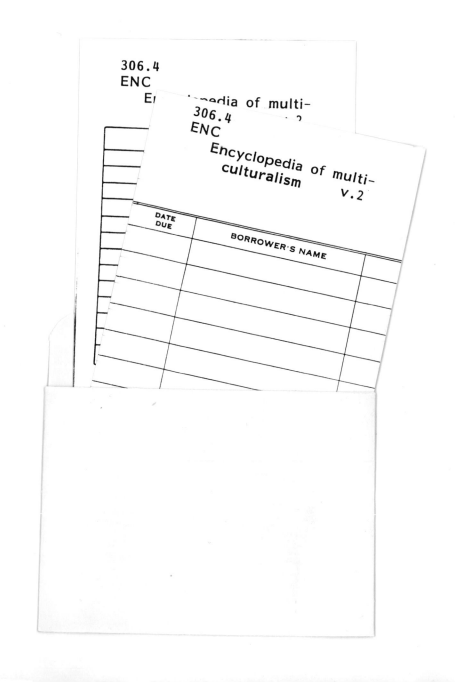

306.4
ENC
Encyclopedia of multi-

306.4
ENC
Encyclopedia of multi-
culturalism
v.2

DATE DUE	BORROWER'S NAME	

Encyclopedia of
MULTICULTURALISM

Encyclopedia of

MULTICULTURALISM

Volume 2

Mother Cabrini – Estonian Americans

Editor

SUSAN AUERBACH

Marshall Cavendish
New York • London • Toronto

Published By
Marshall Cavendish Corporation
2415 Jerusalem Avenue
P.O. Box 587
North Bellmore, New York 11710
United States of America

∞ The paper in these volumes conforms to the American National Standard for Permanence of Paper
for Printed Library Materials, Z39.48-1984.

Library of Congress Cataloging-in-Publication Data

Encyclopedia of multiculturalism / editor, Susan Auerbach.
   p. cm.
   Includes bibliographical references (p. 1767) and index.
   Contents: v. 1. A. Philip Randolph Institute–Business and corporate enterprise; v. 2. Mother Cabrini–
Estonian Americans; v. 3. Ethnic and minority group names–Inner city; v. 4. Daniel Ken Inouye–
Mythology, American Indian; v. 5. Names and name changes–Six Nations; v. 6. Slavery–Zoot-suit
riots.
   ISBN 1-85435-670-4 (set : alk. paper). — ISBN 1-85435-672-0 (v. 2 : alk. paper)
   1. Pluralism (Social sciences)—United States—Encyclopedias.   2. Multiculturalism—United
States—Encyclopedias. 3. Ethnology—United States—Encyclopedias. 4. United States—Ethnic re-
lations—Encyclopedias. 5. United States—Race relations—Encyclopedias.
I. Auerbach, Susan, 1956-
E184.A1E58   1993
306.4′46′0973—dc20   93-23405
                                                                                  CIP
                                                                                  AC

First Printing

Contents

Encyclopedia of
MULTICULTURALISM

C

Cabrini, Mother (Marie Francesca Xavier; July 15, 1850, Lombardy, Italy—Dec. 22, 1917, Chicago, Ill.):

Mother Cabrini, the first American saint of the Catholic faith, worked with Italian immigrants beginning in the nineteenth century. (Library of Congress)

First American saint. Supposedly white doves circled the house the day of her birth, and from the age of seven she wanted to be a missionary. After heading an orphanage, she founded the Missionary Sisters of the Sacred Heart in an empty Franciscan convent in 1880. By 1887 seven more convents were opened. Two years later, Mother Cabrini opened a mission in New York among Italian immigrants, the first American Motherhouse of the Missionary Sisters of the Sacred Heart. She became a U.S. citizen in 1909 and was canonized in 1946.

California: By the late 1980's, California had an extremely diverse population, a high rate of immigration, and innovative educational and social programs, all of which placed it in the vanguard of the debate on MULTICULTURALISM. The state had the nation's largest con-

centrations of Latinos, Asian Americans, and Pacific Islander Americans; these three groups accounted for more than three-fourths of the state's population increase of 6.2 million people between 1980 and 1990. The state's white population dropped from 78 percent in 1970 to 57 percent in 1990, while the combined population of ethnic minorities rose from 22 percent to 43 percent.

California has always had a large and diverse American Indian population, despite the decimation caused by resettlement near the SPANISH MISSIONS and by the onslaught of westward expansion in the eighteenth and nineteenth centuries. Native tribes were joined by Indians from other parts of the country during the period of termination and urbanization in the mid-1900's when U.S. policy urged Indians to leave their reservations. California cities were also magnets for African Americans from the South during the GREAT MIGRATION in the interwar years of the twentieth century; many blacks came to the state seeking better housing and defense jobs during and after World

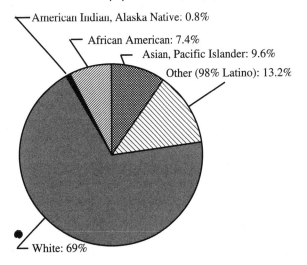

California Population by Race/Ethnicity: 1990
Total population: 29,760,021

American Indian, Alaska Native: 0.8%
African American: 7.4%
Asian, Pacific Islander: 9.6%
Other (98% Latino): 13.2%
White: 69%

Source: Bureau of the Census
Note: Californians of Latino origin (any race) made up 25.8 percent of the population.

S. I. Hayakawa was the first Japanese American from California to be elected to the U.S. Senate. (AP/Wide World Photos)

War II. The state's unique demography, however, comes from waves of immigration of Latinos and Asians in the nineteenth and twentieth centuries.

Latinos have been important to the development of the area since the Spanish colonial period. People of Spanish and Mexican descent were among the state's early governors and landholders. Numerous Mexican immigrants, especially since the Mexican Revolution (1910), have helped to transform a vast, undeveloped land into one of the most productive agricultural regions in the United States. Traditionally, however, Mexican Americans have shared little in the affluence they helped to create. Immigrants, especially undocumented workers, have typically worked in low-wage jobs as MIGRANT WORKERS, garment industry workers, food service employees, domestic help, and factory workers. Despite efforts to curb their growing economic and political clout in the 1970's, new generations of Chicanos have made significant gains, enter-

ing the middle and upper class. Growing numbers have become entrepreneurs and 617 Latinos had won elected office by 1990. The educational, health, and social service needs of this fast-growing population continue to challenge the state's public services and institutions.

The second largest ethnic minority in California is Asian, which amounted to almost three million people in 1990. The six largest Asian national groups were Filipinos (732,000), Chinese (705,000), Japanese (313,000), Vietnamese (280,000), and Koreans (260,000); other Asian-Pacific groups comprised another 251,000 people. These Asians, too, have had a long and bitter struggle.

Early Chinese immigrants, for example, worked mainly in mining; forced from the gold fields, they turned to railroad construction and later, agriculture or fishing. Like the Mexicans, the Chinese became a powerless community in a state they had helped to develop and feed. With the CHINESE EXCLUSION ACT of 1882, the Chinese population declined and remained low throughout California's peak growth years. After 1965, the Chinese American population boomed with new immigration from Hong Kong and Southeast Asia. Both newer immigrants and long-established Chinese with traditional ideals of hard work and education have succeeded. For example, Chinese have purchased about one-third of the land and at least 15 percent of the businesses in one Los Angeles suburb. CHINATOWNS such as the one in San Francisco continue to be prime tourist attractions and provide livings for thousands of Chinese Americans.

Japanese people began arriving in the state in the late 1800's; by 1990, they numbered more than 300,000. They were also the victims of anti-Asian prejudice and NATIVISM. The INTERNMENT of Japanese Americans during World War II completely disrupted this population. After the war, however, Japanese Americans rebuilt their lives and communities, with the Nisei (second) and Sansei (third) generations achieving marked success in terms of education and income. By 1980, a U.S. senator, two Congress members, two state assembly members, and dozens of local office holders in California were Japanese American.

Throughout the 1980's, California remained the top state of residence for immigrants and refugees from Southeast Asia. Indeed, immigrants from a variety of countries continue to list California as their intended home. They are attracted to the state's strong immigrant communities, healthy economy, and tradition of generous social services, despite the economic troubles of the early 1990's.

SUGGESTED READINGS. For details on cultural diversity in California, see *California, Inc.* (1982) by Joel Kotkin and Paul Grabowicz; Albert Camarillo's *Chicanos in a Changing Society: From Mexican Pueblos to American Barrios in Santa Barbara and Southern California, 1848-1930* (1979); Warren Beck and David A. Williams' *California: A History of the Golden State* (1972); *California: Five Centuries of Cultural Contrasts* (1976) by Julian Nava and Bob Barger; and *The Fourth Wave: California's Newest Immigrants* (1985) by Thomas Muller and Thomas Espenshade.—*Victoria Price*

California Agricultural Labor Relations Act (1975): Fulfilled the request made by Governor Jerry Brown at his inauguration in 1975 for a law which was fair to both growers and farm workers. The bill was designed to alleviate tensions between César CHÁVEZ's UNITED FARM WORKERS (affiliated with the AFL-CIO) and the International Brotherhood of Teamsters, the leading unions representing farm laborers. It included several important provisions. First, it guaranteed agricultural workers essentially the same benefits guaranteed to industrial workers by the National Labor Relations Act of 1935. Second, it allowed workers to vote by secret ballot to select which union, if any, they wish to represent them. The bill also limited the use of secondary boycotts against supermarkets and other distributors of farm produce by sanctioning only demonstrations that urged consumers to avoid those outlets that handled produce from employers with whom the unions had disputes.

California Rural Legal Assistance (CRLA): Nonprofit organization established in 1966 to provide free legal services to the poor. It was funded by the Office of Economic Opportunity and emphasized services of benefit to farmworkers, including many Mexican Americans. In the 1980's the group handled more than thirteen hundred cases annually. A CRLA task force studies the legal needs of the rural poor in education, housing, agricultural work, and other areas of employment. CRLA headquarters is in San Francisco, and it has a bimonthly publication called *Noticiero*.

Calvinists: Adherents of the Protestant theology associated with John Calvin (1509-1564), a religion which had immense influence both throughout Europe and in the founding of America.

Calvin's *Institutes* was published in 1559, and although Calvinism assumed many different forms during the sixteenth and seventeenth centuries, the *Institutes* constitutes its basis. Calvin's fundamental dogma was the total depravity of humanity, in contrast to the majesty, omniscience, and omnipotence of God. Because of Original Sin, the first disobedience of Adam and Eve, human nature is incontrovertibly corrupt and therefore damned. Nevertheless, through God's mercy and love, He has chosen for salvation those people whom He foreknew. This doctrine of ordained salvation was known as predestination.

These Elect, those chosen by God for salvation from the beginning of time, are responsible for proclaiming God's work in His world. Calvin therefore stressed the importance of the church, the community of visible saints by which God's intention is made visibly manifest. True revelation for the saved comes from reading the Scriptures. The church is also responsible for administering the Sacraments, the most important being the Eucharist, called by Calvin the Lord's Supper. Only those saved, those who had undergone a conversion experience, could partake of the Lord's Supper. In America, these restrictions on church membership were reinterpreted and liberalized throughout the seventeenth century.

The world, though an expression of God's handiwork, is meant for the Calvinist as a sojourn in exile: Since the true home of the Elect is in heaven, the petty pleasures of the world must be rejected. For Calvinists, human beings by themselves cannot perform good works in the world; they require God's strength, imparted to the human spirit, for moral action. Nevertheless, the early New England Calvinists known as PURITANS were called for a mission, a "covenant" or binding agreement with God to prepare His way. In America, they were, as Perry Miller has stated, "on an errand into the wilderness" to prepare for the millennium.

One of the most important Calvinist ministers in American history was Jonathan Edwards (1703-1758). Edwards, though opposed to excessive emotionalism in religion, was rigorous in his defense of predestination; his sermon, "Sinners in the Hands of an Angry God," is remembered as contributing to the religious revivalism sweeping America in the mid-eighteenth century, called the "GREAT AWAKENING."

Calvinism was extremely influential in America for other reasons as well. R. H. Tawney, for example, has argued that there is a close connection between Calvinism and capitalism—Calvin was the first important Christian thinker to accept usury. Many Calvinists in England and on the Continent immigrated to the New World to form communities where their religious beliefs would be accepted and would flourish. In Germany, Calvinists came from established centers in Brandenburg and the Palatinate; the French Protestant Church (or HUGUENOT) was founded in 1559 and many of its persecuted followers fled to America. Scotland adopted Calvinism officially in the year 1560, through the efforts of John Knox. The Anglican Church reflected many of Calvin's ideas, and Calvinism is the foundation of the following English dissenting churches whose adherents immigrated to America: PRESBYTERIANS, CONGREGATIONALISTS, and BAPTISTS. In America, the Pilgrims were Calvinist Congregationalists.

SUGGESTED READINGS. For Calvin's influence in the founding of America, consult Perry Miller's books:

Errand into the Wilderness (1956) and *The New England Mind: From Colony to Province* (1953). See also Sydney E. Ahlstrom's magisterial *A Religious History of the American People* (1972). For the connection of Calvinism and capitalism, see R. H. Tawney's *Religion and the Rise of Capitalism* (1937). For Calvin's theology, see Francois Wendel's *Calvin: The Origins and Development of his Religious Thought* (1963).

Cambodian Americans: Cambodian Americans are one of several Southeast Asian REFUGEE groups who came to the United States as a result of the VIETNAM WAR. Their population, as of 1992, numbered about 180,000.

History. The vast majority of Cambodians are Khmer who speak the Khmer language, although some Cambodians belong to Chinese and Muslim minorities. Khmer culture is rooted in the Buddhist religion, rice cultivation, and the civilization that peaked in the twelfth century with the completion of the great palace and temple compound of Angkor Wat. Contact with Asian Indian traders and emissaries influenced almost all aspects of Khmer culture, including the design and construction of the 215-foot towers of Angkor Wat. In the United States, Cambodians often watch Indian films dubbed in Khmer and decorate their apartments with posters depicting scenes from Hindu myths. Angkor Wat, the symbol of Khmer culture, appears on the country's flag and on the walls of many Cambodian American homes.

France made Cambodia a colony in 1864, and it remained part of French Indochina until independence in 1953. The lasting French influence on Cambodian culture is evident in loan words describing new technologies and administrative procedures, the inclusion of French bread at meals and cognac at weddings, and sports such as soccer and the ball-throwing game of *boules*. An independence movement began in 1942, but violence never reached the intensity that it did in Vietnam. Japan occupied Cambodia during World War II. In the early 1970's, Cambodian Communist guerrillas known as the Khmer Rouge expanded their control of rural areas and encircled cities. Extensive American bombing of Cambodia, as part of the Vietnam War, did further harm by driving Cambodians into the cities, thereby reducing food production in the countryside. In April, 1975, the Khmer Rouge captured the capital of Phnom Penh.

Over the next four years, the Khmer Rouge conducted a cruel revolution. The entire population of 7 million, including children, was forced to work with little food on collective farms modeled on those in China during the Cultural Revolution of the 1960's. Anyone associated with education, wealth, or urban lifestyles and occupations could be executed. The Khmer Rouge urged children to monitor their parents for signs of disloyalty to the new regime. Forced marriages were common (Cambodian marriages had traditionally been arranged by families). The Khmer Rouge taught disrespect for Buddhist monks, who had previously been central to community life. By the time Vietnamese troops drove the Khmer Rouge from power in 1979, about 1 million Cambodians had died, and their culture had been fundamentally disrupted.

The scope of this GENOCIDE for a small country like Cambodia would be equivalent to killing all Americans in the New York City and Los Angeles areas.

Migration. Only after the Vietnamese invasion in 1979 were Cambodians able to flee in large numbers. By 1980, a dozen camps just inside the Thai border sheltered more than 500,000 REFUGEES. The largest camp, Khao I Dang, was home to more than 140,000 Cambodian refugees, making it the second largest Cambodian "city" at the time. Conditions in the camps were harsh. The refugees established temples and schools, but food, water, and cooking fuel were limited. Thai guards and Cambodian bandits threatened the refugees' safety. Some camps came to be controlled by Cambodian guerrilla factions.

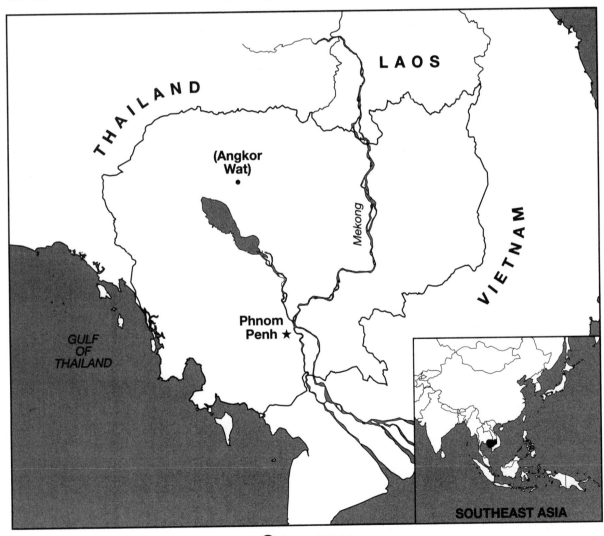

CAMBODIA

Many Cambodians fled to border villages in Thailand in the wake of the 1979 invasion of Cambodia by Vietnamese troops. (AP/ Wide World Photos)

Refugees arriving in Thailand before 1980 could register with the United Nations and then be interviewed for resettlement by immigration officials from Western countries. Many refugees waited for years in the camps before being accepted for resettlement elsewhere. More than 25,000 Cambodians arrived in the United States in 1981. By 1992, the United States had admitted 150,000 Cambodian refugees; smaller numbers had been resettled in Australia, Canada, and France. In 1993, the last of the approximately 350,000 Cambodian refugees in Thailand returned to Cambodia to vote in the country's first free election in more than two decades.

Community Life. The Cambodian refugee migration to the United States is unique because there were only a few hundred Cambodians in the country when the first REFUGEES arrived. Unlike other newcomers, they could not rely on help from an established ethnic community. Many were still suffering from the loss of family members, the uprooting of Khmer culture, and the harsh conditions of the Khmer Rouge years. Although most Cambodians came from villages and small towns, they were suddenly thrust into large American cities. American voluntary agencies reset-

tling the refugees were forced, by the high cost of apartment rentals, to locate Cambodians in marginal neighborhoods such as the Tenderloin in San Francisco and Uptown Chicago. Despite the adversity of their surroundings, Cambodians have contributed to the economic and cultural vitality of these areas. With their Vietnamese neighbors they have opened businesses, filled public schools and community colleges, and become involved in local politics. More than two-thirds of the refugees live in California, Massachusetts, Washington, Texas, and Pennsylvania. The Cambodian community in Long Beach, California, numbering more than 20,000, is the largest in the country.

Most Cambodian American communities have a BUDDHIST temple supported by community contributions. Each temple has several monks. A group of lay men and women visit or live at the temple to help provide for the monks, who perform weddings, exorcise bad luck, and preside over annual holidays such as the New Year in April.

The most important Buddhist ceremony among Cambodians is Pchum Ben, the Festival of the Ancestors, in September. Families prepare food at home and then bring it to a central location, usually a high school or community hall. Family members offer dishes and rice to the monks, and donate money and items for use in the temple, such as incense and candles. By eating a small portion of the food, the monks assure that a family's ancestors will not be hungry. After the monks have eaten, the remaining food is distributed to all participants. Eating a dish that has been prayed over before being served to a monk is thought to remove old sins and bring good fortune.

Mutual assistance associations (MAAs) operated by refugees are also found in most Cambodian communities. In many respects, these organizations have replaced the American voluntary agencies that initially supervised refugee resettlement. The MAAs employ caseworkers who help refugees with virtually all the problems of adapting to a new environment: family crises and mental health, employment and public assistance, housing, and sponsoring relatives to the U.S. Some refugees complain that the associations only refer them to low-paying jobs. Others think the associations are too involved in Cambodian politics. Never-

theless, the associations perform vital functions for the community, such as providing translators when non-English speaking refugees interact with courts, hospitals, and social welfare bureaus. Many associations have also raised funds to buy houses for use as Buddhist temples. Gang prevention is an increasingly important activity in urban communities.

Social Adjustment. A film titled *The Killing Fields* (1984), about how a Cambodian journalist survived the Khmer Rouge and came to the United States, symbolizes for Cambodians their community's integration within American society. The leading Cambodian role is played by Haing NGOR, a former refugee. The film gave Americans a greater understanding of their government's responsibility for Southeast Asian refugees and of the horrors of the Khmer Rouge regime.

Like other Asian Americans, Cambodians place a high value on the family. Single brothers and sisters may live with a married sibling, and grandparents often reside with their children and grandchildren. Adjusting to American family forms is one of the greatest difficulties for Cambodians. Children become Ameri-

A Cambodian couple is resplendent in their wedding finery. (Smithsonian Institution)

canized and want more independence than would be permitted in Cambodia. Because they often have greater English skills and knowledge of American society than their parents, Cambodian American children are no longer subordinate to their elders—the reverse of traditional family roles. Youth are increasingly reluctant to have kin select their marriage partner, although arranged marriages are still common. These problems can be especially acute, because many Cambodian households are headed by a widow whose husband was killed by the Khmer Rouge.

Employment has been particularly difficult for Cambodian Americans, since many arrived with little formal education and no knowledge of English. With hard work, some Cambodians have become successful professionals and entrepreneurs, like the hundreds of refugees in Southern California who operate doughnut shops. Frequently, however, the REFUGEES are only qualified for unskilled and semiskilled jobs. Jobs such as soldering electronic parts, bagging candy, and packaging frozen food do not usually provide enough in-

This San Francisco market is owned by Cambodian Americans from Battambang, the westernmost province of Cambodia. (Eric Crystal)

come to support a large family and may not include health insurance. It is often necessary to have a younger sibling, a boarder, or even another family live with a working husband and wife so that the whole household can share expenses. Cambodians are also among the heaviest users of welfare and other public assistance within the immigrant population.

Cambodians come to terms with these and other hardships with remarkable equanimity. BUDDHISM helps them accept the inevitability of change. Their history exemplifies the selective incorporation of new cultures. Further, they survived much worse conditions in Cambodia.

SUGGESTED READINGS. More information on Cambodian history can be found in David P. Chandler's *The Land and People of Cambodia* (1972). See William Shawcross' *Side-Show* (1979) for the period of American military involvement and Elizabeth Becker's *When the War Was Over* (1986) for the Khmer Rouge period. Cambodian refugees' own experiences are related by Haing Ngor and Roger Warner in *Hang Ngor: A Cambodian Odyssey* (1987) and by Molyda Syzmusiak in *The Stones Cry Out* (1986). David W. Haines provides an overview of Southeast Asian refugee resettlement in his edited volume *Refugees in the United States.—Jeremy Hein*

Camp Grant Massacre (Apr. 30, 1871): Vicious campaign of Apache extermination. Early in 1871, Congress appropriated seventy thousand dollars to be used for gathering the Arizona and New Mexico APACHES on reservations, promoting peace and "civilization" among them, and avoiding an outbreak of warfare. A band of Arivaipa Apaches, who hoped to settle down and lead peaceful lives, and who had put themselves under U.S. military protection, was encamped near Camp Grant, Arizona. In an early morning attack, the sleeping Apaches were slaughtered by a party of armed Tucson citizens, assisted by Papago Indians.

Relations between the Apaches and the surrounding white population had been strained for some time because of economic conditions. Some area residents bitterly resented the local ranchers' practice of buying hay from the Apaches, since this jeopardized one of the few dependable sources of their own income in the territory. Moreover, on April 10 an Apache raiding party, in an act of retaliation, drove off some of the Papagos' cattle and horses. Three days later a white settler was killed. Those who pursued the raiders ran into a large war party, and during the ensuing skirmish three more Anglos were killed. Although it was denied that any Camp Grant Apaches were involved, the citizens of Tucson were irate. On April 30, some 150 Tucson residents attacked the Apache encampment. In thirty minutes the battle was over. Nearly all of the dead had been mutilated.

Most of the Arivaipa men were away at the time, hunting with their chief, Eskiminzin. Thus, of the Indians slain (108, by one count, about one fourth of the entire camp), only eight were men. Of the twenty-nine children who were taken prisoner, only two escaped. Five were later recovered from Arizona citizens. The rest were taken to Mexico to be sold as slaves.

The perpetrators of the massacre were arrested, but they were almost immediately acquitted by a Tucson jury. In the weeks following the massacre, no word of remorse was ever uttered. Instead, all statements were calculated to justify what had been done. Newspaper reports of the carnage, however, shocked readers all over the nation and ultimately influenced the formulation of a new federal Indian policy, which came to be known as President Ulysses S. Grant's "peace policy." Its objective was to assemble all the Apaches on reservations and to promote peace and "civilization" among them. This new policy, which was intended to conciliate the Apaches, was partly successful, but hostilities in Arizona and New Mexico continued until 1886, when Chief GERONIMO surrendered. Subsequently, remnants of Apache tribes were sent to reservations in the Southwest.

SUGGESTED READINGS. For a fine introduction to the Camp Grant Massacre, see *Death Song: The Last of the Indian Wars* by John Edward Weems (1976) and Dan L. Thrapp's *The Conquest of Apacheria* (1967). A definitive biography of one of the most notable participants in the event, the Apache chief Geronimo, is Angie Debo's *Geronimo: The Man, His Time, His Place* (1976). Another excellent work and first-hand account of the battle is *The Truth About Geronimo* (1929) by Britton Davis.

Campbell, Ben Nighthorse (b. Apr. 13, 1933, Auburn, Calif.): American Indian politician. Of Cheyenne tribal descent, Campbell was born in northern California. After serving in the Air Force during the Korean War from 1951 to 1953, Campbell attended San Jose State College and received his B.A. in 1957. An interest in judo led him to train and compete as an amateur; he received a gold medal at the 1963 Pan-Am Games and was a member of the U.S. judo team in 1964. After establishing himself as a rancher and jewelry designer in Colorado, Campbell decided to campaign for political office. From 1982 to 1986, he served in the Colorado State Legislature. In 1986, Campbell was elected to Congress as a representative·from Colorado's third congressional district. Campbell then campaigned for a seat in the Senate and, in 1992, became the first individual of American Indian descent to be elected to the Senate. Controversy surrounding the selection of a direct descendent of Christopher Columbus to serve as a grand marshall of the 1993 Rose Parade in Pasadena, California, prompted the parade committee to invite Campbell to serve as well. Sensitive to issues concerning the status of American Indians, Campbell accepted the invitation.

Campbell, Kim (Avril Phaedra Campbell; b. 1947, Vancouver, British Columbia, Canada): Canadian lawyer and politician. She studied political science at the University of British Columbia, where she went on to earn her law degree. Eager to launch a career in politics, Campbell won a seat on the Vancouver school board in 1980. In 1988, she won election as a conservative candidate for a seat in the Canadian Parliament and soon won appointment as the nation's minister of Indian affairs. Prime Minister Brian Mulroney appointed Campbell to be Canada's first woman attorney general and justice minister in 1990; by January of 1993, she had been promoted to serve as defense minister. In February of 1993, Mulroney announced his intention to step down as prime minister, and Campbell became a front-runner in the campaign to succeed him as leader of Canada's ruling Progressive Conservative Party. After winning election on June 13, 1993, Campbell became the first woman prime minister in Canadian history. Her party was defeated in October, 1993, and she lost her post to Liberal Party leader Jean Chrétien.

Canada—Asian immigration: Asian immigrants to Canada may be divided into three major groups: East Asians, South Asians, and Southeast Asians. The East Asian group includes people of Chinese, Japanese, Korean, or Filipino ethnic ancestry. South Asians are those people from India, Pakistan, Sri Lanka, or Bangladesh. Some Asian Indians and other South Asians immigrated from countries such as Tanzania, Kenya, Uganda, South Africa, Guyana, Trinidad, and the Fiji Islands rather than directly from South Asia. Southeast Asians came to Canada from Vietnam, Cambodia, or Laos. Chinese immigrants were originally attracted to Canada by gold

A busy shopping district in Hong Kong; the announcement that control of Hong Kong would revert to mainland China in 1997 prompted many wealthy Hong Kong Chinese to migrate to Canada during the 1980's and early 1990's. (AP/Wide World Photos)

mining and by work building the Canadian Pacific Railroad. The period of greatest Chinese immigration occurred between 1858 (the beginning of the Fraser River Gold Rush) and 1923. Before the 1960's, most came from rural areas of China. More recently, there has been a large increase in immigration from Hong Kong; these immigrants have a more urban, cosmopolitan background. In the early 1990's, Hong Kong, India, Sri Lanka, and the Philippines all provided large numbers of immigrants to Canada.

Chinese Canadians are either descended from men who immigrated before 1947 or from families who arrived after 1947. The Japanese in Canada are more heterogeneous in that they are a mixture of ISSEI, NISEI, SANSEI, and YONSEI people. The first Japanese immigrants arrived in Canada between 1877 and 1907. The Koreans arrived later than 1907. In 1967, Canadian immigration laws were changed to be far less restrictive with regard to racial, national, or ethnic criteria; the new laws have allowed much more Third World immigration. After the fall of President Thieu in South Vietnam in 1975, six thousand political refugees immigrated to Canada. They were typically well educated and skilled. From 1979 to 1980, sixty thousand Southeast Asians, including many BOAT PEOPLE, were accepted as political REFUGEES in Canada through both government and private sponsorship.

East Asians tend to live in distinct ethnic communities in Canada, such as CHINATOWNS. They have often maintained their native languages, which means that their children grow up bilingual in their native language and English.

Group solidarity is very important among East Asian Canadians. Social and physical segregation in their work and residential environments has helped to strengthen their sense of community. For Koreans and Filipinos, local and regional associations, including churches, have served as important community institutions. The majority of East Asians are Christians even though among Chinese, ANCESTOR WORSHIP is still quite strong. The early Japanese immigrants were more often Buddhists.

South and Southeast Asians who immigrated to Canada live in Canada's major metropolitan areas. For these immigrants, job availability, housing, community support, and chain migration have resulted in geographical localization. From British Columbia to Quebec, some entire streets or neighborhoods have become commercial and educational centers for South Asian people.

Many South Asian Canadians speak English as a second or commercial language, since their home countries were part of the British Empire. Almost all immigrant adults, however, use their Asian mother tongue at home, in the community, and in the workplace. South and Southeast Asians try to maintain their traditional values and customs while assimilating into the Canadian cultural mosaic.

SUGGESTED READINGS. See *The Voyage of the Komagata Maru: The Sikh Challenge to Canada's Colour Bar* (1989) by Hugh Johnston; *From India to Canada: A Brief History of Immigration, Problems of Discrimination, Admission, and Assimilation* (1986), edited by S. Chandrasekhar; *Freedom Isn't Free: A Boat People Story* (1985) by Evelyn Friesen (as told by Phu Sam); and *Jin Guo: Voices of Chinese Canadian Women* (1992), compiled by the Women's Book Committee of the Chinese Canadian National Council. More general sources include *Coming Canadians: An Introduction to a History of Canada's Peoples* (1988) by Jean R. Burnet and *Between Two Worlds: The Canadian Immigration Experience* (1983), edited by Milly Charon.

Canada—black immigration: Although most Americans are familiar with the role played by Canada as a destination for fugitive slaves before the outbreak of the Civil War, few are aware that the history of blacks in Canada is at least as old as their history in the United States.

In the French colonial era, economic dependence on the fur trade and reliance on American Indians virtually eliminated demand for black slaves to serve as agricultural laborers or as domestic servants. By the end of the seventeenth century, however, serious colonization efforts by the French began to change the demands for labor. Royal governors and citizens of the colony requested and received permission to import black slaves; by the time British forces conquered Montreal in 1759, more than 1,000 black slaves resided in New France, and most were employed as domestic servants.

The most noticeable early influx of blacks to Canada came during and after the American Revolution. Some 30,000 Loyalists chose to resettle in Nova Scotia and New Brunswick once the 1783 American peace treaty was signed. Among their prized possessions were black slaves who worked as personal servants and highly skilled craftsmen. Other black immigrants came as a result of the British military policy that offered freedom and land grants to any slaves who joined their forces. More than 3,000 free blacks entered Nova Scotia from the port of New York as part of the withdrawal of British and Loyalist troops from the United States.

In 1796, British transport ships brought more than 550 MAROONS, or black guerrilla fighters, from Jamaica to be settled in Halifax, Nova Scotia, where they would pose less of a threat to British colonial interests. Although they agreed to labor on military fortifications in Halifax and were settled in homes vacated by emigrants to Sierra Leone, the Maroons were dissatisfied with conditions in Canada. After lengthy negotiations with the Sierra Leone Company, the British government agreed to allow the Maroons to set sail for Sierra Leone in 1800.

The next large wave of black immigrants to Canada came as a result of the War of 1812. Once again, the British forces offered freedom to American slaves as a reward for military service. Free black Loyalists were eager to join Canadian forces in order to avoid the prospect of a return to slavery that might well occur if Americans invaded Canada. Between 1812 and 1815, more than 2,000 American slaves arrived in Nova Scotia, and many others took refuge in Upper Canada. After the war ended, many American slaves continued to seek refuge in Canada.

The UNDERGROUND RAILROAD provided another source of black immigrants. While it had its origins in a network of routes developed to assist slaves to safety as early as the 1780's, the Underground Railroad became the most active conduit for American fugitive slaves in the wake of the FUGITIVE SLAVE LAW of 1850. Rather than allow the extradition of runaway slaves who had sought refuge in the North, American abolitionists stepped up their efforts to transport fugitives to Canada. Many free blacks from northern states were also encouraged to migrate to Canada in pursuit of economic gain and equality. In the month after the act was signed into law, some 3,000 blacks crossed the border into Canada, and by 1860 it is estimated that nearly 40,000 more black immigrants had followed, bringing the total estimated black population to more than 50,000. The outbreak of the Civil War in the United States did not initially stem the flow of refugees and immigrants, since the Fugitive Slave Law of 1850 remained in effect. Once the Emancipation Proclamation was issued in 1863 and the Lincoln Administration began to allow the military recruitment of African Americans for the war effort, many refu-

Families of West Indian and African descent celebrate their heritage at cultural festivals such as this one in Edmonton, Alberta, Canada. (Photo Search Ltd./Murty)

gees were convinced to take up arms. Many of these Canadian recruits decided to take up permanent residence in the United States after the war ended and their families often followed them south. By 1871, the black population of Canada was reduced to approximately 20,000 and remained at that level through the turn of the century.

By the early twentieth century, Canada had adopted restrictive immigration policies and created racial quotas that inhibited the growth of the black population. This situation was dramatically reversed in the early 1960's. Canadian immigration reforms in 1962 and 1966 eliminated quotas at the same time that new restrictions in Great Britain made it a less desirable destination. Blacks from former British colonies in Africa as well as those from Jamaica, Haiti, and Trinidad in the Caribbean migrated to Canada and formed large immigrant communities in cities such as Montreal, Toronto, and Vancouver. By the late 1970's, researchers estimated that residents of West Indian descent made up nearly 80 percent of the black population of Canada. Caribbean immigrants and their descendants infused black Canadian society with their rich cultural heritage in music, religion, sports, food, and the arts.

SUGGESTED READINGS. Robin W. Winks's *The Blacks in Canada: A History* (1971) provides an overview of the black experience in Canada. For a more up-to-date account of the influx of West Indian immigrants and their impact on Canadian society, see *Identity: The Black Experience in Canada* (1979). Leo W. Bertley's *Canada and Its People of African Descent* (1977) provides demographic analysis of the black Canadian population.

Canada—Latino immigration: Canadian immigrants who emigrated from Spanish-speaking countries can be divided into three groups. The largest group came from any of the nineteen Spanish-speaking Latin American countries in Central America, the Andean region, and the Southern Cone area. A smaller group came from Spain and the Canary Islands. The smallest group is immigrants from North African Spanish-speaking countries such as Morocco. Many Latinos who emigrated to Canada, especially during the 1970's, did so because of political persecution or the loss of family members, jobs, or political positions in their native countries. This was particularly true of people from Argentina, Chile, and Uruguay. The war in El Salvador also drove many Salvadoran REFUGEES to emigrate to Canada. Latino Canadians vary widely in their ethnic community links, educational levels, political ideologies, and socioeconomic status.

Latino immigration to Canada has its roots in a series of sociopolitical events in Latin America and in Canada's response to those events. Canada's economic expansion necessitated changes in its immigration policy, which allowed Latinos to enter and look for employment. Latinos immigrated to Canada in four major waves or phases: the lead, Andean, coup, and Central American waves. The first two waves were economically driven, while the last two were linked to war and political persecution.

The lead (or first) wave is typified by Latinos who entered Canada between World War II and 1973. These immigrants, who were professionals and skilled workers, came from industrialized countries such as Argentina, Brazil, Mexico, Venezuela, and Uruguay. Many of them had a Spanish ethnolinguistic link to European immigrants already in Canada. Religion played a very important part in this wave. For example, MENNONITE churches in countries such as Argen-

tina, Paraguay, and Mexico helped in the immigration and settlement of Latinos in Canada. The 1973 Canada Amnesty legislation made possible the Andean wave, in which thousands of Ecuadorians and Colombians became Canadian immigrants. People in this wave were highly motivated to succeed economically. The Andean wave encountered social problems such as language and cultural barriers, job disruption, and lack of job promotion opportunities in Canadian society.

The coup wave was typified by those who left countries such as Chile, Uruguay, and Argentina after those states became military dictatorships. Many of these immigrants were very highly educated professionals. This wave has regularly supplied the Canadian economy with both white-collar and blue-collar workers.

The Central American wave was a direct result of the civil wars in El Salvador and Guatemala and the Sandinista Revolution in Nicaragua in 1979. Compared with immigrants in the other three waves, the Central Americans are generally less educated, less skilled, and less proficient in the English language.

SUGGESTED READINGS. For more information see *Ontario Ethnocultural Profiles* (1981) by the Ontario Ministry of Culture and Recreation. Mata Fernado's *Latin American Immigration to Canada, 1946-1981* (1983) is a very helpful source. Also see Rene Rodas' *Children of a Postponed Dream* (1993). For migration statistics see *Immigrants in Canada: Selected Highlights* (1990), published by Statistics Canada: Housing, Family, and Social Statistics Division. For information on Canadian refugees, see Gerald E. Dirks's "A Policy Within a Policy: The Identification and Admission of Refugees to Canada," in *The Canadian Journal of Political Science* 17 (June, 1984), pp. 279-307. *Ethnic Demography: Canadian Immigrant, Racial, and Cultural Variation* (1990), edited by Shiva S. Halli, Frank Trovato, and Leo Driedger, is a good general source.

Canada—native population: Three major groups—Indians, MÉTIS, and INUITS—compose Canada's native people; the Canadian constitution identifies them as aboriginal peoples. The Métis are primarily descendants of French Canadian and Scottish Canadian trappers and Indians. The term "Inuit" is supplanting "Eskimo," and the two words are commonly used synonymously. Canadian natives are found in six main cultural areas: the Northeast, sub-Arctic, Great Plains, Plateau, Northwest Coast, and Arctic. There are eleven broad linguistic groupings of native languages, each of which branches into several languages and dialects. As of 1991, the combined Canadian native population was approximately 405,000.

Most registered Indians belong to one of 595 Indian bands formed in almost every region of Canada. Most of these bands have one or more Indian reservations set aside by the government for their exclusive use. Since the passage of the 1876 Indian Act, Indians in Canada have been making steady political, social, and economic progress, but unemployment is higher and educational attainment significantly lower, proportion-

on various socioeconomic indicators such as employment or postsecondary educational degrees.

The Canadian Inuits, or Eskimos, primarily live in small communities in areas such as the Mackenzie Delta, the Arctic Islands, and the Northwest Coast Territories. They speak a language called Inuktitut. Their small communities are usually located on bays, river mouths, inlets, or fjords. The location of these communities reflects a culture that was formerly tied to fishing, hunting, and gathering. Since the arrival of the whalers and fur traders in the nineteenth century,

These Canadian youngsters wear outfits that reflect the cultural traditions of their Indian heritage. (Photo Search Ltd./Marilyn McAra)

ally speaking, than figures for the general Canadian population.

The Métis are known for their drive for self-government, which was manifested in the Red River Valley Rebellion (1869-1870) led by Louis Riel. The actual number of Métis is not known. Even though there has been a Métis cultural awareness movement in Canada, many people of Métis origin have not identified themselves with it. Like the Canadian Indians, the Métis lag behind the general Canadian population

traditional Inuit life has changed from fishing and hunting to fur trapping. Life for the Inuit people has also changed because of modern technology such as communication satellites, telephone, radio, and television programs, some of which are aired in Inuktitut. The general health of the Inuit people has improved significantly, and a variety of government programs in areas such as education, social affairs, local government, and economic development have also improved. The majority of the Inuit communities are now incorporated into villages or hamlets that are managed by their own elected councils. Native Canadians are known for their masterful arts and crafts.

SUGGESTED READINGS. For more information, see E. Palmer Patterson's *Indian Peoples of Canada* (1982), Joseph F. Krauter and Morris Davis' *Minority Canadians: Ethnic Groups* (1978), and Susan Cowan's edited volume of first-person Inuit accounts, *We Don't Live in Snow Houses Now: Reflections of Arctic Bay* (1976). Robert McGhee's *Canadian Arctic Prehistory* (1978) reconstructs ancient native life in the Arctic.

important "receiving" countries in the world for immigrant groups.

This constant, large-scale immigration replenishes the population and adds arrivals from all continents of the world. Most important, Canadian immigration laws were altered in 1967: Criteria for admittance were changed to be far less concerned with race, ethnicity, and nationality. This has resulted in greater numbers of Third-World peoples entering Canada and contributing to its ethnic diversity. The country has an official policy of MULTICULTURALISM that stresses tol-

Residents of Alberta, Canada, celebrate their diverse ethnic roots at the Heritage Day festival. (Photo Search Ltd./Murty)

Canadian ethnic diversity: The multiethnic character of Canadian society is increasingly inclusive. It is also far more complex than the obvious division of Canadians into English-speaking and French-speaking communities. Except for historic native Indians and Inuits (Eskimos), Canada has been populated by immigrant groups for the past three-and-a-half centuries; moreover, the so-called native peoples of Canada were almost certainly immigrants from earlier centuries. Canada, along with the United States and Australia, remains one of the most

eration in intergroup relations and support for the preservation of ethnic heritage.

Visitors to Canadian cities note the variety of ethnic communities and the ways in which this multiethnicity is comparable to that of New York or Los Angeles. Increasing numbers of Asians populate Vancouver; Toronto has sizable southeastern European communities; African Americans live in Halifax and all other major urban centers; and French-speaking Caribbean nationals, including Haitians, are prominent in Mont-

Ethnic Origins of Canadians: 1991

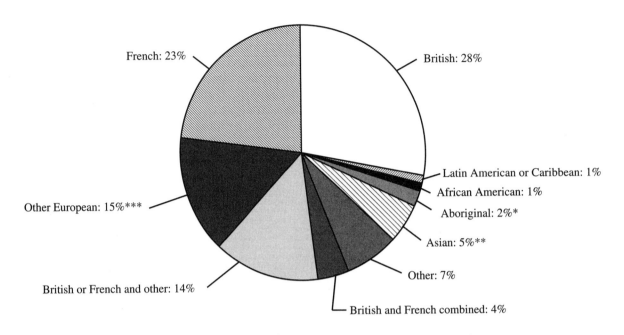

French: 23%

British: 28%

Latin American or Caribbean: 1%

African American: 1%

Aboriginal: 2%*

Asian: 5%**

Other: 7%

British and French combined: 4%

British or French and other: 14%

Other European: 15%***

Source: Data are from "The Daily," Statistics Canada, February 23, 1993.
*Includes American Indian, Inuit, and Métis
**Especially Chinese and Asian Indian
***Especially German, Italian, and Ukranian

real. Each of these groups contributes to an ethnic mosaic.

Native Populations: Aboriginal Canadian groups may be divided into four categories: status Indians, who are registered under the Indian Act of Canada; non-status Indians, who are not officially registered; Métis, whose ancestry is mixed, consisting of both Indian and non-Indian peoples; and Inuits or Eskimos, northern natives who live mainly in the Arctic regions of Canada, including the Northwest Territories and northern Labrador and Quebec. Each of the four groups remains a functioning community or group of communities. Archaeological research in the Yukon Territory of Canada since the 1950's has suggested that there may have been human habitation there approximately 120,000 to 150,000 years ago. This was the time of the emergence of *Homo erectus*, or modern man. These people had the ability to hunt large animals, produce functional cutting edges, and domesticate animals. They may have been the ancestors of the current aboriginal population of Canada.

Europeans began to settle in Canada in the 1500's.

At that time, there were an estimated 200,000 Indians and 10,000 Inuits. These numbers soon declined dramatically. One reason was the wars that were fought with the immigrating Europeans; another reason was disease, much of which was introduced by the Europeans. By the 1870's, there were only 80,000 Indians left in Canada. This declining ethnic presence changed dramatically in the 1940's, when the native population saw accelerated growth. By 1985, census figures indicated that more than 700,000 Canadians reported that they or their ancestors belonged to at least one native group. Since the numbers of native Canadians cannot be replenished by additional immigration, the question of ASSIMILATION into Euro-Canadian culture is particularly acute. The erosion of traditional Indian cultures combined with an enforced "CULTURE OF POVERTY" have led to both increasing dependence on Euro-Canadian cultures and increasing unease about this dependence.

Canadian native groups, along with others in the United States and Brazil, have produced a new Indian leadership that explicitly opposes forced Indian assimilation into Canadian society. Some of these leaders contend that Indians should not have to be concerned about becoming Canadians culturally, since they are the original Canadians. Others emphasize that they must continue to be concerned about being accepted as Canadians, since there are powerful groups within the nation that continue to discriminate against non-European Canadian cultures. By 1991, this leadership had developed political movements that fought for native rights including the recovery of historically native-owned lands in the north and west of Canada. The increasing political power of native Canadian groups has been recognized at the provincial level, as in the Manitoba assembly, as well as nationally. Political activism is supported by a continuously increasing native population which, in 1992, was estimated at one million people. This large community now includes 533 "bands," or individually distinctive Indian groups and settlements.

English and French Communities. The "charter groups" in Canada are those whose ancestors originated in either France or the British Isles. Both historically and presently, the two communities are dominant in their own geographic areas. French speakers predominate in the province of Quebec, and English speakers predominate in much of the rest of Canada. There are increasing numbers of French speakers throughout the nation, however, especially in regions such as the maritime provinces in the southeast. A sizable minority of English speakers also remains in the urbanized centers of Quebec, especially in the city of Montreal.

These two major groups, along with some native peoples, represent a federalist type of ethnic integration in Canada—in other words, they are largely regionally based. Other ethnic groups tend to have no regional geographic base with which they especially identify or that specifically encourages their cultures to be dominant in that region. An exception to this pattern are very small religious groups such as the HUTTERITES, whose regional and cultural bases are not legally protected.

Canada's black population continued to grow in the 1990's as a result of immigration, typified by this University of Alberta student from Africa. (Aneal Vohra/Unicorn Stock Photos)

This federalist approach to ethnic integration is reflected in Canada's linguistic dualism. Quebec province residents generally speak French, while English predominates in most of the rest of the country. There are some Indians and INUITS who speak neither language, but they are a small minority of the total national population. The vast majority of recent immigrants to Canada become committed to the use of one of the two major languages, with most speaking English. These groups include the newest arrivals from Asia, Africa, and Latin America. This is a concern for French-speaking Canadians and is accentuated by lower birthrates among them; contemporary English speakers have higher birthrates nationally than French speakers, a reversal of historic trends. Whether French Canadian culture can remain functional with fewer people and most immigrants becoming English speakers is a continuing ethnic dilemma in Canada.

An attempt in 1992 to write a new constitution for Canada that would give French speakers as well as aboriginal groups and some western provinces more political power was defeated in a national referendum. Fifty-four percent of the voting population rejected the idea. The rejection implied substantive differences among Canadians as to their country's cultural identity and the role of the French-speaking province of Quebec.

French speakers are engaged in ongoing debate on the most appropriate means to maintain their identity. While a minority is assimilating into English-speaking society, the majority prefer cultural continuity, with French as their first language. This is especially true of French speakers who live in Quebec. Some prefer that Quebec be in a loose federation with the rest of Canada; some want to be certain that Quebec in the future controls its own tax monies and has self-determination in domestic affairs. Others, called separatists, would like Quebec to become a separate nation rather than only a distinct society within Canada. In 1992, most opinion polls showed that only about one-third of the residents of Quebec preferred full separation from Canada. The issue of French culture in Canada is "ethnic": It concerns whether and how language, values, and folkways should be preserved by the second-largest ethnic community in the country.

Black Settlers. The black community in Canada differs from that in the United States in a number of ways. It has enjoyed political and legal freedoms longer, has always been a much smaller ethnic minority in Canadian provincial populations, and, until the 1960's, was far less aggressive in seeking and claiming civil rights. Most important, black Canadians are from very heterogeneous backgrounds.

There were blacks among Canada's earliest seventeenth century settlers. Others came to Canada via the UNDERGROUND RAILROAD before the American Civil War. Additional black immigrants arrived directly from Caribbean colonies and countries. The diversified history of the black community has been one reason that blacks have not united until relatively recently to work for social change in Canada. This pattern is shifting in spite of the fact that many blacks claim they have been less rigidly defined than in other nations, such as the United States.

In the early 1990's, for example, there was intensified publicity about the treatment of blacks by urban police forces, especially in Toronto. The question of whether there was an increasing "Americanization" of attitudes by the police and others toward blacks was raised. These questions helped to create a more unified

In the 1960's, René Levesque became one of the leaders of the separatist movement, seeking independence for the Canadian province of Quebec—an enclave of French-speaking culture. (Library of Congress)

black response to the larger society. They also encouraged a new militancy and strengthened the idea that blacks are a distinct category in Canada's ethnic mosaic rather than another assimilable group. The idea of a distinct community is likely to be reinforced by newer immigration trends in which blacks are shown to be arriving in Canada in increasing numbers, mostly because of changes in immigration laws that are more favorable to immigrants from black nations.

Asian Immigration. One of the fastest-growing immigrant communities in Canada is from Asia, with the majority of Asian immigrants coming from Hong Kong. In the early 1990's, the bulk of these immigrants resided in western coastal areas such as Vancouver. There has also been a large Chinese community since the 1960's in major Canadian cities such as Toronto. These new Asian immigrants are culturally different from previous Chinese communities: Before the 1960's, most Chinese immigrants were from agrarian villages in southern China and were resilient in maintaining traditional customs. More recent immigrants from Hong Kong tend to be cosmopolitan and international in their culture before arrival.

Generally, the Hong Kong immigrants have a strong civic identification of being "Canadians." Simultaneously, they have resisted ASSIMILATION in particular cultural areas such as language. They maintain ethnic pride in the Chinese component of their Canadian affiliation. Unlike many immigrant groups arriving in Canada, immigrants from Hong Kong are typically entrepreneurs with sufficient funds to establish businesses, buy real estate, and contribute to Chinese and other charitable organizations. Large-scale Asian immigration to British Columbia in the 1990's has benefited that province's trade and financial markets as well as added to the ethnic diversity of its major cities. It has also, however, led some residents to attempt a revision of immigration codes to restrict Asian immigrants. There was also controversy in the 1980's when Canada admitted large numbers of Southeast Asian refugees, especially BOAT PEOPLE.

Immigration and Population Trends. The major growth factor affecting Canada's population is not immigration but natural increase, which accounts for 80 percent of the increase of births over deaths. Yet Canada remains one of the three main immigrant-receiving nations in the world when the numbers of immigrants are compared with the existing population. Between 1991 and 1992, the largest numbers of arrivals came from Hong Kong, India, Sri Lanka, Poland,

the Philippines, China, and Iran. More people arrived in Canada from each of these countries than arrived in the United States.

These figures demonstrate that the changes in Canada's immigration laws have resulted in a dramatic shift away from Western European and United States immigrants seeking permanent resident status in Canada. They also indicate how global the ethnic mosaic of Canada is.

What no figures can describe, however, is how Canada's multiethnic society actually functions. Canadians continue to formulate not only the relationships among ethnic communities but also what those relationships imply for national stability and consensus. Canada's ethnic groups are united in addressing the issue of Canadian identity. They are not united, however, as to what models are appropriate for the future, covering a spectrum of visions from ASSIMILATION to separatism.

SUGGESTED READINGS. Jean Leonard Elliot's *Immigrant Groups: Minority Canadians* (1971) looks at Canada's major immigrant groups, such as Italians, and less-researched groups, such as black Canadians. *Ethnic Demography: Canadian Immigrant, Racial, and Cultural Variation* (1990), edited by Shiva S. Halli, Frank Trovato, and Leo Driedger, is a comprehensive contemporary discussion of the country's diversity. See also *Ethnic Encounters: Identities and Contexts* (1977), edited by L. Hicks and Philip E. Leis, and *The Canadian Ethnic Mosaic: A Quest for Identity* (1978), edited by Leo Driedger.—*William T. Osborne*

Canadian policy of multiculturalism. *See* **Multiculturalism—Canadian policy**

Canadians in the U.S.: Canada and the United States share a peaceful border that is thousands of miles long. Relations between the two countries have long been so stable that much of the border is unpatrolled and goes nearly unnoticed. Because the two countries are neighbors and because English is the dominant language both in the United States and in much of Canada, there are strong similarities in the cultures and lifestyles of the two countries. For these same reasons, the contributions of Canadian culture to the United States have been subtle and have often, like the border between the two countries, gone almost unnoticed.

Migration to North America from Europe was extensive in the early nineteenth century. Between 1820 and 1860, more than five million Europeans came to

A U.S. Navy submarine proceeds through the locks in honor of the 1959 opening of the St. Lawrence Seaway between the U.S. and Canada. (AP/Wide World Photos)

the United States; at the same time, many other millions went to Australia, Latin America, Africa, and Canada. All these receiving countries and continents experienced growth that allowed their populations to expand into interior regions and, in the cases of the United States and Canada, to move westward.

Yet Canada, in addition to receiving immigrants, was also a "sending" nation; people left Canada to immigrate to the United States. These immigrants can be divided into two groups: those who were born in Canada and moved to the United States, and those who first immigrated to Canada from Europe and then, in what has been termed a "second immigration," moved southward to the United States. In the first half of the nineteenth century, it is likely that several hundred thousand people moved permanently to the United States from Canada. Many of these immigrants were European-born. The second migration of Europeans via Canada to the United States continued into the twentieth century.

Historical Reasons for the Second Immigration. Through much of the nineteenth century, Western Europe experienced radical economic downturns. Many Irish and French (and some English) people re-

alized that immigration to either Canada or the United States was their only option for escaping continued poverty. The British government encouraged immigration to Canada, because it wanted its colony to be populated with British citizens who would counteract French influences. The inducement to immigrate was supported by very low fares on ships from Great Britain to Canada. Irish immigrants, in particular, had reservations about resettling in British territory; privately, their true destination was often the United States. Hundreds of thousands of Irish people and others took advantage of the cheap rates for passage to the mouth of the St. Lawrence River and the free transportation offered to the city of Quebec. After arrival, however, many immigrants simply walked to the United States from these Canadian locations. In the case of the Irish, it is suspected that a majority did not remain in Canada but relocated to the eastern United States. Thus, passing through Canada became the most economical way for the very poor to reach the United States. With its unpatrolled border, Canada also enabled relatively easy entrance to the United States for people who might have been rejected by American authorities at immigration centers in New York.

After immigration laws were strengthened by the United States via the IMMIGRATION ACT OF 1924 and other legislation, the total number of people allowed to enter from other continents was only 150,000; further, because of ancestry regulations, more than half these spaces were reserved for immigrants from the British Isles. The same laws, however, allowed exceptions for immigrants from the Americas, including Canada: There were no restrictions placed on persons entering from Canada in the early part of the twentieth century. The result was continuing legal and illegal immigration from Canada to the United States. A majority of the immigrants from Canada were poor and Catholic, and many of them were culturally French. The reception of these large numbers of entrants from or through Canada altered the ethnic and cultural orientations of some American towns, especially the small cities throughout New England where many immigrants first settled.

Economic Contributions of Canadian Immigrants. In the middle of the twentieth century, there was a constant movement of Canadian-born immigrants to the Northeast, Florida, and California. In New England, many French Canadians were brought in to work at brick-laying or in cotton mills. Some were temporary workers, returning to Canada in the winters when the types of jobs they performed were not so available; others settled permanently. These skilled and unskilled laborers often became the focus of debates in the United States. They were charged with breaking strikes and with accepting low wages and poor working conditions. They were defended, however, for helping businesses to staff seasonal employment slots that many Americans would not accept. Those who settled permanently, especially in New England, have contributed to the multilingualism of some northeastern cities, strengthened the Catholic church

from the Canadian border. The cotton mills once typical of New England, for example, are now found in the Carolinas. Canadian laborers who might have been willing to work in Massachusetts are less likely to travel to southern states.

Two-thirds of the Canadians living in the United States in the early 1990's had immigrated before 1960. Nearly 30 percent of Canadian immigrants in the United States in 1990 were age sixty-five or older. Most of the Canadians who immigrated before 1960 continue to live in the northeastern part of the United

This accordion maker from Quebec is one of many Canadians involved in cultural exchange with the U.S. (Smithsonian Institution)

in the area, and created alternative French-speaking social and business ventures, including newspapers, nightclubs, and retail businesses.

Beginning in the late 1960's, the majority of Canadians settling in the United States were professionals, skilled artisans and technicians, managers, or sales and service workers. Very few were classed as laborers, household workers, or farmers. The low-wage jobs that had once attracted unskilled Canadian laborers gradually became more concentrated in the southern and southwestern parts of the United States, away

States, but those who immigrated after 1960 are more likely to live in the Sunbelt states, especially California and Florida. In the 1990's, immigrants from Canada had higher income and educational levels than Americans on average.

Although more than 100 million people cross the United States-Canadian border each year, fewer than twenty-five thousand people a year immigrated from one country to the other in the 1980's and early 1990's. This is far less than the 140,000 who migrated between the two countries in 1910 or even the 59,000 who migrated in 1960. Immigration by Canadians to the United States declined by nearly two-thirds between 1960 and 1990.

Social and Cultural Contributions. Since the 1970's, most Canadian immigrants have had origins similar to the majority of the U.S. population, sharing a common language, common religions, and similar customs. ASSIMILATION into American society has been relatively easy for these late twentieth century immigrants. Further, the newest immigrants have been much less restricted by geography than the unskilled laborers of previous immigrations were. Their professions may locate them outside the northeastern states, and their consequent dispersion contributes to faster and more complete assimilation. Their social and cultural contributions are not geographically limited.

Among the social, commercial, and cultural contributions of Canadians in the United States is the journal *Canada Today*, published in Washington, D.C. Newspapers are published by Canadian immigrants in many states. Canadians have a foundation in New York City that promotes projects in the United States that relate to Canada. Canadian fraternal organizations are located throughout the United States, including Boston, New York, Florida, and Chicago. "Canada day" is celebrated wherever there is a concentration of Canadians or where Canadians make up a significant percentage of tourists; for example, there are "Canada day" festivals in Desert Hot Springs, California; Daytona Beach, Florida; Myrtle Beach, South Carolina; and at Walt Disney World in Orlando, Florida. Many commercial and trade organizations promote commerce between the United States and Canada, and veterans groups such as the Royal Canadian Legion draw members from British Commonwealth Forces now residing in the United States.

Canadian social and cultural contributions are not limited to those people who have immigrated to the United States: They also include the contributions of Canadians who may visit infrequently but communicate Canadian perspectives on social and political matters to Americans. Some residents of Canada attempt to influence American life through legislation and international agreements. Canadians have been particularly influential in environmental issues, insisting, for example, that the United States change certain policies about air pollution and acid rain that affect Canada. Canadians, along with Mexicans, have also attempted to work out free-trade policies, arguing for legislation that does not adversely affect Canadian business. In

addition, Canadian governmental social programs were examined by politicians in the early 1990's as the United States considered altering its health and human services policies. Finally, Canadian immigration policies have occasionally directly affected American international politics. The main example of this occurred during the Vietnam War era, when some American draftees fled to Canada on a temporary or permanent basis. Canada's acceptance of the young men was criticized by some Americans and praised by others.

One area in which Canadian culture has influenced the United States is in the world of sports. Two sports played widely in the United States came from Canada: ice hockey and lacrosse. A number of places in Canada have claimed to be the "birthplace" of ice hockey, which developed in the nineteenth century. The National Hockey League (NHL), created in Canada in 1917, accepted its first United States team, the Boston Bruins, in 1924. In 1993 there were sixteen U.S. teams competing in the NHL. Many Canadians play on the U.S. teams (as many baseball players from the United States play on the two Canadian teams in major league baseball). For example, one of hockey's most famous players, Wayne Gretzky, joined the Los Angeles Kings in 1988.

Lacrosse is directly descended from a game that was played by North American Indian tribes and copied by Canada's French colonists. It became widely popular in the 1860's and in 1867 was declared Canada's national game. By the late nineteenth century, lacrosse had become popular in the United States as well. Although hockey is played professionally in the United States, lacrosse has remained a sport played mostly by high school and university teams, primarily in the eastern United States.

Many Canadians have moved to the United States to pursue careers in film, television, and the music business. William Shatner, Michael J. Fox, and Leslie Nielsen are among the well known Canadian-born actors working in the United States, as are comic actors Martin Short and John Candy. Newscaster Peter Jennings and television personality Alex Trebek are also Canadian. In the world of music, jazz pianist Oscar Peterson and singers and songwriters Joni Mitchell and Neil Young are from Canada. Canadian literature is increasingly appreciated in the United States. Canadian writers who moved to the United States include mystery writer Ross Macdonald (actually born in California, Macdonald grew up in Canada) and influential literary critic Hugh Kenner. Although fiction writers William Kinsella and Margaret Atwood reside in Canada, they are well known in the United States.

The long border between Canada and the United States remains one of the most peaceful in the world. Two-way immigration has not compromised that peace, but it has altered both countries politically, socially, and culturally.

SUGGESTED READINGS. James Hill Parker's *Ethnic Identity: The Case of the French Americans* (1983) presents detailed studies of French-speaking communities that have migrated to the United States from Canada. *Migration Between the United States and Canada* (1990) by John F. Long et al., delineates the demographics of migration patterns. See also Roger Neville Williams' *The New Exiles: American War Resisters in Canada* (1971).—*William Osborne*

Captain Jack [Kintpuash] (c. 1840, Calif.—Oct. 3, 1873, Fort Klamath, Oreg.): Chief of the Modoc Indians who led resistance to removal to the reservation. In 1864, the Modocs, who lived in Southwest Oregon and Northern California, ceded their territory to the United States

Captain Jack, an Oregon Modoc chief, was hanged for leading the resistance to removal to the reservation. (National Archives)

and were required to go to a reservation. Discontented there, the chief of the Modocs, Kintpuash, better known to white settlers as Captain Jack, led the Modocs back to the California border and refused to return. The attempt to bring the runaways back precipitated the Modoc War of 1872-1873. Kintpuash and his followers retreated to the lava beds of California, where they carried on a remarkable defensive movement for several months. Finally, they were overcome, and Captain Jack and three other leaders were hanged on October 3, 1873.

Hattie Caraway was the first woman to be elected to the U.S. Senate. (AP/Wide World Photos)

Caraway, Hattie (Hattie Ophelia Wyatt; Feb. 1, 1878, near Bakerville, Tenn.—Dec. 21, 1950, Falls Church, Va.): First woman U.S. senator. After ten years of marriage, including rearing three children and managing a farm, Caraway's husband, Thaddeus Caraway, then U.S. senator for the state of Arkansas, died. His wife took over his position in 1931. In 1932, when asked to preside over the Senate for a day, she announced that she was seeking renomination. She won, becoming the first woman elected to the U.S. Senate. Caraway was elected for a second term in 1938. She served on a number of committees, and in 1943 cosponsored the EQUAL RIGHTS AMENDMENT.

Carlisle Indian School: First off-reservation American Indian school in the United States, founded by General Richard Henry Pratt in 1879. By the late nineteenth century, Indian reformers and the U.S. government were encouraging Indian youth to be taught white habits of hygiene, clothing, work ethic, and worship. Thus started the Indian school system. General Pratt, a Civil War cavalry officer, opened the U.S. Training and Industrial School at Carlisle, which later became the Carlisle Indian School, in Carlisle, Pennsylvania. The school was a model for subsequent American Indian boarding schools, which taught the idea, in Pratt's own words, of "immersing the Indians in our civilization." One of the most famous graduates of the school was legendary athlete Jim THORPE.

Carmichael, Stokely (Kwame Toure; b. June 29, 1941, Port-of-Spain, Trinidad): African American political activist. A native of Trinidad, Carmichael attended New York City's Bronx High School of Science and was graduated from HOWARD UNIVERSITY in 1964. He

Stokely Carmichael, a radical leader of the Civil Rights movement, eventually settled in Guinea, Africa. (AP/Wide World Photos)

worked for civil rights in various roles before becoming the leader of the STUDENT NONVIOLENT COORDINATING COMMITTEE (SNCC) in the early 1960's. After 1963, and especially after his "BLACK POWER" speech in 1966, Carmichael pushed SNCC away from the idea of non-

violent integration and toward "black liberation," splintering and eventually destroying the group. Carmichael later became a BLACK PANTHER, but resigned when he found that group too conciliatory toward whites. He married the African singer Miriam Makeba and moved permanently to Guinea.

Carr, Vikki (Florencia Bisenta de Casillas Martínez Cardona; b. July 19, 1940, El Paso, Tex.): Mexican American singer. Carr began singing with the Pepe Callahan Mexican-Irish Band in Los Angeles. She recorded numerous albums with Liberty Records from 1961 to 1969 and then with Columbia Records from 1970 to 1975. By 1993, she had recorded nearly fifty best-selling records, including fifteen gold albums. Her hits include "Can't Take My Eyes Off of You" and "It Must Be Him"; among her twelve albums with CBS-Mexico are *Disculpame* and *Ni Princesa*. Carr was named Woman of the Year for 1970 by the *Los Angeles Times*, made numerous television appearances through the 1970's and 1980's, and received a Grammy Award in 1985 for her Spanish-language album *Simplemente Mujer*. In 1981, she founded the Vikki Carr Scholarship Foundation to provide higher education opportunities for Mexican American young people. Carr has served on the World Vision Hispanic Advisory Board and has been active in several other charity organizations.

Carson, Kit [Christopher] (Dec. 24, 1809, Madison County, Ky.—May 23, 1868, Fort Lyon, Colo.): Frontiersman, Indian agent, and general. Carson migrated to Taos, New Mexico, in 1825, serving as a cook, guide, and hunter for exploring parties, most notably John C. Frémont's expeditions into Wyoming and California (1842-1846). In 1853 Carson became an Indian agent. He served as a Union general in the Civil War and was instrumental in subduing the NAVAJOS (1863-1864).

Carson, Rachel (May 27, 1907, Springdale, Pa.—April 14, 1964, Silver Spring, Md.): Conservationist, naturalist, and writer. An article published in *Atlantic Monthly* evolved into her first book, *Under the Sea-Wind: A Naturalist's Picture of Ocean Life* (1941). After World War II, she wrote a series of twelve booklets on national wildlife refuges for the U.S. government. Carson's first widely received book was *The Sea Around Us* (1951). After a friend came to her because her bird sanctuary had been sprayed with the experimental pesticide DDT, Carson wrote *Silent Spring* (1962), a thoroughly researched work on the irresponsible use of industrial

Rachel Carson, shown in her study, wrote Silent Spring, *which lambasted the use of DDT and launched the environmental movement.* (AP/Wide World Photos)

pesticides world-wide. The book, attacked by the agricultural chemical industry, was instrumental in inspiring the environmental movement.

Cart War of 1857: Incident at the Mexican-Texas BORDER that received international attention. Trade between the Texas coast and San Antonio had been controlled by Mexican teamsters since colonial times. After Anglo businessmen unsuccessfully attempted to take over the lucrative business in 1857, they began attacking and murdering Mexican teamsters along the route between San Antonio and Indianola, Texas. Attacks continued until the Mexican minister to the United States protested in October, 1857, resulting in a company of Texas Rangers being sent to the area by the legislature. By December, 1857, the attacks stopped and the "war" ended.

Carver, George Washington (1865, near Diamond Grove, Mo.—Jan. 5, 1943, Tuskegee, Ala.): Early African American scientist. Born a slave, Carver earned a B.S. (1894) and an M.A. (1896) in agricultural science at Iowa State College. He spent his working life at TUSKEGEE INSTITUTE in Alabama, where he promoted land conservation and helped poor southern blacks—and the South generally—during the Depression. His research led to revolutionary discoveries in agriculture and the development of numerous products from peanuts, sweet potatoes, and soybeans. He also found ways to utilize cotton waste and to extract pigments from clay. Carver left his estate to a research foundation at Tuskegee.

Cassatt, Mary (May 22, 1844, Allegheny City, Pa.—June 14, 1926, Château de Beaufresne, France): Impressionist painter. In 1872 her painting *Pendant le Carnavel* was accepted by the Paris Salon. In 1874 Impressionist painter Edgar Degas noticed one of her paintings and invited her to join the Impressionists. She showed works in four out of eight of the Impressionist salons before she and Degas split from the group in 1882. Cassatt's famous paintings include *The Tea Cup* (1881), *Woman and Child Driving*, and *The Bath* (1891). She is noted for her paintings of children. Cassatt was the most widely recognized female artist of her time.

Castañeda, Carlos [César Aranha] (b. Dec. 25, 1925, Cajmarca, Peru?): Peruvian American anthropologist and writer. Castañeda came to the United States in 1951, where he began his studies in 1958 at the University of California at Los Angeles and received his Ph.D. in 1970. He is best known for a series of autobiographical, philosophical, anthropological narratives describing his apprenticeship with an American Indian Yaqui *brujo* (medicine man or sorcerer) named Don Juan (*Matus*). In *The Teachings of Don Juan: A Yaqui Way of Knowledge* (1968), *A Separate Reality: Further Conversations with Don Juan* (1971), and numerous sequels, Castañeda attracted a strong and loyal readership with his portrayal of the mysticism of Yaqui beliefs and metaphysics.

Cather, Willa (Willa Cather Sibert; Dec. 7, 1873, Back Creek Valley, near Winchester, Va.—Apr. 24, 1947, New York, N.Y.): Writer. When she was a child, Cather's family moved from stable colonial Virginia to Nebraska, where she lived among impoverished immigrants and other uprooted families. She kept her hair short, called herself William, and generally preferred the company of women. Her first published works were a book of poetry, *April Twilights* (1903), and a collection of short stories, *The Troll Garden* (1905). Her novels portray strong female characters in the Nebraska frontierland of her childhood. They include *O Pioneers!* (1913), *The Song of the Lark* (1915), *My Ántonia* (1918), and *A Lost Lady* (1923), which won the Pulitzer Prize.

Catholic–Protestant relations: Catholics are the largest group of Christians in the world, totaling about one billion people, or about a fifth of the world's population.

About fifty-seven million Catholics live in the United States. Protestant churches include hundreds of Christian denominations and claim a membership of about 420 million people worldwide and about seventy-nine million in the United States.

Historically, Catholics and Protestants in the United States have often been at odds. Yet the differences between them were only partly religious; they were also ethnic, because the two religions were strongly identified with certain national groups. Competition between different national and ethnic groups helped to foster religious antipathies. Even today, in many people's minds, terms such as "WASP" (WHITE ANGLO-SAXON PROTESTANT) and "Irish Catholic" immediately conjure up certain cultural traits and STEREOTYPES. Relations between Catholics and Protestants since the 1960's have in general been increasingly marked by ecumenical movements (promoting Christian unity) and cooperative involvement in social causes.

Historical Background. Protestant denominations grouped because they all together stem from the Reformation, a religious and political movement that began in the 1500's in Germany. Resulting from criticism of the Catholic papacy and failed attempts to "reform" the Catholic church, the Reformation led to the emergence of the major Protestant denominations, such as the LUTHERANS, PRESBYTERIANS, METHODISTS, BAPTISTS, and CONGREGATIONALISTS. The Reformation also resulted in the schism of Europe into Protestant and Catholic countries. The historical animosity between these two interpretations of Christianity, as well as the political implications of their separation in Europe, is still reflected in their relations throughout the world, including the United States.

As European nations moved into the lands of the New World, only the colonies in what would become the United States and parts of Canada were founded by Protestants. French, Spanish, and Portuguese colonists established Catholic strongholds in much of Canada and all of Central and South America. The early American colonists, with links to England, were generally anti-Catholic as a result of the historical separation of the Anglican church (the Church of England) from the ROMAN CATHOLIC church.

Although the colonists rebelled against the English in order to obtain their independence, most Americans in positions of power maintained their linkages to the Protestant (Anglican) tradition. Many also shared the animosity of the British toward Irish Catholics. The anti-Catholic bias that existed in the colonial period persists in the contemporary United States to a certain extent. Yet this bias was, and is, tempered by the principles of religious freedom and SEPARATION OF CHURCH AND STATE upon which the United States was founded.

Early immigrant groups often sought religious freedom in the United States, since their Protestant sects were being discriminated against by Catholic powers in Europe. These included the Pilgrims and the BAPTISTS. New Protestant groups, such as the QUAKERS, the Separatists, and the SHAKERS, developed in the colonies.

Although most of the early colonists were Protestant, a large group of Catholics lived in Maryland. During the years of the major waves of immigration to the United States, the Catholic population grew rapidly. From 1790 to the mid-1860's, more than two million Catholics immigrated, mainly from Germany and Ireland. From 1870 to 1900, more than three million Catholics came, most of them from Italy, Austria-Hungary, and Poland. By 1900, Irish Americans had become the most powerful force in the Catholic church in the United States. Since they tended to immigrate to major industrial cities and to take extremely low-paying jobs, Catholics were often found in pockets of extreme poverty.

In spite of the large immigration of Catholics, the United States remained essentially a Protestant nation and has, in general, maintained its Anglo-Saxon, liberal, and Protestant culture and leadership. American frontier conditions helped to extend the range of new Protestant groups, which then spread beyond the United States. Major Protestant groups in the United States include the Baptists, the LUTHERANS, the Churches of God, the Churches of Christ, the EPISCOPALIANS, the MORMONS, the PRESBYTERIANS, and the METHODISTS. The South, dominated by the Southern Baptists, is sometimes called the "Bible belt" because of the inhabitants' emphasis on God and religion as the center of their lives. By contrast, ROMAN CATHOLICS are a minority in all regions of the United States except in the large cities of the Northeast, such as Boston, and the Southwest, such as Los Angeles.

Ethnic Struggles. Some Protestant Americans subjected Catholic immigrants to a form of prejudice called "NATIVISM," questioning and denigrating their patriotism, morals, and religion. This prejudice led to neighborhood conflicts and to separation between Protestant and Catholic groups, even long after their immigration to the United States. Nativism sometimes led to violence, such as the burning of the Ursuline convent in Charlestown, Massachusetts, in 1834, and to blatant job discrimination such as that against Irish Catholics.

Catholic groups managed to gain extraordinary political power in certain cities, such as Boston, New York, and Chicago, where Irish and Italian Catholics predominate. In more recent years, Latino Catholics in states such as Texas have also gained political in-

cation system and recommending that Catholics educate their children in this system of parochial schools, rather than in public schools. They have developed an extensive system of schools and universities with outstanding reputations, staffed by several of the orders of Catholic priests and nuns.

Theological Relations. Catholic-Protestant relations have been defined to a large extent by the theological differences between the two groups. Catholics long professed that only they were true Christians and that

The Vatican II Council, called by Pope Paul VI in the early 1960's, broke ground in building unity among all Christians. (AP/Wide World Photos)

fluence. In general, Catholics were not considered acceptable candidates for national political office, including the presidency, until John F. Kennedy was elected president in 1960. That event was a watershed in American history and served to break down the barriers between the groups to a large extent.

Catholics have in general practiced a separatist policy in the United States, establishing a Catholic edu-

they should therefore not associate with Protestants. This attitude has made Catholics insular, dampening an evangelistic spirit among them and preventing the building of bridges between the two groups.

Protestants agree with Roman Catholics on the foundations of Christianity, namely the belief that there is only one God and that in God there are three Persons: the Father, Son, and Holy Ghost, who together form the Trinity. Protestants, however, have disagreed with Catholics about the nature of faith in God and the grace of God, and about the authority of the Bible. Protestants stress grace whereas Catholics emphasize sin. Protestants believe that people "are saved by faith through grace," not by good works, which Catholics emphasize. God is loving and forgiving, Protestants assert, and God's grace comes to people through Jesus Christ. To Protestants, salvation is consequently a gift and is not based on one's own merit,

raments and rituals, which are major parts of Catholic worship. In addition, Protestants emphasize the importance of the laity—church members who are not clergy. Lay members teach Sunday school, perform major church functions, lead worship, and even preach, evangelize, and manage the church in Protestant denominations. In Catholicism, clergy perform these functions almost exclusively.

The Catholic focus on sin and the Protestant focus on grace has made dialogue difficult, since the Catho-

The first meeting of the World Council of Churches took place in Evanston, Ill. (National Archives)

as Catholics assert. Catholics base their beliefs both on the Bible and on their own church traditions, which come from the declarations of popes, church councils, creeds, and dogmas. Protestants do not agree that the pope should be the highest Christian authority on earth; they look instead to the authority of the Bible. Most Protestant religious services stress the minister and his sermon on the Word of God rather than sac-

lic church has been unwilling to change its position on basic issues such as clerical celibacy, women in the ministry, birth control, abortion, and homosexuality. Many Protestant groups have compromised biblically based positions on these issues in accordance with social trends. Yet Protestants are by no means united on their positions regarding these controversies. Certain denominations, such as the BAPTISTS, remain conservative and in essential alignment with Catholic positions, whereas other denominations, such as the EPISCOPALIANS, have veered far from literal interpretations of the Bible in response to social trends.

The Vatican II Council was called by Pope Paul VI in the early 1960's in an attempt to build unity among all Christians and to open up the Catholic church. Since then there has been more dialogue and more movement toward ecumenism. In 1965, the Joint Consultation Committee was established by the World Council of Churches, a Protestant body, and the Vatican Secretariat for Christian Unity to attempt some formal linkages. In the United States, the National Council of Churches heads the ecumenical movement. In 1966, the National Council and the Catholic Bishops' Commission on Ecumenical Affairs established a joint group to keep in touch with each other and work together. In addition, the Episcopal, LUTHERAN, and Catholic churches developed a liturgy that was essentially interchangeable in an effort to achieve some sense of commonality.

After Vatican II, several state church councils included Catholic members, especially in Texas, where ten Catholic dioceses joined; in Arizona, where Protestants and Catholics joined to form the Ecumenical Council; and in Ohio.

Political and Social Relations. Catholics and Protestants have worked together in a number of social and political arenas to spread the Christian gospel. In the area of religious education, they have joined forces to establish ecumenical theological seminaries. The Graduate Theological Union at Berkeley, California, for example, includes twelve different denominations that have joined to provide a program of advanced studies for graduate degrees. The Boston Theological Institute represents seven institutions. Both schools contain ROMAN CATHOLIC and Protestant influence.

Catholics and Protestants joined together in the 1960's for social action, prompted by the challenge of the CIVIL RIGHTS MOVEMENT. In the momentous MARCH ON WASHINGTON in 1963, Catholics and Protestants joined forces. *Living Room Dialogues,* a guide for Catholic-Orthodox-Protestant lay discussion on social issues, put out in 1965 by the National Council of Churches and the Paulist Press, was used by thousands of groups throughout the country. In 1966, the first annual Faith and Order Colloquium met in Chicago to launch a continuing forum on basic questions affecting Christian unity. Other watershed events in ecumenism during the 1960's included the World Council of Churches assembly in Sweden and the Interreligious Committee in 1968, which brought American Protestants and Catholics closer together.

Certain elements of the Catholic church in the United States that have supported social causes and rejected the rigid control of the Vatican have begun to align themselves more closely with Protestants, but this alignment has brought criticism from the Catholic hierarchy. Protestant groups have also joined in the protests of Catholics who have been reprimanded by the pope for their political opposition to certain U.S. government policies.

SUGGESTED READINGS. For a discussion of Catholic-Anglican relations, see *Call to Full Unity: Documents on Anglican-Roman Catholic Relations* (1986) by Joseph Witmer and Robert Wright and *So Near and Yet So Far: Rome, Canterbury, and ARCIC* (1986) by Hugh Montefiore. Lutheran-Catholic relations are explored in *Justification by Faith: Lutherans and Catholics in Dialogue VII* (1985), edited by George Anderson et al. *Exploring the Faith We Share* (1980) by Charles LaFontaine and Glenn Stone discusses the common beliefs that Catholics and Protestants share that override their differences. Kenneth Underwoods' *Protestant and Catholic* (1972) presents the many facets of these two parts of Christianity. *The Ecumenical Revolution: An Interpretation of the Catholic-Protestant Dialogue* (1967) by Robert Brown discusses the major issues that separate the groups. Brown's *An American Dialogue: A Protestant Looks at Catholicism and a Catholic Looks at Protestantism* (1961) discusses the difference between the two.—*Randal Joy Thompson*

Catholics, Roman: The Roman Catholic church has been present in the Americas since European explorers and colonists first arrived in the fifteenth and sixteenth centuries. There were early Spanish Catholic settlements throughout California and the Southwest; Louisiana and Florida also had significant Catholic communities.

As COLONIAL AMERICA, then the United States, grew, the Catholic church was profoundly affected by the ways in which its members became Americans.

The largest group entered the United States as immigrants seeking to escape harsh conditions in their homelands. This includes the arrivals of Irish, French Canadians, and Germans in the mid-1800's; the enormous wave of immigrants around the beginning of the twentieth century (eastern Europeans, Hungarians, Lebanese, and Italians); and more recent waves of immigrants (Vietnamese, Filipinos, and Middle Easterners). The early groups tended to assimilate into American society, to cease being bilingual by the third generation, and to lessen contacts with extended family in their countries of origin. Their religious practice is standardized and interchangeable, following universal American models.

The second group, predominantly Latino, consists of those who were resident in territories seized or dominated by the United States in its various expansionist thrusts. Periodic crises such as the Mexican Revolution (1910), the Castro coup in Cuba (1959), and U.S. interventions in Central America in the 1970's and 1980's have accelerated the immigration of Latino Catholics. Those from Mexico, the Caribbean, and Central America maintain close contacts with their countries of origin, especially within extended families. This has helped them to preserve their language and cultural identity as well as unique religious customs and indigenous styles of worship. Latino clergy are very few, however; Anglos have usually controlled Latino parishes.

The third group includes African Americans and American Indians, who, because of racism, have been excluded from the mainstream of American society. Catholicism among them is the result of efforts of white missionaries. Since 1966, African American Catholics have been allowed a measure of secondary leadership within their own churches. The first American Indian bishop was appointed in 1986.

Catholics of European Descent. The largest bodies of American Catholics are of European origin. The major groups for many years were the Irish and the Germans. Persecuted for their religion in their homeland, the Irish became the commanding force in the American Catholic hierarchy, dominating positions of leadership. In areas with few local priests, such as the South and the West, Irish immigrant priests continue to supply a substantial part of the clergy. Conservative Irish morals and faith in the clergy strongly influenced American Catholic values and theology. The Irish often held back the development of subordinate ethnic groups such as eastern Europeans.

Irish leadership did not go unchallenged. In the late nineteenth century, Germans promoted the parochial school system as a means of preserving and extending the faith. The Irish were cool to Catholic schools initially. Tensions between the better-educated, bourgeois Germans and the working-class Irish persisted for several generations.

In the secular world, Irish Catholics were strong supporters of the labor movement, founding the Knights of Labor and defending it from its critics. The Irish also gave the United States its most famous Catholic—President John F. Kennedy, grandson of Irish immigrants, elected as the country's first Catholic president in 1960.

The worst example of ethnic colonialism was the treatment accorded eastern European and Ukranian Catholics, who followed the Byzantine or Eastern Rite. Attempts by leaders of the Latin Rite to force the Byzantines to abandon their customs caused more than five hundred parishes to transfer to Eastern Orthodoxy. The main conflict was over the acceptance of married clergy, an ancient Byzantine tradition that was unacceptable to the dominant Latin bishops. Clerical celibacy was finally imposed upon all Eastern Rite Catholics in the United States, although married immigrant priests continue to function. Eastern Rite Catholics are fully represented in the National Conference of Catholic Bishops.

Many other European ethnic immigrants brought their own Catholic clergy to the United States and established "national" parishes. Preservation of the faith was tied to maintaining language and customs. This became increasingly difficult after World War II. Suburbanization and intermarriage with those of other faiths made the national parish obsolete. Such parishes, however, made important cultural contributions to cities in the American industrial heartland, notably Germans in Cincinnati, St. Louis, Louisville, Milwaukee, and Chicago; eastern Europeans in Cleveland and Detroit; Portuguese in New England; and Italians in the middle Atlantic states. As these European Catholics entered the mainstream of economic, political, and religious life, anti-Catholic sentiment waned.

In a niche by themselves are Catholic Americans of Middle Eastern descent. The earliest arrivals were the Maronites of Lebanon, who for many years constituted half of all Arab Americans. Well educated and well established in business, Maronites have been among the most accepted Arab Americans, including nationally known personalities and members of Congress. Middle Eastern conflicts since the 1960's have accelerated emigration of Arab Christians, such as some Palestinians. The Chaldeans of Iraq are established in Detroit. With the exception of the Palestinians, who are of the Latin Rite, Middle Eastern Catholics belong to various Eastern Rite churches.

A Latino priest in San Antonio, Tex., celebrates the Mass (James L. Shaffer)

Latinos. More than one-fourth of American Catholics are Latino. They are the dominant Catholic group, not only in their traditional heartland, the Southwest, but also in cities such as Boston, New York, Miami, Los Angeles, and Chicago. They are made up of three major groups: Mexican Americans and Chicanos; Caribbeans (Cubans, Puerto Ricans, and Dominicans); and Central Americans (Salvadorans, Guatemalans, Nicaraguans, and others). Historically, they have been dominated by Anglo church leaders; only since the 1960's have a number of Latino bishops been appointed.

Latinos have resisted cultural ASSIMILATION, even as they move into the economic mainstream. They are more likely than any other group in American society to be bilingual.

Latino religious traditions, especially forms of popular religion, remain strong. Distinctive forms of worship and celebration usually center on family and community, as in cemetery observances on the DAY OF THE DEAD (November 2) or the processions called *LAS POSADAS* before Christmas. Church music may incorporate *MARIACHI* and other popular forms. The icon of Our Lady of Guadalupe is widely revered, especially among Mexicans, for whom she has become a symbol of Mexican American identity.

Asian Americans. Catholics of Asian origin either came to the United States as Catholic immigrants or entered the church as Americans. Predominant among the first group are the Filipinos. Like Latino Catholics,

the source of their Catholicism is Spanish, and many emigrated to the United States as a result of American imperialism. Filipinos are concentrated on the Pacific Rim of the United States and are one of the largest elements of the Catholic church in Hawaii—the only state where the majority of Catholics are of Asian descent. While Filipinos often retain family religious customs, they have not developed unique liturgical patterns.

The Vietnamese are recent arrivals who came as a result of the Communist victory in the Vietnam War. They settled across the country, with large concentrations in California and Louisiana. About half the Vietnamese refugees in the United States are Catholic, and they have built thriving communities, often around ethnic parishes. Their chief religious community is the Congregation of the Mother Coredemptrix, a society of Vietnamese priests and brothers who came to the United States as BOAT PEOPLE. Apart from their native clergy, Vietnamese are disproportionately represented among seminarians preparing for priesthood in the United States.

Among other Asian American groups, such as those of Japanese, Korean, and Chinese descent, Catholicism has been only moderately successful. The great majority of Asian Catholics are found in California and Hawaii. The Diocese of Honolulu has the only significant presence of Pacific Islanders, mostly from Guam.

African Americans. Although black Catholics have suffered second-rate status in the church since emancipation, they are an important presence. Catholicism is the third-largest African American religious group in the United States and is the largest of any integrated church body. There are more than 1.5 million African American Catholics, with large communities in New Orleans, Chicago, Washington, D.C., New York City, and Los Angeles. A host of African American Catholic institutions and more than a dozen African American bishops have maintained the faith among African Americans. Where all-black parishes have continued, distinctive African American worship and preaching styles have been embraced, often with influences from Catholic Africa.

After a period of decline, African American Catholic institutions revived, and they provide identity and cultural pride. Xavier University of New Orleans, the only historically black Catholic university, is an important center. The fraternal organization Knights of St. Peter Claver fosters leadership and social activities.

Vietnamese parishioners have established thriving religious communities served by their native clergy, as seen here in the Midwest. (James L. Shaffer)

Ironically, earlier African American groups, such as the Federated Colored Catholics, were undermined by the Catholic Interracial Councils, which rarely tolerated African American leadership and avoided civil rights advocacy. Contemporary African American institutions are often open to people of other races, but they maintain their distinctive role in the African American community.

For many years, seminaries and religious orders were segregated and hostile to African Americans. The oldest African American Catholic community is the Oblates of Providence, a sisterhood established in Baltimore in 1828. The main religious orders working among African American Catholics are the Society of the Divine Word, the Josephites, and the Edmundites.

All have African American members, including bishops. There is an office of African American affairs within the National Conference of Catholic Bishops. National Black Catholic Congresses in 1987 and 1992 resulted in a new evangelical program among African Americans.

American Indians. Early Catholic attempts at conversion of Indians had little lasting success. With the acquisition of the West after the Mexican War, further mission work was undertaken by the Franciscans in the Southwest and the Jesuits in the northern plains. Taking advantage of the reservation system and the restrictions on Indian cultures enacted by Congress, Catholic missions and schools brought large numbers of American Indians into the church but at the same time contributed to the breakdown of indigenous culture. The Tekakwitha Society, named for Kateri Tekakwitha, the first Indian Catholic to be declared a saint, has pioneered in recovering native customs and giving Indians a voice in the church. The writings of Black Elk, both a practicing Catholic and a traditional Indian holy man, have inspired many young Indian Catholics.

Women. Church authorities have always been ambivalent about the place of women in the church. On one hand, through women's religious orders, the church has promoted unique roles, historically far surpassing the opportunities open to women in general in American society. On the other hand, leadership in the Catholic church has been effectively limited to men because of the restriction of the clergy to males.

Since Vatican Council II, feminist groups have agitated for an increased voice in the church and for priestly ordination. The bishops have strongly upheld the tradition of a male priesthood, leading to an impasse. In 1992, after nine years of debate, the bishops rejected a national pastoral letter on women in the church, unable to agree on its main thrust. Catholic feminist groups have also challenged church teaching on BIRTH CONTROL and, to a lesser degree, on ABORTION.

Gays. Catholicism teaches that homosexuality itself is not sinful but that gay sexual acts are immoral. This has led to a discordant response to gay civil rights. Eastern dioceses generally have opposed gay rights legislation, while western and many midwestern dioceses have supported antidiscrimination laws. The Catholic gay association, Dignity, is the largest gay religious group in the country, with chapters in most major cities. It has argued for acceptance of gay lifestyles in the church, but without much success. Like most American institutions, the Catholic church is HOMOPHOBIC, and Catholic institutions commonly discriminate against gay employees, especially teachers in parochial schools. At the same time, the church has been active in providing hospices and care for victims of the ACQUIRED IMMUNE DEFICIENCY SYNDROME (AIDS) epidemic.

SUGGESTED READINGS. Of the many basic histories of the Catholic church in the United States, the best single-volume work is *American Catholics* (1981) by James Hennesey. The standard study of African Americans is *The History of Black Catholics in the United States* (1990) by Cyprian Davis. Antonio Stevens Arroyo's *Prophets Denied Honor* (1980) brings together wide-ranging essays on Latino reli-

gious history and contemporary issues. Extensive research has been done on white ethnic Catholics. Two excellent examples are Colman Barry's classic work, *The Catholic Church and German Americans* (1953), and a fine collection of smaller studies on Eastern European groups, *The Other Catholics* (1978), edited by Keith P. Oyrud, Michael Novak, and Rudolf J. Vecoli.—*Norbert C. Brockman*

Catt, Carrie Chapman (Jan. 9, 1859, Ripon, Wis.—Mar. 9, 1947, New Rochelle, N.Y.): Suffragist, teacher,

Carrie Chapman Catt was a major force in obtaining passage of the Nineteenth Amendment. (Library of Congress)

and journalist. In 1895 Catt was elected chair of the National American Woman Suffrage Alliance, and in 1900 she succeeded Susan B. ANTHONY as president. In 1912 she headed the SUFFRAGE MOVEMENT in the state of New York and succeeded in passing a measure for suffrage there in 1917. Her books include *Woman Suffrage and Politics: The Inner Story of the Suffrage Movement* (1923), with Nettie Rogers Shuler, and *Why Wars Must Cease* (1935). She founded the LEAGUE OF WOMEN VOTERS and was a member of the Committee for the Cause and Cure of War. She was also a major force in gaining passage of the NINETEENTH AMENDMENT in 1920 giving women the right to vote.

Lauro Cavazos introduces a drug education program during his tenure as U.S. Secretary of Education. (AP/Wide World Photos)

Cavazos, Lauro Fred (b. Jan. 4, 1927, King Ranch, Tex.): Latino health professional and educational leader. Cavazos studied zoology and physiology at Texas Technical University and Iowa State University from 1949 to 1954. He began his career teaching anatomy at the Medical College of Virginia and then moved on to Tufts University Medical School, where he served as dean from 1973 to 1980. 48 x 4In 1988, Cavazos was appointed to serve as U.S. Secretary of Education by President Ronald Reagan and was reappointed by George Bush in 1989. He was selected as one of ten influential Hispanic Americans by *Hispanic Business Magazine* in 1987, received a National Hispanic Leadership Award from the LEAGUE OF UNITED LATIN AMERICAN CITIZENS (LULAC) in 1988, and was awarded a Medal of Honor from the University of California at Los Angeles in 1989. In 1990, Cavazos resigned his government post, but continued as a private education and business consultant.

Census, Bureau of the: U.S. government agency responsible for the periodic counting of the American population. As required in the U.S. CONSTITUTION, the census has been conducted every ten years since 1790 to help determine the fair apportionment of tax dollars and government representation.

In the early years, the census was accomplished by temporary workers with temporary facilities. In 1879 and 1880, laws were passed establishing a more permanent Census Office within the Department of the

Interior, and on March 6, 1902, the Bureau of the Census, with full-time staff and facilities, was created. William R. Merriam, the former governor of Minnesota, was appointed by President Theodore Roosevelt as its first director.

At first, the Bureau of the Census was little more than a government statistics factory. States still conducted their own censuses, and many federal departments were unwilling to relinquish fact-finding authority to the new bureau. As a result, the best social scientists and statisticians avoided the bureau for the comfort and challenge of university posts. World War I, however, brought out the nation's need for improved statistical services, and President Herbert Hoover expanded the bureau in the 1920's.

The bureau's work engaged it in controversial issues. During the 1910's and 1920's, those concerned over immigration policy—controlling the numbers of foreigners entering the country—used census figures to sound panic calls. The GREAT DEPRESSION and the emergence of NEW DEAL programs in the 1930's focused attention on urban migration, unemployment, and the apportionment of government benefits. The bureau became of paramount importance during World War II, when great segments of the population were mobilized for military or industrial support. In 1942, the bureau moved into its permanent home in the Washington, D.C., suburb of Suitland, Maryland.

Though the Bureau of the Census has always been nonpartisan, underreporting has been a constant issue. Specifically, younger people, males, nonwhites, and the poor have been routinely undercounted, resulting in less representation and fewer benefits. It is estimated that the 1970 census missed only 1.9 percent of whites but 7.7 percent of African Americans. Minority and civil rights groups voiced concern about the problem, and the bureau held conferences and created advisory committees to guarantee fair counts. After the 1980 census, fifty-four lawsuits were brought against the bureau, mostly by cities and states seeking more funding. This led to census readjustments in the courts. As the census' purpose is to count all persons living in the United States, the bureau devised methods for calculating the undocumented immigrant population and made questionnaires available in Spanish. In the early 1990's, innovative strategies were being recommended to reach a more accurate count of the homeless population.

By 1990, the bureau had twelve regional offices and nine thousand full-time employees, including statisticians, geographers, economists, and political and social scientists. For the census itself, another 450 temporary district offices were set up with a total of 300,000 "enumerators," or census-takers, across the country. The census of 1990 provided more detail on the nation's multicultural population than any previous count, with more breakdown on national origin and ethnicity. In addition to the decennial count, the bureau conducts many special censuses on issues such as health care, crime, and consumer activities and provides personal documentation services.

SUGGESTED READINGS. For more information on the Bureau of the Census, consult Daniel Halacy's *Census: 190 Years of Counting America* (1980); Margo J. Anderson's *The American Census: A Social History* (1988); or Ann Herbert Scott's *Census U.S.A* (1968). A good treatment aimed at younger readers is *Counting America* by Melissa and Brent Ashabranner (1989).

Census of 1990, U.S.: Twentieth official population count of the United States, which showed the continuing trend of dramatic growth in minority numbers, despite

These boys are growing up in an increasingly multicultural America, as documented in the Census of 1990. (James L. Shaffer)

charges of an undercount of these populations. The Bureau of the Census found that about one in every four Americans is of minority ethnic or racial background, compared to about one in five in 1980. The greatest growth in the 1980's was among people of Asian (107.8 percent) and Latino (53 percent) background, because of immigration and—in the case of Latinos—a high birth rate. By contrast, the black and white populations grew only by 13.2 percent and 6 percent, respectively. A 37.9 percent increase in American Indians may be traced to the larger number of Americans who had come to identify themselves as having some Indian ancestry.

The census revealed regional differences in population trends, such as the general population growth of the Sunbelt states and the role of CALIFORNIA as a microcosm of rapid demographic change. For example, rates of growth since 1980 were higher than the national average in California for Asians (127 percent), Latinos (69 percent), and African Americans (21.4 percent). The states or districts with the largest percentage of specific minorities were Washington, D.C., for African Americans, Oklahoma for American Indians, Hawaii for Asian Americans, and New Mexico for Latinos.

Controversies continued to plague the census process, especially around the endemic problem of the "differential undercount." This refers to the census' tendency to undercount African Americans, Latinos, immigrants, poor people, and other disadvantaged groups of the inner city. To address this issue, some areas engaged in special census outreach efforts to persuade people of the importance of being counted for political reasons. For example, there were efforts by local activists to locate and count local homeless people. Meanwhile, Asian Americans successfully lobbied to have the ten Asian nationality group categories retained on the census form to show the diversity of the Asian American population, and members of the MULTIRACIAL MOVEMENT continued to press unsuccessfully for a separate "multiracial" category rather than "other."

Central American Refugee Center (CARECEN): Nonprofit legal advocacy and human rights organization founded in 1981 to defend and advance the fundamental human and civil rights of Central American REFUGEES. It is composed of a national network of independent offices located in Houston, Los Angeles, San Francisco, New York, and Washington, D.C. The organization's stated goals are direct legal and social services, advocacy, education and empowerment, and human rights. CARECEN receives no state or federal funding and relies on volunteer service and private contributions. It publishes a newsletter called *Carecen Notes.*

Central Pacific Railroad—Chinese workers: When the U.S. government guaranteed the construction of a railroad connecting the Missouri River to the Pacific coast, two railroad companies, the Union Pacific and the Central Pacific, were responsible for building the track from the Missouri River westward and from Sacramento eastward, respectively. Since each company was to be paid according to the number of miles completed, competition was fierce. This project and its brutal pace in turn would become a landmark of both opportunity and suffering for Chinese immigrants to the United States.

Since white labor was scarce in the 1860's, in part because of the Civil War, Charles Crocker of Central Pacific thought of hiring the Chinese men who had arrived in the United States to work in mining camps a decade earlier. His supervisor, initially skeptical of the physical stamina of the Chinese, eventually agreed to experiment with fifty Chinese laborers. They turned out to be excellent workers in arduous and dangerous tasks including leveling roadbeds, digging tunnels, and blasting mountainsides. Eventually more than ten thousand Chinese were hired. Even though they worked faster than white workers, they were derided as "Crocker's Pets." The average Chinese laborer worked twelve hours a day and received less than his white counterpart (who was given room and board as well).

The construction of the railroad proved treacherous on the snowy and rocky slopes of the Sierra Nevada. Vying fiercely with Union Pacific, Central Pacific became determined to speed up construction and forced the Chinese to work through the winter. In the winter of 1866, for example, half of the nine thousand Chinese—generally from the southern regions of Guangdong—were put to work clearing the snow, and many were killed by avalanches. Their bodies were not found until the following spring; some still clutched their shovels in their hands. The total Chinese death toll for the railroad construction project is believed to exceed twelve hundred.

In the spring of 1867, Chinese workers demanded a wage increase to forty five dollars as well as an eight-hour work day; five thousand workers threatened to walk out. The company offered to raise their wages by four dollars to thirty five dollars, but the Chinese stood by their original demands, seeking treatment equal to their white counterparts. Central Pacific fought to break the strike and even wired New York to request ten thousand black laborers to replace the Chinese. Crocker isolated the Chinese workers and cut off their food supply. Near starvation, the strikers finally gave in.

In 1869, at Promontory Point, Utah, the two sets of railroad tracks were finally connected. Despite their

mented anti-Chinese violence and legal restrictions on Chinese immigrants. For decades, those events eclipsed the heroic triumph of the Chinese in opening the American West.

SUGGESTED READINGS. The central experience of railroad building among most nineteenth century Chinese immigrants has dominated both historical scholarship and literary grapplings with Chinese American identity. Aspects of the former can be found in Ronald Takaki's *Strangers from a Different Shore:*

This wood engraving depicts the mingling of European American and Chinese American workers as they complete the last mile of the Central Pacific Railroad. (Library of Congress)

hard work and casualties, the Chinese were not invited to the ceremony that marked the completion of the first American transcontinental railroad.

Chinese workers also were hired to construct local lines, such as the Virginia City and Truckee lines, and nearly all the major railroad lines along the Pacific coast. Some also went east of the Rockies to work on railroads in Alabama, Tennessee, and Texas. Yet increasing competition and economic recession fo-

A History of Asian Americans (1989), Sucheng Chan's *Asian Americans* (1991), and the museum catalog prepared by Him Mark Lai, Joe Huang, and Don Wong entitled *The Chinese of America, 1785-1980* (1980). Fictional/memoir treatments include Frank Chin's *Donald Duk* (1991), "The Dance and the Railroad," in *FOB and Other Plays* (1990) by David Henry Hwang, and *China Men* (1980) by Maxine Hong Kingston.

Chain migration—Asian immigration: In its most general sense, refers to any pattern of migration in which the first people who move to a new area induce and assist others from their homeland to move there as well. Kinship networks and special knowledge are used in overcoming quotas and other restrictions on immigration. For many Asians, such chains epitomize responses to historical obstacles of racism and exclusion. After immigration reforms in 1965, there was a rapid growth of Asian networks employing preferential and nonquota categories for family unification. After 1978, this practice became more widespread among all immigrants.

Nineteenth century Chinese immigration exemplified early manipulations of family relationships. Streams of immigrant males from Guangdong brought over relatives and relied on family, regional, or clan associations for help. Problems arose, however, with the CHINESE EXCLUSION ACT of 1882. Until it was lifted in 1943, Chinese Americans met economic and social needs by bringing in their own offspring as "legal" entrants. Returning to the United States from China, in fact, many men reported the birth of sons; these created later opportunities for their family and for others who bought false entry to the United States. Such "PAPER SONS" had to memorize lengthy family histories while officials cross-checked their stories against detailed files at ANGEL ISLAND. This suspicion constrained the minuscule legal immigration as well.

The IMMIGRATION AND NATIONALITY ACT of 1965 eliminated restrictive ASIAN-PACIFIC TRIANGLE quotas, and placed a premium on immediate family reunification. Although it was assumed that this would reproduce the Eurocentric balance of previous American immigration, many earlier immigrant groups actually did not maintain ties within preferential degrees of kinship. Reforms favored recent immigrants as well as those who entered under new professional quotas—the latter encompassing many Chinese, Koreans, Filipinos, South Asians, and others who brought the burgeoning expertise and training of their developing home societies to the United States.

Each chain begins with one person who might arrive as a student, business professional, or health practitioner. Over a decade, such individuals could sponsor a range of kin, constrained by different rights for residents and citizens as well as kinship distance. Spouses and unmarried children under twenty-one, for example, are considered nonquota immigrants who may join permanent residents, while siblings and married children may only be sponsored by citizens and need

to await visas under appropriate quotas. Parents are nonquota arrivals, although they only may be sponsored by U.S. citizens over twenty-one. Together, the conditions favoring migration in Asia and the use of family unification strategies have created an Asian immigration boom since the 1970's.

After the 1978 combination of Eastern and Western Hemisphere quotas, family unification gained precedence in all cases. Chain migration, however, became a target for criticism by those alarmed by the rapid, cohesive growth of new immigrant communities; family unification entries reached 215,000 in 1988. Thus, in congressional debates, immigration rights for spouses and children were stressed and reductions proposed for siblings and their offspring. Family preferences as both goal and strategy, however, were ratified

Inspection station at Angel Island, Calif., in the 1920's. (National Archives)

by the IMMIGRATION ACT OF 1990. Moreover, special extended quotas for Hong Kong, separate plans for Asian refugees, and the structures for admitting immigrants by occupational preferences that encourage Asian professionals together sustain a strong flow around which new chains continue to form.

SUGGESTED READINGS. For information on post-1965

Tennis player Michael Chang displays his winner's trophy at the 1989 French Open. (AP/Wide World Photos)

Asian chain migration, see David Reimers' *Still the Golden Door: The Third World Comes to America* (2d ed., 1992). Many sources depict the historical experience of chain migration among various Asian American communities, including Ronald Takaki's *Strangers from a Different Shore* (1989) and Sucheng Chan's *Asian Americans* (1991).

Chamber of Commerce: National organization of businesses founded in 1912. Membership consists of local chapters, trade organizations, professional associations, and private companies. The primary functions of the Chamber of Commerce are to prioritize and publicize important issues to be addressed on the local level, to make recommendations on problems affecting the country's economy and general welfare, and to train and empower members to participate in policy-making at all levels of government. While the Chamber is often associated in the public mind with defense of the status quo, some urban chapters have been active in efforts for improved public education, better intergroup relations, and other controversial issues.

Chang, Michael (b. Feb. 22, 1972, Hoboken, N.J.): Chinese American tennis player. Chang was born to Chinese parents who had immigrated to the United States. He began playing Ping-Pong as a small child and soon moved on to tennis. After moving with his family to California, Michael began training seriously with his father and worked with several tennis coaches. At the age of fifteen, he won a match at the U.S. National Junior Championships; at age sixteen, he turned professional. In 1989, Chang became the youngest male player ever to win the French Open and the first American to do so in thirty-four years. That same year, he was the youngest player to compete on center court at Wimbledon. A smooth, intelligent, and entertaining player, Chang helped lead the U.S. team to a Davis Cup championship in 1990.

Chang, Yin-huan (Feb. 8, 1837, Fo-shan, China—Aug. 20, 1900, Sinkiang, China): Chinese diplomat. Chang began his career as a magistrate and in the 1870's worked with the government to fortify Chinese ports after Japan's invasion of Formosa (later Taiwan). He came to the United States in 1886 as China's minister to the United States, Peru, and Spain. During the next three years, he successfully negotiated financial reparations to families of Chinese miners killed in the 1885 Rock Springs Massacre. He also negotiated a treaty regulating Chinese laborer immigration and seeking to protect Chinese Americans from discrimination and violence. After returning to China, Chang was banished to Sinkiang by government conservatives and executed there in 1900.

Charles, Ray (Ray Charles Robinson; b. Sept. 23, 1930, Albany, Ga.): African American musician. Charles is a singer, pianist, and band leader with broad appeal to both the general public and jazz professionals. Blind from the age of six, he learned music in a Florida school for the blind. He left school at age fifteen and over the next ten years played with and organized several bands; cut his first record (1952); and issued his first record album (1957)—a mix of pop, jazz, and gospel. A "down home" style links his music to early American jazz. He has received ten Grammy Awards and has been elected to various musical halls of fame.

Chávez, César Estrada (Mar. 31, 1927, near Yuma, Ariz.—Apr. 23, 1993, San Luis, Ariz.): Mexican American farm labor organizer. Born to a family of Mexican American MIGRANT WORKERS, Chávez knew from a young age the abuses suffered by the oppressed labor force. He became a volunteer organizer for the Community Service Organization in San Jose, California, in 1950, and served as its general director from 1958 to 1962. In 1962, he became head of the United Farmworkers Organizing Committee, which eventually became the UNITED FARM WORKERS union and was affiliated with the AFL-CIO. Chávez's efforts to organize workers

Ray Charles performs on a CBS television special. (AP/Wide World Photos)

César Chávez founded the United Farm Workers and served as an inspiration to Latino Americans. (Library of Congress)

and strikes—including his own hunger strikes—and to inform the general populace of the living standards endured by agricultural workers throughout the Southwest helped him become the standard-bearer of the farm workers' movement. At the time of his death, he was eulogized for also galvanizing the CHICANO MOVEMENT as a hero of young Mexican Americans.

Chávez, Linda (b. June 17, 1947, Albuquerque, N. Mex.): Political appointee and commentator. Born to parents of Spanish and Irish descent, Chávez completed her undergraduate work at the University of Colorado and pursued graduate studies at the University of California at Los Angeles, where she earned her Ph.D. in 1972. From then through 1977, she served as a lobbyist or staff member for various organizations in the public and private sectors, including the American Federation of Teachers, the House Judiciary Committee, and the Department of Health, Education, and Welfare. From 1983 to 1985, Chávez served as staff director for the U.S. Commission on Civil Rights during the Reagan Admini-

stration. She has attended many international leadership conferences on women's, minority, and educational issues. She became a syndicated columnist in 1988 and was a frequent guest on television news shows. In 1991, Chávez published *Out of the Barrio: Toward a New Politics of Hispanic Assimilation.*

Cherokees: Branch of the IROQUOIS Indian tribe, originally occupying the southern Appalachian region, part of Georgia, and Alabama. Cherokees, who called themselves *Anti-Yun'Wiya* ("the real people"), were named *Chillaki* ("people who live in caves") by their neighbors, the Choctaws.

By the time of the revolutionary war, many Cherokees bore the names of their British fathers, such as Cochran, Ross, and Adair. Cherokees began to adopt the ways of white culture, and in 1801 they allowed white missionaries to set up schools for Cherokee children. In 1821 Sequoya invented a Cherokee alphabet; soon many books, including the New Testament, were printed in the Cherokee language. A Cherokee/English language newspaper, the *Cherokee Phoenix,* began publication in 1821.

Political appointee and commentator Linda Chávez served as staff director for the U.S. Commission on Civil Rights for the Reagan Administration. (AP/Wide World Photos)

One of the great leaders of the Cherokees was a full-blood known as "The Ridge," born in 1771. He believed the Cherokees could retain their traditions while adapting to white encroachments. His son John Ridge was instrumental in negotiating the relocation of the tribe to Oklahoma. John Ross, a mixed-blood, blue-eyed Cherokee, waged a lifelong struggle against the Ridges to oppose the tribe's relocation. A small group of Cherokees led by the Ridges signed away the Cherokee lands in Georgia, and the tribe was forced to leave for Oklahoma (Indian Territory) in 1838. Nearly one quarter of the Cherokee population died en route on the "TRAIL OF TEARS."

The survivors rebuilt their society in the new land. In 1841 they established a system of public schools, and in 1851 they built two institutions of higher education in their capital city of Tahlequah in northeast Oklahoma. The *Cherokee Phoenix* was replaced in 1844 by *The Cherokee Advocate*, edited by the nephew of John Ross, who had been educated at Princeton University.

In 1861 STAND WATIE organized a Cherokee cavalry to fight for the Confederacy. Principal Chief John Ross was captured by Union troops in 1862 and taken to Washington, D.C., as a prisoner of war. In 1887 Congress directed that Indian lands be divided into allotments, a practice which violated Cherokee concepts of "Mother Earth." This policy continued as American Indians' control of their lands almost disappeared. The Cherokees agreed to a treaty in 1905 which compensated them for lands ceded to create the new state of Oklahoma in 1907.

A small group of Cherokees managed to remain in the Carolinas during the "Trail of Tears," and their heirs have established themselves as the Eastern Tribe of the nation. Most contemporary Cherokees, however, identify with the main body descended from the founder of the nation in the Oklahoma (Indian) Territory.

Before statehood, Cherokees possessed more than 4 million acres of land in Oklahoma Territory; less that three decades later, they held less than one-eighth that amount. Cherokees did not succeed as small farmers. Many lost their land allotments, and several developed dependency habits, drawing welfare checks as their main source of income. The rocky forested hills they chose to inhabit have become valuable for tourism, and so they are pressured to sell and move into nearby towns and cities, such as Muskogee and Tulsa, Oklahoma. Many full-bloods resent the presence of mixed-bloods, whom they call "White Indians," and who compete with them for medical and financial benefits directed to Cherokees through their modern tribal government, formed in 1949.

Federal courts have ruled that the Cherokees are entitled to receive financial compensation for underpayment from sale of the Cherokee Outlet. Tribal government used these resources to build a cultural center in Tahlequah and to establish several programs of social assistance for tribal members. In 1985, WILMA MANKILLER became Principal Chief; she was elected to her office in 1987 and reelected in 1991. She administers a multimillion dollar budget for support of health, education, and housing benefits to members of the Cherokee Nation in modern Oklahoma.

SUGGESTED READINGS. A brief but powerful study of the Cherokees is Peter Collier's *When Shall They Rest? The Cherokees' Long Struggle with America* (1973), narrating the tragic experiences of the tribe as it broke into factions before the removal and gradually disintegrated. A short book written for children is Alex W. Bealer's story of the Removal in *Only the Names Remain* (1972). Major histories include Grace Steele Woodward's *The Cherokees* (1963) and Marion Starkey's *The Cherokee Nation* (1946). A specialized study is *Cherokees and Missionaries, 1789-1839* (1984) by William G. McLoughlin, and James W. Parins' *John Rollin Ridge: His Life and Works* (1991), is a biography of the Cherokee leader.

Chesnut, Mary Boykin (Mar. 31, 1823, Pleasant Hill, near Camden, S.C.—Nov. 22, 1886, Sarsfield, S.C.): Diarist. When she was a child, Chesnut's father took her to Mississippi, removing her from what he felt was the threat of thirteen-year-old suitor James Chesnut. After her father's death, she married Chesnut, who was then appointed to the United States Senate (1859-1860). This put her in an invaluable position as an observer and recorder of history. Around 1860 she began compiling her 400,000-word diary, which provides accurate details of the Civil War period and strongly condemns slavery.

Cheyennes: American Indian tribe of the Great Plains. Called by themselves *Tsistsistas*, or "alike people," the Cheyennes' common name is derived from a Sioux term meaning "red [alien] speakers." In other Plains languages they are called "striped arrows" for their use of turkey feather fletching.

When the Lewis and Clark expedition met them in the Black Hills in 1804, the Cheyennes already had a

This drawing depicts the defeat of the Cheyennes by Colonel Forsyth in September, 1863. (Library of Congress)

CHEYENNE TERRITORY

long history of migration and integration. They emerged from the forests north of Lake Superior at an undetermined date and were found farming in Minnesota by the French in 1680. During the 1700's they were forced through the Dakotas by more easterly tribes. Along the way they allied with the Sutais, another people of Algonquian language stock, and eventually absorbed them. Yet another Algonquian tribe in the region, the ARAPAHOS, joined with the Cheyennes in a confederation which continues to the present day.

Moving southwest across the High Plains in the early 1800's, the Cheyennes vied for hunting and grazing territory and access to horses. They were harassed by the Assiniboines from behind while battling the Kiowas and COMANCHES ahead of them. Firm alliances were struck with the latter tribes and the SIOUX by 1840 in the midst of American expansion. Trade and treaty inducements prompted the Cheyennes to split into northern and southern populations which located along the North Platte and Yellowstone headwaters in Wyoming and the Arkansas River in Colorado, respectively. These divisions kept in contact even though their separation was formalized with the es-

tablishment of reservations in Montana and Oklahoma. Modern populations remain at both locales.

Because of their central position and many alliances, the Cheyennes bore the brunt of fighting during the INDIAN WARS. The southern Cheyennes suffered infamous massacres led by Captain John CHIVINGTON at SAND CREEK, Colorado (1864), and by Colonel Armstrong CUSTER at the Washita River, Oklahoma (1858). Embittered by these episodes, they fought vigorously until the overwhelming army campaign of 1874-1875. The northern Cheyennes fought alongside the Sioux to defeat Custer in the BATTLE OF THE LITTLE BIGHORN (1876). In 1878-1879, some northerners who had been relocated to Oklahoma fought their way back north in a final show of resistance.

Cheyenne traditions clearly reflect the tribe's history of migration and cultural contact. Folktales about stolen corn signify the move onto the Plains, when gardening was forsaken. The SUN DANCE (learned from the Sutais) and the Sacred Arrow ceremonies, emphasizing social unity, hunting, and warfare, also represent a commitment to Plains life. Many Cheyenne customs survived government suppression on the reservation; their Sun Dance was a model for the modern Sioux Sun Dance revived after 1920.

SUGGESTED READINGS. Donald Berthrong's *The Southern Cheyennes* (1963) is a forthright history of that group. Colorful first-hand accounts of the Plains battles are recorded in George Grinnell's *The Fighting Cheyennes* (1915). Compare *The Cheyenne Way* (1941) by Karl Llewellyn and E. Adamson Hoebel with John Moore's *The Cheyenne Nation* (1987) for contrasting analyses of Cheyenne social and political life. In *The Wolves of Heaven* (1987), Karl Schlesier traces elements of Cheyenne worldview deep into prehistory.

Chicago, Ill.: With a 1990 population of 2,783,726, Chicago is the largest city in Illinois and the third largest in the United States. Situated on the southwest shore of Lake Michigan, the city grew around fur trade early in the late eighteenth century. White settlers acquired the land on which it is located from Indians in 1795. With the opening of the Erie Canal in 1827, shipping traffic from the East came to ports along Lake Michigan, particularly Chicago. When the city was destroyed by a fire in 1871, it took nearly two decades to rebuild.

Always a transportation center and melting pot, by the late nineteenth century Chicago had attracted large numbers of immigrants from eastern Europe. It continues to have the largest Polish population of any city other than Warsaw, Poland. It is also home to large numbers of Germans, Irish, Scandinavians, Greeks, Italians, Czechs, Bohemians, and Russians. Since 1970, the Spanish-speaking population has increased to the point that it and the Asian population are among the city's two fastest-growing minority groups. In the mid-North area of the city is the second largest urban concentration in the United States of American Indians, sharing the area primarily with whites who have relocated from Appalachia.

Members of the large Irish population, which early settled the South Side, became active in ward politics and eventually produced five Democratic mayors of Chicago. Polish neighborhoods are found primarily in the Near Northwest, and Czech neighborhoods in the southwestern suburb of Cicero, while Greeks have settled in the area west of the Loop, Chicago's downtown. The north and northwest parts of the city retain strong Scandinavian and German enclaves. CHINATOWN and other Chinese areas are concentrated on the South Side, whereas Korean and Japanese residents are found on the North Side.

During World War I, many southern blacks migrated to the city to work in war-related industries. This population, which reached 233,000 by 1930, had swelled to 1,100,000—two-fifths of Chicago's total population—by 1990. African Americans originally gravitated to Chicago's South Side, but as their numbers grew, blacks moved into the West Side and the Near North, which originally had been heavily Jewish. The city is home to important black organizations such as OPERATION PUSH and elected Harold Washington as its first black mayor in 1983.

The city has expanded, particularly to the north along the shores of Lake Michigan and to the west. Many Jewish residents, leaving the West Side as it came increasingly to be occupied by blacks, moved to the northern suburbs outside the city limits. Some affluent, upper-middle-class black neighborhoods have flourished on the West Side.

SUGGESTED READINGS. Peter D'Alroy Jones and Melvin G. Holli's *Ethnic Chicago* (1981) and Richard Lindberg's *Passport's Guide to Ethnic Chicago* (1992) are solid guides to Chicago's ethnicity. Stephen Longstreet's *Chicago: 1860-1919* (1973), although somewhat dated, provides excellent insights into the historical development of the city and the complexity of its ethnic composition. *Chicago Magazine's Guide to Chicago* (1988) is compact and provides a sound orientation to the city and its attractions.

Chicano. *Use* **Latino**

Chicano Moratorium (1970): Protest march on August 29, 1970, of more than twenty thousand Mexican Americans and their supporters from Belvedere Park in East Los Angeles to Laguna Park. The demonstration was organized by Rosalio Munoz, former student body president of the University of California, to protest the high percentage of Mexican American casualties in the Vietnam War. Violence broke out between the marchers and law enforcement officers. Police cars were damaged, and stores were burned when police used tear gas. Some officers were injured, as were hundreds of marchers. Three Mexican Americans were killed, including Ruben Salazar, a Chicano activist and journalist.

Chicano movement: Coalescence of political organizations, academic efforts, and cultural activities that promoted Chicano rights and a vision of Chicano peo-

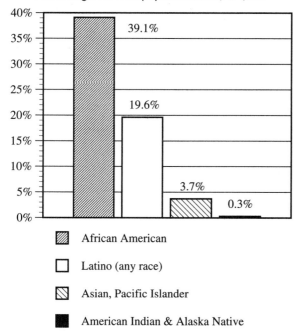

Chicago Minority Population: 1990

Percentages of total population of 2,784,000

- African American — 39.1%
- Latino (any race) — 19.6%
- Asian, Pacific Islander — 3.7%
- American Indian & Alaska Native — 0.3%

Source: Data are from *Statistical Abstract of the United States, 1992.* Table 38. Washington, D.C.: U.S. Government Printing Office, 1992.

plehood, especially from about 1965 to 1975. The term "Chicano," originally a pejorative way to refer to people of Mexican descent in the United States, came to be associated with a strong sense of group identity and political activism as a result of the movement. Movement activists encouraged intense ethnic pride by linking contemporary Chicanos with AZTLÁN, the mythical home of the ancient Aztec people, and promoted unity by invoking "La Raza," a general term for the language, culture, and heritage of Spanish-speaking people.

movement because they saw it as male-dominated. Not all Mexican Americans identify themselves as Chicanos, finding the Chicano movement's agenda too politically radical. Yet they, too, have been affected by the movement, which brought greater public attention to the experience of the largest Latino group in the United States.

Historical Background. There is no exact time or place, or particular group or person responsible for the rise of the Chicano movement. Rather, it developed

César Chávez, founder of the United Farm Workers, shown here (right front) picketing a government office, was considered one of the Four Horsemen of the Chicano movement. (AP/Wide World Photos)

Perhaps the greatest achievements of the Chicano movement were to foster a unique Chicano identity and to develop a leadership that continues to promote the advancement and cultural heritage of Chicano people. The movement's legacy could be seen most clearly in the 1990's in the activities of Chicano youth as well as Chicano educators in American colleges and universities. The movement also created an atmosphere in which Mexican American women could become more involved in public life, although a number of feminist Chicanas eventually broke with the

as a "people's" cause through the efforts of various Mexican American organizations and talented, politically minded individuals. The Chicano movement as an ongoing, nationally recognized minority voice had its roots in both the university community and the Mexican American working class.

Two important leaders founded organizations that served as forerunners to the emerging Chicano movement. They were Bert Corona, a militant activist in California who formed the MEXICAN AMERICAN POLITICAL ASSOCIATION (MAPA) in 1959, and Dr. Hector

Garcia who founded the AMERICAN G.I. FORUM in Corpus Christi, Texas, in 1948. The forum, originally for Mexican American veterans from World War II, later included Korean War veterans and opposed discrimination against Latino veterans.

In the 1960's several American ethnic minorities, such as African Americans and Native American Indians, were also bringing their concerns as oppressed peoples before both the university community and the American public. The great inspiration to African

lege students in Crystal City, Texas. In 1970, he founded a new political party, PARTIDO DE LA RAZA UNIDA. One of its main objectives was to achieve a sociopolitical power base so that Chicanos could enter mainstream American society. It also aimed to safeguard the uniqueness of Chicanos as a viable, bicultural, bilingual subculture within a multicultural American society. The success of La Raza Unida in Crystal City became a symbol to Chicanos of strength achieved through unity.

José Gutiérrez, shown here in 1967, organized La Raza Unida Party to sweep through local governments in Texas in the 1960's. (AP/Wide World Photos)

Americans and others in this process was the nonviolent protests of civil rights leader Martin Luther KING, Jr. A number of Mexican American community activists from the Southwest followed his example. Four of these leaders became popularly known as "The Four Horsemen," namely, José Angel Gutiérrez, César CHÁVEZ, Reies López TIJERINA, and Rodolfo "Corky" GONZÁLES.

"The Four Horsemen": Movement Leaders. Gutiérrez, the youngest of the four, first founded the Mexican American Youth Organization (MAYO) for col-

Meanwhile, César CHÁVEZ, born in Arizona to a migrant worker's family, moved to the West Coast and became active in organizing Mexican American MIGRANT WORKERS, especially in the grape industry of Southern California. Within a short period of time, after moving to Delano, Chávez not only became known for his leading role in the creation of the National Farm Workers Association (later the UNITED FARM WORKERS) but also for inaugurating the Delano grape strike on September 16, 1965. The MEXICAN AMERICAN POLITICAL ASSOCIATION (MAPA), led by Bert

Corona, gave its full support to the strike. Chávez became highly respected for his political activities among Americans from diverse socioeconomic backgrounds. For example, in the same month that he began the Delano strike, he visited Stanford University and the University of California at Berkeley, appealing for support in his fight for migrant workers' rights—thus uniting Chicanos from all walks of life. Because of his charismatic appeal to the Mexican American community, he became the first nationally recognized leader in the Chicano movement.

Reies López TIJERINA, born in Texas, moved to New Mexico and became active in the Chicano movement around the same time as Chávez. He organized the Alianza Federal de Mercedes (Federal Alliance of Land Grants) in 1963 to fight land-grabbing by Anglos in northern New Mexico and to demand that lands be returned to their rightful owners. Part of his argument was based upon the rights of Mexican landowners as provided for in the Treaty of GUADALUPE HIDALGO, signed by Mexico and the United States on February 2, 1848, shortly after the end of the MEXICAN-AMERICAN WAR (1846-1848). Tijerina and his Alianza believed that many Chicano problems were the result of loss of their lands to abusive, scheming Anglo Americans.

Rodolfó "Corky" Gonzáles, the fourth member of the "Four Horsemen," was a civil rights leader and Chicano activist in Denver, Colorado. Like Chávez, Corky was the son of a MIGRANT WORKER family, thus realizing first-hand the need for social reform. He founded a nationalistic group known as the CRUSADE FOR JUSTICE in 1965. Its main objective was to attain quality social services with a focus on education, law, health, and finance for Chicanos, thus providing them with the necessary political power base to be viable participants in Anglo American society. González wrote a powerful poem, "Yo Soy Joaquín" (I Am Joaquín), an introspective narrative that succinctly stated the plight of Chicanos as a subjugated people. The poem begins, "I am Joaquín,/ lost in a world of confusion,/ caught up in the whirl of a/ gringo society"; exploring his own struggle for identity, Joaquín concludes by saying, "I withdraw to the safety within the/ circle of life—/ MY OWN PEOPLE." The poem had great appeal for Mexican American youth and teachers in the Chicano movement, and it became a rallying cry for those questioning their own identities and seeking social justice.

Other Organizations. In Los Angeles in 1967, a militant youth group called the BROWN BERETS began espousing support for the civil rights of urban Chicanos as called for by the CRUSADE FOR JUSTICE. They established chapters throughout the Southwest and made one of their most recognized contributions to the Chicano movement by calling for the review of the killing of a Chicano youth by an Anglo policeman in Albuquerque, New Mexico. This group focused on the needs of poor, urban Mexican Americans and drew its members from the *BARRIOS*.

Several other youth activist groups sprung up during the most vital years of the Chicano movement from 1965 to 1975. In addition to the group MAYO formed in Texas by Jóse Angel Gutiérrez in the late 1960's, a chapter of the United Mexican American Students (UMAS) was formed in Albuquerque, New Mexico. It consisted of Chicano students from middle-class backgrounds and was best known for requesting that the University of New Mexico include more courses on Mexican and Indian cultures in the curriculum.

After attending the 1969 National Chicano Youth Liberation Conference sponsored by the Crusade for Justice in Denver and later meeting at the Coordinating Council on Higher Education in Santa Barbara, California, MAYO, UMAS, the Mexican American Student Confederation, and the Mexican American Student Association formed EL MOVIMIENTO ESTUDIANTIL CHICANO DE AZTLÁN, or the Chicano Movement of Aztlán (MEChA). This group symbolized the emergence of a new youth society to carry forth the ideals of the Chicano movement.

MEChA helped organize student protests, as when students from EAST LOS ANGELES boycotted their high schools in March, 1968. With clenched fists and *gritos* (cries) from the barrio, they called for Chicano Power. "Education—not Eradication" was their motto. In the spirit of MEChA and the Crusade for Justice, the high school students demanded that their mainly Anglo American teachers stop denying them their Chicano culture and language, distorting their history and identity without offering a viable alternative. Chicano student organizations were a major force in prompting the establishment of CHICANO STUDIES PROGRAMS at American colleges and universities.

Literature and the Arts. Chicano writers became highly visible as intellectual fighters for the principles of the Chicano movement. Abelardo Delgado, once called "the Don of Chicano Poetry," wrote his famous political poem, "Stupid America," in 1969. Its message was primarily addressed to a naïve Anglo American public holding a stereotypical view of Mexican American youth:

> stupid america, see that chicano
> with a big knife
> on his steady hand
> he doesn't want to knife you
> he wants to sit on a bench
> and carve christfigures
> but you won't let him.

This poem became a classic, earning Delgado national recognition. In 1969, Octavio Romano-V., editor of the landmark Chicano journal *El Grito*, set forth an eight-point plan for developing a positive Chicano self-image. He suggested that Chicanos view themselves not as traditional and unchanging but as creators of systems; as participants in the historical process; as creators and generators of social forms, proclaiming their *mestizaje* (mixed cultural heritage) within a pluralistic society; as a people continuously engaging in social issues; and as capable of their own system of rationality. The image of the illiterate Mexican American must be discarded, Romano-V. said, and Chicanos must continue to pursue intellectual activity while maintaining their unique symbiotic relationship with the earth. Romano-V.'s theory brought together most of the concerns of the "Four Horsemen" and their followers.

Combining the views of Delgado, Romano-V., and Gonzáles in a symbolic mixture of English and Spanish, Alurista (Alberto Horedia) wrote "when raza?," a 1971 poem that calls Chicanos to action with the lines, "mañana/ mañana doesn't come/ for he who waits." Additional Chicano and Chicana writers who aided the cause include Thomas Rivera, Jesus Maldonado, Irene Castaneda, and Estela Portillo, among many others.

In theater, the leading figure was Luis VALDEZ, who founded El Teatro Campesino in Delano, California, in 1965. He wrote short plays called "actos" that were highly political. A firm supporter of CHÁVEZ, both men took these plays to schools and Chicano communities in Southern California. Not only was Teatro Campesino important to the civil rights quest of the Chicano movement but it also played an important role in the development of Latino theater in the United States.

Muralists were also active in the Chicano move-

ment. Leo Tanguma, originally from Houston, Texas, did work there and in Denver. One of his most famous murals, titled "La Antorcha de Quetzalcoatl" ("The Torch of Quetzalcoatl"), is a 72-foot multicultural work depicting Mexican, Latin American, Chicano, African American, and American Indian peace activists. Like poems associated with the movement, Chicano murals present a vivid portrait of Chicano history, culture, and political demands. Other important muralists were Jose Treviño of Austin, Texas; Ray Patlan, who worked in California and Chicago; and Carlota Espinosa who did murals in schools and churches in Denver, to name but a few. Many young people got their political as well as artistic education by assisting professionals on community mural projects in cities such as Los Angeles.

SUGGESTED READINGS. Diego Vigil's *From Indians to Chicanos* (1980) looks at the dynamics of Mexican American cultural history, focusing on the diversity of these peoples' experiences within Mexico and the United States. Gerald Paul Rosen in *Political Ideology and the Chicano Movement: A Study of the Political Ideology of Activists in the Chicano Movement* (1975) offers a clear view of the activities of Chicano youth groups. Carlos Muños, Jr.'s *Youth, Identity, Power* (1989) presents an intensive study of Chicano students and the Chicano Power movements they generated, especially focusing on the Los Angeles high school strike and the ramifications of El Plan Espiritual de Aztlán (The Spiritual Plan of Aztlán), adopted at the first National Chicano Youth Liberation Conference in Denver, Colorado. Essays compiled by Renato Rosaldo, Gustav L. Seligmann, and Robert A. Calvert in their book *Chicano: The Beginnings of Bronze Power* (1974) expose the reader to various popular stereotypes such as the "sleepy Mexican." Francisco J. Lewels, Jr.'s *The Uses of the Media by the Chicano Movement* (1974) contains a detailed account of how the Mexican Americans astutely learned to use the power of the mass media for their cause.—*Silvester J. Brito*

Chicano studies programs: Originally defined as "the formal, institutionalized, and dynamic study of Chicano culture in all its diversity and unity," Chicano studies evolved on university campuses in the late 1960's and early 1970's. Chicano studies involves interdisciplinary programs that include the examination of language, literature, arts, philosophy, FOLKLORE, history, and social sciences as these affect Chicanos. Viewed as vehicles to train individuals who could serve the needs of their communities through education, research, and public service, such programs were conceived as part of a struggle for equality and equal justice in the CHICANO MOVEMENT.

Early History. Chicano studies is primarily a product of California, though programs do exist in other states. One reason is California's large Mexican American population; another is that California's Chicano student activists made Chicano studies their top priority. Student groups such as the United Mexican American Students (UMAS), the Mexican American Youth Organization (MAYO), and the Mexican American Student Conference (MASC) had shaped their political perspectives through exposure to the black CIVIL RIGHTS MOVEMENT as well as through involvement with farmworkers' struggles in California, land grant issues in New Mexico, and local urban problems faced by the Mexican working class. This loosely formed coalition came to be known as the Chicano movement. In late 1967, a group of graduate students at Berkeley under the guidance of Octavio Romano-V.

published its first volume of *El Grito: A Journal of Contemporary Mexican American Thought.* The journal's essays challenged the traditional views of social scientists who traced the social problems of Mexican immigrants to their tenacious clinging to their traditional culture and their inability to assimilate into the American culture.

During the 1968-1969 academic year, a number of student demonstrations placed increasing demands on universities to respond to the needs of minority communities. Universities responded for purposes of political expediency and created several Chicano studies programs of differing organizational structures. At California State University, Los Angeles (UCLA), Chicano studies took the form of a program with two class offerings. At San Francisco State College, La Raza studies focused on the Latino population in the United States and Latin America. At the University of California, San Diego, Chicano studies was incorporated into the Third World College, which adopted a socialist and internationalist perspective. At the University of California, Berkeley, and at San Fernando

In 1993, Chicano studies students at UCLA went on a hunger strike to try to establish a separate Chicano studies department. (Bob Myers)

Valley State College, the move was to create a Chicano studies department with a strong community focus. The University of California, Los Angeles, set up a research center rather than a department. The University of California, Santa Barbara, established an ambitious program including a department, research program, and community outreach. Some programs addressed students' cultural identity crises or focused on training community organizers, while others took a more traditional academic approach.

In order to address variations in structure and focus in Chicano studies programs, the Chicano Coordinating Committee on Higher Education (CCHE) was formed. One of its first activities was a conference in April, 1969, to develop a plan of action to gain more equal educational access for Chicano students. This document came to be known as *El Plan de Santa Bárbara*. An important element of the document was the linkage of Chicano studies with the student movement, which stressed the needs of the Chicano community outside the university. Another important step was the creation of a statewide Chicano student organization, Movimiento Estudiantil Chicano de Aztlán (MEChA) whose focus would be statewide communication, improved university-community relations, campus organization, and political action. The conference issued a mandate to California universities and colleges to take action to provide: "1) admission and recruitment of Chicano students, faculty, administrators and staff; 2) a curriculum program and an academic major relevant to the Chicano cultural and historical experience; 3) support and tutorial programs; 4) research programs; 5) publications programs; 6) community cultural and social action centers." Finally, the plan's philosophy was opposed to ASSIMILATION and RACISM and in favor of radical social change to address Chicano concerns.

Chicano Paradigm. The objectives of Chicano studies were to develop an institutionalized discipline; a body of critical and empirical knowledge; an interdisciplinary approach; and a group of practitioners whose work in teaching, research, and community service upheld the intent of creating a Chicano paradigm.

Drawing on the pioneering work of writers such as George I. Sánchez, Carlos Castañeda, and Ernesto Galarza, Chicano scholars such as Octavio Romano-V. in anthropology, Nick Vaca in sociology, and Ralph Guzman in political science built an important foundation for Chicano intellectual work through their critiques of social science. They pointed out bias and deficiencies in social science research; they also noted a paucity of reliable data and a failure to consider the needs of people of Mexican descent. The Chicano paradigm rejected romanticized descriptions; explanations of Chicano conditions based on genetics or cultural determinism; and the use of unethical research methodologies.

At San Fernando Valley State College, activists tried to design a program that would enable "noncollege-track" students to succeed and ultimately, graduate. A unique arrangement evolved with the first two years of the curriculum designed to build students' self-image through courses in history, culture, and the arts, as well as courses to improve reading, writing, and other communication skills. This plan, achieved through negotiations with the administration, permitted students to take their general education courses and fulfill state requirements through Chicano studies rather than conventional departments. The primary objective of the B.A. program was to prepare students to enter the professions.

Dilemmas. After an intense beginning, Chicano studies programs began to dwindle in the mid-1970's because of falling enrollments, budget cuts, denial of tenure, and internal conflicts between faculty and students.

The response of campus administration to issues of control, funding, objectives, the role of students, and staffing was largely negative. Confrontations and violence at San Francisco State College, San Fernando Valley State College, and UC Berkeley left the universities in a state of siege and relations strained. At California State College, Fresno, the Chicano studies faculty was fired and replaced by faculty considered more in line with the administration. University administrators were seen as having sabotaged programs by withholding sufficient resources, which contributed to an overworked faculty. Controversy erupted at UCLA in 1993 when Chicano students went on a hunger strike after the university refused to establish Chicano studies as a separate department. The strike ended when UCLA agreed to establish a center for Chicano and Chicana studies.

Internal problems in Chicano studies also served as barriers to successful programs. In some cases, Mexican American administrators collaborated with university administrators to stall program development by simply following their own agendas and ignoring departmental needs. In other cases, students saw their role in developing and implementing Chicano studies decline once programs were approved and staffed. This led to divisions between MEChA students and faculty. At UCLA a Chicano faculty member was asked to resign on the grounds that he was not pursuing the needs of students or the Chicano community. At California State University, San Diego, Chicano professors with a Marxist orientation were ousted by those who represented more nationalistic views.

Accomplishments. In spite of internal and external problems, the field of Chicano studies has made inroads in a number of areas and has come to be viewed as a viable academic discipline. While programs initially focused on Chicano/Latino students, over time large numbers of non-Mexican students have enrolled in courses, especially at the general education level. Curriculum offerings have grown to include courses in Pre-Columbian Mexico, feminist perspectives, literary theory, and contemporary Mexican and Latin American history.

The most noticeable achievements can be observed in the area of research and intellectual work. Contributions in research have expanded from the social sciences to the humanities and public policy. Moving beyond critical reaction to traditional social science, intellectual work has reflected the development of a Chicano perspective. Juan Gomez-Quiñones has asserted that the ideological struggle, ideas, critiques, and knowledge pursued by Chicano studies assured that stereotypical ideas about Chicanos from pre-1966 social science would never again gain credence. Chicano research has also helped strengthen cultural awareness among the general community.

The founding of *Aztlán: Chicano Journal of the Social Sciences and the Arts* in 1970 allowed regular scholarly analysis and discussion of myriad Chicano issues. Complementing the work of *Aztlán* was the formation of the National Association of Chicano studies, the only professional association dedicated to Chicano studies, which has helped to promote research in the social sciences and humanities.

On a more practical level, Chicano studies has helped train numerous teachers for the public schools, especially in the area of BILINGUAL EDUCATION. This contribution, and the increase in Chicano/Latino students at colleges and universities, have perhaps been the discipline's greatest accomplishments.

Since the advent of Chicano studies, numerous developments have elicited changes in focus. Students of the 1990's often are not even aware of the history of Chicano studies or the CHICANO MOVEMENT. Early

Chicano activists moved on to graduate study or the world of work. Thus, while the activist tradition continues, it lacks the intensity of the 1960's and 1970's. Many Chicano faculty believe themselves to be perceived as second-class academic citizens whose research is considered illegitimate. Lack of resources and tenured positions continue to plague Chicano studies departments and programs.

SUGGESTED READINGS. To capture the development of Chicano critical inquiry, see the following works: *Occupied America* (1985) by Rodolfo Acuña; *Race and Class in the Southwest: A Theory of Racial Inequality* (1979) by Mario Barrera; *Gunpowder Justice: A Reassessment of the Texas Rangers* (1979) by Julian Samora; *La Chicana: The Mexican-American Woman* (1979) by Alfredo Mirandé and Evangelina Enríquez; and *Twice a Minority: Mexican American Women* (1980), edited by Margarita Melville. Although the definitive history of Chicano studies has yet to be written, consult the following sources *El Plan de Santa Bárbara: A Chicano Plan for Higher Education* (1969) by the Chicano Coordinating Council on Higher Education; Carlos Muñoz, Jr.'s "The Development of Chicano Studies, 1968-1981," in *Chicano Studies: A Multidisciplinary Approach* (1984), edited by Eugene Garcia et al.; Muñoz' *Youth, Identity, Power* (1989); and Juan Gomez-Quiñones' "To Leave to Hope or Chance: Propositions on Chicano Studies," in *Parameters of Institutional Change: Chicano Experiences in Education* (1974), edited by the Southwest Network.—*Carlos F. Ortega*

Child, Lydia Maria (Feb. 11, 1802, Medford, Mass.— Oct. 20, 1880, Wayland, Mass.): Writer and reformer. Child's first book, *Hobomok,* a romance about a white woman and an American Indian, was published in 1824. In 1826 she was editor of *Juvenile Miscellany,* the first American magazine for children. Three books offering household tips followed. In 1833 her writing shifted drastically with the publication of *An Appeal in Favor of That Class of Americans Called Africans.* The domestic society she had previously represented turned against her. She continued to publish research pamphlets and other works on slavery, including "Authentic Anecdotes of American Slavery" (1935), despite drastic drops in book sales.

Child abuse: Child abuse can be defined as harm inflicted upon children by adults that is not the result of an accident. It encompasses physical, emotional, and

Instances of Child Abuse Reported to U.S. Authorities, 1976-1986

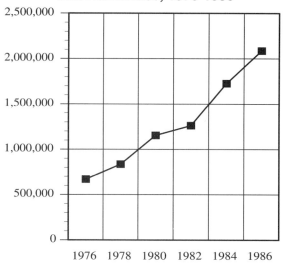

Source: From Elizabeth Dale Schetina, *As a Child: Safeguarding Children's Rights.* Human Rights series, p. 18. Vero Beach, Fla.: Rourke Corp., 1992.

sexual abuse. Child abuse is a serious social problem in the United States; some experts believe it to be a problem of epidemic proportions. How extensive child abuse is, however, and even what constitutes child abuse are subjects of debate. Four criteria are often used in determining abusive behavior: willful malnutrition, sexual trauma, physical abuse, and the isolation of the child in a dark area such as a closet. Abusive behaviors always involve direct intent on the part of the abuser to bring injury or harm to a child.

Child abuse has serious consequences which may remain as permanent painful scars throughout the victim's life. The violence and negligence of parents and caregivers serve as a model for children as they grow. It is very likely that the child victims of today, without protection and treatment, will become child abusers of tomorrow.

A victim of child abuse is defined as an unmarried person under the age of eighteen, who has been intentionally injured, either physically or mentally. This abuse can be either actual or threatened harm to a child. According to laws in many states, threatened harm means substantial risk of harm to a child's health and welfare. There is no single social level that is free from incidents of child abuse. There is, however, sociological evidence suggesting that child abuse and

neglect are related to certain social problems, including POVERTY, unemployment, and drug abuse. A study in New Jersey in the 1970's concluded that child neglect was particularly prominent among impoverished families; poor parents are less able to obtain the CHILD CARE services available to the affluent.

All child abusers have in common a particular type of parent-child interaction that often includes expecting and demanding much from children. Many of these parents lack basic information on normal child development and parenting. Sexual abusers violate the trust that a child places in them. They usually threaten the victim "not to tell," thus creating a conspiracy of silence about the assault.

Between 1963 and 1967, all fifty states and the District of Columbia passed laws that require teachers, doctors, and other professionals to report suspected child abuse. The U.S. Congress, in 1974, created the National Center for Child Abuse and Neglect. The center funds projects to study and prevent child abuse. A number of other groups are also involved in preventing child abuse and safeguarding the rights of children. Among them are the National Committee for the Prevention of Child Abuse and Neglect; Parents Anonymous, a self-help group for troubled parents; and the CHILDREN'S DEFENSE FUND. Organizations and individuals that seek to protect children are sometimes collectively known as the CHILDREN'S RIGHTS MOVEMENT.

Among different cultures there is a tremendous variety of accepted customs, including various approaches to health care and CHILD REARING. These cultural differences have sometimes created controversies regarding perceptions and accusations of child abuse. One such case that has received attention in the United States involves a Vietnamese practice known as *cao gio*, or "coining." A traditional treatment for fever and illness, it involves applying tiger balm ointment rubbed into the skin with the edge of a rough coin. The process can leave red marks on the skin, and American school and health officials have sometimes seen the marks as evidence of child abuse.

SUGGESTED READINGS. For a precise discussion of the effects of child abuse in the United States, see Donna Gollick and Philip Chinn's *Multicultural Education in a Pluralistic Society* (1990). Perhaps the most comprehensive summary of the issue is a book entitled *Recognizing and Reporting Child Abuse and Neglect* (1988) by Diana L. Roberts. Other good sources include Sander J. Breiner's *Slaughter of the Innocents:*

Child Abuse Through the Ages and Today (1990) and Vincent Fontana's seminal *Somewhere a Child Is Crying* (1973).—*K. Paul Kasambira*

Child care: In the United States, child care has traditionally been wholly a function of the family, with the child's education provided by the state from the age of approximately five onward. During the twentieth century, changes in the makeup of the work force and shifts in family life and American work habits have taken many traditional child care functions out of the home, and the term "child care" has also come to refer more specifically to services provided outside the home and family.

Health. A parent's first responsibility is assuring the health of the child. Child care effectively begins with the confirmation of pregnancy. Many American mothers have enhanced their children's health with careful prenatal care and abstention from harmful substances, including cigarettes, alcohol, and most drugs.

Conversely, many mothers give birth to children who have already inherited their mothers' disorders or addictions. The prevalence of the street drug known as "crack" in the 1980's resulted in the 1990's in growing numbers of crack kids, whose development and learning were adversely affected by the influence of the drug in the womb. In addition, a primary concern in the fight against the ACQUIRED IMMUNE DEFICIENCY SYNDROME (AIDS) epidemic is the transmission of the human immunodeficiency virus (HIV) through the blood from mother to child. The child of an infected mother not only is born HIV-positive but also faces the possibility of orphanhood in the untimely AIDS-related death of one or both parents. The effects of drug addiction and HIV are more common among children raised in poorer, inner-city communities, many of which have primarily African American or Latino populations.

During the first decade of the twentieth century, it is estimated that twenty-seven infants per thousand died within the first year of life. Infant mortality rates have declined in the ensuing decades, and by 1990, disease treatment and child care had improved to such a degree that 97 percent of children lived not only beyond their first birthday but also into full adulthood. According to 1980 estimates, however, infant mortality rates among African Americans are double those of white Americans, and American infant mortality rates generally are among the highest of any industrialized nation.

A number of life-threatening diseases, including diphtheria, whooping cough (pertussis), tetanus, measles, mumps, and rubella, are now widely controlled by standardized immunizations. Most American children receive these vaccines before entering school. The most frequent illnesses affecting children are respiratory infections, colds, ear infections, bronchitis, pneumonia, and influenza. With adequate medical care, they are all manageable.

Yet the health care system in the United States, depending as it has for decades on employer-based health insurance or public health facilities, leaves many families with inadequate health care, or none at all. Among the poor, simple childhood illnesses can thus be serious and result in permanent impairment. Furthermore, it is estimated that as many as 20 percent of children in the United States suffer from malnutri-

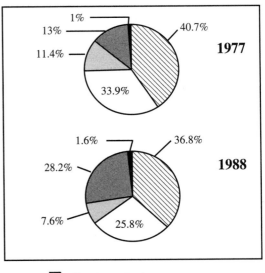

Preschool-Age Child Care Arrangements of Working Mothers: 1977 and 1988

Care in another home

Care in child's home

Mother cares for child at work

Organized child care facilities

Other

Source: Data are from *Statistical Abstract of the United States, 1992.* Table 600. Washington, D.C.: U.S. Government Printing Office, 1992.

tion. In such children, the body's defenses and immunities are weakened, making the threat of disease much greater.

Emotional Development. Nearly as important as the child's physical health is his or her emotional development. Modern social science, including the disciplines of psychology, sociology, and anthropology, has identified basic psychosocial needs that must be satisfied for the child's healthy growth. All children, regardless of class or ethnicity, need to be wanted and needed, to be cared for, to be valued and accepted, to be guided and educated, and to be given opportunities for independence and self-expression. Child psychology pioneers such as Erik Erikson and Jean Piaget have analyzed child development into distinct stages moving from infancy through adolescence, involving such issues as trust, autonomy, initiative, industry, and identity.

The responsibility for the child's psychosocial development ultimately rests with the parent or guardian. The importance of early mother-child contact is both instinctual and supported by clinical findings, and natural breastfeeding has become preferred by many doctors and mothers. In recent decades, more fathers have come to appreciate the nurturing and supportive aspects of fatherhood as well. Psychologists believe that children need a balance of love and discipline from both mother and father. In early adolescence, the child must be helped to accept and integrate physical changes and the onset of sexual maturity into his or her psychological matrix.

While the vast majority of parents and guardians facilitate the child's emotional development in a positive and natural way, the problem of CHILD ABUSE in the United States has received increased attention. Studies in 1986 and 1988 found between 1.5 and 2 million cases of maltreatment or neglect reported annually. Many parents who physically abuse their children are merely reproducing patterns from their own childhoods. A 1988 study estimated that 8.9 of every 10,000 American children are sexually molested or abused by a family member; 75 percent of these cases involve girls and their fathers or stepfathers.

Such figures may represent increases in actual incidents, reporting, or both. They certainly have raised concern over the general level of child care in the nation and focused attention on the transformations that have been seen in the American family over the past century.

Changes in the Family. Historically, humans have

This Rochester, N.Y., man is a nurturing caregiver. (Don Franklin)

used five major social arrangements for the care of children: sole care by mother; care within a nuclear FAMILY; tribal care through the extended family; family care with extensive community involvement; and community-based care. While formal education in the United States has always been community-based, the overwhelming model for child care has been the nuclear family.

The traditional family model, with a working father, a homemaking mother, and two or more children, is all but obsolete. One of every two marriages in the contemporary United States is likely to end in DIVORCE, and broken families, single-parent families, and stepfamilies are commonplace. Teen pregnancy and spousal desertion contribute further to such trends.

The greatest factor affecting children has been the entry of women into the labor force. While single mothers have always had to provide for their children, the preponderance of dual-income families is a relatively recent development. In 1900, only 19 percent of American women participated in the work force. Beginning with World War II, women entered the job market in such numbers that by 1988 their participation had risen to 74 percent. According to the Bureau of Labor Statistics in 1990, 96 percent of fathers and

65 percent of mothers work outside the home. In 1991, only 10 percent of American families depended solely on a male breadwinner.

These factors have combined dramatically to affect child care practices. In 1988, the number of children under the age of six whose mothers were working was estimated at 10.5 million. This included more than 50 percent of young African American children and more than 40 percent of young white and Latino children. Care and supervision traditionally administered by home-based mothers has to be provided elsewhere. Many parents and guardians, especially in minority communities, look to extended families for help.

settings with no adult supervision.

Government Programs and Policies. Many schools offer before- and after-school programs, as do synagogues, churches, and community centers. In addition, the federal government has responded with various programs, including Aid to Families with Dependent Children, which served 7.3 million children in 1966. Project HEAD START, established in 1964, is a federally funded, comprehensive program for low-income preschoolers. In 1988, Head Start's thirteen hundred branches served nearly half a million children, two-thirds of them nonwhites. The Family and Medical Leave Act of 1993 allows workers to take temporary

Children attending a day care center in Madison, Wis., play an "imagine" game. (Mary M. Langenfeld)

Given the increased mobility of modern society, however, grandparents, aunts, uncles, or cousins often live too far away to be of assistance.

One result has been the phenomenon of "latchkey" children, who spend part of the day in the home alone. A 1982 estimate placed the number of such children at seven million; surprisingly, they were not more likely to be members of single-parent families. A 1988 study of eight-year-old children in Dallas, Texas, found that 23 percent returned from school to home

leave to care for newborn or sick children. Such programs and laws have not fully answered the vast need, and many parents and guardians have been forced to find alternative paid child care situations, including nannies, in-home babysitters, job-based child care, and, most frequently, some form of day care.

Day Care. Institutional child care, or day care, began in the United States in 1854 with the Nursery for Children of Poor Women in New York City. A cooperative nursery school was established at the University of Chicago in 1915; day care greatly expanded during World War II with the Communities Facilities Act (the Lanham Act), but most of the Lanham Centers closed after the war.

The SOCIAL SECURITY ACT of 1962 defined day care as a public child welfare service. With the WOMEN'S LIBERATION MOVEMENT in the early 1970's, public policy toward child care facilities became a women's issue; the lack of such facilities was considered a factor in the continuing societal oppression of women, especially single and poor mothers. President Richard Nixon vetoed the Comprehensive Child Care Act in 1971, and the 1980's brought funding cuts on both the federal and state levels. The United States is the only major developed nation in the world without a comprehensive child care policy.

Family and Institutional Day Care. While supply still runs short of demand, millions of children receive some sort of day care in the United States. In 1982, the largest portion of them, approximately 37 percent, were enrolled in family day care homes, situations in which a mother brings other children into her home setting. Twenty-seven percent were placed in day care centers or preschools. Such facilities are licensed and regulated by state law as to safety, group size, space, and personnel credentials. Most family day care situations accept up to ten children, while day care centers can accommodate up to one hundred. In addition, during the 1980's the number of companies with on-site child care increased from one hundred to forty-five hundred, with many more offering child care assistance.

Psychologists and parents have long debated the relative value of child care provided outside the home. Early fears about the deleterious effects of separating small children from their mothers have been allayed by some research, but the practice of full-time day care is still too new for reserachers to have measured its long-term effects. Some day care centers have sparked controversy because of charges of unsanitary conditions, neglect, or CHILD ABUSE. As with parenting itself, the quality of care in centers and day care homes varies, but so long as sufficient nurturing and attention are provided, day care can be an effective adjunct to parenting.

Moreover, day care offers important benefits not always found in the home. When well administered, day care helps young children gain a sense of independence; offers a variety of experiences; teaches important early socialization skills; accelerates educa-

tion; and facilitates parent networking. It also reduces the stress that children may feel upon entering elementary school itself. From an anthropological viewpoint, modern child care practices recapture some of the social dynamics of traditional kinship systems.

Child care practices and public policy continue to be a major concern in the United States. Parents search for the best way to raise their children, and governments strive to provide effective and affordable services. With the ongoing transformation of work, home, and family life, how and where American children are raised will continue to change as well.

SUGGESTED READINGS. Definitive books on rearing children include *Dr. Spock on Parenting* by Benjamin Spock (1988) and Penelope Leach's *The Child Care Encyclopedia* (1984). Ann Muscari and Wanda Wardell Morrone take a practical look at child care alternatives in *Child Care That Works* (1989). A broader theoretical discussion is found in *Child Care: Facing the Hard Choices* (1987) by Alfred J. Kahn and Shiela B. Kamerman. Ruth Sidel's *Women and Children Last: The Plight of Poor Women in Affluent America* (1986) is a rigorous examination of child care in the larger context of sexism and poverty.—*Barry Mann*

Childbirth and child rearing: In societies throughout the world, reproduction—bearing and caring for children—has traditionally defined the role of women. A woman often spent much of her adult life pregnant, nursing babies, or caring for young children. She learned to incorporate the demands of child rearing into the busy and often strenuous routine of her domestic role. In the industrialized world, including the United States, this changed gradually in the twentieth century with the advent of effective methods of BIRTH CONTROL AND FAMILY PLANNING. The availability and wide acceptance of birth control pills in the early 1960's was a particularly significant development.

The many different cultures—from American Indian to European immigrant to African American to Latino—that have found places in the United States have historically had widely differing ideas about the proper approach to childbirth and child care. These differences have included the number of children a family should have, how infants should be cared for, approaches to disciplining children, and even what "childhood" means.

There have also been changes over time about how to approach giving birth. At one time virtually all births were home births. Then, as hospitals and medical care became more widely available, the trend was toward births in delivery rooms, with the mother under some type of medication or anesthesia. Finally, since the 1970's, increasing numbers of women have chosen to give birth without medication. Although the once common practice of giving birth in the home assisted by a MIDWIFE is today followed only by a minority, it does continue, despite legal and medical controversies.

rounded by female relatives and a midwife. After the birth, a woman was generally secluded for as long as three months while she cared for her baby and recuperated. Indian women nursed their babies and kept them close by, often on a cradle board, for a year or more.

After children learned to walk, they played games that emulated their same-sex parent. Mothers taught little girls how to prepare and preserve food and do other chores, while boys emulated their fathers. Gen-

Many of the most valuable parenting secrets are exchanged when mothers meet. (Dale D. Gehman)

American Indian Women. Pregnancy for the Indian woman was traditionally governed by a strict set of rituals and taboos. For example, neither the mother or father of an unborn baby among the Flathead Indians could leave the lodge walking backward; if they did, a breech birth would follow. Customs varied from tribe to tribe, but most tribes shared the notion of a segregated lodge or other structure for giving birth. The woman would either be alone or, more often, sur-

erally Indian boys and girls enjoyed extensive play time and were not separated until they reached puberty. Corporal punishment was very rare. Discipline might include setting the child apart until he or she stopped crying or, among the Crows and Iroquois, the "water treatment," which entailed pouring water in the child's nose or throwing water in his or her face. Some traditional child-rearing customs are preserved by contemporary Indians. The Cherokees honor a matrilineal structure in which the maternal aunt and uncle, or the grandmother, are responsible for a child's education and discipline.

Colonial Patterns. The first European culture arrived in the Indians' land with the various colonists of the seventeenth century: Huguenots from France, Puritans from England, Dutch from Holland, and Germans from Moravia. Despite a difficult colonization process, the birthrate for the colonists was nearly double that of Europeans overseas by the mid-eighteenth century. Women often bore eight children and sometimes as many as sixteen, even though most women did not marry until their early twenties. They were assisted in the birth process by other women and by midwives. Usually one woman sat behind the laboring woman and held her upright while a second prepared to receive the child. Once the child was born, the mother and child rested for some time in an effort to ensure the survival of both.

In colonial America there was no concept of childhood as it is understood today. In this preindustrial agrarian world, boys and girls were reared for the first six years in a close relationship with both parents. By the age of six, most children were considered little adults. Education was a high priority among the Puritans of New England, and "Dame" schools for children were established within the first fifty years. Among the New England settlers, children after the age of seven were sometimes "bound out" to other families to rear. They were taught a trade, but they were often also used as servants. Though the notion of "binding out" did not outlast the 1600's, children continued to work very hard. By the age of seven, many girls had finished their first quilts at their mother's knee, while male children had been instructed in a trade or farming. Children of both sexes were very strictly disciplined, and corporal punishment was typical.

The lives of children became somewhat less rigorous after 1693, when philosopher John Locke published *Thoughts on Education*. Locke suggested that children were not miniature adults and that they needed special care and education. In the years following the American Revolution, white women bore fewer children. Because of economic changes, men often worked away from home while women governed the domestic sphere. Women were now seen as guardians of the New Republic's virtue. They reared the children and were responsible for discipline, education, and the instilling of morals. These changes were most evident on the Eastern Seaboard and in urban areas. Meanwhile, women on the western frontier had a preindustrial lifestyle, and they bore their children on labor benches with the help of either MIDWIVES or, in remote areas, their husbands.

At the time of the American Revolution, childbirth as a momentous and life-threatening event for a woman generally began in her late teens or early twenties. Most communities had a "healer" or midwife to care for women in childbirth. The maternal death rate in the nineteenth century was one death for every 154 births; if a woman delivered five children, her chance of death was closer to one in thirty. As the process of childbearing changed from being woman-centered to being controlled by the male medical establishment with its new technology, the fear of death diminished along with women's control over their bodies and experiences.

Immigrant Women. By 1850 thousands of Irish, German, and Scandinavian people had immigrated to the United States in hope of a better life. These women generally delivered their children in the new land with the aid of a midwife; some went to hospitals, however, where doctors discovered that some mothers had illnesses such as tuberculosis. These immigrants maintained high birthrates of more than six children per woman. The children were reared by the mother, since the father was generally a day laborer working twelve to sixteen hours a day in a factory. Many women took in "piece work" to help the family make ends meet, expecting children to help with the grueling work. By 1900, with increasing numbers of immigrants crowding the cities, more women and children began working in factories. The new immigrants from southern and eastern Europe lived in largely ethnic neighborhoods where women still depended on other women to help them with childbirth and child care. Poverty and unsanitary conditions endangered the lives of the women and their newborns.

African American Women. Since the middle of the seventeenth century, African men and women had been imported into the colonies under the system of slavery. For these women, bearing children was a mixed blessing. A "good breeder" was more likely to remain on the plantation where she was born, but pregnancy and childbirth were risky propositions. A female slave usually bore her first child in her teens. In her early twenties, the young woman formed a permanent alliance, and the "husband" welcomed the woman's other children as he later did his own. Legal marriage was not recognized for enslaved persons, and the parents of a child could be sold before the child was grown. Older men and women in the slave quarters were called Aunt and Uncle so that if the parents were separated from the child, he or she would still have the support of a large extended family. RAPE and sexual abuse were common on the plantation, and enslaved women were often forced to bear and rear the slaveowner's children.

Enslaved women became pregnant frequently, but the conditions of slavery precluded very large fami-

The economic hardships of black sharecroppers, such as these tobacco workers in 1939, put a strain on family life in the Jim Crow era. (Library of Congress)

lies. Women were expected to return to the fields three weeks after giving birth and were allowed a break to breastfeed only four times a day. Children were often born premature because of the mother's poor health and nutrition. Corporal punishment for pregnant Africans was accepted; the overseer simply dug a hole for the woman's pregnant belly and had her lie down to be beaten. If a baby was carried to term, it was delivered by a MIDWIFE within the slave quarters. Older enslaved women in the quarters who could no longer work in the fields took care of children under six years of age until the children were put to work on the plan-

tation. Discipline for an enslaved child was a strange mixture of parental input and the constant threat of corporal punishment by white slave owners.

During the Civil War, enslaved pregnant women or women with babies tried to escape behind Union lines. One woman carried her dead baby all the way to a Union camp so he could "at least be buried free." After the war, African American women worked hard to make ends meet, to establish viable families, and to instill in their children both learning and an ability to "get along" in the world where Black Codes and tenant farming controlled their lives.

Women in the Southwest. In the southwestern United States, Latino women inherited a strong sense of community from their towns and villages that was grounded both in strong kin networks and in the CATHOLIC religion. They tended to marry young and have several children. Women were supported through childbirth by *parteras* (MIDWIVES) and strong matrilineal ties; grandmothers and even great-grandmothers were typically involved in rearing children. After the Mexican Revolution in 1910, many Mexicans worked primarily in seasonal agricultural jobs or moved to the cities, both of which eroded female support networks. LATINAS were vital both to child rearing and to the family business. By the end of the twentieth century, Mexicanas could claim a high percentage of nuclear families with both parents present, healthy babies with good birth weights, and extended families to provide child care.

One of the last groups to settle the western United States was the Asian immigrants who began arriving as laborers during the California Gold Rush. Few women came with this early group of travelers; many who did were imported as prostitutes. Many Japanese women entered the United States in the early 1900's through marriages arranged at home through "PICTURE BRIDE" exchanges. Typically, a young girl in her teens was sent to the United States to meet a man who had established himself economically and therefore was usually about twenty years older than she was; the marriage took place by proxy in Japan. After arrival, these Asian women often bore children every two or three years, supported by midwives from their communities. The household was the center of their lives, but some women worked both in the home and in the family business while rearing the children to respect both the American and Asian traditions. By the end of the twentieth century, Asian Americans had a reputation for success nurtured by mothers who instilled a strong work ethic in their children.

Trends After World War II. By the mid-twentieth century, most American women of all backgrounds bore their children in hospitals, where they were confined to labor and delivery rooms and sedated on their backs with their feet in stirrups. When they took their babies home, women were encouraged to bottle feed rather than nurse the infants. New birth techniques, such as the Lamaze and Laboyer methods, entered the mainstream after the 1960's. These advocated a drug-free birth, the support of the woman's partner as a labor coach, and alternative birth centers (ABCs) to create a more comfortable, home-like atmosphere. Women were again encouraged to nurse their children. By the 1970's, women of all classes had entered the work force, and nursery schools or "mother's helpers" filled in for "mom" as she tried to work and be a mother. "Baby boomers" typically had two children, frequently reared in single-parent households as the DIVORCE rate neared 50 percent by 1973. In 1990 the infant mortality rate in the United States remained high among industrialized nations, cesarean sections accounted for 30 percent of all births, and infertility became a problem for many couples as child bearing was postponed until after women established their careers.

Women of the late twentieth century also faced other challenges in childbirth and child rearing. African Americans and Latinos of the inner city faced the risks and child-endangering effects of drug use and poor prenatal care. The ACQUIRED IMMUNE DEFICIENCY SYNDROME (AIDS) epidemic threatened women and their unborn children. Yet despite such problems, women had come full circle, once again placing themselves and their babies at the center of the birth experience.

SUGGESTED READINGS. For further discussion of childbirth and trends in the United States see *Brought to Bed: Childbearing in America 1750 to 1950* (1986) by Judith Walzer Leavitt and *The American Way of Birth* (1992) by Jessica Milford. An overview of American family life can be found in Steven Mintz and Susan Kellogg's *Domestic Revolutions: A Social History of American Family Life* (1988) and Carl Degler's *At Odds: Women and the Family in America from the Revolution to the Present* (1980).—*Michael Crawford Reaves*

Children and minimum wage laws. *See* **Minimum wage laws for women and children**

Children's Defense Fund (CDF): Private nonprofit organization, created by Marian Wright EDELMAN in 1973, dedicated to protecting the rights of all children and families. It is highly respected for its annual conference addressing the needs of poor and minority children in the United States. The goal of the organization is to educate the nation about the needs of children—especially poor and minority children and children with disabilities—and encourage preventive investment in children before they get into trouble. CDF is also politically active by bringing important matters to the attention of lawmakers at the federal level.

Children's rights movement: Organized efforts to protect the human rights of minors (people under the age of eighteen or twenty-one, depending on the state). Children are at risk for exploitation for a number of reasons, including their small size, lack of education, and lack of voice in the political system. Reformers in the early 1900's agitated for child labor laws to prevent American children from being exploited in the workplace. In 1959, the United Nations Declaration of the Rights of the Child spoke of the need of children everywhere for "special protection" with the chance for healthy development "in conditions of freedom and dignity." The contemporary American children's rights movement took shape in the 1970's, when alarming increases in reported CHILD ABUSE became a national issue. Organizations such as the CHILDREN'S DEFENSE FUND, founded in 1973 by Marian Wright EDELMAN, have raised awareness of this and other issues, lobbying political leaders for better child care, teenage pregnancy prevention, child welfare, education, and family support programs. Despite increased recognition of children as a sector of American society that has suffered exploitation and discrimination, in 1990, children represented 40 percent of Americans below the poverty line and the U.S. Labor Department found eleven thousand violations of child labor laws.

Chilean Americans: Chile is a narrow ribbon of a country that lies along the west coast of South America. It is almost as long as the United States is wide: approximately 2,500 miles. Chile is separated from its neighbor to the east, Argentina, by the Andes mountains. The SPANISH LANGUAGE is spoken by a majority of its people.

Aboriginal people, principally the Mapuche tribe, have inhabited the territory that is now Chile for about ten thousand years. In 1541, Pedro de Valdivia was the first European to arrive in Chile. He claimed it for Spain, declaring it part of the Viceroyality of Peru.

A young Chilean girl celebrates the victory of Patricio Aylwin, who took office in 1989 as Chile's first elected president in nineteen years. (AP/Wide World Photos)

Spain ruled Chile until 1810, when Napoleon usurped the Spanish throne. Chileans took advantage of this power struggle to establish their own government. When the Spanish king returned to power, the Chileans refused to acknowledge him. Under the leadership of Bernardo O'Higgins, they successfully repulsed the Spanish *Reconquista*. In 1818, Chile formally declared its independence.

Chile is a nation of immigrants and prides itself on its European heritage. A majority of modern Chileans claim some Spanish descent. A small but influential group of Irish and English people established themselves in Chile in colonial times. Many Germans migrated to the southern part of the country in the nineteenth and early twentieth centuries. French, Balkan, and Italian groups have also found a home in Chile.

The number of Chileans immigrating to the United States has always been relatively small. The first Chileans may have come to the United States in 1849 in response to the GOLD RUSH in California. Since then, Chileans, along with other South Americans coming to the United States, have generally assimi-

lated into the general population by the third or fourth generation. Some immigrants from Chile have actually been first-generation Europeans who used Chile only as an intermediate stopover on the way to their ultimate destination in the United States.

Chilean Americans, like other immigrants from South America, tend to be well-educated and highly skilled. A majority are ROMAN CATHOLIC, and many hold what could be considered middle-class American values. These characteristics have allowed Chilean immigrants to achieve success in American society relatively easily.

Chin, Frank Chew, Jr. (b. Feb. 25, 1940, Berkeley, Calif.): Chinese American writer. A fifth-generation Californian, Chin attended the University of California, Berkeley, wrote film and television scripts for King Broadcasting in Seattle, and then in 1969 moved to San Francisco, where he was a consultant and lecturer on Chinese American culture and creative writing. In 1974, he received playwriting grants from the Rockefeller Foundation and the National Endowment for the Arts. He helped found the Asian American Theatre Workshop and in 1976 he became its artistic director. Among Chin's writings are dozens of television scripts, plays including *Year of the Dragon* (pr. 1974) and *The Chickencoop Chinaman* (pr. 1972), numerous short stories, and a novel, *Donald Duk* (1991). He also coedited *Aiiieeeee!* (1974), an anthology of literature by Asian Americans. Chin uses his writing to oppose anti-Asian racism and to explore traditional Chinese stories and legends.

Chin, Vincent (1955—June 22, 1982, Detroit, Mich.): Chinese American engineering draftsman. In June of 1982, two days before his wedding, Chin, a twenty-seven-year-old Chinese American, was involved in a fight at a local bar with an autoworker named Ronald Ebens, who had taunted him and expressed anti-Japanese sentiments. Ebens and his stepson Michael Nitz chased Chin to a nearby fast-food restaurant and beat him to death with a baseball bat. Ebens and Nitz were allowed to plead guilty to the lesser charge of manslaughter. The light sentences received by the assailants—a $3,780 fine and three years of probation each—outraged the Asian American community and led to protests and demands for justice. Chin's mother made a cross-country tour to raise funds for legal expenses involved in pursuing a civil case. The FBI investigated, and in the subsequent case Ebens was sentenced to twenty-five years in prison. The conviction was reversed on appeal because of judicial errors, but the case was retried in 1987. Ebens was freed, but in a subsequent civil suit he was ordered to pay $1.5 million to Chin's estate as part of a court-approved settlement agreement. In 1989, Renee Tajima and Christine Choy made a documentary film based on the case entitled *Who Killed Vincent Chin?*

China lobby: Unofficial political coalition primarily consisting of conservative Republican politicians, journalists, business tycoons, and publishing magnates who avidly supported the Chinese Nationalist government of Chiang Kai-shek in the 1940's and 1950's. The China lobby reflected the views of the dominant political faction within the Chinese American community, where issues relating to internal Chinese politics and U.S.-

political contributions in Washington, D.C., and to establish a lobbying base for the Guomindang, Chiang's government. When World War II ended in 1945, a struggle for control of the Chinese mainland erupted into civil war. The contending elements were the Chinese Communists, under the leadership of Mao Zedong, and Chiang's Nationalist forces, which had been armed and financially supported by the United States throughout China's struggle with Japan.

By 1947, Soong was Chiang's official foreign minister, and his influential anticommunist allies were many. They included publishers Henry Luce and William Randolph Hearst as well as William C. Bullitt, former presidential adviser and ambassador to both the Soviet Union and France. Bullitt's article, entitled "Report on China," published in October, 1947, in

The China lobby, a political coalition in the U.S., supported the nationalist government of Chiang Kai-shek (shown here at center leaving the tomb of Sun Yat Sen). (National Archives)

China relations were highly significant and hotly debated.

The inception of the China lobby can be traced back to 1940 when Chiang's brother-in-law, the independently wealthy T. V. Soong, first began to make

Luce's *Life* magazine, charged that the Washington bureaucracy was undermining Chiang's opposition to Communism and urged immediate, full-scale military intervention in support of the Guomindang.

The lobby was successful in pressuring the Truman

Administration to approve the China Aid Act of 1948, which provided Chiang with $125 million to use at his discretion. Chiang, however, continued to suffer a series of military defeats, and his position became increasingly desperate. Despite extensive propaganda efforts by the lobby, including goodwill visits to the United States by Madame Chiang Kai-shek, Chiang's Nationalist army was forced in 1949 to evacuate the mainland and reestablish the Guomindang on the offshore island of Formosa (Taiwan).

The loss of China to Communism seemed to the China lobby to be the result of a deep-seated Communist plot developed by a procommunist state department. Secretary of State George C. Marshall became the central target of the lobby's enmity. It was Marshall, the lobby contended, who had erroneously advised Roosevelt to relinquish Manchuria to Stalin in return for military alliance against Japan. Furthermore, Marshall's 1945-1947 truce mission that temporarily ended hostilities and attempted to bring about a Nationalist/Communist coalition had only served to enable the Communists to consolidate their mainland position, according to the lobby.

China's involvement in the KOREAN WAR (1950-1953) fueled fears of Communist aggression in Asia. Aided by COLD WAR paranoia and an alliance with the infamous Senator Joseph McCarthy, the China lobby continued to forestall recognition of Communist China by the United Nations. Although the lobby survived in increasingly diminished strength into the 1970's, President Richard Nixon's historic visit to China in 1972 and the death of Chiang Kai-shek in 1975 signaled the group's demise. In 1979, the United States formally recognized the People's Republic of China and restored diplomatic relations.

SUGGESTED READINGS. The most thorough examination of the China lobby's political network is Ross Y. Koen's *The China Lobby in American Politics* (1974). Sterling Seagrave's *The Soong Dynasty* (1985) offers interesting insight into the control of the lobby maintained by Taiwan. Also helpful are Michael Schaller's *The United States and China in the Twentieth Century* (1979) and A. T. Steele's *The American People and China* (1966).

Chinatowns: Urban neighborhoods with a concentration of Chinese American homes, businesses, and community organizations. Like other American immigrant enclaves in the nineteenth century, Chinatowns started as involuntary urban GHETTOS. Additionally, since the Chinese faced both verbal and physical abuse as well as legal restrictions on immigration and citizenship, large-scale Chinatowns had become places of refuge by the 1880's. Their subsequent histories have reflected shifts in Chinese immigration as well as adaptations to American life.

Early Chinatowns were predominantly "bachelor" societies in which the male-to-female ratio reached twenty-seven to one in 1890. Since most Chinese immigrants were SOJOURNER male laborers, they left their wives in China, seeking to earn enough money to return successfully one day. Only merchants and professionals established families in the United States. Generally from the southern province of Guangdong, these Toishan/Cantonese speakers established complex "towns" harboring shops and living quarters as well as many associations. These included religious, social, political, and trade organizations, as well as fraternal societies (TONGS), and family and district associations. Each served different functions, and to some extent they replaced the traditional familial support the bachelors had left behind in China. They provided jobs, money, mail, lodging, fellowship, and recreation. In San Francisco's Chinatown, the major association, called the Chinese Six Companies or the CHINESE CONSOLIDATED BENEVOLENT ASSOCIATION, also spoke for the Chinese community to the outside world.

The only major non-Chinese fixtures in Chinatowns were the missionaries, especially those from Protestant churches. As early as 1853, a Presbyterian mission was established in the San Francisco Chinatown. By 1890, 275 missions and Sunday schools could be found throughout the country's Chinese communities.

As Chinese immigration progressed, Chinatowns were gradually transformed. Second-generation Chinese Americans, although born and raised in Chinatowns, were citizens who could leave to pursue careers elsewhere. They also formed new organizations to express their voices, such as the CHINESE AMERICAN CITIZENS ALLIANCE.

Since the abolition of the CHINESE EXCLUSION ACT in 1943, the establishment of the Communist People's Republic of China in 1949, and finally the repeal of the 105-person Chinese immigration quota in 1965, Chinese immigration has grown continuously. Chinatowns continue to provide familiar surroundings for those with little knowledge of English or American culture. Many low-skilled workers can find jobs only in the restaurants and sweatshops of Chinatowns. With little knowledge of their rights, they have faced exploitation by their Chinese employers, working long hours for little pay and benefits. Despite crowded and unsanitary living and working conditions, many immigrants, such as the elderly, still prefer to stay in Chinatowns because of the accessibility of medical and legal services and recreational opportunities.

Today's Chinatowns retain some of their traditional features and associations, but their importance has declined with integration and the rise of government social agencies such as the Chinatown Planning Council in New York. Some Chinatowns also face serious problems of gang activities, large elderly populations,

China, Taiwan, and Hong Kong as well as Southeast Asia, adapting to the ever-changing Chinese experience in the United States.

SUGGESTED READINGS. Peter Kwang has constructed a detailed portrait of New York's Chinese enclave in *The New Chinatowns* (1987). Ronald Riddle has brought together issues of music and culture on the West Coast in *Flying Dragons, Flowing Streams: Music in the Life of San Francisco Chinese* (1983). John Kuo Wei Tchen has made Arnold Genthe's turn-of-the century photographic record of San Francisco available in *Genthe's Photographs of San Francisco's Old*

In Los Angeles, Chinatown is located just north of the main downtown business center. (David Fowler)

and clashes with encroaching urban groups and projects. At the same time, newer Chinese communities have grown in such areas as Queens, New York and Los Angeles' suburban Monterey Park as well as in smaller American cities and towns. These communities incorporate diverse Chinese populations from

Chinatown (1984). A variety of Chinatowns are examined in Betty Lee Sung's *The Story of the Chinese in America* (1971) and Sucheng Chan's *Asian Americans* (1991), as well as in Himm Mark Lai, Joe Huang, and Don Wong's *The Chinese of America, 1785-1980* (1980).

Chinese American Citizens Alliance: Organization of American-born Chinese working for equal treatment. The group was first established in San Francisco in 1895 and was known as the Native Sons of the Golden State. By 1915, other chapters had developed in cities throughout the country, and the group took the name Chinese American Citizens Alliance. The organization published the largest Chinese newspaper in the United States, the *Chinese Times,* and was influential for a time. Its leaders tended to be conservative Republican businessmen. Eventually, as the Chinese American population grew larger, the group was unable to maintain its influence on Chinese Americans of other classes or ideologies.

working for the British East India Company, established a shipbuilding center on Victoria Island, Canada, with shipbuilders, carpenters, metal workers, and sailors from Guangdong, China. These workers built a 40-ton schooner, the largest ship of its time built on the coast of the Americas, evidence that Chinese were working on the West Coast well before the Lewis and Clark expedition arrived there in 1804.

Emigration from one's country is affected by both "push" and "pull" forces. The push factors affecting Chinese emigration were primarily economic and political. The first large wave of Chinese that emigrated to the United States left China in the mid- to late nine-

Early meeting of the Chinese American Citizens Alliance. (Asian American Studies Library, University of California, Berkeley)

Chinese Americans: Although large-scale Chinese immigration to the United States did not begin until the 1850's, Chinese contact with the Americas dates to the eighteenth century—if not centuries earlier, as some traditions suggest. In 1788, John Meares, an Englishman

teenth century to escape famine as well as political and social unrest in southern China. A small number of Chinese students also arrived in hope of securing knowledge that they could take back to China to help with their country's modernization process. The pull

CHINA

factors included exaggerated tales of extreme wealth and opportunity in America surrounding the California GOLD RUSH of 1848. The Chinese name for California

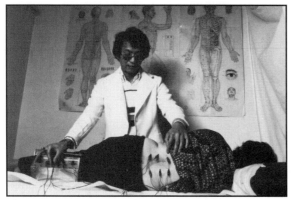

A Chinese American practitioner treats a patient with acupuncture. (Asian American Studies Library, University of California, Berkeley)

was "GOLD MOUNTAIN." Despite imperial edicts that forbade emigration from China, many Chinese, mostly young males, began emigrating to other countries in Asia and the Americas, as well as moving to other areas within China itself. Their purpose in leaving southern China was to earn money to support their families and then return home. To secure passage to the United States, many Chinese indentured themselves to a merchant or a labor agent, a "CREDIT-TICKET" arrangement by which merchants advanced immigrants money for passage and kept collecting on the loan for years. Others paid their own fares, while still others were sponsored by relatives already in the United States and other countries.

For many Chinese, the journey to the United States was, in some ways, analogous to the African slave trade. The ships were very old, and the immigrants traveled in the most wretched conditions: densely packed into poorly ventilated, unsanitary compartments with meager food supplies. Many did not survive the long journey. Once in the United States, the labor agents gained almost complete domination of their INDENTURED workers, who were kept in isolated communities that became known as CHINATOWNS. Many Chinese, not wanting to remain permanently in the United States, had little incentive to become Americanized. Their unwillingness to become acculturated fueled American prejudices against all Chinese. Although most Chinese wanted to return to China, many could not secure sufficient money for return passage.

After the outlawing of the international slave trade by the United States in 1862, the large port cities in southern China became centers of "COOLIE labor" for wealthy entrepreneurs in the Americas. When volunteers were not forthcoming, agents resorted to tricks and intimidation. Often men were simply kidnapped (shanghaied) and put into barracks where they were terrorized before being sent to South America and the Caribbean to work on plantations. As a result of the ethnic wars taking place in southern China, captured prisoners were sometimes sold to the agents of what was called the "pig trade." By 1900, there were thirty thousand Hakka Chinese in the Western Hemisphere, partly as a result of this barbarous trade.

Life in California in the late 1800's was difficult at best for the Chinese. The Chinese communities organized *Hui-Guan* (merchant guilds) that served as welcoming committees and MUTUAL AID SOCIETIES for new immigrants. Chinese immigrants were also organized by the CHINESE CONSOLIDATED BENEVOLENT ASSOCIATION (the Six Companies) and later by TONGS, secret societies that originated in China.

Building the West. The California GOLD RUSH drew people from all over the world, including Europeans, Latin Americans, and Asians, as well as people from the eastern parts of the United States. As California's

The herbal pharmacy at Emperor's College in Santa Monica, Calif., is stocked with myriad potent natural treatments. (Alon Reininger, Unicorn Stock Photos)

population increased and the gold supply decreased, violence against "foreigners" and other nonwhites increased. American Indians were the first to be driven out, followed by African Americans, Chileans, Peruvians, French, Mexicans, and Chinese.

As the gold supply declined, many Chinese moved on to other states. Chinese mined silver and other minerals in Utah, Nevada, Colorado, Montana, Wyoming, and Idaho, as well as coal in Northern California, Oregon, and Wyoming, and gold in South Dakota. Chinatowns or Chinese quarters flourished for years in these areas. By 1870, Chinese laborers accounted for more than 27 percent of all miners in the United States.

Approximately half of the Chinese living in the United States in 1870 were involved in mining, while and Rocky Mountains—called the greatest engineering accomplishment of the nineteenth century—was completed largely by Chinese laborers. After the completion of the transcontinental railroad in 1869, many Chinese went to work on other railways in the United States, Canada, and in Panama.

In 1849, the year of the great California Gold Rush, there were only 325 Chinese living in California. By 1882, there were 107,488 Chinese in the United

TEN STATES WITH HIGHEST CHINESE AMERICAN POPULATIONS

Source: Data are from John Wilson, *Chinese Americans*. American Voices series. Vero Beach, Fla.: Rourke Corp., 1991.

others were involved in a variety of occupations. Some Chinese established restaurants, laundries, shops, and home delivery services for flowers, fresh vegetables, cloth, and exotic wares from China. As a result of the small number of women in the West at that time, Chinese men were commonly employed as domestics and cooks in homes and on ranches. Chinese in San Francisco were also involved in street leveling and grading and construction with some buildings imported in their entirety from China. Some Chinese were employed in the Chinese theater and the traveling opera troupes that were popular at that time.

As the mining industry declined, many Chinese went to work on the railroads. The extremely difficult and dangerous track that was laid through the Sierra States, representing 0.2 percent of the total U.S. population.

Early Chinese immigrants to the United States contributed greatly to the economic development of the West. The Chinese made an enormous contribution in mining the minerals needed to industrialize and modernize the West. California's gold and financial power went into commerce, harbor facilities, transport, industry, irrigation, and reclamation of farmland, all of which helped create the infrastructure of a modern agricultural and industrial state that helped transform the United States into the richest and most powerful nation on earth.

The special tax that Chinese paid as foreign miners provided substantial revenue to the state of California for many years, funding hospitals, schools, and other social services. Chinese farmers helped plant the vineyards in the Napa and Sonoma valleys; by 1886, Chinese made up 85.7 percent of California's farm labor. In addition, Chinese laborers performed much of the difficult, underpaid manufacturing work in industries such as textiles, clothing, shoes, and canneries. In the 1880's, Chinese accounted for 86 percent of the work force in the salmon canneries of California and the northwest coast, 80 percent of the shirtmakers in San Francisco, 70 to 80 percent of the work force in the wool industry, 84 percent in the cigar industry, and 50 percent of the fisheries workers.

The Anti-Chinese Movement. Despite their significant contributions, the Chinese living in the western United States met with extreme RACISM and violence. The first anti-Chinese riot took place in Tuolumne County in 1849, where sixty Chinese miners were driven out of town by white miners. In the 1860's and 1870's, many unions and political parties, including the Democratic and Republican Parties, adopted anti-Asian platforms. In 1871, eighteen Chinese were lynched in a riot in Los Angeles. A similar incident occurred in San Francisco in 1877. The violence also spread to other western states. In 1885, twenty-eight Chinese were murdered and three hundred others were driven out of town in Rock Springs, Wyoming. There were anti-Chinese riots in Colorado and Wyoming and, in 1887, thirty-one Chinese miners were robbed, murdered, and mutilated in the Snake River massacre in Oregon. Sometimes Chinese were not only lynched or shot but also dismembered, disemboweled, battered to death, or burned alive. It is no wonder that the phrase "not a Chinaman's chance" became popular in the United States.

Exclusion. The first law to restrict immigration into the United States was the CHINESE EXCLUSION ACT of 1882. This act, along with the Congressional Acts of 1888, 1892, 1894 and 1904, prevented the naturalization of Chinese living in the United States; banned future immigration of Chinese laborers; limited and later barred altogether the re-entry of Chinese laborers formerly residing in the country; and required that Chinese, alone among the residents of the United States, must register themselves and always carry photo identification papers. In 1871, the U.S. Supreme Court upheld a California state law declaring Chinese ineligible for citizenship; in 1893, the Court ruled that the federal government could deport Chinese aliens without going to court or showing just cause. Federal

legislation in 1898 and 1902 extended the exclusionary acts to Hawaii and the Philippines. By 1943, the year the Chinese Exclusion Act was repealed, the Chinese population in the United States had shrunk to 0.05 percent of the total U.S. population.

These racist laws and discriminatory practices, coupled with legal and illegal harassment and violent attacks, caused many Chinese to abandon most farming, fishing, manufacturing, and other relatively high-paying jobs. The severe racist policies and practices of U.S. immigration officials led to a boycott of American goods by students and merchants in China from 1904 to 1906.

During the period of exclusion, the Chinese American community gradually became overwhelmingly urban. Most of the small CHINATOWNS that had dotted the nation disappeared, and the major Chinatowns became part fortress, part ghetto, and part haven in which Chinese could escape harassment and ANTI-CHINESE VIOLENCE.

Integration and Assimilation. In the latter part of the twentieth century, attitudes toward Chinese Americans began to improve. A major impetus to improved relations was the support and direct participation of Chinese Americans in World War II. Chinese Americans organized patriotic associations, raised funds to defend China and the United States, and led strikes against scrap iron sales to Japan. The thirteen thousand Chinese Americans who fought in the war represented

These Chinese American combatants practice an ancient form of martial arts. (Asian American Studies Library, University of California, Berkeley)

17 percent of that ethnic population. In addition, fifteen thousand Chinese seamen served in the merchant marine during the war. Chinese American women joined the war effort by working in nursing, shipbuild-

ing, and various trades.

Once they were accorded the same rights and privileges as other immigrants with the passage of the Magnuson Act in 1943, more Chinese Americans began to move into the mainstream of American society. The population swelled after the IMMIGRATION AND NATIONALITY ACT OF 1965 removed national quotas, encouraging new arrivals from Hong Kong and Taiwan as well as frequent CHAIN MIGRATION of relatives.

**Chinese in the Contiguous
United States, 1860-1990**

Source: From John Wilson, *Chinese Americans*. American Voices series, pp. 42, 46. Vero Beach, Fla.: 1991.
Note: 1990 includes Hawaii

Many of these newcomers were well-educated professionals.

Chinese Americans and other Asian American groups have been dubbed the "MODEL MINORITY" because of their successful adjustment to American life. By 1990, 40 percent of Chinese Americans above the age of twenty-five had four or more years of college education (twice the national average) and earned five thousand dollars more per year than the median family income; 30 percent held professional or managerial jobs; 6 percent owned their own businesses; and many had moved out of CHINATOWNS into the suburbs.

Despite these accomplishments, Chinese Americans still face significant barriers to equal opportunity in education and employment; they also lack equal access to many public services, including police protec-

tion, health care, and the court system. ETHNIC SLURS and HATE CRIMES against Chinese Americans have surfaced on high school and college campuses, in print and nonprint media, in the workplace, and in other public places.

In 1990, there were more than 1.3 million Chinese in the United States, including 92,684 university students from mainland China, Taiwan, and Hong Kong. More than 60 percent live in California and New York. Most recent immigration has been related to the "push" factors of continuing political problems in mainland China and Hong Kong and the "pull" factors of educational and economic opportunities in the United States.

Cultural Contributions. The cultural values the Chinese immigrants brought with them meshed well with those of a country struggling to become a nation and an industrial power: a respect for a job well done and the view that hard work was a way to get ahead. The strong sense of family that is central to Chinese culture and the prime ambition of giving their children a good education also fit well into the American tradition. Coupled with the traditional CONFUCIAN respect for elders, authority, and social stability, these values have contributed to the molding of American culture.

Undoubtedly the most obvious and pervasive Chinese contribution to American life is the widespread American acceptance of Chinese cuisine. Traditionally, Chinese restaurants primarily offered Cantonese food. In the late decades of the twentieth century, however, Chinese restaurants have emphasized a greater variety of Chinese foods, including the regional cuisines of Shanghai, Szechuan, and Hunan. Another aspect of Chinese culture that has been studied and practiced by many Americans is traditional Chinese healing practices, such as herbal medicine and acupuncture. Chinese art and calligraphy have also been influential.

Chinese Americans have excelled in many fields of endeavor, ranging from science and medicine to architecture. Chen Ning YANG and T. D. LEE, who shared the Nobel Prize in Physics in 1957, are among the many renowned American scientists of Chinese descent. Another is chemist Yuan T. Lee, who shared the Nobel Prize in Chemistry in 1986. Internationally recognized Chinese American architects include I. M. PEI, who designed a wing of the National Gallery in Washington, D.C., and Maya Ying Lin, who designed the Vietnam Veterans Memorial.

A Chinese American worker waits for the Chinese Benevolent Association to open its doors in Sacramento, Calif., 1936. (Library of Congress)

Prominent Chinese Americans have also left their marks in journalism, politics, and the arts. Known for their work in journalism are NG POON CHEW, who published the country's first Chinese-language newspaper (in 1898), and, more recently, television journalist Connie CHUNG, named by the Columbia Broadcasting System (CBS) in 1993 as coanchor of its evening news broadcast. In politics, Hiram L. FONG of Hawaii was the first Chinese American senator. Chinese Americans have been making increasingly influential contributions to artistic fields. Renowned playwrights include David Henry HWANG and Frank CHIN; prominent among fiction writers are Amy TAN and Maxine Hong KINGSTON. Chinese American filmmakers include Wayne WANG and Felicia Lowe. In the world of music, cellist Yo-Yo MA has received international acclaim.

SUGGESTED READINGS. A thorough historical account of Chinese Americans from a Chinese perspective is provided in Jack Chen's *The Chinese of America* (1980). A broader view is offered in Ronald Takaki's *Strangers from a Different Shore: A History of Asian Americans* (1989), Roger Daniels' *Asian America: Chinese and Japanese in the United States Since 1850* (1988), and Linda Perrin's *Coming to America: Immigrants from the Far East* (1980). For a brief, unbiased account of Chinese Americans see Stanley Karnow and Nancy Yoshihara's *Asian Americans in Transition* (1992). An excellent overview of Chinese American history and discrimination against Chinese Americans is provided in the United States Commission on Civil Rights report *Civil Rights Issues Facing Asian Americans in the 1990's* (1992). An excellent high school level book is Dana Ying-hui Wu and Jeffrey Dao-Sheng Tung's *Coming to America: The Chinese American Experience* (1993).—*Gregory A. Levitt*

Chinese Americans from Hong Kong. *See* **Hong Kong, Chinese Americans from**

Chinese Consolidated Benevolent Association: Outgrowth of the Chinese Six Companies that was founded to fight anti-Chinese discrimination. Chinese immigrants in California formed community groups, called *huiguan*, composed of people who had come from the same districts in China. To settle disputes among the groups, six *huiguan* formed a group in 1862 that whites came to refer to as the Chinese Six Companies. In 1882, when the CHINESE EXCLUSION ACT went into effect, various *huiguan* in San Francisco united to fight discrimination. They called the organization the Chinese Consolidated Benevolent Association, but it was often still known as the Chinese Six Companies as well. The group hired white lawyers to bring antidiscrimination lawsuits and established CHINESE LANGUAGE schools. The Association became powerful in CHINATOWNS across the United States, even determining who was permitted to emigrate and to operate businesses in Chinatowns.

Chinese diaspora: Chinese people living outside their original homeland. In 1990, the conservative estimate of this population stood at approximately thirty-five million people. This number refers only to people who immigrated to their new countries within recent memory, and who maintain distinct ethnic, cultural, and emotional ties to the land of origin of their ancestors.

Chinese Americans, most of whom immigrated to the United States after 1965, account for about 1.8 million of the diaspora. They came from Taiwan, China, Hong Kong, and Southeast Asia, and live throughout the United States, though San Francisco, Los Angeles, and New York account for a large percentage. For example, since 1965 the number of Chinese in New York City has more than quadrupled, and now accounts for 5 percent of the total population of greater New York City.

Chinese immigrants in the United States fall into two categories. The first are well-educated, skilled, and moneyed; most of them came from Taiwan or Hong Kong. They assimilate easily, become business and professional people, and tend to settle in the suburbs. Many among the second group came from mainland China or Hong Kong to join family members. These tend to have less education and money. They tend to live in crowded housing in CHINATOWNS and take low-paying work in the GARMENT INDUSTRY and

in restaurants. Few, however, resort to public assistance for fear of losing face and because of ignorance of welfare procedures. Despite sensational reports of Chinese youth gang crimes, crime is low among Chinese immigrants.

General American perception of Chinese Americans has changed in accord with the nature of recent Chinese immigrants. They are regarded as a high achieving minority, and their children characteristically do well in school. Many Chinese language newspapers, some affiliated with papers in Taiwan and elsewhere, keep Chinese Americans informed on events both in their adopted home and in their former homelands. Others are aware of events abroad as the result of frequent travel. Chinese Americans draw investments and trade to the United States from Taiwan, Hong Kong, and Southeast Asia; they also invest in their former homelands.

Historical Background. Peoples throughout the world have always moved to find new homes and work, either voluntarily or by forced migration and

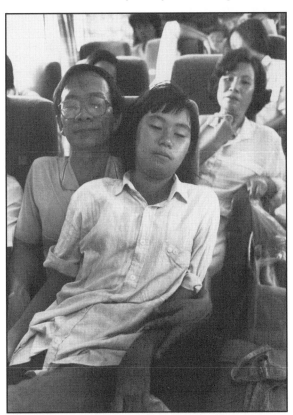

Vietnamese boat people of Chinese descent en route to their new homes in the U.S. (A. Hollmann/UNHCR)

slavery. From the beginning of Chinese civilization some four thousand years ago, Chinese from the middle and lower Yellow River Valley have been moving to open new lands. Many of these new lands, such as the Yangtze and Pearl River valleys and the coast, eventually became Chinese.

More than two thousand years ago, Chinese immigrants brought an advanced culture to Korea and

This Chinese American woman makes her home in San Francisco, Calif. (Jim Hays, Unicorn Stock Photos)

northern Vietnam. Although for hundreds of years both areas were part of the Chinese empire, they developed their own distinctive Chinese-influenced cultures and absorbed the Chinese immigrants. For more than a thousand years, successive waves of Chinese merchants have gone to mainland and island Southeast Asia, where some settled and intermarried with local peoples. Early European explorers, traders, and colonial administrators throughout Southeast Asia have noted the thriving Chinese communities. In time most of these became assimilated and lost contact with China.

The millions of Chinese in the contemporary diaspora are found in every continent and more than a hundred countries. They are part of the universal population movements of the nineteenth and twentieth centuries, motivated by economic and political forces. During the modern era, the migration of Chinese to other lands can be subdivided into three periods, each with distinct characteristics.

First were the commercial migrants, who like their forebears, sailed to Southeast Asia for trade, or to ply their highly sought skills as weavers, miners, or potters. These were the industrious and prosperous Chinese early Europeans observed, most notably in Manila in the Philippines, Bangkok in Thailand, and Batavia (Jakarta) in the Dutch East Indies. Most came from China's two southernmost provinces, Fukien and Guangdong. They built up important trading networks and thrived despite periodic persecution by locals and European colonial governments.

The second wave, estimated at more than two million people, left China in the nineteenth century. Most were originally poor farmers or landless workers, also from Fukien and Guangdong provinces. They left because of economic hardships and political turmoil caused by the Taiping Rebellion (1851-1864), First Anglo-Chinese War (1839-1841), and the Second Anglo-Chinese War (1856-1860), which were especially devastating to Guangdong. Many left China as contract laborers (also called COOLIES) and resembled late twentieth century guest workers in Europe. They were often called "SOJOURNERS," rather than immigrants. They went to Southeast Asia, the United States, and Peru, among other places, to build railroads, open mines, clear land, and work in plantations. When their contracts expired, many returned to China; hence there was a constant rotation of Chinese in lands where they worked. Records are incomplete, but those for 1881-1882 show that while 57,271 Chinese arrived in the United States, only 26,788 departed, leaving a net gain of 30,483. The reasons were probably a combination of delays in the realization of unrealistic goals set by the sojourners and changes in plans as some sojourners became settlers.

Chinese laborers were not particularly important in Southeast Asia to the formation of local perceptions of Chinese, as the laborers were subordinate to the well-regarded Chinese merchants. In the United States, Australia, and Canada, however, the sojourners were the first Chinese encountered by nineteenth century white settlers. The latter formed their impressions of Chinese people based on this group of gold rushers, miners, and railway builders. Rapid transformations in the economies of Western countries soon outgrew demand for coolie labor. Moreover, hostile white reactions to perceived racial and social differences with the predominantly male Chinese sojourners—often led by labor unions—resulted in the enactment of laws that ended the importation of Chinese laborers before the end of the nineteenth century. The U.S. CHINESE EXCLUSION ACT was passed in 1882, effectively ending immigration. By the 1920's, most doors in Southeast Asian lands had also been closed.

Overseas Chinese and Relations with the Homeland. Many Chinese emigrants not only sent money to kin back home but also became active in seeking political change in China. Sun Yat-sen, a native of Guangzhou educated in Hawaii and later in British Hong Kong, relied heavily on Chinese emigrants in Southeast Asia, Hawaii, and the United States for membership and financial support of his revolutionary society (later named the Kuomintang or Nationalist Party) that in 1911 overthrew the Ch'ing dynasty.

By the early twentieth century, the term *hua-ch'iao*, or "overseas Chinese," was used to denote Chinese who lived outside the boundary of China. The early Ch'ing government tended to neglect this population; until the late nineteenth century, emigration was officially illegal though not enforced. The Nationalist government, established in 1928, cultivated overseas Chinese through its embassies and consulates, and sought to protect their interests. It established schools for overseas Chinese children in their new lands and set aside special scholarships for returning overseas Chinese students in China. Many overseas Chinese reciprocated by investing money in and contributing their expertise to modernize China. The patriotic feelings of overseas Chinese toward their homeland were strongly expressed during World War II. After 1949, the governments of the People's Republic of China on the mainland and the Republic of China on Taiwan competed for the allegiance of overseas Chinese throughout the world.

These policies fostered political, cultural, and emotional ties with the mother country, but also fed the belief among local peoples that the Chinese were unassimilable. This feeling was especially strong in parts of Southeast Asia where Chinese were numerous. When former colonies in Southeast Asia gained independence after World War II, many nationalistic governments of newly independent countries looked on local Chinese as politically untrustworthy; the mistrust

was exacerbated by the rise of the People's Republic of China whose Communist ideology and military might were feared throughout the region. Many countries passed laws discriminating against Chinese minorities, whose economic success also made them the targets of envious locals.

Modern Trends. By the late twentieth century, Chinese nationalism had dissipated among many overseas

Chinese American family residing in the suburbs of Chicago, Ill. (Jim and Mary Whitmer)

Chinese, who considered their adopted country, not China, their home. In Southeast Asia, where most overseas Chinese live, ethnic Chinese have found a mixed reception to their quest to assimilate. For example, the Chinese of Vietnam have been intensely persecuted by its Communist government since the late 1970's; the resulting flight of ethnic Chinese reduced their number from 1,550,000 in 1975 to about 700,000 by 1990. Many of the "BOAT PEOPLE" who fled Indochina and eventually settled in the United States were ethnic Chinese.

The number of ethnic Chinese in the United States dropped drastically from 1890 to 1945 because of ex-

Artist's depiction of Chinese railroad workers; xenophobia and fear of labor competition prompted the passage of the Chinese Exclusion Act in 1882. (Asian American Studies Library, University of California, Berkeley)

clusionary laws, and because many of the predominantly male nineteenth century SOJOURNERS remained bachelors. In time, the largely uneducated sojourners were replaced by an acculturated generation of American-born Chinese.

The nature of Chinese immigration changed dramatically after 1949. With Communist conquest of China, thousands of Chinese graduate students in the United States sought immigrant status. They were joined by thousands more who came from Taiwan for graduate study after 1949 and stayed on in the United States to work. These mid-twentieth century Chinese came from all parts of China, belonged to an urban, westernized elite. They were not ghettoized in inner-city CHINATOWNS, but lived in middle-class suburbs. The liberalized IMMIGRATION AND NATIONALITY ACT OF 1965 allowed the entry of 20,000 Chinese immigrants annually from Taiwan; after 1979, China was also allowed 20,000 annually, and later Hong Kong received its own annual allotment of 5,000. As a result, the Chinese community became one of the fastest growing immigrant communities in the United States, reaching 1,800,000 in 1988.

Similarly, Canada and Australia have rescinded their previously anti-Asian immigration laws; as a result, the number of ethnic Chinese climbed rapidly to 635,000 in Canada and 410,000 in Australia by 1989. Liberalized immigration laws in Great Britain and France have also resulted in a wave of recent Chinese immigration, boosting the number of Chinese to 230,000 in Britain and 150,000 in France respectively.

Number and Characteristics. By far the largest number of overseas Chinese live in East and Southeast Asia. Their estimated numbers are 7.2 million in Indonesia, 5.8 million in Thailand, 5.2 million in Malaysia, 5.8 million in Hong Kong, 2 million in Singapore, 1.5 million in Burma, 800,000 in the Philippines, 700,000 in Vietnam, and 450,000 in Macao. (Hong Kong and Macao are anomalies in that they are British and Portuguese colonies on the southern China coast and are scheduled to be returned to China in 1997 and 1999 respectively.) The remaining countries in the region, namely Japan, Korea, Cambodia, and Laos combined, have under a million Chinese. In South Asia and the Middle East, the total number of ethnic Chinese is less than a quarter of a million. Most of these are culturally not Han Chinese (who account for about 94 percent of Chinese citizens); those in India are mostly Tibetans and those in the Middle East (chiefly in Turkey and Saudi Arabia) are Chinese Muslims.

Both these groups fled after the establishment of Communist power in China in 1949.

After Asia, North America has the largest number of ethnic Chinese, with 1.8 million in the United States and 650,000 in Canada. Approximately a third of a million live scattered in Central and South America and the Caribbean islands with Brazil accounting for the largest aggregation (about 100,000). Most ethnic Chinese in Europe are found in Britain and France, in addition to seventy thousand in the Netherlands, forty thousand in Germany, and smaller numbers in other western European countries. Recent Chinese immigration to Australia has raised the number there to more than 400,000. Aside from about 200,000 Chinese in South Africa who entered in the early 1900's as laborers and traders, there are few Chinese in Africa.

The character of post-World War II Chinese emigrants differed from that of earlier eras. Most of the later emigrants fled China for political or economic reasons to escape the Communist regime. Thus they were largely from urban and middle-class backgrounds, and many were highly educated and cosmopolitan. Some fled with capital. Many are re-migrants, some several times over; that is, they are Chinese who were born and domiciled abroad in Hong Kong, Macao, Vietnam, and Malaysia, for example, who re-emigrated to escape impending Communist takeover (from Hong Kong or Macao, and earlier from Indochina) or for other reasons, by migrating to North America, Australia, and western Europe.

SUGGESTED READINGS. See Barth Gunther's *Bitter Strength* (1964) on early Chinese immigration to the United States. Charles P. Fitzgerald's *The Southern Expansion of the Chinese People* (1972) is a good, scholarly survey. Clarence E. Glick's *Sojourners and Settlers* (1980) deals with changing attitudes among Asian immigrants. Francis L. K. Hsu's *The Challenge of the American Drama: The Chinese in the United States* (1971) offers thoughtful analysis of cultural confrontation. *The Chinese in Southeast Asia* (2 vols., 1983), edited by Linda Y. C. Lim and L. A. Peter Gosling, presents a comprehensive overview. Lynn Pan's *Sons of the Yellow Emperor: A History of the Chinese Diaspora* (1990) is an informative book written in a conversational style.—*Jiu-Hwa Lo Upshur*

Chinese Exclusion Act (1882): Law passed by the U.S. Congress in 1882 forbidding the entry of unskilled laborers from China. Over the years, amendments to the law made it harder and harder for Chinese to immigrate,

Chinese hand laundries organized an alliance in New York to challenge high city tariffs and other questionable practices. This engraving shows a Chinese laundry in the 1880's. (Library of Congress)

effectively limiting the growth of the Chinese American population. The act required Chinese already in the country to carry registration papers with them at all times, and forbade their reentry if they went back to China for any reason. The law was passed not only because of economic worries about job competition in California but also because of widespread anti-Chinese prejudice. The act was originally to last for ten years, but was renewed repeatedly at ten-year intervals until it was finally repealed in 1943.

Chinese Hand Laundry Alliance: An organization formed in the early 1930's by owners of Chinese laundries in New York City. When the efficient and inexpen-

sive Chinese laundries in the city posed a threat to white-owned businesses, the city passed new laws imposing high fees on the Chinese-owned shops. Chinese launderers found that they could get no support from their own CHINESE CONSOLIDATED BENEVOLENT ASSOCIATION (CCBA); it refused to help unless the launderers paid an additional fee to the association. The launderers formed their own group, which continued for years as a more progressive alternative to the conservative CCBA.

Chinese language: Language spoken by more than one-fourth of all people in the world. The Chinese language has many variations. If a person from Guangzhou, in southern China, met a person from Beijing, in northern

China, it is likely that although they are both Chinese, they could not understand each other. The different forms of spoken language are called dialects. Among the Han nationality, which makes up 95 percent of China's population, there are many different dialects but only one written language. In fact, there are thirty-two national minorities in China, many with their own spoken and written language. Most Chinese living in the United States came from southern China and speak the Cantonese dialect. Nevertheless, because the national television stations use the Beijing or Mandarin (also called national language) dialect, most recent immigrants can understand the Beijing dialect.

The Beijing dialect consists of four tones—high, rising, dipping, and falling—plus a neutral tone. The

A San Francisco man creates elegant Chinese calligraphy. (Robert Fried)

same sound with a different tone results in different words and meanings. For example, the word *ma* in first tone means mother, in second tone it means hemp or rope, in third tone it means horse, in fourth tone it means to scold, and in the neutral tone it is a word used to indicate that the speaker is asking a question. The Cantonese dialect consists of nine tones plus the neutral tone.

The earliest examples of Chinese writing consist of characters written on bones, tortoise shells, and bronze vessels from the Shang Dynasty, 1500-1028 B.C.E. In three thousand years, there have been some modifications to the characters, yet the basic principles have remained the same. Some contemporary characters, such as the one for horse (*ma*) are formalized pictographs whose origin can be traced back to ancient times. Most older characters have been changed, however, and new ones have been added, making it almost impossible to trace their origins.

There are more than 90,000 characters, including single and compound ones, used to make words. To read a newspaper, it is necessary to recognize nearly 3,500 characters. Traditional Chinese characters are difficult to remember and to write. As a result of this difficulty, Chinese government leaders in the early 1950's introduced simplified characters which consist of fewer strokes. For example, the traditional character for horse 馬 consists of ten strokes, while the simplified character consists of four strokes 马. The traditional characters are still used in Hong Kong, Taiwan, and by most overseas Chinese throughout the world.

The pleasing appearance of written characters is extremely important to the Chinese, who consider calligraphy—characters written with a writing brush and ink—a fine art. There are several styles of written characters. In the regular style, each character is written separately and each stroke is made distinctly. In the running hand style, some strokes are run together. In the grass writing style, the flow of line, relative thickness of strokes, and other elements give each character an art form. The grass writing style is most often used by calligraphers on Chinese scrolls and paintings.

SUGGESTED READINGS. Excellent resources for understanding Chinese written and spoken language include John De Francis' *The Chinese Language: Fact and Fantasy* (1984), Robert S. Ramsey's *The Languages of China* (1987), and Cecilia Lindqvist's *China: Empire of Living Symbols* (1991). An informative and enjoyable introduction to Chinese characters is provided in Peggy Goldstein's *Long Is a Dragon: Chinese Writing for Children* (1991).

Chinese New Year: Most important holiday in Chinese communities worldwide. In the United States, Chinese Americans have maintained the traditional festival while introducing new elements. Celebrations often involve the cooperation of the whole Chinese community, a

Participants in Chinese New Year celebration in New York City. (Richard B. Levine)

statement to or proclamation from the city, and invitations to other communities to attend the parades and festivities.

The fifteen-day celebration of New Year begins on the first day of the first moon in the Chinese lunar calendar, which in most cases falls between late January and late February. Also called the Spring Festival, its name and emphasis on certain flowers reflect its geographic heritage. Families must clean the house to usher in a prosperous year, while blossoming peach and cherry branches bring good fortune. All debts should be settled, and animosity should be resolved among friends and family on New Year's Day. Families join together for dinner on New Year's Eve to complete the old year.

Preparations begin a few days before the New Year with the cooking of festive foods. Popular items include fried shredded taro ball, a chip medley that includes fried taro, sweet potato, peanut, and broad bean; fried dumplings with sweet fillings; parsnip cake and taro cake; and sweets such as sweet rice cake and coconut cake. Special dishes whose names resonate with good wishes are also prepared for celebratory meals.

On New Year's Day, everyone dons new clothes as families visit relatives, friends, and business associates. Children (and, theoretically, all unmarried people) receive red envelopes containing gifts of money from married couples. People greet one another saying "Kow Hei Fat Choy" ("I wish you much prosperity")

and everyone turns one year older.

Urban Chinese American communities have retained these customs for many decades: San Francisco's Chinatown has celebrated Chinese New Year since 1851. Most shops close on New Year's Day, if not for a few days, and establishments bear placards with words of wisdom and greetings. Firecrackers explode on the streets. Many CHINATOWNS have added Chinese New Year parades. This Sino-American invention recalls the main street parade of other American towns, with floats and marching bands mingling with lion and dragon dancers. These draw Chinese people who live elsewhere to Chinatowns, and they attract non-Chinese, who may remain for restaurant banquets. Many Chinese communities try to hold their parade on New Year's Day; however, in order to cater to the American work calendar, they sometimes move the parade to a nearby weekend.

Those Chinese Americans who live or work far from Chinatowns or areas with large Chinese populations tend to celebrate Chinese New Year on a reduced scale at home or in Chinese restaurants. Other Asian New Year celebrations, such as Tet of the Vietnamese Americans, occur at about the same time of year and involve many similar customs.

SUGGESTED READINGS. The festival and its attendant customs and their adaptations can be found in most descriptions of Chinese people in the United States. Frank Chin provides a strong, impressionistic portrait of the events and experiences of a San Francisco New Year's fortnight in *Donald Duk* (1991). Ronald Riddle discusses relevant issues of music and performance in *Flying Dragons, Flowing Streams: Music in the Life of San Francisco Chinese* (1983).

Chinese workers and the Central Pacific Railroad. *See* **Central Pacific Railroad—Chinese workers**

Chisholm, Shirley (b. Nov. 30, 1924, Brooklyn, N.Y.): African American congresswoman. Early in her life Chisholm worked with children, eventually running her own nursery school. At Hamilton-Madison Child Care in New York, she advised city officials on the quality and needs of day care facilities. In 1946 she was elected New York State Assemblywoman and directed her attention to minimum wage laws and labor conditions. In 1968 she was elected to the U.S. Congress from the 12th District in Brooklyn. She is a member of the LEAGUE OF WOMEN VOTERS and the NATIONAL ASSOCIATION FOR THE ADVANCEMENT OF COLORED PEOPLE (NAACP).

Chivington, John Milton (Jan. 27, 1821, Warren County, Ohio—Oct. 4, 1894, Denver, Colo.): Methodist preacher turned soldier, known as the Fighting Parson. As colonel of the Colorado Volunteers, Chivington led the attack upon CHEYENNES at SAND CREEK in which two hundred Indians were gunned down, clubbed, or knifed to death, most of them women and children. Cheyenne chief BLACK KETTLE escaped; the massacre spread a wave of revulsion against Chivington and his men and gave the Cheyennes, SIOUX, and ARAPAHOS renewed strength. Partly because of Chivington's actions at Sand Creek, the U.S. Army had to spend $30 million in campaigns to subdue the Indians.

Choctaw Nation of Oklahoma: Tribe formed when the Choctaws of the Southeast were compelled to move west in the 1820's and 1830's. In 1820 Chief PUSHMATAHA and others negotiated with General Andrew Jackson and signed the Treaty of Doak's Stand, wherein the Choctaws ceded part of their southeastern lands for a vast amount of land in the eastern part of Indian Country (present Oklahoma). In the 1820's only about one-fourth of the Choctaws of Mississippi and Alabama moved west. After white settlers increasingly encroached on Choctaw lands and harassed the tribe, most Choctaws accepted the Treaty of DANCING RABBIT CREEK in 1830. This committed them to move to Indian Country within three years. About 4,500 Choctaws, however, chose to stay in Mississippi and accept land allotments.

Because of hostile whites who honored no treaty and who immediately began seizing tribal property, most Choctaws migrated westward long before their treaty deadline. Several thousand, leaving late, traveled on a "TRAIL OF TEARS" in the dead of winter. Probably as many as 16,000 Choctaws finally reached Oklahoma, but at least 4,000 perished on the Trail of Tears.

Once in Oklahoma, the Choctaws established a society that mirrored the one they had left behind. They set up a constitutional tribal government based on a written code of laws. They reestablished their excellent educational system and welcomed missionaries such as Cyrus Kingsbury, who followed the tribe as it moved west. A breakthrough occurred in the mid-1830's when the Anglo missionary Cyrus Byinton reduced the Choctaw's spoken language to a written form based on the English alphabet. Choctaw readers established academies, seminaries, and boarding schools, and many mixed-bloods sent their children to American or European colleges.

In their economic life, the tribe likewise reestablished old patterns. Most became small, yeoman farmers who raised beans, squash, potatoes, tobacco, and other crops. The diet was supplemented by fishing as well as hunting deer, bear, boar, wildfowl, and an occasional "woodlands" bison.

Urban life also flourished in Miller Courthouse, Perryville, Skullyville, Boggy Depot, and Doaksville. These Choctaw towns all had a blacksmith shop, cotton gin, gristmill, sawmill, post office, and hotel, as well as retail stores, warehouses, tribal government buildings, schools, and churches.

In its trading patterns, the tribe found that numerous military posts in the region provided a ready market for all the vegetables, eggs, butter, and meat that the tribe could spare. Further, the Choctaws had long been known as excellent stockmen, and there was a ready market for all the hardy horses the Choctaws could breed and train.

An American Indian woman participates in the 1992 "Trail of Tears," a re-enactment of the tribe's relocation to reservation land in Oklahoma. (Elaine S. Querry)

Mississippi Choctaw woman weaves baskets at a 1992 Choctaw Indian Fair. (Elaine S. Querry)

Eventually there were strains between the full-bloods and the mixed-bloods. Full-bloods tended to isolate themselves on small farmsteads and to venture into settlements only when in need of supplies. Mixed-bloods tended to locate near towns and continue to adopt the "white man's ways." They also established large plantations, complete with African slaves, and produced vast quantities of cotton.

The downfall of the Choctaw Nation began during the American Civil War. Its warriors split in their allegiance, with many fighting for the Confederacy; at war's end the victorious Union punished the tribe by taking part of its land and thus beginning the ultimate destruction of the nation. From the 1870's through the early 1900's, the Choctaw holdings were slowly stripped away by Anglos. Only in the 1930's, under the enlightened direction of the Indian Commissioner John Collier, were steps taken to heal old wounds and restore tribal government and religion.

SUGGESTED READINGS. Two general histories provide considerable information: Arrell Gibson's *Oklahoma: A History of Five Centuries* (1981) and Edwin C. McReynolds' *Oklahoma: The Story of Its Past and Present* (1967). Other worthwhile accounts include *The Five Civilized Tribes* (1934) by Grant Foreman, *The Rise and Fall of the Choctaw Republic* (2d ed., 1961) by Angie Debo, and *A Guide to the Indian Tribes of Oklahoma* (1951) by Muriel Wright.

Choctaws, Mississippi band: Choctaw Indians who remained in the Southeast rather than relocating in Oklahoma in the nineteenth century. The original home of the Choctaws—before the coming of European settlers—was in present-day southern Mississippi and Alabama. The tribe's language was of the Muskhogean family. In the 1540's the Spanish explorer Hernando de Soto reported that the tribe had large stockaded towns on river terraces surrounded by fields and gardens; in some of the towns there were as many as a hundred dwellings that circled around a central square used for religious ceremonies and celebrations. Made of grass, plaster, or thatch attached to a pole frame, Choctaw houses showed architectural ingenuity, as did the temple or community house that dominated their towns.

Farming was the principal occupation of the Choctaws, who raised tobacco, cotton, beans, squash, potatoes, and other crops; children and women supplemented the tribe's diet by gathering nuts and berries. The Choctaw men were excellent hunters who brought home small game along with deer, bear, and wildfowl. The tribe also had superb fishermen who supplied enough fish to keep everyone fed even in hard times. Women made jelly from wild roots and berries, cakes from corn flour and hominy, as well as a sweet, honey-like syrup from corn. Choctaw ponies were noted for endurance and general hardihood and were preferred by traders and travelers to all other mounts. So widely did Choctaw horse-breeders travel that Mobilian, a Choctaw dialect, became the trade language of the entire Southeast.

As contact with Europeans and Anglo Americans became more common, the Choctaws increasingly adopted some of the "white man's ways," with some INTERMARRIAGE with whites producing a mixed-blood population. Indeed, along with the CHEROKEES, Creeks, Seminoles, and Chickasaws, the Choctaws became known as one of the FIVE CIVILIZED TRIBES, with many of the mixed-bloods developing plantations like their white neighbors and even adapting African slavery.

The Choctaws numbered at least twenty-five thousand when the Anglo Americans began casting greedy eyes on the tribe's land in the 1790's and early 1800's. In 1820 Chief PUSHMATAHA and some lesser chiefs agreed to sign the Treaty of Doak's Stand, which General Andrew Jackson negotiated for the United States. By its terms the Choctaws ceded part of their southeastern lands for a vast estate in INDIAN TERRITORY (present eastern Oklahoma). Only about one-fourth of the tribe moved to the western lands. As they settled Mississippi and Alabama and took the reigns of government, Anglos unmercifully harassed the remaining Choctaws with a series of laws that abolished their tribal government, made Choctaws subject to state law, and put chiefs in prison if they insisted in exercising their tribal duties. White settlers, individually and in groups, heaped indignities on tribal members. Consequently, most Choctaws accepted the Treaty of DANCING RABBIT CREEK of 1830, which ceded all the tribe's southeastern lands; most Choctaws agreed to move to Indian Territory.

Approximately forty-five hundred Choctaws elected to remain in Mississippi as was allowed under the treaty of 1830. They received land allotments of up to 640 acres. Over time, however, corrupt Anglo Americans managed to swindle most of the Choctaws and steal their lands. Many Choctaws sank into poverty. By the late 1900's, approximately twenty-five hundred of the tribe remained in Mississippi and were known as the Mississippi band of the Choctaw Nation.

SUGGESTED READINGS. General histories that include coverage of this group include Arrell Gibson's *Oklahoma: A History of Five Centuries* (1981) and Edwin C. McReynolds's *Oklahoma: The Story of Its Past and Present* (1967). See also Wilcomb Washburn's *Red Man's Land, White Man's Law* (1971) and Arthur De Rosier's *The Removal of the Choctaw Indians* (1970).

Cholos: Term used for poor, lower-class Mexicans and Mexican Americans, especially common in California. During the Spanish and Mexican periods in the Southwest, a person of mixed Spanish and Indian ancestry or an acculturated Indian was referred to as a cholo, but the term was most commonly applied to such a person who was lower class. In modern times it has been used to refer to a member of a PACHUCO gang, and by the 1960's it had largely replaced the term pachuco. Sometimes cholo has been used to mean any Mexican, especially one who is young and rowdy.

Christian–Jewish relations: Interaction between Christians and Jews has been troubled and often violent since the two religions split at the beginning of the Christian era. Although many early Christians were originally devout Jews, the two groups vied for the loyalty of the masses, and Christianity rapidly gained ascendance. Since then, Christians and Jews have generally related to each other in terms of their majority or minority group status and as rivals rather than as coequals. Indeed, from the perspective of many Jews, the world has been an overwhelmingly Christian-centric place in which Christian beliefs have dominated the portrayal of history, religion, and even the passage of time (as in the abbreviations B.C. for "Before Christ" rather than the more neutral B.C.E. for "Before the Common Era" preferred by Jews).

The roots of Christian-Jewish conflict, many scholars believe, are theological. For Christians, Jesus was the fulfillment of the messianic promise, whereas Jews believed that the Messiah had not yet arrived. The Jews' refusal to accept and worship Jesus angered Christians; the Christians' insistence (after Paul and especially after the Reformation) that faith mattered more than observance of the laws and ethics of the holy Torah angered the Jews. The two groups even came to disagree about the name and extent of the holy books on which they were based, with the Christians dubbing the Torah and other Jewish writings the Old Testament and adding their own New Testament.

The chief hallmark of Christian-Jewish relations in most Christian cultures at most periods has been various forms of ANTI-SEMITISM. Some modern Christian and Jewish theologians have come to believe that official church anti-Judaism—what one calls "the teaching of contempt"—was the basis of both religious and political anti-Semitism. The power of anti-Semitism in the United States was never as threatening as it was in other countries. By the late twentieth century, a number of forces had combined to bring increasing numbers of American Christians and Jews into dialogue, INTERMARRIAGE, and other forms of harmonious interaction.

Relations Before World War II. There were few Jews in colonial America. The Jewish population did not really grow significantly until the immigration of GERMAN JEWS in the mid-1800's. They came to the United States determined to leave behind their Old

Country ways and become assimilated. They worked hard to establish themselves in peddling and certain urban businesses, mingling with Christians in the world of commerce. Most of these immigrants were REFORM JEWS who succeeded in Americanizing their Jewish practice to be more akin to Christian customs; for example, they called their houses of worship "temples" rather than synagogues, introduced organ music, and stressed the role of the sermon in the service. They

marked the beginnings of widespread anti-Jewish social discrimination that would peak in the 1920's and not really subside until after the 1960's. Through much of this period, Jews and Christians had extensive contact through the public school system and the business world in large cities such as New York or Chicago, but Jews tended to be restricted to certain neighborhoods and professions.

The influx of hundreds of thousands of eastern

Jews and Christians have traditionally mingled in the commercial arena, such as the garment industry or bustling streets of New York's Lower East Side. (Kim Iacono)

continued, however, to marry among themselves and to take pride in their distinctive identity.

Before the late 1800's, there was little systematic persecution of Jewish Americans by the dominant culture of WHITE ANGLO-SAXON PROTESTANTS (WASPs), although there were BLASPHEMY LAWS, occasional riots, and other measures that targeted Jews or excluded them from positions of power. In 1877, Joseph Seligman, a Jewish banker, was refused accommodation at a prestigious resort on the grounds of "race." This

European Jews around the beginning of the twentieth century inflamed existing anti-Jewish feeling. The "new" immigrants were far less inclined to assimilate than the "old" German waves, holding on to their YIDDISH LANGUAGE and more traditional religious practices and lifestyles. Congressional testimony suggests that much of the impetus for restricting immigration in the early 1920's was an effort to exclude eastern European Jews, who were viewed as alien by many Christians (as well as by many German Jews).

The nadir in Christian-Jewish relations in the United States was from the 1920's to the 1940's, when the immigrant community had reached a critical mass and sought greater opportunity. A Jewish businessman had been lynched in George in 1915, and the KU KLUX KLAN stepped up its efforts to discredit and terrorize Jews in their homes and synagogues. Through his newspaper *The Dearborn Independent,*

in Christian-Jewish relations in the United States. Americans gradually became sensitized to the extreme state of ANTI-SEMITISM in Europe and to its milder forms in their own country. Many Jewish war refugees were admitted under the DISPLACED PERSONS ACT of 1948, and some discriminatory practices began to ease. As Jews became more integrated into the American mainstream in education, housing, and employ-

The Holocaust brought new awareness of anti-Semitism. Here, Nazis arrest Jews in Berlin, 1933. (Simon Wiesenthal Center)

auto magnate Henry Ford waged an anti-Semitic campaign that was only stopped when some prominent Jews sued him for libel. At the same time, restrictive covenants excluded Jews from residing in certain neighborhoods, and unofficial admissions quotas strictly limited their access to higher education. Neither Christian religious organizations nor the U.S. government responded with help for European Jews under Nazism in the 1930's and 1940's until it was too late.

The Impact of the Holocaust. Hitler's murder of six million Jews during World War II was a turning point

ment, they remained relatively quiet about their religion and the special concerns that their community might have. Some Jewish theologians such as Abraham Heschel, however, began to lecture on Judaism at the Protestant Union Theological Seminary, while the HEBREW UNION COLLEGE started a Christian Fellow program in 1947 to train Christian seminary students in religious and cultural tolerance.

In the early postwar years, there was a conspiracy of silence about the HOLOCAUST on the part of both religious communities. It took decades for Jewish survivors to begin speaking out publicly and frequently about their experiences and for Christian religious leaders to exhort their flocks to learn lessons from Hitler's debacle. As time progressed, religious leaders of every persuasion were forced to confront the Holocaust as demarking the end of the "moral world." This caused great introspection among both Jews and Christians not only about their mission but also about the necessity for better relations. Slowly, Jewish organizations began to bring attention to the "righteous Gentiles" who had risked their lives to save Jews during the war. Significantly, it was not until 1980 that HEBREW UNION COLLEGE sponsored a major conference called "Religion in a Post-Holocaust World," attracting some twelve hundred Jewish and Christian religious leaders and seminary students for an unprecedented theological and educational exchange.

Some American Jews were also motivated by their link to the Holocaust as well as Jewish traditions of social justice to reach out to other persecuted minorities such as African Americans and Latinos. One of the mainstays of the early Civil Rights movement was Jewish activist and financial support, often arranged through courageous religious leaders.

Efforts at Dialogue Since 1967. By the late 1960's and 1970's, the time was ripe for more Christians and Jews to seek dialogue. Pope John XXIII, who convened the council known as Vatican II in 1962, made important steps in this direction when he absolved Jews of the charge of having killed Christ—a notion that had fueled many anti-Semitic acts—and composed a prayer stressing common roots and asking for forgiveness. Although the Vatican's "Jewish Declaration" issued in 1965 after the pope's death was a much weaker statement, the door had been opened. Indeed, Vatican II had opened the way for a new ecumenical spirit in Christian life as well, setting the stage for broader interfaith efforts.

Around the same time, Jews were emboldened by the Israeli victory in the 1967 Arab-Israeli war. They were ready to speak out against Christian silence in what they feared could be another Holocaust. Moreover, coinciding with the ETHNIC HERITAGE REVIVAL of the 1970's, some Jews were involved in religious renewal movements or a return to orthodoxy that made them more assertive about their separate religious and cultural identity. They were ready to challenge Christians about what they believed to be entrenched religious ANTI-SEMITISM.

The late twentieth century has been an explosion of conferences, publications, and organizations devoted to improving Christian-Jewish relations, at least among mainstream Protestants and CATHOLICS and REFORM and CONSERVATIVE JEWS. The National Conference on Christians and Jews promotes interreligious and other forms of intergroup tolerance, while most large Jewish Federations have Community Relations Councils, and Christian bodies such as the National Conference of Bishops have a Secretariat for Catholic-Jewish Relations. Theologians increasingly stress the shared heritage and ethical foundations of the two religions in a climate in which comparative religion is no longer threatening. Jews ask that Christians relearn history from a Jewish perspective, much as American Indians or African Americans in debates on multiculturalism ask that school districts discard their Eurocentric curricula. Liberal congregations have banded together in common political and humanitarian causes, from supporting the SANCTUARY MOVEMENT to aid for the homeless. With about one in three Jews marrying non-Jews in the United States, larger numbers of both groups are learning about each other's religion, converting, or finding that the differences no longer matter.

Yet certain issues continue to divide many Christians and Jews. Primary among them is SEPARATION OF CHURCH AND STATE, which some Jews prize as a principle that protects religious minorities and removes public life from Christian dominance. Liberal Jewish organizations have generally been opposed to prayer, the teaching of creationism, and certain types of Christmas observances in the schools, for example, believing that even Christmas trees and carols represent the imposition of the dominant religion. Views on Israel are contentious, with many Christian leaders insisting that Israel get no preferred treatment from the U.S. government and others (often Christian fundamentalists) strongly defending the needs of the Jewish state, often to the discomfort of mainstream Jewish organizations. Militant actions of the JEWISH DEFENSE LEAGUE (JDL) are widely condemned across the religious spectrum; the ORTHODOX JEWS, with whom some JDL members are affiliated, generally refuse to take part in interreligious dialogue.

African American-Jewish American relations have also been tense over racial violence in Brooklyn, the allegedly anti-Semitic rhetoric of some black (especially NATION OF ISLAM) leaders, and the resistance of some Jews to Black Power or affirmative action. In an effort to bridge the divide, Dillard University, a historically black college in New Orleans sponsored by the United Methodist Church, founded the National Center for Black-Jewish Relations in 1991. Individual churches and synagogues have also forged partnerships.

SUGGESTED READINGS. For more information, see the essays in *Introduction to Jewish-Christian Relations* (1991), edited by Michael Shermis and Arthur E. Zannon, and *In Our Time: The Flowering of the Jewish-Christian Dialogue* (1990), edited by Eugene Fischer and Leon Klenicki. *A Bridge to Dialogue: The Story of Jewish-Christian Relations* (1991) by John Rousmaniere offers a Christian viewpoint on the issue, while Stuart E. Rosenberg's *Christians and Jews: The Eternal Bond* (1985) provides a Jewish perspective.—*Susan Auerbach*

Christian Scientists: Christian Science is a system of physical and spiritual healing founded by Mary Baker EDDY (1821-1910) during the tumultuous final decades of the nineteenth century. Born on a farm near Concord, New Hampshire, Eddy was an imaginative but emotionally tormented child. Illness, early widowhood, a broken marriage, and periodic emotional disturbances turned her adult life into an unceasing quest for mental and physical health.

In February, 1866, after a serious fall on ice, Eddy experienced a miraculous healing that led her to discover the religious truths she would name Christian Science and later publish in her seminal work, *Science and Health with Key to the Scriptures* (1875). An organizational genius, she overcame seemingly insurmountable odds in carving out an enduring religious organization, the Church of Christ, Scientist (originally organized in 1879), and initiating such important publications as *The Christian Science Monitor*. Her religious organization, with headquarters in Boston, Massachusetts, was immediately successful, in part because it provided a haven for women who were otherwise cut off from avenues of power in a male-dominated society. As Eddy's success grew, she outlasted persistent attacks by prominent male leaders in religion, politics, education, and medicine.

While Christian Scientists believe Eddy's truths to be part of a unique and final religious revelation, most outside observers place Christian Science in the metaphysical family of religions with roots in Platonic Idealism. The theological underpinnings of Christian Science reverberate with the thoughts of nineteenth century writers such as Phineas Parkhurst Quimby,

Ralph Waldo Emerson, and Warren Felt Evans.

As part of the metaphysical tradition, Christian Science makes a radical claim for Divine Mind as the controlling factor in human experience: God is Mind, the material realm is illusory, all is spirit. Health, wealth, and happiness are available to anyone who gives up negative, limited thinking and recognizes his or her self as a perfect thought reflected in the Divine Mind. Particularly noteworthy is Eddy's articulation of God as both a father and mother principle, present in all reality. The "Christian" element of Christian Science emerges in the teaching that Jesus was the ultimate "Christian Scientist" who demonstrably overcame sin, sickness, and death through his superior perception of the allness of Spirit and the nothingness of matter.

SUGGESTED READINGS. The best compilation and explanation of the complex teachings of Christian Science is Stephen Gottschalk's *The Emergence of Christian Science in American Religious Life* (1973). Robert Peel offers an exhaustive historical account of the movement in a three-volume set, *Mary Baker Eddy* (1971). Judah Stillson's *The History and Philosophy of the Metaphysical Movements in America* (1967) and Catherine Albanese's *America, Religions and Religion* (2d ed., 1992) are recommended for students who wish to place the Christian Science movement in a broader religious-historical context.

Christmas (Dec. 25): Since the fourth century, December 25 has been celebrated by Christians as the commemoration of the birth of Jesus of Nazareth. No other festival has been celebrated so widely or with such a variety of customs. Roman Christians adopted the December date in an attempt to counteract and replace the week-long Roman Saturnalia festival (December 17-24), which celebrated the harvest and the Roman god of agriculture, and December revelry surrounding the festival of the Iranian god Mithras, the "unconquered sun."

By the sixth century, Christians had extended the celebration to include twelve days after the four-week season of austerity, Advent. Because the Advent fast did not end until December 24 at midnight, there are many national Christmas Eve dinners that include fish.

Many pre-Christian and non-Christian elements have become part of American Christmas traditions. The rites of Dionysius contributed the use of ivy. Scandinavians and Germans contributed the yule log from their winter solstice festivals. Druids had long used mistletoe for decorations around the time of the winter solstice, but its modern use is a revived custom rather than one surviving from antiquity. The Christmas tree, long dormant as a winter ornament, became popular in Germany in the seventeenth century and was brought to America by German immigrants. It was nineteenth century England that began the custom of exchanging Christmas cards.

The uniquely Christian tradition of the crèche is usually attributed to Saint Francis of Assisi in the early thirteenth century. Since then, manger scenes have become widespread in public settings as well as homes. Some Italian cribs have become so elaborate that they contain thousands of pieces. Mexican American women in some communities also assemble intricate, impressive *nacimientos*, which become the focus for family prayer and visiting during the holiday. Public crèches, such as those erected by city governments and schools, have been the source of controversy and lawsuits over the issue of SEPARATION OF CHURCH AND STATE.

A West Indian import to the American South, especially North Carolina, is the festival of John Kunen. This has its origins in the period of slavery, when African Americans sang carols for plantation owners and were paid some small token. In Bladen County, North

Las Posadas is a Mexican American tradition that re-creates Mary and Joseph's search for shelter. (Robert Fried)

Carolina, women and girls go to the woods on Christmas eve. Later, in a candlelight procession, they walk to a church where the men and boys await them. Together they "watch in" Christmas, singing songs in pidgen.

Some of the oldest continuing folk celebrations of Christmas on the North American continent are the *Coloquios* of Northern New Mexico. Every village has a play script, some dating back to the seventeenth century, of the story of Christmas. The story of Mary's conception and pregnancy, especially the search for a suitable place for the birth, and the adoration by shepherds and Magi are consistent elements in the plays. There are many opportunities for local variations, improvisation, and subplots in these communal celebrations leading up to Christmas.

Even more widespread is *Las Posadas,* the reenactment of the search for suitable lodging for Joseph and the pregnant Mary. Wherever in the Southwest there is a sizable Mexican American population, one can find this celebration. For nine days before Christmas, lighted candles placed along streets and yards illuminate the way for the family to find a place for the coming birth.

Santa Claus is largely an American phenomenon, even though his origins are German and Dutch. Saint Nicholas of Myra, whose feast is celebrated on December 6, was a saintly bishop known for having saved the honor of several young women by some timely gifts. To recall the saint's generosity, the Germans and Dutch gave gifts to children on December 6. Americans moved the day to Christmas and extended the gift-giving to adults as well as children. The purchase and exchange of gifts has become such a prominent part of this festival that many merchants

Nativity drama enacted by members of New York's Eastside Children's Ministry to benefit children with disabilities. (Odette Lupis)

A Korean adoptee enjoys a visit with Santa Claus. (James L. Shaffer)

rely on the month before Christmas to determine their survival in business. As much as 90 percent of the retail trade of some companies comes in the weeks immediately preceding Christmas.

SUGGESTED READINGS. Sue Samuelson's *Christmas: An Annotated Bibliography* (1982) lists most of the relevant literature on this festival, placing special emphasis on anthropological studies. Franz Xavier Weiser's *The Christmas Book* (1952) examines Christmas traditions, especially those of European origin. *The Folklore of American Holidays* (1987), edited by Hennig Cohen and Tristram Potter Coffin, provides rich anecdotal accounts of the many American ways of celebrating Christmas.

Chu, Louis H. (Oct. 1, 1915, Toishan, China—Feb. 27, 1970, Queens, N.Y.): Chinese American novelist and social worker. Chu immigrated to the United States in 1924 and received an M.A. from New York University in 1940. He served in the Signal Corps of the U.S. Army in World War II. Chu is probably best known for the novel *Eat a Bowl of Tea* (1961), a lively account of life among the "bachelor societies" of New York's Chinatown in the early 1940's. Chu was active in community life in New York's Chinatown, directing a day center for

older Chinese Americans and, between 1951 and 1961, hosting a popular radio program called "Chinese Festival."

Chung, Connie (Constance Yu-Hwa Chung; b. Aug. 20, 1946, Washington, D.C.): Chinese American broadcast journalist. After graduating with a degree in journalism from the University of Maryland in 1969, Chung was hired as a secretary for a local Washington, D.C., television station in 1969. She was quickly promoted to newswriter and editor and within two years moved to on-the-air reporter. She was a Columbia Broadcasting System (CBS) correspondent from 1971 to 1976, a coanchor on a Los Angeles affiliate from 1976 to 1983, and an anchor on various National Broadcasting Company (NBC) news programs from 1983 to 1989. In addition, she has done many news specials on various topics of public interest. Chung has received three Emmy awards for individual achievement and numerous honors from women's, ethnic, and professional organizations. In 1989, she returned to work for CBS News and in June, 1993, she joined Dan Rather as coanchor of the CBS Evening News. Her success has paved the way for other Asian Americans, particularly women, in television news.

In 1993 Connie Chung joined Dan Rather as coanchor of the CBS Evening News. (AP/Wide World Photos)

Chung, Myung-Whun (b. Jan. 22, 1953, Seoul, Korea): Korean American conductor and pianist. Chung grew up in a very musical family and made his debut with the Seoul Philharmonic Orchestra at the age of seven. In late

Myung-Whun Chung served as assistant conductor of the Los Angeles Philharmonic Orchestra in the late 1970's. (AP/ Wide World Photos)

1961, his family came to the United States, where he completed high school in Seattle, Washington. Upon graduation, Chung moved to New York to attend the Mannes College of Music. He received a Kosciusko Foundation Chopin Fellowship in 1971. In 1974, he won second prize at the Tchaikovsky Piano Competition in Moscow and had his first solo recital at New York's Carnegie Hall. Chung was selected as assistant conductor with the Los Angeles Philharmonic Orchestra in 1978, and in the 1980's pursued his conducting career in Europe. He has played and conducted with orchestras and opera companies in Europe, served as music director for the Opera de la Bastille's 1989 gala celebration of the bicentennial of the French Revolution, and won Italy's Abbiata and Toscanini prizes in 1988 and 1989.

Church and state, separation of: One of the fundamental principles of the political system in the United States. The separation of church and state means, minimally, that government shall not establish an official religion or coerce citizens to believe any particular religious doctrine. Although the settlers of the country were intensely religious and governmentally established religions were common in colonial America, the First Amendment to the U.S. Constitution explicitly stated that "Congress shall make no law respecting an establishment of religion, or prohibiting the free exercise thereof." This amendment reflected the emerging consensus in the late eighteenth century that religion was a matter of private conscience and that religiously motivated struggles for political power were a primary cause of civil instability. Although unconventional and unpopular religious sects have experienced periodic legal and illegal discrimination and persecution, the principle of separation has afforded religious groups a strong measure of legal protection and has been a prime factor encouraging religious pluralism in American culture.

Throughout the nineteenth century, church-state relations were shaped by state governments that were largely in the control of men wishing to advance Protestant religious values. Massachusetts, for example,

Prayer in the schools, like the "Pledge of Allegiance" shown here, is controversial because of issues of separation of church and state. (James L. Shaffer)

denied Jews the right to hold public office until 1828. Protestant prayer in public schools was common, as were laws against BLASPHEMY. Occasionally, a religious group would run directly afoul of traditional Judeo-Christian values. The MORMON church's practice of polygamy, for example, came under sustained attack in the late nineteenth century. Driven out of the states of Missouri and Illinois, the Mormons eventually were compelled to renounce polygamy after the federal government seized their property, an action upheld by the Supreme Court in 1890.

In the twentieth century, church-state relations took a decidedly secular turn. Beginning in 1947, the Supreme Court erected legal barriers against religious influence in public schools and against many forms of state aid to religious organizations. The Court regularly struck down direct state financial grants to parochial schools as well as state-endorsed prayer in public schools as violations of the "establishment" clause. The Court generally requires that state programs have a secular purpose, that their primary effect neither advance nor inhibit religion, and that the program not foster excessive government entanglement with religion. In 1987, for example, the Court struck down Louisiana's law requiring the teaching of creationism because it did not have a secular purpose; in 1992, the Court ruled that a rabbi's benediction at a public junior high graduation ceremony was unconstitutional. Despite criticism from conservatives that it is hostile to religion, the Court has made decisions that generally, though not invariably, maintain a suspicious view of any state support or endorsement of religion.

SUGGESTED READINGS. An excellent source of primary documents on church-state separation in the U.S. is John T. Noonan, Jr.'s, *The Believer and the Powers That Are* (1987); a multicultural perspective on religious groups and the law is presented in Jill Norgren and Serena Nanda's *American Cultural Pluralism and Law* (1988); a historical perspective can be found in Leonard Levy's *The Establishment Clause: Religion and the First Amendment (1986).*

Cinco de Mayo: Second most important Mexican holiday, celebrated on or around the fifth of May. (The most important holiday is September 16, which commemorates the beginning of the War of Independence against Spain in 1810.) Cinco de Mayo commemorates the defeat of the invading French army at Puebla in 1862 by the Mexican Army under the leadership of the Texas-

A pint-sized señorita rides on a float in San Francisco's Cinco de Mayo Day parade. (Robert Fried)

born general Ignacio Zaragoza. The holiday has been celebrated by Mexican Americans since the latter part of the nineteenth century. In the late twentieth century it was marked by parades, festivities including music and dance, speeches, and school programs.

Cisneros, Evelyn (b. 1955, Long Beach, Calif.): Latino ballet dancer. Cisneros began dancing at age eight and studied as a teenager at the San Francisco Ballet School and the School of American Ballet in New York. In 1971, she apprenticed at the San Francisco Ballet and six years later joined the company. Major performances include *Scherzo*, *Romeo and Juliet*, *Cinderella*, and *A Song for Dead Warriors*. Cisneros has received awards from Hispanic Women Making History in 1984, the MEXICAN AMERICAN LEGAL DEFENSE AND EDUCATION FUND (MALDEF) in 1985, and the California League of United Latin Citizens in 1988. In 1989, she was named spokesperson of the Chicano/Latino Youth Leadership Conference.

Cisneros, Henry Gabriel (b. June 11, 1947, San Antonio, Tex.): Latino politician. After receiving his B.A. and

Henry Cisneros served as Secretary of Housing and Urban Development under Bill Clinton. (AP/Wide World Photos)

a master's degree from Texas A&M University in 1970, Cisneros moved to Washington, D.C., where he worked for the National League of Cities and became a White House fellow while pursuing graduate studies at George Washington University. Cisneros returned to San Antonio after earning a second master's degree at Harvard and a Ph.D. from George Washington University. He became a city councilman in 1975 and served as San Antonio's mayor from 1981 to 1989. In 1982, Cisneros was named one of ten Outstanding Young Men in America by the U.S. Jaycees; in 1986, he served as president of the National League of Cities and was a member on two bilateral commissions on Latin American affairs. After declining to seek reelection in 1989, he founded Cisneros Asset Management Company, but four years later returned to public service as secretary of Housing and Urban Development (HUD) under President Bill Clinton.

Civil rights: Nonpolitical rights of personal liberty guaranteed to all Americans by the U.S. CONSTITUTION as well as other key acts and documents. Civil rights are considered to be the backbone of a free modern state. They provide a yardstick to measure the relationship between individuals and the government in a democratic society. At times, the concept of civil rights has been misconstrued as referring only to the rights of minority races and ethnic groups within a country or as rights that are purely political in nature.

The idea of civil rights originated in the West and found its first formal comprehensive documentation in the first ten amendments to the U.S. Constitution, known as the BILL OF RIGHTS. In the post-World War II period, the inclusion of a list of fundamental rights of individuals and citizens has become a characteristic of all written constitutions of democratic and psuedo-democratic countries around the world. Theoretically, civil rights are considered to be sacrosanct.

Civil Liberties and Civil Rights. A distinction is sometimes made between civil liberties and civil rights. The former consists of negative restraints on the conduct of government, as in the phrase, "the state shall not . . . ," whereby it must refrain from interfering with the freedom of individuals, thereby creating an area of liberty. Civil rights, on the other hand, expressly confer upon an individual a positive power to act, such as the right to own property, to travel freely, and to have equal access to public facilities. In common usage, however, the terms civil liberties and civil rights are interchangeable. A charter of civil rights in any constitution is usually a combination of civil liberties and civil rights.

In the context of the ever-changing meaning of civil rights, the area of civil liberty is no longer defined as constituted exclusively by the absence of governmental interference. In the latter half of the twentieth century, government's positive intervention has been utilized and sought in many instances as the best means of widening the sphere of liberty for equal enjoyment of freedom by all individuals. Furthermore, civil rights protection is sought not only against infringements by government but also against arbitrary discrimination and harassment by other individuals and groups in society.

Civil rights, then, include political guarantees to individuals and citizens within a state but are not solely political in nature. They refer to a variety of political, social, economic, cultural, and psychological freedoms. The enjoyment of civil rights, however, is not absolute and unrestrained but is subject to "reasonable restrictions," which are either defined by the constitution itself or left for the interpretation and judgment of the courts. For example, the right to "freedom of speech" cannot be justified if it results in inciting a riot or a massacre that threatens the basic freedoms and rights of others.

Historical Sources. Despite its widespread usage,

the concept of civil rights has not been consistently or adequately defined. At best, it has been variously defined in different contexts, places, and times. The idea of civil rights is generally associated with the modern concept of democracy. Although the idea of civil rights existed in rudimentary form in ancient societies such as Greece and Rome, women, males without property, slaves, and immigrants were generally excluded from protection. The concept of natural law, which originated with the Greek Stoics, is generally considered the main philosophical source of modern civil and human rights.

The idea of civil rights has evolved considerably over time. The Magna Carta of 1215 was the first landmark charter of civil liberties in England. It restrained the power of the Crown, though initially in the interests of the nobility rather than the masses. The humanism of the European Renaissance of the fifteenth and sixteenth centuries, which underlined individualism, was influential, as was the emergence of the principle of SEPARATION OF CHURCH AND STATE and the consequent establishment of "nation-states" in Europe. The English Petition of Right of 1628 and the Bill of Rights of 1689, following the Glorious Revolution of 1688, strongly entrenched the principles of restrained authority of the government and the people's right to dissent under certain circumstances.

The relationship between the government and the governed began to be viewed as contractual in nature, as discussed by philosophers Thomas Hobbes, John Locke, and Jean Jacques Rousseau. Locke became the intellectual father of civil rights and the liberal democratic state in England and the United States. He claimed that natural law bestowed upon men certain basic and "indefeasible" rights. It was for the sake of protection of those fundamental rights that men decided to give up some of the freedoms that they enjoyed in the state of nature by entering into a social contract with the artificial state.

The New American Republic. The United States became the first country in the world to include a list of specific civil rights in a formal, documented form as an essential part of its written constitution. It should, however, be noted that the original U.S. CONSTITUTION, as adopted at the Philadelphia Convention of 1789, did not include such a list. The BILL OF RIGHTS was created by the first ten amendments to the Constitution, which were ratified by the required number of states in 1891.

The idea of civil rights in the American political system is generally believed to have been influenced by both the political philosophy of Locke and the intellectual currents of the eighteenth century French Enlightenment. These influences may be seen in the American DECLARATION OF INDEPENDENCE (1776), written by Thomas Jefferson, which states that "all Men are created equal, that they are endowed by their Creator with certain unalienable Rights; that among these are Life, Liberty, and the Pursuit of Happiness."

The United States was founded by those seeking freedom of religion. Here a Virginia Mennonite family goes to worship. (Photo Agora)

This document expanded existing concepts of civil liberties by referring to the pursuit of happiness, which implied the opportunity for individuals to develop to their fullest potential. Here the impact of the Utilitarian school of thought of the English political philosopher John Stuart Mill, stressing that individual fulfillment is best promoted by restricting the powers of the government, cannot be underestimated.

During the proceedings of the Philadelphia convention, a proposal by George Mason for adding a bill of rights to the Constitution was rejected by Alexander Hamilton and other Federalists, who believed that there was no need for such guarantees as the power

Fight for civil rights goes on at 1983 anniversary of March on Washington. (Hazel Hankin)

of the national government had been formally limited to only its delegated powers. The general feeling was that the national government could not abuse powers that it did not even have. When the Constitution was submitted for ratification to states, however, Anti-Federalists, most of whom had not been delegates to the Philadelphia convention, campaigned in favor of Jefferson's argument that the omission of a bill of rights was a major imperfection of the new Constitution. In order to get the Constitution ratified by the required number of states, the Federalists had to make an unwritten pledge to include a bill of rights.

The addition of a bill of rights to the U.S. Constitution became the first task of the first Congress, which met in April, 1789. The first ten amendments to the Constitution, known as the American Bill of Rights, were ratified by the states on December 15, 1791.

The Nature of the Bill of Rights. The BILL OF RIGHTS is a charter of civil liberties and civil rights of American citizens. Originally, the document consisted of a series of negative restraints on the conduct of the government, thereby creating an area of civil liberty protected from the improper conduct of government. Some of these restraints were substantive and others procedural in nature. In the former category, restraints were put on what the government did not have the power to do—for example, establishing a religion, quartering troops in private homes, or seizing property without just compensation. The latter category consisted of prescriptions on how the government was supposed to act. For example, the principles of "due process of law" and "innocent until proven guilty" were to guide the conduct of the government in exercising its judicial powers.

The first four amendments to the Constitution bestow positive civil liberties on the American people. These are freedom of religion, of speech, and of the press; the right to keep and bear arms, protection against the quartering of soldiers in private homes without the consent of the owner; and security from unwarrantable search and seizure. The Fifth to Seventh Amendments establish procedural restraints on the conduct of the government in dealing with the rights of accused persons. The Ninth and Tenth Amendments, respectively, clarify that residual pow-

to the Supreme Court in matters of conflict over the interpretation of the Constitution. Hence, the Bill of Rights, throughout its history, has been what the majority of the Supreme Court justices at any given time said it was. The Supreme Court's judgments have not been consistent or static; periodically, the Court has reversed its own past decisions by reinterpreting the Constitution. In its application, the Bill of Rights has become broad, progressive, and widely democratic only in the late twentieth century.

Where To Find Civil Rights in the U.S. Constitution

Right	Amendments to the U.S. Constitution													
	1	2	3	4	5	6	7	8	9	10	14	19	24	26
Freedom of religion	✔										*			
Freedom of speech	✔										*			
Freedom of the press	✔										*			
Freedom of assembly/petition	✔										*			
Right to bear arms		✔												
No unlawful quartering			✔								*			
No unreasonable searches or seizures				✔							✔			
Right to due process					✔						*			
Speedy trial by jury						✔								
Jury trial in civil cases							✔							
No excessive bail or cruel and unusual punishments								✔						
Recognition of unnamed rights									✔		*			
Powers reserved to states and to the people										✔	*			
Equal protection of the law											✔			
Voting rights												✔	✔	✔

Source: From William C. Lowe, *Blessings of Liberty: Safeguarding Civil Rights.* Human Rights series, Vero Beach, Fla.: Rourke Corp., 1992.
*Rights that have been incorporated into the Fourteenth Amendment by Supreme Court decisions.

ers that are not enumerated in the Constitution, expressly given to the national government, or expressly denied to the states "are reserved to the States respectively, or to the people."

Though it has been in force since 1791, the Bill of Rights has never been completely understood or consistently applied. Its meaning and interpretation have varied from time to time and still remain controversial and vague in many respects. The Congress, the executive branch, and the Supreme Court have often held conflicting and competing views of the Bill of Rights. The American political system, based on the principle of "judicial supremacy," gives an upper hand

Nationalization of the Bill of Rights. The BILL OF RIGHTS was originally binding only on the federal government, not the states. Most of the states later adopted similar guarantees in their individual state constitutions. Furthermore, federal and state statutes, subject to the judicial review of the Supreme Court, have supplemented and provided details to the constitutional provisions concerning individual liberties and rights.

The First Amendment is perhaps the only part of the Constitution that is explicit in its intention to put limits on the national government, as it begins by stating that "Congress shall make no law" that would re-

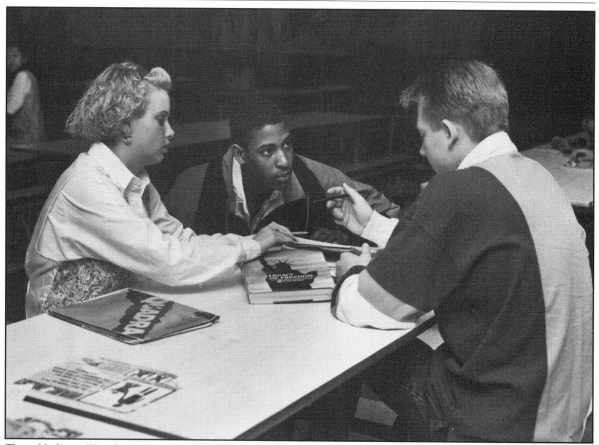

These Madison, Wis., history students study the rights guaranteed to all Americans by the U.S. Constitution. (James L. Shaffer)

strict freedom of religion, the press, free speech, or peaceful assembly. It has been questioned time and again in American history whether the remaining amendments of the Bill of Rights limit state governments or only the national government.

The question whether the Bill of Rights also limits state government was decided for the first time in 1833 by the Supreme Court in *Barron v. Baltimore* in the negative. The judicial opinion in 1833 confirmed "dual citizenship" for American citizens: Each American citizen was a subject of the United States as a national entity and was separately also a citizen of one of the states. This meant that the Bill of Rights did not apply to decisions or procedures of the state or local governments. As a result of this decision, the system of slavery was allowed to continue in those states that did not outlaw it. For more than a century, a system of near-slavery and segregation reinforced by JIM CROW LAWS could legally continue in the South.

In fact, the Bill of Rights did not become a charter of civil liberties for all Americans until after the bloody Civil War and the subsequent passage of the THIRTEENTH, FOURTEENTH, and FIFTEENTH AMENDMENTS to the Constitution. From a constitutional standpoint, the end of the Civil War in 1865 settled the question of federalism by determining that the states were to be more "united" than "states," but that fact did not amount to a reversal of the *Barron v. Baltimore* ruling. Furthermore, the provisions of the FOURTEENTH AMENDMENT that "All persons born or naturalized in the United States, and subject to the jurisdiction thereof, are citizens of the United States and of the State wherein they reside," and that "No State shall make or enforce any law which shall abridge the privileges or immunities of citizens of the United States; nor shall any State deprive any person of life, liberty, or property, without due process of law" clearly appear to provide for a single national citizenship and to nationalize the Bill of Rights. Such was not the interpretation of the Supreme Court, however, for the next hundred years.

Gradually during the course of the twentieth century, Supreme Court rulings began to expand the application of the Bill of Rights in the light of the Fourteenth Amendment. As early as 1897, the principle of "just compensation" in the protection of property rights was made mandatory for states. In 1925, freedom of speech was declared to be "among the 'fundamental' personal rights and 'liberties' protected by the due process clause of the Fourteenth Amendment from impairment by the states." In 1931 and 1939, freedom of the press and freedom of assembly, respectively, were added to the preceding list. The Supreme Court was not yet willing to go beyond the First Amendment in nationalizing the complete charter of civil liberties and rights of American citizens.

In the mid-twentieth century, the limited nationalization of the Bill of Rights still left states free to violate the spirit of this charter through their unrestricted power to practice racial segregation, to engage in search and seizure without a warrant, and to deprive accused persons of their right to trial by jury. People were not nationally protected against double jeopardy or against testifying against themselves. It was in this climate that the Jim Crow system was legally maintained in at least thirteen southern states until the early 1960's.

It took a second constitutional revolution, which began around World War II and culminated in the mid-1960's, to nationalize the Bill of Rights. This was achieved mainly through congressional acts (such as the CIVIL RIGHTS ACT OF 1964, the VOTING RIGHTS ACT OF 1965, and their subsequent amended forms), the executive orders of presidents, and Supreme Court cases such as *BROWN V. BOARD OF EDUCATION* (1954). The Supreme Court has not been inclined to declare formally that the entire Bill of Rights is included in the Fourteenth Amendment.

Minorities and Women. Originally, the U.S. CONSTITUTION, based on liberal democratic principles, neither recognized nor denied differences among individuals. Because of the brevity of this document, its interpretation and expansion were left for future generations. Three main flaws in the Constitution related to civil rights were the nonresolution of the question of slavery; the ambiguity surrounding the definition of citizenship; and granting power to the states to determine voter qualifications. As a result, there was no uniform definition of a citizen or a voter in the United States.

It would take organized social movements and group struggles throughout American history to demand and win greater legal equality. The EMANCIPATION PROCLAMATION of 1863—as much a response to the ABOLITIONIST MOVEMENT and slave rebellions as to Union Army victories in the Civil War—declared all slaves free. The THIRTEENTH AMENDMENT of 1865 made slavery unconstitutional. The FOURTEENTH AMENDMENT of 1868 was designed to guarantee directly the rights of freed slaves, and indirectly of other powerless minority groups. It provided that no state shall "deprive any person of life, liberty or property, without due process of law; nor deny to any person within its jurisdiction the equal protection of the laws." The FIFTEENTH AMENDMENT, ratified in 1870, was intended to safeguard the voting rights of African Americans.

Soon after the radical developments of the RECONSTRUCTION period, the Supreme Court turned conservative and restricted the interpretation of the "equal protection" clause of the Fourteenth Amendment in such a way as to justify "private DISCRIMINATION" against blacks by whites, and "public SEGREGATION" of races by governmental agencies as long as "separate but equal" facilities were provided for blacks. The landmark decision in this regard was *PLESSY V. FERGUSON* (1896), which came on the heels of the Court's invalidation of the congressional Civil Rights Act of 1875. The "separate but equal" status of African Americans, particularly in the southern states, was to prevail by law until the Court's reversal of the *Plessy* decision in *Brown v. Board of Education* in 1954.

Originally, the U.S. Constitution, both in theory and practice, was male-oriented. As a result of years of struggle by the women's SUFFRAGE MOVEMENT, which intensified around the beginning of the twentieth century, the NINETEENTH AMENDMENT to the Constitution enfranchised women in 1919.

The civil rights of nonwhite and nonblack minority groups were not to be addressed until after the mid-twentieth century. American Indians did not qualify for civil rights until as late as 1968, when Congress extended the guarantees of the first eight amendments to Indians living under tribal authority on reservations through the Civil Rights Act of 1968.

Early Asian Americans, who immigrated from China, Japan, South Asia, Korea, the Philippines, and other areas, followed an uneven path to citizenship between the late 1800's and 1947. Individually, many Asians were made eligible for naturalization after the passage of the Fourteenth Amendment. Yet, following the passage of the CHINESE EXCLUSION ACT and the Asian Exclusion Acts, reflecting the mass anti-Asian prejudice and hysteria, naturalized citizens of Asian origin were stripped of their citizenship by the Supreme Court between 1917 and 1922. Asian naturalization was thenceforth banned, since Asians did not qualify either as members of the "White" race or as "Negroes." The Filipinos in the United States, as American colonial subjects, remained an exception to this naturalization rule. The ban on naturalization remained in force until after the end of World War II.

California and other western states passed alien land laws that deprived Asian Americans of the right to own land, because a majority of Anglo Americans in the West were farmers or engaged in agri-business and perceived Asian immigrants as a threat. The civil rights of Asians were to become a mockery with the INTERNMENT of Japanese Americans during World War II, when thousands of West Coast Japanese, including the American-born, were placed in internment camps by an executive order of President Franklin D. Roosevelt.

The Mexican Americans and many other Latino groups were deprived of their basic rights because of the prejudice of government agencies against them. Even American-born Latinos were deported numerous times throughout the twentieth century without the "due process of law."

The Civil Rights Movement and Its Aftermath. It required a mass movement of the magnitude of the Civil War, though without comparable violence, to make the BILL OF RIGHTS effectively applicable to all Americans. The movement had been in the making at a slow but steady pace in African American commu-

A Japanese American shop owner in Oakland, Calif., protests his upcoming internment during World War II. Some reparations for civil rights violations were eventually paid by the U.S. government. (National Japanese American Historical Society)

Police officers are supposed to protect, but sometimes violate, the civil rights of citizens. (Hazel Hankin)

nities since the end of RECONSTRUCTION. Besides on-going grass-roots mobilization and political activism among black organizations, other factors set the stage for the movement in the 1950's and 1960's. These included upward mobility of African Americans in the North; black participation in both the military and civilian war effort during World War II; reaction to competing international ideologies such as communism and fascism that challenged liberal democratic ideals and the capitalist system; and the beginning of the Cold War, with the United States assuming the role of the leader of the "free world."

The CIVIL RIGHTS MOVEMENT began to emerge under the leadership of Martin Luther KING, Jr., after the *BROWN V. BOARD OF EDUCATION* decision. The Supreme Court's ruling in 1954 that "separate is inherently unequal" gave legitimacy to the movement's struggle to change the JIM CROW system of legal racial SEGREGATION in the South. The movement culminated in the federal government's initiative to nationalize the definition of citizenship and the conditions for voter qualification by providing for universal adult suffrage. The government finally removed race, religion, and gender as acceptable categories for discrimination.

Inspired by the African American Civil Rights movement, other nonwhite ethnic and racial minorities began to organize themselves around renewed group identities, reexamine their experiences of deprivation and discrimination, and demand equality of treatment and compensatory justice. Asian Americans, American Indians, and Chicanos all formed civil rights movements of their own to pursue distinct ethnic agendas.

The organization of groups for equal rights took place on nonracial/transracial lines as well. The WOMEN'S MOVEMENT also received new impetus from the Civil Rights movement. Inspired by Title VII of the CIVIL RIGHTS ACT, groups identified by disability, age, and sexual preference began to organize to fight against discrimination. Overall, consciousness about civil rights among the American public has been unprecedented in the years since the heyday of the Civil Rights movement in the 1960's. This has sometimes given rise to divisive tendencies among the population and intensified competition and conflict.

The universalization of the Bill of Rights and the removal of barriers to equality of treatment has become a political and legal reality. Yet this legal reality is not the same as having equality of treatment in practice, which is a difficult process full of obstructions and conflicts. This became clear soon after the implementation of the *Brown v. Board of Education* decision in the South. Most southern states refused to cooperate until they were sued. Many ingenious schemes were employed to maintain actual segregation. The problem of segregation was perhaps even more acute outside the South. Segregated housing and residential patterns made schooling virtually segregated. Mandatory busing as a means of integrating schools ultimately proved controversial with both whites and blacks.

Widespread RACISM and PREJUDICE among the American population was, and is, a serious hurdle to implementing equality of treatment and equal protection. To overcome this, the federal government resorted to positive or AFFIRMATIVE ACTION to dispense "compensatory justice." Civil rights acts were supplemented with the Equal Employment Opportunity Act (1972), which mandated preference and "protected status" to minorities and women, especially in education, employment, and housing.

Affirmative action programs gave rise to yet another controversy related to the Bill of Rights, as they were accused of violating the First Amendment freedoms of white males. A legal suit charging "reverse discrimination" reached the U.S. Supreme Court in RE-GENTS OF THE UNIVERSITY OF CALIFORNIA V. BAKKE (1978). Such charges have contributed to a new phase of civil rights history. The Court has not held a consistent position in its judgments in cases of REVERSE DISCRIMINATION, thus adding to the confusion in legal interpretations. The justices ruled against preferential admissions quotas based on race in *Regents of the University of California v. Bakke*, but in both *United Steelworkers of America v. Weber* (1979) and *Fullilove v. Klutznick* (1980) the Court was permissive about the efforts of employers to experiment with AFFIRMATIVE ACTION programs. Then, in 1989, it returned to its earlier position in the *Richmond v. J. A. Croson Co.*, holding that a "rigid numerical quota" is suspect. The Civil Rights Act of 1991 attempted to undo many of the Supreme Court's decisions of the 1980's by shifting the burden of proof back to the employer and making it more difficult to mount later challenges to agreements in affirmative action cases.

At the political level, debate on AFFIRMATIVE ACTION had reached a stalemate by the early 1990's. Conservatives and neo-conservatives argued for a hands-off policy whereby the government neither favors nor hinders one group over another, citing the principles of liberal democracy based on individualism and equality of opportunity. Liberals, on the other hand, debated the pros and cons of "compensatory justice" versus "redistributive justice," recognizing that affirmative action may be an imperfect way to correct injustices. It is noteworthy that the critics of affirmative action have seldom questioned the legitimacy or constitutionality of certain other forms of quotas, such as the Veterans' preference or "alumni legacy" quotas in educational institutions.

While political debate over civil rights continues, it is ultimately the American public—its conscience and its level of tolerance—that determines the pattern of the struggle to make full civil rights a reality for all Americans. The role of the main branches of the government, particularly the U.S. Supreme Court, continues to be crucial in defining the nature and extent of civil rights.

SUGGESTED READINGS. For a general discussion of the principles of justice, see John Rawls's *A Theory of Justice* (1971). For a history of civil rights and liberties in the United States, the following works are useful: Lucius Barker and Twiley Barker, Jr.'s *Civil Liberties and the Constitution* (1982); Jack R. Pole's *The Pursuit of Equality in American History* (1978); Ronald Dworkin's *Taking Rights Seriously* (1979); and *Statutory History of the United States: Civil Rights* (1970), edited by Bernard Schwartz. For varied perspectives on the affirmative action and reverse discrimination controversy, detailed summaries are provided in Kathanne W. Greene's *Affirmative Action and Principles of Justice* (1989) and in Herman Belz's *Equality Transformed* (1991).—*Indu Vohra*

Civil Rights Act of 1964: Most sweeping piece of legislation on civil rights at least since the Reconstruction period following the Civil War and perhaps in all of U.S. history. The bill outlawed DISCRIMINATION based on race and gender in public facilities, public accommodations, employment, and institutions on federal contract. Because women as well as racial minorities were included, the bill affected a majority of Americans.

Background of Civil Rights Movement. The Supreme Court ruling in May, 1954, in BROWN ET AL. V. THE BOARD OF EDUCATION of Topeka, Kansas, which outlawed racial segregation in public schools, was only the first of many steps toward realizing the national ideal of equal rights for all. The next decade was eventful but frustrating for proponents of civil rights.

The MONTGOMERY BUS BOYCOTT of 1955 and 1956 made Martin Luther KING, Jr., a nationally known figure and ended bus segregation in one town. The LITTLE ROCK, Arkansas, CRISIS of 1956 showed how the full power of the federal government could be used to enforce integration, but it resulted in the integration of only one school. Against the backdrop of "massive resistance" mounted by southern states, the gradual gains for blacks achieved by voter registration drives, FREEDOM RIDES, lunch counter SIT-INS, and department store picketing seemed puny indeed. It became clear

The landmark Civil Rights Act of 1964 was drafted during the administration of President John F. Kennedy (left). Attorney General Robert F. Kennedy (right) was instrumental in enforcing it. (John F. Kennedy Library)

to leaders of the most active civil rights organization, the SOUTHERN CHRISTIAN LEADERSHIP CONFERENCE (SCLC), that desegregating the South town by town would be a neverending task. National legislation was needed which would decisively end SEGREGATION and make discrimination illegal across the country.

When John F. Kennedy became president in 1961, winning a narrow victory that included 68 percent of the African American vote, civil rights supporters hoped they had placed a champion for their cause in the White House. They were soon disappointed. Ken-

nedy wanted to pass domestic legislation through Congress, including a tax bill. To accomplish this, he needed the support of senior Southern Democrats who were chairmen of various committees. In order to get their support, Kennedy held back on civil rights bills.

In the spring of 1963, Martin Luther King, Jr., head of the SCLC, decided to put pressure on the conscience of the entire nation to support civil rights legislation. To do this, King needed a situation that would show the evils of segregation and expose it as an oppressive system. He found the situation he needed in Birmingham, Alabama.

Birmingham Police Commissioner Eugene "Bull" Connor reacted in a manner worthy of his nickname when the SCLC began a series of peaceful demonstrations in an attempt to bring DESEGREGATION to Birmingham. Police dogs and high-pressure fire hoses were deployed against the demonstrators. King shrewdly sent hundreds of schoolchildren marching down the streets into the police lines. Thanks to journalists and television cameras, the whole world watched and listened as the children were led off to jail.

The nation was appalled. The waves of protest and concern generated in Birmingham swept Kennedy into the maelstrom of the fight for civil rights. On June 11, 1963, Kennedy promised, in a nationwide television broadcast, to press for passage of major civil rights legislation. Eight days later, his bill was submitted to Congress. By August 28, Kennedy's bill had begun its journey through the appropriate congressional committees. The same day, several hundred thousand people of all races thronged the Mall in Washington, D.C., to hear King deliver his masterpiece of oratory, the "I Have a Dream" speech, in the historic MARCH ON WASHINGTON.

Content of the Bill. Kennedy's bill contained eleven titles or sections. They outlawed DISCRIMINATION based on race and gender in virtually every sector of public life. These included voting rights and registration; public accommodations, such as businesses; public facilities, such as parks; public education; and federally assisted programs. Other parts of the bill strengthened the authority of the COMMISSION ON CIVIL RIGHTS; called for equal opportunities in employment; allowed intervention by federal courts in discrimination cases; established the Community Relations Service to deal with prejudice and mandated jury trials in certain civil rights cases.

The final content of this lengthy bill was not

worked out quickly. Attorney General Robert Kennedy, lawyers from the Justice Department, and leaders of both the House and the Senate met often to determine the content. The goal of those writing the legislation was to have a bill strong enough to end legal discrimination but not so strong as to alienate moderate or conservative members of Congress. Such change was accepted, so women were better protected from discrimination.

By the time the content of the bill was set, civil rights had become not merely a "black" issue but a broad "people" issue for many Americans. White liberals and church groups all over the nation had joined in the cause.

President Lyndon Johnson passes out some pens used to sign the Civil Rights Act of 1964, (left to right, standing): Representative Roland Libonati, Representative Peter Rodino, the Reverend Martin Luther King, Jr., Representative Emanuel Celler, and Whitney Young, executive director of the National Urban League. (AP/Wide World Photos)

members came from midwestern and western states with few minority constituents. With no groups lobbying strongly for the bill, it would be easy for these members of Congress to be alienated by an overly demanding bill.

While the legislation was being debated in the House of Representatives, Howard Smith of Virginia, an opponent of the bill, rose to offer an amendment. He suggested that the word "sex" be added to Title VII so that women, as well as racial minorities, would be protected. Smith thought this would make the bill unacceptable to many moderates and thus would kill the legislation. Much to his—and others—surprise, the

Contest in the House. Every piece of legislation introduced into Congress must undergo committee hearings. These hearings can be quite lengthy and, if the committee chair is opposed to the bill, can become a graveyard for the proposed law. President Kennedy introduced his bill into the House of Representatives, instead of the Senate because the House Judiciary Committee was dominated by liberal Democrats. This would ensure the bill a friendly reception, at least initially. Representative Emanuel Cellar was chair of this committee and served as official sponsor of the bill. The hearings in the Judiciary Committee were sometimes heated as its proponents and opponents clashed. When the hearings ended, Celler unexpectedly had a very strong bill and a good bargaining position to take to other committees and to the debate on the House floor.

There was a certain amount of political maneuver-

still pending in the Rules Committee when Kennedy was assassinated on November 22, 1963.

Vice President Lyndon Johnson had served in Congress much longer than Kennedy and knew how to get things done faster. As the new president, Johnson

Lady Bird Johnson, Robert Kennedy and various members of Congress look on as President Lyndon Johnson signs the Civil Rights Act of 1964. (National Archives)

ing over the bill. Many conservative Republicans did not care for it but did not want the onus of being the ones to weaken it. They decided to leave the bill strong so that Southern Democrats would oppose and, perhaps, kill it.

The next step was for the bill to go to the House Rules Committee. This body was chaired by Howard Smith of Virginia, who was opposed to the legislation. Until this committee granted a "rule," or date for debate, no further action could be taken. The bill was

made a speech to a Joint Session of Congress only a few days after Kennedy's death to make clear his determination to see speedy passage of the civil rights bill. Realizing that African Americans did not have sufficiently broad support, Johnson quietly urged church leaders to begin lobbying on behalf of the bill. He worked furiously to achieve progress on the bill, even to the point of giving congressional leaders rides to work so he could talk with them about it. The president spent so much time at the Capitol campaigning for the bill that it almost became a second home. On January 30, 1964, Johnson's efforts brought results, as the bill was sent to the floor of the House for debate. Thanks to close cooperation between Democratic and Republican leaders, all the amendments intended to weaken the bill failed, and on February 10, the bill passed the House by a vote of 290 to 130. Hard work still remained to be done in the Senate.

Passage in the Senate. Senator Mike Mansfield, Majority Leader of the Senate, knew that he needed Republican support to pass the bill, so he began to work closely with Senator Everett Dirksen of Illinois. This partnership paid immediate dividends in bypassing the Senate Judiciary Committee chaired by a hostile senator, James Eastland of Mississippi, and placing the bill before the Calendar Committee. Even there, however, Senator Hubert Humphrey, the floor manager of the bill, faced slow going. The opposition was skillfully led by Senator Richard Russell of Georgia, who used every tactic to delay progress. On one occasion Russell used up three weeks over a mere procedural vote.

The opposition was aided by a group called the Coordinating Committee for Fundamental American Freedoms, headed by William Loeb of New Hampshire. Loeb's group aroused many people and, for a time, generated considerable anti-civil rights mail to members of Congress.

Throughout all the delays and debates, Senate leaders worked closely with House leaders to keep the bill intact. Humphrey also orchestrated a grass-roots effort to counter the influence of Loeb's group. As the public learned more about the civil rights bill, support for it increased. By April, 1964, a Gallup Poll showed that about two-thirds of all Americans approved of the bill. This did not deter the bill's opponents, mainly Southern Democrats, from engaging in a favorite delaying tactic, a filibuster. Day after day the talk droned on until the Senate broke a record for length of debate set in 1846.

By this time many senators were becoming frustrated with the delay and were feeling increasing pressure from constituents who favored the bill. Prominent among these were church groups who looked on civil rights as a moral issue. Finally, on June 10, 1964, the Senate voted to shut off debate. The filibuster had lasted just over 534 hours.

Once debate was ended, events moved swiftly. At 7:40 P.M. on June 19, the Senate passed the bill with a vote of 73 to 27. Since a few amendments had been added by the Senate, the bill had to return to the House for final approval. Liberals in the House brought the issue to a head swiftly and passed the bill on July 2, 1964. President Johnson signed the bill into law the same day.

The Civil Rights Act of 1964 is not only the most massive piece of legislation on the subject since the Civil War; it is also sweeping in its coverage. Its provisions protect all Americans, regardless of race or gender. The bill also represents a high point of cooperation among Americans of diverse races and religions working for a common goal.

SUGGESTED READINGS. Charles and Barbara Whalen's *The Longest Debate* (1985) is the best discussion of the passage of the bill. The role of Kennedy in the civil rights field is discussed by Arthur Schlesinger in *A Thousand Days* (1965), while Johnson's contributions are detailed in *To Heal and to Build: The Programs of Lyndon B. Johnson*, written by Johnson and edited by James M. Burns (1968).——*Michael R. Bradley*

Civil Rights Commission. *See* **Commission on Civil Rights**

Civil rights legislation: Acts of the legislative branch of government that attempt to apply constitutional guarantees, particularly equality of privileges and immunities, to all citizens. In the United States, civil rights laws have been used to combat discrimination against racial, ethnic, and religious minorities, as well as women, gays and lesbians, and people with disabilities. The federal government's efforts fall into two historical periods: the decade following the Civil War (RECONSTRUCTION) and the period beginning in the late 1950's (the modern era). While individual states also enacted a wide range of civil rights laws during the same periods, their actions have been less systematic than those of Congress. Despite occasional setbacks on both the state and national levels, the historical trend has been toward an expansion of civil rights to more and more people.

Reconstruction and Congress. Immediately after the Civil War, states of the former Confederacy were not represented in a Congress dominated by "radical" Republicans. A series of sweeping laws was passed to give African Americans, especially former slaves, broad protection of basic rights such as voting, access to public accommodations and transportation, jury service, and property ownership. The purpose of such laws has often been described as the elimination of

Despite civil rights laws passed during Reconstruction, an antiblack backlash led to scenes like this during the long Jim Crow period of segregation. (National Archives)

all "incidents and badges of slavery" and of racial distinctions in governmental and public acts. Yet because these laws usually prohibited discrimination on the basis of race or color generally, they have subsequently been applied to protect the civil rights of members of racial minorities other than African Americans as well.

The Civil Rights Act of 1866 was enacted to override the 1857 U.S. Supreme Court decision in SCOTT V. SANDFORD (the Dred Scott case), which held that slaves and former slaves were not citizens of the United States and thus were not protected by the Constitution. After the Civil War, "unreconstructed" southern state legislatures sought to limit the rights of former slaves and used *Scott v. Sandford* to legitimize such discrimination. The 1866 act, passed by Congress over President Andrew Johnson's veto, conferred full citizenship rights on "all persons born in the United States . . . excluding Indians not taxed." The act became superfluous after ratification of the FOURTEENTH AMENDMENT in July, 1868.

Congress then passed the Civil Rights Act of 1870, in many respects a restatement of the 1866 act, because it feared that the Supreme Court would declare the Fourteenth Amendment unconstitutional. The new act also protected voting rights previously conferred by the FIFTEENTH AMENDMENT upon all citizens regardless of "race, color, or previous condition of servitude." By criminalizing actions that interfered with the exercise of civil or voting rights, the act put "teeth" in the constitutional amendments. It was the first of a series of federal civil rights laws known pejoratively in the South as the "Force [or Enforcement] Acts."

Two civil rights acts were passed in 1871 by a Congress that was suspicious of southern officials' enforcement of civil rights. The "Second Enforcement Act" prohibited any person from hindering or preventing another from voting and it authorized the federal appointment of election commissioners to oversee voting procedures and practices. Less than two months later, Congress passed another civil rights law, unofficially known as the "Ku Klux Act" or the "Third Enforcement Act." While the KU KLUX KLAN and other secret groups that terrorized African Americans were the immediate targets of the law, several of its provisions have been applied to various contexts. It prohibits any conspiracy (of at least two people) that in any way interferes with the execution of any federal law or deprives any person(s) of the equal protection of the laws, and it extends that prohibition to anyone who acts under the guise of any state law or authority. Now codified as Title XLII United States Code Sections 1981 and 1983, these provisions can be used by any citizen as the basis for a lawsuit against government officials who may have violated his or her civil rights. Examples include police brutality claims and charges of educational discrimination.

With the Civil Rights Act of 1875, Congress sought to extend the scope of civil rights protection from public, government-related activities to more private, social acts. This law imposed civil and criminal penalties on private citizens who denied equal access to public accommodations (such as hotels and restaurants), transportation, and entertainment on the basis of race or color. It was declared unconstitutional by the Supreme Court in the *Civil Rights Cases* (1883).

Congress did not enact another civil rights law for eighty-two years. Some historians attribute this inaction to a political deal negotiated between Republicans and southern Democrats in which the former agreed to withdraw federal troops from the South in return for the latter allowing the election of Rutherford B. Hayes as president by the House of Representatives in 1876. Others argue that RECONSTRUCTION was doomed to fail because of poor policy design, administration, and implementation. Most of the federal civil rights laws of the Reconstruction era were severely restricted, if not invalidated, by judicial decisions in the late nineteenth and early twentieth centuries. In 1894, Congress itself repealed forty-two of the forty-nine sections of the Enforcement Acts.

From Reconstruction to the Modern Era in the States. The civil rights record of the state legislatures was decidedly mixed. While several Reconstruction governments in the South, such as Louisiana and Florida, passed laws covering equal access to accommodations and public education, few northern and western states did so. In the early 1870's, limited protection was accorded racial minorities in Massachusetts and Kansas for accommodations and transportation, as well as for education in New York. Generally, however, states deferred to the federal government on civil rights policy during RECONSTRUCTION.

After the decision in the *Civil Rights Cases* and the continuing judicial retrenchment thereafter, the burden fell to the states to ensure civil rights protection for

The Supreme Court's decision in Brown v. Board of Education, *invalidating the concept of "separate but equal" schools for whites and blacks, spawned a desegregation crisis in Little Rock, Ark.* (The Associated Publishers, Inc.)

their citizens. Various states adopted piecemeal measures that dealt with particular civil rights. By 1900, the greatest number of these focused on public accommodations. Women gained through the ongoing passage of Married Women's Property Acts beginning in the 1830's. States were unwilling, however, to address discrimination in other aspects of life such as education, employment, and housing.

Civil Rights Acts of the Modern Era. Congress' long civil rights hibernation was interrupted by the burgeoning black CIVIL RIGHTS MOVEMENT that began after World War II, the Supreme Court's 1954 school desegregation decision in BROWN v. BOARD OF EDUCATION, and the recalcitrance of many states to comply with the Court's ruling. The focus shifted from the notion of equality, which had tacitly allowed "separate but equal" facilities, to that of DESEGREGATION—true equal access to white institutions. Besides civil rights legislation for racial and ethnic minorities, this period has also seen the enactment of laws granting such rights in varying degrees to women, older people, and people with disabilities.

As in the Reconstruction era, the most comprehensive modern legislation was motivated by concern for the rights of African Americans. The early measures, the 1957 and 1960 Civil Rights Acts, were attempts to reinforce existing rights such as voting and jury service. The 1957 act also established the COMMISSION ON CIVIL RIGHTS and the Civil Rights Division within the Department of Justice. The commission was the first federal agency whose sole mission was the study, investigation, and evaluation of civil rights in the United States.

The CIVIL RIGHTS ACT OF 1964 was the most far-reaching omnibus civil rights law ever passed by Congress. Seen by the nation as a tribute to the late President Kennedy, and advocated by a huge movement led by Martin Luther KING, Jr., the act extended civil rights protections to almost all aspects of public life. Especially important were provisions that denied federal aid to any program or activity found to discrimi-

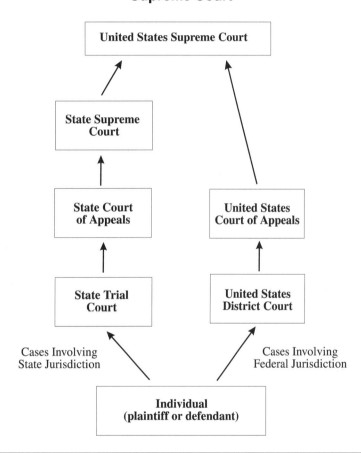

How Civil Rights Cases Reach the Supreme Court

Source: From William C. Lowe, *Blessings of Liberty: Safeguarding Civil Rights.* Human Rights series, p. 14. Vero Beach, Fla.: Rourke Corp., 1992.

nate on the basis of race, color, religion, or national origin, and that prohibited DISCRIMINATION, including on the basis of sex, in employment or union membership. This marked the first time that women were included as a protected group in a civil rights law.

The last sweeping federal civil rights law was the Civil Rights Act of 1968. Even more than the 1964 act, its passage was a memorial to a fallen leader. Originally faced with nearly certain defeat, the act sailed through Congress only a week after the assassination of Martin Luther King, Jr. Its most significant provision prohibited discrimination on the basis of race, color, religion, or national origin in the sale or rental of most housing. It also contained protections for civil rights workers and, in response to growing tension over inner-city and anti-Vietnam War unrest, imposed federal penalties on persons who used interstate commerce to incite a riot.

Only two other pieces of federal legislation have since been designated "civil rights acts." Both were primarily intended to reverse Supreme Court decisions that had narrowly construed civil rights laws. The Civil Rights Restoration Act of 1988 clarified that TITLE IX of the 1972 Education Amendments prohibited federal aid to an entire educational institution if any of its programs is discriminatory (reversing the 1984 decision in *Grove City College v. Bell*). The Civil Rights Act of 1991 reversed nine Supreme Court decisions from 1986 to 1991 that had made it difficult for workers to bring and win employment discrimination suits. It also amended Title VII of the 1964 act to allow limited damages for employment discrimination based on sex, religion, or disability and for cases of SEXUAL HARASSMENT.

Broadening the Civil Rights Agenda. Throughout this period, Congress was also active in protecting the civil rights of groups other than racial and ethnic minorities. Congress has generally viewed women, older people, and people with disabilities as requiring treatment different from racial or ethnic minorities. A brief sampling of laws affecting such groups follows.

The era's first law dealing with women was the EQUAL PAY ACT OF 1963, which mandated "equal pay for equal work," but only in the limited sphere covered by the 1938 FAIR LABOR STANDARDS ACT. Title IX of the Education Amendments of 1972 prohibited sex discrimination in federally funded education programs. The Equal Credit Opportunity Act of 1974 forbade discrimination based on sex or marital status in the granting of credit. The Women's Educational Equity Act of 1974 and subsequent amendments of 1978, 1984, and 1988 gave federal funds to programs to support the fair treatment of women in education. The Retirement Equity Act of 1984 protected spousal retirement benefits and maternity leave for employees in pension plans.

Several federal laws also sought to protect the civil rights of older people. The Age Discrimination in Employment Act of 1967 safeguarded workers from forty to seventy years of age against biased treatment. The Age Discrimination Act of 1975 withheld federal funds from any programs which practiced age discrimination.

People with disabilities have also been the focus of civil rights legislation in the modern era. The ARCHITECTURAL BARRIERS ACT of 1968 required that all new federal construction projects be made accessible to people with disabilities. The REHABILITATION ACT of 1973 prohibited discrimination on the basis of disability in federally funded activities. The Education for All Handicapped Children Act (1975) required that all states receiving federal education funding provide children with disabilities a "free, appropriate public education." The AMERICANS WITH DISABILITIES ACT (1990) extended to people with disabilities most of the basic protections afforded other minorities and women, such as equal employment opportunities and access to public accommodations and transportation.

The extensive involvement of the federal government in the modern era has made much of the states' activity somewhat redundant. Unlike the federal government, states such as California, Connecticut, Hawaii, Massachusetts, New Jersey, Vermont, and Wisconsin have extended some civil rights protections to cover sexual orientation. As of 1990, only seventeen states had equal rights amendments that granted full civil rights to women.

SUGGESTED READINGS. Good historical accounts of civil rights laws, particularly relating to African Americans, include *A Century of Civil Rights* (1961) by Milton Konvitz and Theodore Leskes, and Richard Bardolph's *The Civil Rights Record* (1970). The modern era is covered in many works, including Hugh Davis Graham's *The Civil Rights Era* (1990). Women's legal issues are the subject of *Law, Gender, and Injustice* (1991) by Joan Hoff-Wilson, while Richard Scotch's *From Good Will to Civil Rights* (1984) deals with disability law, particularly the 1973 Rehabilitation Act.—*Bruce Snyder and Jean Schroedel*

Civil Rights movement: Organized efforts by African Americans and their supporters to obtain full and equal rights of citizenship. The movement reached peak effectiveness from 1954 to 1965. It also inspired efforts by other minority groups to press for more equal positions in American society.

Origins and Early Efforts. At the beginning of the twentieth century, Americans of African descent were almost everywhere treated as second-class citizens despite the promise of equal rights in the FOURTEENTH AMENDMENT and of voting rights in the FIFTEENTH AMENDMENT. Discrimination was most evident in the southern and border states, where almost 90 percent of African Americans lived and where state law required separation of the races in nearly all areas of life. This system of JIM CROW LAWS grew with the blessings of the U.S. Supreme Court. In its famous decision in *PLESSY v. FERGUSON* (1896), the court decreed that laws requiring racial segregation were constitutional as long as an attempt was made at main-

cans were entitled to equal treatment and should demand it organized the NATIONAL ASSOCIATION FOR THE ADVANCEMENT OF COLORED PEOPLE (NAACP), a biracial group. The NAACP employed a "law and lobby" approach that sought to influence the actions of government, especially through the courts. By arguing against laws and practices that clearly discriminated against blacks, the NAACP hoped to bring the courts back to the "equal protection of the laws" promised by the Fourteenth Amendment. Early victories, however, were rare.

Martin Luther King, Jr., (left, shown here with Ralph Abernathy) led the Civil Rights movement according to his philosophy of nonviolence. (Library of Congress)

taining a "separate but equal" standard. Yet evidence showed that "separate" almost always meant "unequal." Even in the North, where Jim Crow laws were rare, SEGREGATION was on the increase as blacks were subjected to pervasive DISCRIMINATION in education, housing, and employment. The result was de facto segregation that effectively relegated African Americans to subordinate positions in American society.

The Civil Rights movement began as an attempt to change this pattern of inequality. In 1909, W. E. B. DU BOIS and others who believed that African Ameri-

World War II proved to be a boon to the movement. Many African Americans saw the war as an opportunity to prove their claim to equality and demanded the right to participate fully. NAACP membership increased tenfold. One million blacks served in the largely segregated armed forces. An equal number left the South for war-related work in the North and West. In 1941, President Franklin D. Roosevelt moved to head off a march on Washington by issuing an executive order banning discrimination in defense hiring. White attitudes also began to change. Gunnar Myrdal's *An American Dilemma* (1944) pointed out the gap between the Declaration of Independence's promise of equality and the reality for minorities in American society. Even more influential, perhaps, was the war against Adolf Hitler's Germany, which discredited the very idea of racial superiority. By the mid-1950's, public opinion polls for the first time found a majority of Americans expressing belief in racial equality.

The GREAT MIGRATION of southern blacks to northern and western cities continued after the war, increasing African American political influence. New civil rights organizations appeared on the scene, such as the CONGRESS OF RACIAL EQUALITY (CORE), organized in Chicago in 1942. CORE waged a campaign to integrate eating establishments in northern cities and in 1947 tested a federal ruling that interstate transportation should be desegregated. The NAACP's legal campaign gained momentum and increasingly focused on segregation in public education. Though the judicial system's sympathy was first expressed in efforts to ensure genuinely equal facilities, a major shift came in 1954 when the U.S. Supreme Court reversed the "separate but equal" doctrine in *BROWN V. BOARD OF EDUCATION*. It ordered an end to schools segregated by law. By extension, any legally required separation in other spheres seemed suspect.

The Movement Emerges. The *Brown v. Board of Education* decision was an important catalyst. In 1955, Montgomery, Alabama, witnessed a campaign that many would come to see as marking the start of the Civil Rights movement's golden age. The arrest of Rosa PARKS for refusing to comply with a city law requiring that blacks sit in the back of buses triggered a well-organized boycott of the city's bus system. Led by a young Baptist minister, Martin Luther KING, Jr., the MONTGOMERY BUS BOYCOTT went on for a year. Eventually the Supreme Court ended segregation in the bus system.

Defenders of SEGREGATION did not give in easily, despite the weight of judicial opinions handed down against them. Many states and localities continued to enforce JIM CROW LAWS, and there was much talk by public officials of "massive resistance" to court rulings and executive orders. The prospect that public schools would be shut down rather than integrated was a real one. During the LITTLE ROCK CRISIS, Governor Orval Faubus of Arkansas called out the National Guard rather than integrate Little Rock's Central High School; President Dwight Eisenhower then ordered the guard into federal service and sent in paratroopers to ensure the safety of African American students.

By the late 1950's, it was clear that a major movement for social change had arrived. In many ways the movement took its cue from the Montgomery bus boycott. Influenced by Mahatma Gandhi's advocacy of nonviolent resistance to unjust laws, Martin Luther King, Jr., in 1957 organized the SOUTHERN CHRISTIAN LEADERSHIP CONFERENCE (SCLC) to provide organizational support for a movement of nonviolent direct action. His tactics proved especially effective in an age when Americans were increasingly getting their news from television. The sight of nonviolent demonstrators, including children, confronting upholders of the status quo who seemed much more willing to resort to violence won the movement increasing support in the contest for public opinion.

Though national organizations such as the NAACP, CORE, and the SCLC were prominent in civil rights efforts, much of the real momentum for change came from local communities. A new phase of the movement began in 1960 when four college freshmen in Greensboro, North Carolina, challenged the "whites only" policy at the lunch counter of the local Woolworth's by sitting down and refusing to leave when they were not served. Their "SIT-IN" immediately caught on and soon sit-in demonstrations were underway in many other cities. The tactic was also adaptable to other purposes; "wade-ins," for example, challenged segregated swimming pools. The imagination of the younger generation of African Americans was captured, and pressure for more rapid change grew. The organization of the STUDENT NONVIOLENT COORDINATING COMMITTEE (SNCC) in 1960 showed their determination to press ahead. By the end of 1960, a hundred cities and towns had experienced direct action campaigns and seventy thousand people, mostly young, had taken part in them. The Civil Rights movement had become a mass movement.

The Movement Peaks. By the early 1960's, segregation and racial DISCRIMINATION were being challenged at the grassroots level across the South and in other parts of the country as well. Though the tactics of demonstrators were invariably nonviolent, the response they provoked was often otherwise. The violent reception accorded the CORE-organized "FREEDOM RIDERS" of 1961 (one bus burned, many riders beaten) was a foretaste of things to come. Medgar EVERS, head of the Mississippi NAACP was murdered, as were three civil rights workers during the "freedom summer" of 1964. (Ultimately some forty people, black and white, would lose their lives as participants in the movement.) Some of the movement's most memorable images came from the BIRMINGHAM DEMONSTRATIONS in Alabama. In the spring of 1963, KING organized the largest series of demonstrations yet seen in an attempt to desegregate public accommodations and expand employment opportunities. The pictures of youthful demonstrators, some as young as five, confronting high-pressure fire hoses and police

Kennedy fueled further public support for civil rights legislation. President Lyndon Johnson proved a forceful and persuasive advocate. Congress passed the landmark CIVIL RIGHTS ACT OF 1964, outlawing discrimination in public accommodations, employment, and the distribution of federal funds. After this, the focus shifted to efforts to end practices such as poll taxes, literacy tests, and intimidation that had prevented African Americans from voting in many parts of the

The Montgomery, Ala., bus boycott in 1955 was one of the first successful movement efforts. Here, Martin Luther King, Jr. (second from left) and Ralph Abernathy (left) refuse to sit in the back of the bus. (AP/Wide World Photos)

dogs did much to rally public opinion in favor of the movement. The massive MARCH ON WASHINGTON later in 1963 was attended by more than 200,000 people and highlighted by King's "I have a dream" speech. In many ways the emotional climax of the movement, it prompted the promise of significant legislative action by the Kennedy Administration.

Sorrow over the assassination of President John

South. Though the battle was fought in hundreds of small towns and rural communities, it was Selma, Alabama, that seized the nation's attention. The seat of a county in which blacks were in the majority but only numbered 325 in an electorate of 9,800, Selma typified the lack of black voting power in much of the South. Demonstrations there and a violence-marred march to Montgomery highlighted the problem for all to see. Congress responded by passing the VOTING RIGHTS ACT OF 1965, allowing federally appointed registrars to supervise elections in areas where African Americans did not vote in numbers consistent with their presence in the population. The impact on southern politics was significant. (In 1975, the act was extended to protect the voting rights of American Indians and Latinos in other parts of the country.)

The Movement Fragments. By the end of 1965, the JIM CROW system was dead and African Americans had access to the ballot throughout the country. At this point, however, the movement began to splinter. Troubling to many whites was the prominence in the later 1960's of the BLACK POWER wing of the movement. Though the slogan was never clearly defined, Black Power advocates drew on the thought of MALCOLM X (assassinated in 1965) and other black nationalists who appeared to reject the goal of integration and the methods of nonviolence. SNCC and CORE purged their white members, and separatist rhetoric contributed to a renewed sense of racial division in the country. Ultimately the emphasis on racial pride and self-reliance proved a longer-lasting legacy than the militant statements of Black Power advocates.

Also frustrating was the de facto SEGREGATION that characterized much of the urban United States. Often the result of segregated housing patterns, such segregation was difficult to combat because it was legal if it could not be proved to be the result of conscious efforts to discriminate. Conditions in the cities were dramatized by a series of destructive RACE RIOTS from 1965 to 1967 that rocked Los Angeles, Newark, Detroit, and other cities. Moreover, the assassination of Martin Luther KING, Jr., in 1968 robbed the movement of its most respected and eloquent leader.

The combination of urban riots and Black Power rhetoric, together with the sense that the movement's legislative achievements had erased barriers to equality, caused many whites to turn away. Indeed, a backlash developed that conservative politicians would exploit in the 1970's and 1980's. While the courts continued to oppose any sort of overt racial discrimination, efforts to try to deal with the observable inequalities in American society through AFFIRMATIVE ACTION programs often received a cooler reception. In 1978, the Supreme Court banned the outright use of quotas to benefit minority applicants in education and employment, while efforts to halt the resegregation of urban schools were hurt by judicial reluctance to order cross-district busing. Though the Civil Rights movement continued on into the 1990's, it lacked the focus, leadership, and broad base of support that it had enjoyed in the decade after BROWN V. BOARD OF EDUCATION.

Its impact had been broad and multicultural, however. Not only did CIVIL RIGHTS LEGISLATION protect other racial and ethnic groups, but these as well as women, children, people with disabilities, and homosexuals found the methods and rhetoric of the Civil Rights movement useful as a model in their own quests for a more equal place in American society.

SUGGESTED READINGS. Among a number of good general accounts of the Civil Rights movement are Harvard Sitkoff's *The Struggle for Black Equality, 1954-1992* (rev. ed., 1993) and Juan Williams' *Eyes on the Prize: America's Civil Rights Years, 1954-1965* (1988). The latter is the companion volume to an award-winning television documentary and may be supplemented by a valuable collection of primary sources in *The Eyes on the Prize: Civil Rights Reader* (1991), edited by Clayborne Carson et al. A good oral history is *My Soul Is Rested: Movement Days in the Deep South Remembered* (1977) by Howell Raines. David R. Goldfield's *Black, White, and Southern: Race Relations and Southern Culture, 1940 to the Present* (1990) provides a useful account of the movement from a regional perspective.—*William C. Lowe*

Civil service: Administrative service of a government in which positions are secured through competitive examinations. The progress and changes that American civil service has experienced since its inception in the eighteenth century reflect the country's political development and a growing concern with equal opportunity.

History. Civil service can be defined according to the function of its employees, which is to provide administrative support that connects the state with its people in nonpolitical, nonpartisan ways. Services are organized according to standard bureaucratic practice, with staffing based on the pyramid model: The chain of command extends from the highest office (the apex) to the lowest offices (the base).

The origins of bureaucracy and the pyramid system can be traced to antiquity. Egyptians and Greeks conducted public affairs in this way, as did the Romans, whose vast empire was governed by an elaborate system with separate agencies for the military, foreign affairs, finance, taxation, and other related operations. Changes in government services corresponded to political changes in a given country over time. For example, after the French Revolution of 1789, which abolished the monarchy and created the republic, civil servants owed their service to the state, not to the crown. Napoleon insisted that authority belonged to the office and not to the official, a clear example of the government's attempts to establish universality rather than partisanship.

In the United States, however, the early days of civil service were closely linked to politics, and there were few attempts to base employment on principles other than those of political preferment. The notorious "spoils system," considered a hallmark of the Andrew Jackson administration, handed out public office as a reward to those who had helped a party or candidate win. The tenure of most civil servants was short and uncertain, and their backgrounds and training varied widely. Continuity and stability, the principles that most contemporary administrators consider essential, were almost unknown. Politicians saw in civil service a way to establish bases of power and well-run "machines," which operated at the federal, state, and local levels.

The spoils system, considered by many a legacy of the British model of civil service, became firmly established in the system of American democracy. Members of minorities were not appointed to positions, although the issue of African American employment seems to have surfaced in 1802. In a confidential letter to a Senate committee, the Postmaster General stressed the need to continue the exclusion of African American mail carriers, warning that the dangerous idea that "a man's rights do not depend on his color" might be absorbed by black carriers if they were allowed to deliver mail.

Later legislation stipulated that "no other than a free white person should be employed in carrying the mail of the United States," although in 1828 African Americans were permitted to carry mailbags from the stagecoach to the post office as long as they were supervised by white men.

Reform. Attempts at reforming the civil service did not occur until after the CIVIL WAR when reform organizations campaigned for a merit system, whereby positions would be given on the basis of merit rather than political favor. Although the Grant and Hayes administrations attempted some measure of reform, their efforts collapsed because of dissension and political infighting. In 1883 the Pendleton Civil Service Reform Act was passed, transforming the nature of civil service. This legislation established the bipartisan Civil Service Commission to administer the merit system, which appointed employees on the basis of competitive examinations or—in some fields requiring more advanced, specialized, or technical experience and training—competitive qualifications.

By the beginning of the twentieth century, career service was not unusual, workers were better educated and trained, and political associations were no longer essential ingredients of the system. Personnel sections were part of each government agency, which meant that hiring, firing, and related matters were supervised by specially trained employees who were not directly involved with the machinations of the individual departments. Managerial studies, such as personnel relations and public administration, became part of many universities' curricula and soon became burgeoning fields of undergraduate and graduate studies.

During WORLD WAR II, many of the rules of the merit system were sacrificed to wartime necessities. In 1949, four years after the war's conclusion, more changes were enacted, such as simplified hiring procedures and more uniform salaries. The preferential consideration of veterans for civil service jobs first established in 1919, remained and continues today de-

Civil service workers fulfill many vital functions. Here a small boy assists his neighborhood postal worker. (Mary M. Langenfeld)

spite the occasional opposition of certain groups.

The Civil Service Reform Act of 1978, sponsored by the Carter Administration in part in response to the Watergate scandal during the Nixon Administration, abolished the Civil Service Commission and relegated its previous functions to a politically appointed agency, the Office of Personnel Management, and the Merit Systems Protection Agency, containing its own

1883, the merit system has determined the nature of the examining process for most entry-level, middle-level, and managerial positions, while higher positions have tended to be political appointments.

Under the merit system, the candidate whose application has been approved takes a written test, administered and scored by a neutral examining agency, that is designed to correspond to the duties and require-

Hiring practices used in filling federal civil service jobs use testing and other evaluation procedures to preclude any type of discrimination. (Jim West)

Office of Special Counsel. This act has been considered the most important civil service reform since the reform legislation of 1883, which in effect created the modern civil service.

Examinations and Eligibility Requirements. In Great Britain, whose early system served in many ways as a model for the United States, the civil service examining process was closely linked to the country's universities; thus, successful candidates had performed well in a rigorous classical curriculum. There were few attempts to connect performance of a particular job with an examination. In the United States, since the Civil Service Commission was established in

ments of the job. After a stipulated time on the job, the worker may then take another test to obtain a promotion. Thus hiring and promotion are usually handled by neutral, third-party agencies. Occasionally in lieu of a written test there is an oral examination; this, too, is usually governed by a neutral examining board.

In the case of more technically trained or specialized workers such as engineers, lawyers, or physicians, professional qualifications such as degrees and previous experience are ordinarily considered in place of examinations.

The examination system, although designed to be fair and impartial, does have its disadvantages in that it tends to restrict eligibility because of its close connections to the minutiae of job specifications. Critics contend that under such limitations, the system overlooks promising possible candidates. Attempts to make open job classifications more accessible have met with mixed results, however; they seem to be the most successful at state and local levels.

Representative Bureaucracy. When one considers bureaucracy in its neutral sense (the administration of government through agencies or bureaus) and not pejoratively (usually synonymous with "red tape"), the importance of equal representation becomes apparent. Ideally, equality should exist both within the general population of a democracy and within the civil service. The servants of government (and therefore, in a democracy, of the people) should reflect the nature of those being governed. When racial, ethnic, or gender imbalances are found to exist in the staffing of the civil service, the problem of how to correct the imbalances arises. The goal of equal representation comes into conflict with the goal of an impartial system based strictly on merit.

Aggressive recruitment of minorities has been suggested as one vehicle for change. Studies addressing the possible cultural biases of written examinations, particularly those at the entry level, have succeeded in creating revisions of tests and test materials. Affirmative action policies have been instituted in many government agencies to boost minority representation. Indeed, civil service jobs have been a route to economic security for large numbers of minorities, especially in urban areas. Civil service, like other areas of government, has never been completely depoliticized and will always be sensitive to political change.

Employee Restrictions and Codes. Most civil service systems allow workers to form unions. Workers and middle management often affiliate with mainstream trade unions, such as the AMERICAN FEDERATION OF LABOR, paralleling their counterparts in industry. Yet because civil servants are agents of public government and provide services that are essential to the health and welfare of the people, most systems prohibit union-sponsored strikes. Thus, civil servants' workers organizations are considerably weakened. In order to resolve this problem, many agencies have created special mediation boards, periodic reviews, and other measures giving workers greater power in changes and reforms.

Political activity and direct political involvement remain contentious issues. The standard to which most civil servants must adhere holds that discreet political interest and commitment on the part of the individual are accepted but active proselytizing or campaigning are not. Civil servants are not allowed to engage in any activity that might conflict with the function and nature of their positions, such as engaging in related businesses or accepting gifts.

Continuity and Reform. Since the merit system was firmly established and the spoils system abandoned, civil service has stressed equality of opportunity. Because in a democratic society government responds to the needs and demands of the people, fundamental changes in both the structure and the internal machinery of civil service inevitably occur. Reformers continue to grapple with the questions of how a civil service meritocracy can be sensitive to demographic changes or rectify countless years of discrimination and oppression. It is perhaps reassuring to note that civil service reform has been, and continues to be, addressed by outstanding scholars and institutions throughout the world. The results suggest a healthy situation: lively exchange of ideas and opinions and a persistent desire to increase the strengths as well as to eliminate the weaknesses of the system.

SUGGESTED READINGS. *History of the United States Civil Service* (1958) by Paul P. Van Riper provides a comprehensive historical analysis. Ari Hoogenboom's *Outlawing the Spoils: A History of the Civil Service Reform Movement, 1865-1883* (1968) presents a cogent study of the critical reform movement. Samuel Krislov's study, *The Negro in Federal Employment: The Quest for Equal Opportunity* (1967) examines the concept of representative bureaucracy and its relationship to civil rights. *Civil Service Reform: An Annotated Bibliography* (1987) by David L. Dillman is another source.—*Jean Gandesbery*

Civil War (1861-1865): Four-year conflict between the Union and the Confederacy which freed the slaves and preserved the federal Union. The Civil War was a defining event for the United States, resulting in "a new birth of freedom," in the words of President Abraham Lincoln.

Causes of the War. Historians have long debated why the Civil War happened but generally agree that three issues were paramount: regional rivalry between North and South; conflict between the doctrine of states' rights and a strong central, federal government; and the festering problem of SLAVERY. While each of these undeniably contributed to the war, slavery was most important as the immediate spark that ignited the conflict.

North-South rivalry had existed even before the AMERICAN REVOLUTION, most notably in the political struggle to promote conflicting economic interests. The agricultural South demanded a trade and tariff system which favored the export of its crops, especially cotton, while the North sought protection for its growing industrial and mercantile economy.

South wished to open this land to slave-holding plantations, whereas increasingly the North was determined to restrict the growth of slavery or even abolish it.

The volatile issue of slavery came to dominate the regional debate. The MISSOURI COMPROMISE and the Compromise of 1850 managed to hold the Union intact yet still allowed slavery to expand. By the 1850's, however, the ABOLITIONIST MOVEMENT was active

The African American 54th regiment served valiantly in the Civil War. (Library of Congress)

To combat northern economic policy and defend slavery, Southern political thinkers developed the doctrine of states' rights. This held that the Constitution had established only a loose union of individual states which retained most of their independence. Under this doctrine, states could choose whether to accept decisions of the national government and could even nullify federal law.

Economic considerations aside, the point of states' rights was to protect the institution of slavery in the South and ensure its spread to the huge territory gained by the United States following the LOUISIANA PURCHASE and the MEXICAN-AMERICAN WAR. The

throughout the North, and Southerners feared that if the new Republican Party came to power it would free the slaves.

The South's fears were confirmed with the election of Republican Abraham Lincoln as president in 1860. A month after Lincoln's victory, on December 20, South Carolina became the first state to secede from the Union. Before Lincoln was inaugurated in March, 1861, seven other states had followed and formed the CONFEDERATE STATES OF AMERICA. They chose as their president Jefferson Davis, a Mississippian who had served as a U.S. Senator and as Secretary of War. After Lincoln's call for troops to suppress the rebellion, more southern states left the Union. In April, 1861, Confederate forces fired on the small Union garrison holding Fort Sumter in Charleston harbor. The American Civil War had begun.

Political and Military Strategies. When the southern states left the Union, they embarked upon a conservative revolution to preserve the status quo, specifically slavery. Because of this, the Confederacy adopted a defensive strategy to maintain its borders, establish itself as an independent nation, and win recognition from foreign powers such as Great Britain and France.

Lincoln and the North, on the other hand, had to fashion a political and military strategy that both denied southern claims to independence and returned the rebellious states to the Union. Inevitably this required defeating Confederate armies in battle and occupying southern territory, both of which were enormously difficult tasks. Despite the advantages the North seemed to hold over the South in terms of population, industrial capacity, railroad mileage, and other factors, the South had one key advantage: While the North had to prevail, the South needed only to endure.

The Confederacy maintained a defensive strategy throughout the war with only a few, dramatic exceptions. The most notable of these were the moves north by Robert E. Lee's Army of Northern Virginia in 1862 and again in 1863. These were not invasions but large-scale raids to replenish southern supplies, draw Union forces away from Confederate territory, encourage the northern peace movement, and gain foreign recognition. Both incursions, however, ended in Confederate defeats, the first at Antietam and the second at the three-day battle of Gettysburg.

The more complex northern strategy evolved throughout the course of the war. Early hopes of a quick, decisive victory were dashed by Confederate success on the battlefield, and by 1863 the Union had settled in for a prolonged war of conquest and attrition. A naval blockade of the Confederacy interrupted the flow of much-needed supplies, especially military equipment. The capture of New Orleans in 1862 and Vicksburg in 1863 gave the North control of the Mississippi River, splitting the Confederacy in two. Meanwhile, powerful Union armies advanced steadily and bloodily across southern territory, returning states and their people to the Union by force of arms.

The Soldiers. Civil War armies were remarkably varied in their composition. There were significant numbers of foreign-born troops and American Indians in both Union and Confederate armies, while African Americans made an indispensable contribution to the Union war effort.

More than half a million foreign-born soldiers fought in the war, most for the Union. That army had a number of distinctly ethnic units such as the Polish Legion, Martinez' Militia (Mexican Americans), the Swiss Rifles, the Gardes Lafayette (French), and the Garibaldi Guard (Italian). Federal forces were also swelled by more than 200,000 German nationals, most scattered throughout the Union armies rather than grouped into special units.

Large numbers of Irishmen were found on both sides of the battle lines. As many as 150,000 served in the Union Army, including those in the famous "Irish Brigade" which performed bravely at Antietam and Gettysburg. There were several Irish units on the Confederate side as well, with equal reputations for valor.

West of the Mississippi River, both Union and Confederate armies recruited American Indians, who often wore their traditional garb rather than more conventional uniforms. The Confederacy raised three brigades, mostly Cherokees, Choctaws, Chickasaws, and Seminoles. STAND WATIE, a Cherokee from Georgia, rose to the rank of brigadier general in the Confederate Army. The Federals enlisted one American Indian brigade, composed mainly of Creek warriors.

Important as these troops were to their respective armies, the greatest single contribution was made by African American soldiers serving with the Union. Lincoln, who had originally hesitated to recruit blacks into service, later admitted that they had made victory possible. Even the Confederacy tried to enlist African Americans in a last-ditch attempt to stave off defeat. They offered freedom in exchange for military service, but the war ended before the idea could be fully implemented.

On the Union side, the drive to capitalize on this available pool of manpower began in 1861 when fugitive slaves were used as laborers. In July, 1862, Congress authorized blacks to serve in the Union army, although not as combat troops. After the EMANCIPATION PROCLAMATION on January 1, 1863, "United States Colored Troops," as they were designated, were recruited, drilled, and sent into battle.

Before the war ended, more than 200,000 black troops had served bravely, frequently under difficult conditions. Often subject to racial taunts and insults, African American soldiers received only half the pay of white troops until the summer of 1864. Still, they fought with exceptional courage and distinction in battles such as Cold Harbor and Fort Walker and participated in 449 engagements, suffering a casualty rate 35 percent higher than white troops. By 1865 they accounted for nearly two-thirds of the Union forces in the Mississippi valley, and their mere presence in the field contributed greatly to the Confederacy's loss of morale and eventual defeat.

The Emancipation Proclamation and the Gettysburg Address. The Civil War ended slavery and radically redefined the nature of the American Union—both profound changes that were shaped by the words of Lincoln.

In many ways, the Emancipation Proclamation had more symbolic than practical effect since it freed only those slaves outside Union control. Still, the document broadened the purpose of the war into a struggle for human freedom, earned the approval of European powers for the Union side, and committed the Union to continue fighting until victory.

Just as the proclamation radically redefined the nature of the war, so Lincoln's Gettysburg Address reshaped the Union itself, changing it from an association of separate states into a compact among free individuals. When Lincoln declared that government was "of the people, by the people, for the people," he was stating the Union's strongest argument against states' rights. Lincoln's two key points, that the American people constituted the true Union and that, as Jefferson had proclaimed, "all men are created equal," assured the growth of American democracy. In Lincoln's terms, there would be "a new birth of freedom" for all Americans.

Results of the Conflict. The Civil War devastated the South and resulted in an estimated 615,000 deaths. Despite the defeat of the Confederacy in 1865 and constitutional amendments abolishing slavery and extending citizenship, within ten years African Americans were largely reduced to second-class status. In the South, this was accomplished *de jure* (by law), and in the North, just as effectively *de facto* (in fact). It might seem that the gains of the Civil War were, for all practical purposes, delayed for almost a century until the modern CIVIL RIGHTS MOVEMENT in the 1960's.

Still, the Civil War produced three lasting effects on American life which have influenced the nation's diverse peoples and cultures. First, it shifted the balance of political power, ending the South's long domination and allowing the country to develop along modern, industrial, and democratic lines. Second, the war ended SLAVERY as a legitimate institution, a decision protected by laws and upheld by the courts. Finally, as Lincoln had foretold, the war brought forth a new Union, a reinvented nation which placed greater emphasis on the individual. This, in turn, assured that the American government had the mandate to be truly "of the people, by the people, for the people," rather than a loose agreement among competing regions or independent states.

SUGGESTED READINGS. Two classic accounts of the Civil War, emphasizing military events, are Bruce Catton's *American Heritage Picture History of the Civil War* (1960, repr. 1982) and Shelby Foote's *The Civil War: A Narrative* (1958-1974, repr. 1986). The first is exceptionally well illustrated; the second is written with the knowledge of a historian and the talent of a novelist. A work which brings in more of the social and political aspects and highlights the role of African Americans is *The Civil War: An Illustrated History,* by Geoffrey Ward, with Ken Burns and Ric Burns (1990). Material on foreign-born and American Indian troops is found in two books by Bell Irvin Wiley, *The Life of Johnny Reb* (1943) and *The Life of Billy Yank* (1971). Finally, *Why the South Lost the Civil War* (1986) by Richard Beringer and others provides a comprehensive analysis of this momentous American struggle.—*Michael Witkoski*

Class: Group that shares the same socioeconomic status or rank, most commonly characterized as lower-class, middle-class, or upper-class. Like RACE or ETHNICITY, class is a controversial variable that is often used to distinguish one group of people from another. It may also be a predictor of an individual's politics, lifestyle, or values, as well as one's choices in marriage, education, and religion.

The United States is sometimes described as a "classless" society compared with other countries because it has never had an official aristocracy, currently has a middle-class majority, and has generally emphasized individualism and equality of opportunity. According to the American dream, someone born into poverty is free to move into the middle or even upper class through hard work. This view is challenged by sociologists, however, and has been shown to be an ideal rather than an actuality by the actual experiences of people who feel trapped in a cycle of poverty in a growing underclass, particularly in the inner city.

Cleaver, Eldridge (b. Aug. 31, 1935, Wabbaseka, Ark.): African American author and activist. His early years in Los Angeles were troubled, and most of his education—and his adoption of the Muslim faith—came in prison. Cleaver's first book, *Soul on Ice* (1968), was a best-selling collection of essays and letters detailing his militant views on the black experience. Writing for the magazine *Ramparts* and speaking for the BLACK PANTHERS after 1968, Cleaver called for "total liberty for black people or total destruction for America." In the late 1970's, after international travel to avoid prison and a residency in Algeria, he became a "born-again" Christian and renounced his former ideas.

Clemente, Roberto (Aug. 18, 1934, Carolina, Puerto Rico—Dec. 31, 1972, near Carolina, Puerto Rico): Latino baseball player. Clemente began his career in 1950 with the Santurce Cangrejeros. In 1953, he was signed by the Brooklyn Dodgers, but the following year he was drafted by the Pittsburgh Pirates, with whom he remained for the rest of his career. A superb defensive right fielder with a feared throwing arm, Clemente won four National League batting titles and twelve Gold Glove Awards for defensive excellence. He was chosen to be on twelve National League All-Star teams and was voted the National League's Most Valuable Player in 1966. He also won Most Valuable Player honors in the 1971 World Series and ended his career as one of only a handful of players to have amassed three thousand hits. In 1973, while helping to oversee relief efforts after a massive earthquake struck Nicaragua, Clemente was killed in a plane crash in the Caribbean. That same year, he was inducted into the National Baseball Hall of Fame.

Cochise (c. 1812—June 8, 1874, Chiricahua Apache Reservation, Arizona Territory): Chief of the Chiricahua APACHE Indians in Arizona noted for his courage, integrity, and military skill. In 1861, following the unjust hanging of some of his relatives, Cochise warred relentlessly against the United States Army, leading a strong but futile effort to stop white expansion westward. In peace talks in 1872, Cochise was promised a reservation for his people in his native territory, but after he died, his people were forcibly removed.

Code Talkers. *See* **Navajo Code Talkers**

Cold War: State of international tension and breakdown in relations between the United States and the Soviet Union which began after World War II. The world

Former Black Panther Eldridge Cleaver renounced his more radical ideas when he became a "born-again" Christian. (AP/Wide World Photos)

became divided into two hostile camps, East and West, with each trying to outmaneuver the other. Each side used every means short of war to obtain its objectives, sometimes running the risk of provoking the war neither wanted.

The origins of the Cold War lay in deep-seated distrust on the part of both nations, extending back to the Russian Revolution of 1917. In 1945, the two nations found they had drastically different plans for the postwar world. The United States envisioned "one world" characterized by lasting peace and genuine democracy in which no nation would control any other. The Soviets were determined to create a system of satellite states in Eastern Europe as protection against future attacks from the West.

Disagreements emerged before the end of World War II over implementation of the "one world" concept in the Atlantic Charter and at the Yalta Conference over specific postwar plans for Poland, Germany, and Eastern Europe. Each side interpreted the agreements differently and believed that the other was violating their provisions.

President Franklin D. Roosevelt died shortly after Yalta, and Vice-President Harry S. Truman assumed office. An outspoken man who distrusted the Soviet

Union and Joseph Stalin, Truman decided on a "get tough" policy. He stopped financial assistance to the Soviets. He was unable to prevent the Soviets from controlling Poland and Eastern Europe, but he resisted Russian claims on the American, French, and British zones of Germany. The effect was to divide Germany into East and West. The Cold War was not confined to Europe. The Soviets supported their Communist allies in China, and Truman, recognizing that China would fall to the Communists, decided to revive Japan as a pro-Western force in Asia.

The Truman Administration adopted the "containment" doctrine and the Marshall Plan in 1946 and 1947 to prevent Communist expansion and to assist in the economic reconstruction of Western Europe. The United States wanted to make the Europeans partners in the struggle against the Soviets. The military capabilities of the West were strengthened by the creation in 1948 of the North Atlantic Treaty Organization (NATO), a defensive alliance. The Soviets countered with an alliance of Eastern European powers, the Warsaw Pact.

A new phase in the Cold War began in 1949 with the successful explosion of the Soviet Union's first atomic weapon and the fall of mainland China to the Communists. Believing that the United States could no longer depend upon the containment doctrine, Truman accepted the responsibility of defending freedom in the world instead of relying upon allies or any other nations. President Dwight Eisenhower's administration developed a new doctrine, "massive retaliation," based upon the new nuclear weapons technology. The administration also attempted, with little success, to develop a system of mutual defense pacts among non-Communist nations.

The new policy involved the United States in Korea, Vietnam, Latin America, and elsewhere in the Third World. The arms buildup in the United States caused an arms buildup in the Soviet Union. The U.S. struggle became a global effort to resist Communism. Not until the breakup of Eastern Europe and the Soviet Union in the late 1980's and early 1990's did the Cold War officially end.

SUGGESTED READINGS. Thomas Bailey's *America Faces Russia* (1950) emphasizes the aggressive Soviet expansion policy. William Appleman Williams links the Cold War to the American belief in capitalist expansion in *The Tragedy of American Diplomacy* (1959). John Lewis Gaddis' *The United States and the Origins of Cold War, 1941-1947* (1972) states that both

sides share responsibility. Idealistic internationalism in the United States is the emphasis of Walter LeFevber's *America, Russia, and the Cold War, 1945-1966* (1967). The end of the Cold War is discussed in Bogden Denis Denitch's *The End of the Cold War: European Unity, Socialism, and the Shift in Global Power* (1990).

Colleges—African American: There were more than one hundred Historically Black Colleges and Universities (HBCU's) in the United States in the early 1990's, the vast majority in the South. Most share a common commitment to public service and the general improvement of African American life through the training of community leaders. HBCUs have traditionally prided themselves on their efforts to improve the conditions of poor people and further the advancement of their race. As training grounds for new generations of African American leaders, these institutions provide invaluable experience. Martin Luther KING, Jr., and Julian BOND, who attended Morehouse College, W. E. B. DU BOIS of FISK UNIVERSITY, and Jesse JACKSON of North Carolina Agricultural and Technical College are but a few examples of African American leaders educated at HBCUs.

African American colleges have also provided a gateway for disadvantaged youths by providing opportunities for EDUCATION for those who would not otherwise attend college. A focus on supplementary remedial education often provides these students with the necessary tools for completion of an academic degree.

The history and future of HBCUs is inextricably linked to the broader issues of RACISM and race relations in the United States. African American institutions historically have been molded and formed by attitudes of the predominantly white leadership of the nation, as well as by leaders of the African American community.

Early History. Because slaves were legally prohibited from receiving even rudimentary education, most post-Civil War black "colleges" were actually small schools teaching fundamentals of literacy. Only two northern black colleges were formed prior to the CIVIL WAR by African Americans: Lincoln University (1854) in Pennsylvania and Wilberforce College (1856) in Ohio.

The first widespread movement for African American education occurred immediately following the Civil War and was spearheaded by northern white American missionaries concerned with the education and placement of freed slaves. Missionaries met with limited success, however, largely because of their ill-conceived attempts at reforming the slaves in a manner consistent with their own white Protestant New England experiences. They were frequently dismayed by the distinctiveness of African American Christianity.

prohibit such funding. The Second Morrill Act of 1890 provided specifically for African American colleges. Notable land grant colleges include FISK UNIVERSITY (1867) in Tennessee and HOWARD UNIVERSITY (1867) in Washington, D.C., both of which remain principal centers for higher education of African Americans.

Historic Howard University is still a major center for the education of African Americans. (Library of Congress)

Eminently more successful was the FREEDMEN'S BUREAU, a governmental organization designed to assist the settlement and ASSIMILATION of freed African Americans. Many early colleges benefited from the bureau's aid to missionaries and religious institutions in the recruiting of white educators and financial support of colleges. With the passage of the First Morrill Act of 1862, funding was granted to the states for land grant colleges designed to bring HIGHER EDUCATION to poor people. Although the act did not specifically designate funding for black institutions, neither did it

By the late nineteenth century, many of the early gains in DESEGREGATION and in African American education had eroded. RECONSTRUCTION created an upsurge of racism that resulted in the dismissal of black political leaders in the South. Furthermore, the United States was rapidly adopting a policy of official SEGREGATION. In 1896, the landmark Supreme Court decision *PLESSY V. FERGUSON* established a principle of "separate but equal" facilities for blacks and whites and prohibited intermingling of the races. African Americans were thereby forbidden to attend white in-

African American Colleges

Institution	Location	Year Founded	Institution	Location	Year Founded
Alabama A & M University	Normal, Ala.	1875	Meharry Medical College	Nashville, Tenn.	1876
Alabama State University	Montgomery, Ala.	1874	Miles College	Birmingham, Ala.	1905
Albany State College	Albany, Ga.	1903	Mississippi Industrial College	Holly Springs, Miss.	1905
Alcorn A&M College	Lorman, Miss.	1871			
Allen University	Columbia, S.C.	1870	Mississippi Valley State University	Itta Bena, Miss.	1946
Arkansas Baptist College	Little Rock, Ark.	1884			
Atlanta University	Atlanta, Ga.	1865	Morehouse College	Atlanta, Ga.	1867
Barber-Scotia College	Concord, N.C.	1867	Morgan State College	Baltimore, Md.	1867
Benedict College	Columbia, S.C.	1870	Morris College	Sumter, S.C.	1908
Bennett College	Greensboro, N.C.	1873	Morris Brown College	Atlanta, Ga.	1881
Bethune-Cookman College	Daytona Beach, Fla.	1904	Morristown College	Morristown, Tenn.	1881
			Natchez Junior College	Natchez, Miss.	1885
Bishop College	Dallas, Tex.	1881	Norfolk State University	Norfolk, Va.	1935
Bishop State Community College	Mobile, Ala.	1927	North Carolina A&T State University	Greensboro, N.C.	1891
Bowie State College	Bowie, Md.	1865	North Carolina Central University	Durham, N.C.	1910
Central State University	Wilberforce, Ohio	1887			
Cheyney State College	Cheyney, Pa.	1837	Oakwood College	Huntsville, Ala.	1896
Chaflin College	Orangeburg, S.C.	1869	Paine College	Augusta, Ga.	1882
Clark College	Atlanta, Ga.	1869	Paul Quinn College	Waco, Tex.	1872
Clinton Jr. College	Rock Hill, S.C.	1894	Philander-Smith College	Little Rock, Ark.	1877
Coahoma Jr. College	Clarksdale, Miss.	1949	Prairie View A&M College	Prairie View, Tex.	1876
Concordia College	Selma, Ala.	1922	Prentiss Institute	Prentiss, Miss.	1907
Coppin State College	Baltimore, Md.	1900	Rust College	Holly Springs, Miss.	1866
Daniel Payne College	Birmingham, Ala.	1889			
Delaware State College	Dover, Del.	1891	Saint Augustine's College	Raleigh, N.C.	1867
Dillard University	New Orleans, La.	1869	Saint Paul's College	Lawrenceville, Va.	1888
Edward Waters College	Jacksonville, Fla.	1866	Savannah State College	Savannah, Ga.	1890
Elizabeth City State University	Elizabeth City, N.C.	1891	Selma University	Selma, Ala.	1878
			Shaw University	Raleigh, N.C.	1865
Fayetteville State University	Fayetteville, N.C.	1867	Shorter College	Little Rock, Ark.	1886
Fisk University	Nashville, Tenn.	1866	South Carolina State College	Orangeburg, S.C.	1896
Florida A&M University	Tallahassee, Fla.	1877	Southwestern Christian College	Terrell, Tex.	1949
Florida Memorial College	Miami, Fla.	1879	Spelman College	Atlanta, Ga.	1881
Fort Valley State College	Fort Valley, Ga.	1895	Stillman College	Tuscaloosa, Ala.	1876
Grambling State University	Grambling, La.	1901	Talladega College	Talladega, Ala.	1867
Hampton University	Hampton, Va.	1868	Tennessee State University	Nashville, Tenn.	1912
Hinds Community College	Utica, Miss.	1903	Texas College	Tyler, Tex.	1894
Howard University	Washington, D.C.	1867	Texas Southern University	Houston, Tex.	1947
Huston-Tillotson College	Austin, Tex.	1875	Tougaloo College	Tougaloo, Miss.	1869
Interdenominational Theological Center	Atlanta, Ga.	1958	Tuskegee University	Tuskegee, Ala.	1881
			University of Arkansas	Pine Bluff, Ark.	1873
Jackson State University	Jackson, Miss.	1877	University of the District of Columbia	Washington, D.C.	1851
Jarvis Christian College	Hawkins, Tex.	1912			
Johnson C. Smith University	Charlotte, N.C.	1867	University of Maryland, Eastern Shore	Princess Anne, Md.	1886
Kentucky State University	Frankfort, Ky.	1886			
Knoxville College	Knoxville, Tenn.	1875	University of the Virgin Islands	St. Thomas, Virgin Islands	1963
Lane College	Jackson, Tenn.	1882			
Langston University	Langston, Okla.	1897	Virginia College	Lynchburg, Va.	1886
Le Moyne-Owen College	Memphis, Tenn.	1862	Virginia Union University	Richmond, Va.	1865
Lincoln University of Missouri	Jefferson City, Mo.	1866	Voorhees College	Denmark, S.C.	1897
			Wilberforce University	Wilberforce, Ohio	1856
Lincoln University of Pennsylvania	Lincoln, Pa.	1854	Wiley College	Marshall, Tex.	1873
Livingstone College	Salisbury, N.C.	1879	Winston-Salem State University	Winston-Salem, N.C.	1892
Lomax-Hannon Junior College	Greenville, Ala.	1893			
Mary Holmes College	West Point, Miss.	1892	Xavier University of Louisiana	New Orleans, La.	1915

Sources:

Hoffman, Charlene, Thomas D. Snyder, Bill Sonnenberg, eds., *Historically Black Colleges and Universities, 1976-1990.* Washington, D.C.: U.S. Department of Education, Center for Education Statistics, 1992.

Peterson's Guide to Four Year Colleges, 1993. Princeton, N.J.: Peterson's Guides, 1993.

Ploski, Harry A., James William, eds. and comp., *The Negro Almanac: A Reference Work on the African American.* Detroit: Gale Research, Inc., 1989.

Note: This list is a selective compilation of colleges and universities historically associated with educating African Americans. Other lists include schools with predominantly black student bodies that were not originally founded as all-black institutions, including ones that were founded since the 1960's to serve predominantly black communities.

stitutions, and HBCUs became the only source of higher education available to them.

Ideological Disputes. An early and fundamental goal of African American colleges, the training of teachers, was born of necessity. Because few freed slaves were literate, teachers were initially recruited among white northerners. To achieve universal literacy and educational opportunities, the training of African American teachers was perceived as vital. Otherwise, education at HBCUs focused on practical vocational training and on liberal arts.

The great nineteenth century educator and black leader Booker T. WASHINGTON advocated vocational training as the cornerstone of a successful African American society. Washington stressed the inherent dignity of labor and the importance of African American self-sufficiency in the post-Civil War society. The creation of a successful and prosperous African American culture, in Washington's opinion, required industrial and agricultural training coupled with stern moral guidance. Recognizing the peculiar conditions of his era, Washington's shrewd accommodationist policy made him a leading spokesman for black Americans among white Americans. In return for white sponsorship and encouragement of black economic and educational growth, he acquiesced to disfranchisement and tolerated segregation. His moderate philosophy, viewed within the context of the increasingly racist and segregationist post-Reconstruction South, was eminently successful and pragmatic. It earned approval from the dominant white community and aided in improving the quality of life, although in a limited fashion, for African Americans.

To help achieve his ideals, Washington in 1881 became the first president of the newly founded TUSKEGEE INSTITUTE in Alabama. Initially Washington patterned Tuskegee after his alma mater, the vocationally oriented Hampton Institute (established 1869) in Virginia. Through Washington's forceful leadership, Tuskegee quickly became a unique model of vocational education for African Americans. Because he asserted that manual labor was vital for the development of self-discipline and morality, Washington initiated a system in which all students were required to perform some manual labor in addition to their studies. At Tuskegee, strict moral codes were enforced, and drills and inspections were a daily routine.

While his system of vocational education and stance of accommodation remained dominant in the nineteenth century, Washington came under increasing criticism from newer organizations including the NATIONAL ASSOCIATION FOR THE ADVANCEMENT OF COLORED PEOPLE (NAACP) and its chief spokesman, W. E. B. Du Bois.

Unlike Washington, who was born a slave, Du Bois was a New Englander who entered the South as a young adult to attend Fisk University. Although he later earned his Ph.D. from Harvard and studied for a time in Berlin, his undergraduate training in the South had a significant impact on the development of his personal philosophy and his intolerance for racism. Appalled by the poor treatment of African Americans, Du Bois attacked Washington's system of vocational training because he believed it reinforced the subordinate status of blacks and severely limited their options. Du Bois advocated a liberal arts education that he hoped would train an elite leadership of African Americans for the betterment of the entire race. Throughout the early twentieth century, there were factions within and between black colleges over vocational versus liberal arts education. Despite Du Bois' criticisms, however, Washington's system of vocational education remained dominant until the mid-1900's.

While segregation of colleges and universities secured greater African American control of policy during the late nineteenth century, by the twentieth century, vocational training had become a means of ensuring white domination over African Americans. Black administrators were replaced by whites, and college curricula reflected the deeply racist nature of southern society. Government funding for African American colleges was far below that of white institutions. Segregation clearly prohibited African Americans from rising to positions of authority and leadership.

Graduate Education. As colleges increased in number and in enrollment, African Americans were incensed by the lack of opportunity for graduate education, including training for the medical and legal professions. By the beginning of the twentieth century, only Howard University had both a medical school and a law school; the only other graduate option was Meharry Medical College. For approximately ten years, beginning in 1938, several U.S. Supreme Court battles ensued in which African Americans challenged their denial of graduate education in white universities. While the *Plessy* decision had guaranteed black Americans "separate but equal" education, it had become painfully evident that separate would always mean unequal. No comparable African American institutions for graduate education existed. While public expenditures for African American colleges increased in the early twentieth century, the intention of many

responsible for producing a large majority of black lawyers and 75 percent of black veterinarians.

Of the several early black colleges supported by religious organizations, Fisk University in Nashville,

Whether historically African American colleges should be integrated is a controversial issue with today's college students. (Hazel Hankin)

legislatures was to meet the letter of the law by creating enough African American schools to maintain segregation rather than improving the quality of existing schools.

As the century progressed the issue of desegregation of institutions of higher education was perceived to be directly related to the broader issue of segregation at the primary and secondary school levels. It became increasingly obvious to reformers that desegregation at all levels was vital for the assurance of quality education for African American people. The historic Supreme Court decision of Brown v. Board of Education (1954) marked the beginning of public school desegregation, at least in law if not in fact.

College Profiles. Howard University in Washington, D.C., from its inception as a land grant college has remained a leader in black education. With a student body that is 80 percent African American, Howard is

Tennessee, founded as a primary school in 1867 and first admitting college students in 1871, is still a leading institution in the education of African Americans. The school has maintained financial integrity in large part through the efforts of the Fisk Jubilee Singers, a gospel singing group that has toured nationally and internationally. While earning vital funds for Fisk, the acclaimed choir brought the black GOSPEL MUSIC tradition to the world. Meharry Medical College in Tennessee, originally founded in 1876 by the Methodist Episcopal church, offers a full range of medical and dental training and continues to account for approximately one-half of the practicing African American physicians. Other well-known black institutions include Prairie View A&M University in Texas, Spelman College and Morris Brown College in Georgia, Bethune-Cookman College in Florida, and Xavier University of Louisiana.

The Future of African American Colleges. Throughout the first half of the twentieth century, HBCUs pursued a cautious plan for desegregation of institutions of higher education. By the mid-1960's, however, new forces arose, demanding the continuation of all-black colleges and universities. The impetus for this new emphasis on segregation came from African American students at white universities who were involved in the BLACK POWER MOVEMENT. They believed that the interests of the African American community would best be served by separate colleges, much as some feminists have argued for the maintenance of WOMEN'S COLLEGES in the late 1900's.

Several controversial issues surround the future of African American colleges. Their role in African American culture and in the culture of the United States at large is uncertain.

It can be argued that the segregated environment allows African Americans to escape temporarily from the pressures of a racist society while focusing on personal growth and development. Students at HBCUs are nurtured in an emotionally protective environment that fosters a sense of community and social responsibility as well as a means for the transmission of distinctive African American cultural traditions. While some educators argue in favor of black institutions for the perpetuation and growth of black culture, others contest that educational segregation is artificial and detrimental to society.

To some the HBCUs are vital in providing education for those in need of remedial help because of the poor quality of secondary educational systems, particularly those in the inner city. Remedial programs have also been initiated in mixed racial colleges and universities that are specifically directed toward disadvantaged black youths, yet many of these students become discouraged and eventually drop out of mainstream colleges.

Approximately 75 percent of African Americans in the early 1990's who attended college were educated at predominantly white institutions. Many predominantly white colleges actively recruit minority professors in the hope of increasing minority attendance. Whether this trend will eventually result in the elimination of HBCUs is uncertain. While the distant future of HBCUs is indefinite, African American colleges in the late twentieth century play a vital role in the continuation of a unique African American cultural tradition.

SUGGESTED READINGS. The most useful overview of African American education is contained in the *Encyclopedia of Southern Culture* (1989), edited by Charles Reagan Wilson and William R. Ferris, which places these colleges in historical perspective. *Black Colleges in America* (1978), edited by Charles Willee and Ronald Edmond, provides several excellent essays on black education, although others must be read critically because of their obvious bias. The National Center for Education Statistics' work, *Historically Black Colleges and Universities, 1976-1990* (1992), edited by Charlene Hoffman et al., provides useful statistics on HBCUs. Addie Louise Joyner Butler's *The Distinctive Black College: Talladega, Tuskegee and Morehouse* (1977) is a notable example of individual institutional histories of HBCUs.—*Mary E. Virginia*

Colleges—Latino. *See* **Latinos and higher education**

Colleges—women's: Institutions of higher education that have as their primary purpose the provision of quality undergraduate education to women within a single-sex environment. Such colleges arose to fill a gap in the late 1800's and peaked in the early 1900's; though controversial, many continued to play a unique role for women in the 1990's.

History. Women were first admitted to college in 1837, when OBERLIN COLLEGE in Ohio decided to become coeducational. Controversy exists about the founding of the first women's college, since a number of female high school academies and seminaries used the word "college" in their names but were actually precollegiate, admitting students as young as age twelve and providing a less rigorous program. In the 1850's, a dozen or so local women's colleges were begun, but the movement really did not advance until after the CIVIL WAR. Then, first-rate institutions such as VASSAR (1865), WELLESLEY (1870), and SMITH COLLEGES (1875) were founded. Some of the leading female seminaries, such as Mount Holyoke in Massachusetts and Mills in California, were rechartered as colleges in the 1880's.

Prior to this time, in colonial America, the education of women was considered a means for women to learn to read the Bible and to teach their sons at home and other children in school settings. In the nineteenth century, women were not given equal access to higher education opportunities. They were often viewed as intellectually inferior to men, and questions were raised as to whether formal education of any kind would be too much for their physical health, their feminine delicacy, and their purportedly "smaller" brains. Some people were threatened by the idea of women expanding their roles and developing identities outside of their families. Consequently, the early women's colleges were developed by religious individuals who saw their primary mission as producing virtuous, Christian women who would be better prepared for their domestic roles.

The women who attended the all-women's colleges were primarily of the upper class. The programs, which offered a full liberal arts curriculum, were patterned after private men's institutions and soon developed very rigorous academic standards. The academic success of these students began to prove that women were in fact the intellectual equals of men. Within the college community, the students learned how to assume leadership roles and to work and play together in both cooperative and competitive ways. As a result, in spite of the original narrow goals for the higher education of women, these students were being prepared for extended roles outside the family sphere.

As the reputation of women's colleges spread, their student enrollments and their total number increased. These schools were no longer considered experiments. They were seen as important educational options for women, especially since a number of prestigious private colleges excluded women.

Some women's colleges were established as coordinate or annex institutions, attached to male colleges. These schools seemed to be a compromise between single-sex and coeducational schools. Several of the coordinate schools actually began as coeducational colleges and later, due to controversy and lingering questions, were changed to single sex schools (such as Jackson College within Tufts University).

A number of women's colleges were developed for special groups of women. Spelman College, founded as a seminary for black women in 1881, eventually became a liberal arts college for black women in 1925. Unlike many northern colleges for white women, which focused on a classical education, Spelman emphasized a practical education. Black women were trained to be teachers, missionaries, and homemakers. Trinity College in Washington, D.C., the first Catholic institution founded as a college for women, was started in the late 1890's. The number of Catholic women's colleges increased to fourteen by 1915 and to 116 by 1955. Since Catholic men's colleges were slow to become coeducational, separate women's colleges provided an important and "safe" higher education alternative for Catholic women.

The influence of women's colleges peaked at the turn of the twentieth century. By 1890, 20 percent of all U.S. colleges were for women only. By 1930, that number was reduced to 16 percent. Some of the decline resulted from a conservative reaction to women's colleges after World War I. There were fears about the larger societal consequences of women with higher education. Statistics emerged showing that graduates of women's colleges did not marry and have children at as high a rate as other women. Critics urged women who wanted higher education to attend the growing number of coeducational institutions. In fact, more and more female students were choosing to do so. Women's colleges had to struggle with and adjust to changing views of female sexuality and student life. Female college students wanted more frequent opportunities to socialize with men. In spite of the difficulties, women's colleges continued to survive throughout the twentieth century, in large part because of the growing number of women attending college. (In 1890, 56,000 women attended institutions of higher education. In 1930, there were 481,000 women. By 1980, 5,694,000 women were enrolled in institutions of higher education.)

Women's Colleges in Decline. By the early 1960's, only 298 traditional women's colleges existed in the United States. Of these, 96 percent were private; more than 69 percent were church-affiliated (primarily Roman Catholic), and 25 percent were independent, nonprofit colleges.

During the 1960's and 1970's, more than half of the women's colleges in the United States closed or became coeducational. Some blamed this decline on prevailing opinions that educational equality had finally been reached. Nevertheless, enrollment at women's colleges declined for the same reason that enrollment at coed colleges declined: The pool of traditional college age students was shrinking. Rising tuition costs led more students, female and male, to attend public rather than private institutions. Colleges and universities had to deal with federal cutbacks in financial assistance. During this same period, many men's colleges became coeducational. There were many individuals, including some feminists, who believed that women would receive the best possible education in the prestigious, formerly all-male colleges. Women who might have gone to women's colleges were encouraged to attend these coeducational institutions. Thus, a declining enrollment, lessening interest in women-only colleges, and financial pressures led to the many closings and conversions.

Of the 298 women's colleges that existed in the early 1960's, only eighty-four remained open in 1993. Nevertheless, the demise of women's colleges is not as immediate as was once anticipated. In fact, the 1970's was actually a period of great growth for the women's colleges that remained opened, with enrollments rising by more than 18 percent. In 1990,

have been betrayed" was written on a number of banners. Students conducted media forums that helped to educate the general public about the value of women's colleges.

The students' position was not against coeducation; rather, it was for maintaining choices in higher education for women. The actions of the students led the trustees to postpone their decision. Faculty members agreed to teach an extra course each year and to recruit more women students. The response of the stu-

Women's colleges provide a unique experience in higher education; shown here, graduation day at Barnard. (Frances M. Roberts)

Wellesley and BRYN MAWR had a 6 percent increase in applications, evidence of the continued interest in women's colleges.

Students Speak Out. Mills College, an all-women's private college in Oakland, California, was the scene of great controversy in May, 1990. Students at Mills were so disturbed by the board of trustees' decision to go coed (because of financial pressures and a declining enrollment) that they boycotted classes and took control of the campus. Many wore T-shirts with the slogan "Better dead than coed." The message "We

dents seems to suggest that all-women's colleges still provide an important and viable educational alternative for women.

Why Women's Colleges Still Exist. From the beginning of women's involvement in higher education, coeducational institutions have been the primary place where women have received a collegiate education. Studies at coed institutions, however, show that they have not necessarily provided equitable treatment for women. The early mission of coeducational institutions was to produce educated wives and mothers rather than to create equal intellectual and social opportunities for women. Women were often marginal figures, subjected to segregation in educational programs and in living areas. Even in the 1990's there are many old prejudices and problems associated with the teaching of women in coeducational settings. There is a bias toward males that persists in the American educational system. Men talk more in class and receive greater attention from teachers, being seen as more serious students. Since women's styles tend to

They are empowered to take more active roles and to develop a sense of independence. Women at single-sex institutions are often highly satisfied with their academic programs, and their learning and their self-confidence are increased.

Women's colleges have had much success in training women for careers. Some colleges have developed programs in areas that have not been seen as traditional for women. More students at women's colleges major in economics, mathematics, and the sciences

Vassar College was founded in 1865. (Library of Congress)

be less aggressive, they often remain silent in coed classes. This phenomenon has been described even in schools such as Wheaton College, an all-women's college that became coed in 1988.

Women's colleges are committed to providing quality women's education. Women students are able to concentrate on academics and other aspects of college life without the distractions that men can bring. Women's colleges usually provide more female role models and mentors than are found at coed institutions. Women do not need to compete with men for leadership positions or in extracurricular activities.

than do women at coed colleges. They are more likely to go on to graduate school and twice as likely to earn doctoral degrees. According to the Women's College Coalition, based in Washington, D.C., all-female schools produced one-third of the female board members of the top one thousand businesses of 1988 as listed in *Fortune* magazine. Of fifty-four women members of the 103rd Congress, thirteen (24 percent) attended women's colleges.

Past research has found a higher rate of professional achievement in women graduates from women's colleges as compared to women graduates from coed institutions. Yet the interpretation of this data is often a complex issue. Some question how success was defined. Others note that a high percentage of these "successful" women attended the Seven Sisters (seven prestigious women's colleges established during the last half of the nineteenth century—BARNARD, Bryn Mawr, Mount Holyoke, Radcliffe, Smith, Vassar, and Wellesley—that are considered comparable to the male Ivy League schools). These women may have been the best women students in the country. In addition, a large percentage of students attending the Seven Sisters tended to be of a higher socioeconomic status. It has been suggested that their greater rate of success may be attributable in part to their wider opportunities and social network, rather than the collegiate experience itself. Thus, the direct impact on women's achievement of the supportive environment of the women's colleges and the presence of same-sex mentors and teachers is unclear.

Struggle for Survival. Most high school women prefer a college that will provide a coeducational experience. Studies have shown that only a small proportion—between 2 and 11 percent—of high school women say that they would even consider a women's college.

With budget deficits and a shrinking pool of applicants, some women's colleges have had to cut back on faculty and staff. Alumnae have actively assisted them in raising money and finding students. Many schools have tried to increase their endowments; some have become more aggressive and innovative in their recruiting tactics. Women's colleges have included evening, weekend, and part-time programs to attract older, nontraditional students. They have recruited international women and transfer students from two- and four-year coeducational colleges. They have provided support to students from lower socioeconomic backgrounds and increased outreach efforts to women of color. Many women's colleges now have student bodies with upwards of 15 percent minority women. Exchange programs or cross-registration with coed colleges have also been instituted.

Certainly the experience of attending a women's college no longer is the isolated experience it was in the past. Unlike 150 years ago, women today constitute the majority of college students and have vast educational opportunities. It remains uncertain whether enough women will choose to attend women's colleges in order to allow these schools to survive and prosper.

SUGGESTED READINGS. Books that provide information about the history of higher education for women include Barbara Miller Solomon's *In the Company of Educated Women: A History of Women and Higher Education in America* (1985) and Helen Lefkowitz Horowitz' *Alma Mater: Design and Experience in the Women's Colleges from Their Nineteenth-Century Beginnings to the 1930's* (1984). Several chapters in *Reconstructing the Academy: Women's Education and Women's Studies* (1988), edited by Elizabeth Minnich, Jean O'Barr, and Rachel Rosenfeld, and Daryl G. Smith's article on "Women's Colleges and Coed Colleges" in *Journal of Higher Education* 61 (March/April, 1990), pp. 181-195, examine the differential impact for women who attend a women's college versus women who attend coeducational institutions.—*Ricki Ellen Kantrowitz*

Colombian Americans: Colombia sits in the northwest corner of South America, southeast of Panama. It was once inhabited solely by Indians, one notable group of whom was called the *Chibchas*. In the sixteenth century, Colombia became part of a colony of Spain called Nueva Granada. In 1819, it achieved independence from Spain in a revolution led by Simón Bolivar. For a short time, the countries of Colombia, Panama, Ecuador, and Venezuela formed a large republic called Gran Colombia. By 1830, however, Colombia became a separate country encompassing its present borders plus the territory that is now Panama.

Colombia's history has been marked by a bloody struggle between two political parties, the Partido Lib-

A Colombian American dance troupe performs in a New York City parade. (Frances M. Roberts)

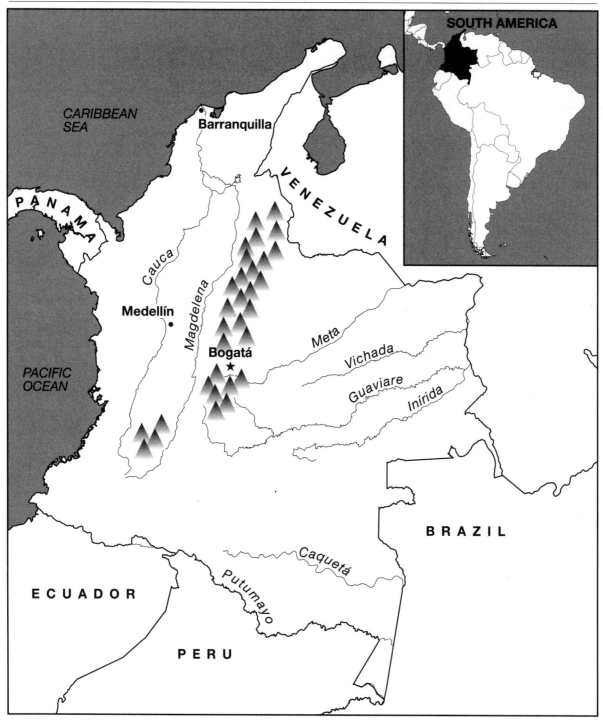

COLOMBIA

eral (Liberal Party) and Partido Conservador (Conservative Party). The conflict became particularly violent during two periods. The first was between 1899 and 1902, which became known as the War of a Thousand Days. As a result of this war, Panama seceded from Colombia and gained independence in 1903.

The second turbulent period lasted from 1948 to 1962 under a series of dictatorships and was called

La Violencia. As many as 300,000 Colombians were killed in this war. Several thousand others escaped to the United States.

Earlier in the twentieth century, a few Colombians had emigrated to NEW YORK CITY to establish a middle-class community. These were white Colombians from the interior of the country, known as Spanish Colombians. They established a base in the United States that could absorb the later immigrants who fled La Violencia.

Another group of Colombians settled in CHICAGO. These people, known as costeños, are of mixed Spanish, African, and Indian heritage, and hail from the coastal region of Colombia. These two groups do not generally mix, although they are both ROMAN CATHOLIC and hold traditional middle-class values.

Most Colombian immigrants have come to the United States in search of economic advancement and are highly skilled. They often eschew involvement in American culture, preferring to concentrate their interest on politics and events in their homeland.

Colonial America: Period between the establishment of the first English colony in North America (1607) and the independence of the United States (1776). The colonial period saw the laying of the foundations of a culturally diverse American society. While the population in 1600 consisted almost entirely of American Indians, by 1776 the thirteen colonies included Africans, English, and many other Europeans.

The European newcomers brought considerable disruption to the native peoples. In the first few decades of the 1600's, the colonies developed policies which bought up the Indian lands (usually under pressure), and kept the Indian population separated from the advancing white settlement. Serious Indian wars developed along the frontier in the 1620's, 1640's, and mid-1670's. Other disturbances accompanied several colonial wars between the British and French empires, when the French often enlisted the Indians to harass English settlements. The final defeat of France in North America after the Seven Years' War in 1763 led to PONTIAC'S REBELLION among the Indians beyond the Appalachians, bringing about the temporary closing of that region to settlement by the British authorities.

Other fateful steps for American society lay in the introduction of SLAVERY into the colonies, beginning with the first importation of Africans to Virginia in 1619. While there were some attempts (particularly in the Carolinas) to use Indians as slaves, the majority of slaves were Africans from the West Indies or West Africa. By the mid-1600's slavery was legally defined and recognized in the Chesapeake colonies as a permanent hereditary status, differing from the indentured servitude of some European immigrants. Slavery became the dominant labor system in the Chesapeake region in the last quarter of the 1600's, and it spread into the newly founded Carolinas. By 1776 slavery was legally established in all thirteen North American colonies, although slaves were much less numerous in the northern colonies.

By the mid-1700's the colonies had developed a diversity of European American cultures. Although the

In Jamestown colony in 1619, the captain of a Dutch ship traded twenty African slaves for food from American settlers. (AP/Wide World Photos)

early Chesapeake and New England colonies drew mostly from the English population, the increasing presence of religious dissenters introduced religious diversity. Beginning in 1624 the Dutch had established a trading post at New Amsterdam, spreading settlements into adjacent regions and taking over Swedish settlements along the Delaware River. All these areas came under English rule in 1664. The colony of Pennsylvania, founded by William Penn in 1681, actively solicited settlement by many national and religious groups. The second quarter of the eighteenth century saw migration by GERMANS and SCOTS-IRISH, people of Scottish descent who came from northern Ireland. Both groups established communities in rural Pennsylvania, from which they migrated down the Appalachians into the southern back country. Thus many of the thirteen colonies were home to a diversity of subcultures by the eve of the AMERICAN REVOLUTION.

SUGGESTED READINGS. Relations between the various peoples in colonial America are dealt with in Gary Nash's *Red, White, Black: The Peoples of Early America* (1974); Winthrop Jordan's *White over Black* (1968); James Axtell's *The Invasion Within* (1985); and David B. Davis' *The Problem of Slavery in Eastern Culture* (1966). On early European migrations see Bernar Bailyn's *Voyagers to the West* (1986).

Colonialism: Imposition of rule by one nation over another foreign territory, usually through settlement for economic gain and political control. While the term "colonialism" is often used interchangeably with "imperialism," most observers agree that the former is a special case of the latter.

Colonial empires can be traced back to antiquity. Yet colonial development is generally associated with European colonialism, lasting from the sixteenth cen-

tury through roughly WORLD WAR II. Colonies (primarily in North and South America, Southeast Asia, and Africa) offered three primary advantages to the various European colonial powers (Spain, Holland, Portugal, France, and England), all of which applied in colonial America. First, colonies added to the political influence of the parent country and provided military bases from which to counter the moves of rival colonial powers. Second, colonization was viewed as a "civilizing" undertaking. Some of the earliest European colonists were Christian missionaries, only too eager to bring Christianity and assist in the spiritual, moral, and material development of the "primitive" inhabitants of the colony (often referred to as "savages" by the colonists). Third, colonies were a source of economic wealth to the parent country. Trade was strictly regulated by the latter and involved the production of food and other raw materials exclusively for the parent country and, in turn, the colony's consumption of the finished products, as in the production of cotton in the American South for English textile production. Indeed, the early history, settle-

Teddy Roosevelt (center) led the Rough Riders during the colonialist Spanish-American War. (Library of Congress)

ment, and development of the United States can only be understood in terms of its functioning as a valued prize among the competing European colonial powers.

The United States itself has also engaged in colonial pursuits. The SPANISH-AMERICAN WAR essentially was motivated by colonial designs. By the last decade of the nineteenth century, many industrialists were searching for expanded international markets for American goods in the Pacific. Under the guise of aiding the downtrodden Cubans against their Spanish colonial masters, U.S. troops were dispatched to Cuba in the spring of 1898. With the defeat of the Spanish, the peace treaty signed later that year gave the United States possession of Guam, the Philippines, and Puerto Rico, for $20 million. Having already annexed the Hawaiian Islands earlier that year, the United States now had not only a firm foothold in the Pacific but in the Caribbean as well. Thus, the nation entered the twentieth century feeling relatively confident that it could successfully compete for "open" international markets with its primary colonial rivals, France and England.

The legacy of European and U.S. colonialism continues. There is no question that colonial ventures contributed significantly to the rise of RACISM, as most colonists, including European settlers in North America, regarded those they colonized as subhuman. The economic development of former U.S. colonies has also been retarded.

SUGGESTED READINGS. For a highly readable account of colonialism as it relates to the emergence of the world economy, see Thomas R. Shannon's *An Introduction to the World-System Perspective* (1989). A more advanced treatment of colonialism is contained in Michael W. Doyle's *Empires* (1986). Harry Magdoff's *Imperialism: From the Colonial Age to the Present* (1978) though somewhat dated, contains classic essays on imperialism and colonialism from a left-wing perspective. John Dobson's *America's Ascent: The United States Becomes a Great Power, 1880-1914* (1978) presents an overview of American colonial pursuits. For an account of American imperialism in the Philippines, see Stuart Creighton Miller's *"Benevolent Assimilation": The American Conquest of the Philippines, 1899-1903* (1982).

Colored Women's League (CWL): Self-help organization of African American women. The league was organized to represent African American women and their achievements at the World Columbian Exposition in Chicago in 1893. The all-white Women's Board of

Managers for the exposition initially rejected the idea of a representative from a black women's organization, but eventually accepted Helen A. Cook as president of the CWL. In 1896, under the leadership of Mary Church TERRELL, the organization joined with the NATIONAL FEDERATION OF AFRO-AMERICAN WOMEN to create the National Association of Colored Women to work for suffrage, self-help, and improved welfare among African Americans.

Coltrane, John (Sept. 23, 1926, Hamlet, N.C.—July 17, 1967, Huntington, N.Y.): African American jazz saxophonist. Coltrane's special technique made him an

Influential jazz saxophonist John Coltrane died in 1967. (AP/Wide World Photos)

influential and controversial player who has had a profound and continuing influence. Some listeners heard Coltrane's "sheets of sound" as harsh, unnerving, and full of dissonance, whereas others found his playing "sonorous and spare." Yet all agreed that he had brilliant technique and emotional force. In the 1940's he played with groups that included big bands and a U.S. Navy band in Hawaii. In the 1950's he linked up with jazz greats such as Miles Davis, Thelonious Monk, and Dizzy Gillespie; his avant-garde style made Coltrane one of the central figures in JAZZ.

Columbus, Christopher (1451?, Genoa, Italy—1506, Spain): One of first European explorers of the New World to reach the Americas, and the first to start colonization there. Born of humble parents, Columbus received little education in childhood and went to sea at age twenty-two. On a voyage to Portugal in 1476, his ship was attacked and sunk by Muslim raiders. Columbus made his way to Lisbon, the center of Portuguese maritime activity. There he got an education, married into the lower nobility, and became a prosperous ship captain.

Columbus became convinced that it was possible to reach the East Indies by sailing west. When he offered his services to King John II of Portugal in 1484, the king rejected his proposal.

For eight years Columbus attempted to interest the kings of Spain, Portugal, England, and France in his voyage. Only in Spain was there any interest. When Columbus moved to Spain in 1485, he was introduced to Queen Isabel and King Ferdinand. Eventually Isabel gave Columbus permission to sail and granted him titles including Admiral of the Ocean Sea. He would also receive one tenth of all royal revenues from lands he might discover.

Columbus sailed on his first voyage on August 3, 1492, in three ships, the *Niña*, the *Pinta*, and the *Santa María*. A five-week voyage brought the expedition to an island in the Bahamas which Columbus named San Salvador. He continued along the coast of Cuba and Haiti, where the *Santa María* ran aground.

When he returned to Spain, Columbus was at the peak of his popularity and easily organized a second expedition in 1494. Between 1494 and 1496 he became the first European to see Jamaica, Puerto Rico, and islands of the Lesser Antilles; however, he did not find the wealth that he and his patrons sought. He lost favor with the sovereigns and the people and had difficulty obtaining financing for his last two voyages (1498-1499 and 1502-1504), on which he reached the mainland of South America and Central America. He returned to Spain, where he died in 1506, still clinging to the belief that he had reached the Orient.

On the second voyage, Columbus started Spanish colonization of the islands; within thirty years, colonization of the mainland began. The Spanish Empire in the Americas emerged, followed shortly by the Portuguese Empire in Brazil.

Until the post-World War II period, Columbus was viewed as the discoverer of the New World and the man who began the colonization and development of the Western Hemisphere. With the rise of anticolonialism, a greater emphasis upon human rights, and efforts such as the AMERICAN INDIAN RIGHTS MOVEMENT and Indian cultural revival, Columbus came under attack. He was pictured as the man responsible for the destruction of Indian cultures and civilizations, the death of millions of natives, and the exploitation of the riches of the area. The four-hundredth anniversary of the "discovery" of America by Columbus in 1992 occasioned protests and counter-marches and exhibits. American Indians and some Latinos referred to Columbus' voyages as an "encounter" rather than a "discovery." Rather than a time for celebration, the quincentennial, according to the protesters, was a time of mourning, repentance, and the rethinking of American culture. Columbus' legacy is still being debated and reconsidered.

SUGGESTED READINGS. The best-known biography of Columbus is Samuel Eliot Morison's *Admiral of the Ocean Sea: A Life of Christopher Columbus* (1942). On the Columbus family, see Troy S. Floyd's *The Columbus Dynasty in the Caribbean, 1492-1526* (1973). John Cummins has translated the journal of Columbus in *The Voyage of Christopher Columbus: Columbus' Own Journal of Discovery* (1992). For a discussion of the geographic ideas of Columbus see George Emra Nunn's *The Geographical Conceptions of Columbus: A Critical Consideration of Four Problems* (1924).

Comanches: American Indian group of the Southern Plains. The tribal name is derived from the Ute *komantcia* ("my adversary"); while the Comanches refer to themselves as *Numina* ("people"). Other early names applied by the French and Americans were *Padouca* and *Ietan*. The Comanches' folklore and Shoshonean language point to origins in the Rocky Mountains of Wyoming. Spanish documents show them in New Mexico by 1706. At this point they had recently acquired horses and were defining the classic Plains lifestyle of buffalo hunting, trading, and raiding. Their core area became western Oklahoma and northwest Texas, though they ranged from the upper Missouri River to the Mexican state of Durango.

During the 1700's, Comanches drove Apaches from the southern Plains while plundering the Pueblo Indians and Spanish on the west and stalling the French on the east. They developed bitter rivalries with other advancing peoples, notably the Pawnees and Osages. To consolidate their position, they allied with their former competitors, the Kiowas and Kiowa-Apaches (by

Quanah Parker was a Comanche chief from Oklahoma. (Library of Congress)

1810) and Cheyennes and Arapahos (around 1840). Friendly relations were maintained with the Caddo and Wichita farmers of eastern Texas, who traded guns and corn for horses and buffalo hides. By 1820, the Comanches ran a horse trading network connecting all the Plains tribes. Their language, considered easy to learn, became an intertribal trade language. They raided deep into Mexico for livestock and bred horses as well. Comanches also took hundreds of European American captives, not only as hostages, but also to increase the tribal population; many were adopted and fully assimilated.

Comanches welcomed the U.S. Dragoons in 1834 but fought Texan settlers for four decades thereafter. Ten Comanche leaders signed the 1867 Medicine Lodge Treaty, agreeing to contain their bands on a combined Comanche, Kiowa, and Kiowa-Apache reservation in Indian Territory (present western Oklahoma). Resistance continued until 1875, however, when the extermination of the buffalo and a concerted campaign by federal troops made nomadic life impossible. Under the DAWES ACT, the reservation was abolished in 1892; the Indians took individual allotments, and non-Indians settled among them. Since World War II, many Comanches have moved to western cities. Their modern tribal government is headquartered in Medicine Park, Oklahoma.

Traditional Comanche culture shows several distinctive features. Their tipis were built around a framework of four poles rather than three, and they favored a buffalo scalp headdress over the familiar feathered war bonnet. The widespread Sun Dance and Ghost Dance ceremonies were never important to them. Reservation Comanches founded a ritual centered on the hallucinogenic PEYOTE cactus, which was the basis for the modern intertribal NATIVE AMERICAN CHURCH. Comanche singers and dancers have been influential in the development of intertribal social gatherings called powwows.

SUGGESTED READINGS. Tribal culture is thoroughly described in *The Comanches: Lords of the South Plains* (1952), by Ernest Wallace and E. Adamson Hoebel. For a precise history of the reservation period, see William Hagan's *United States-Comanche Relations* (1976). Morris Foster discusses modern social organization and cultural identity in *Being Comanche* (1991).

Commission on Civil Rights: Independent, bipartisan, nonregulatory panel established by Congress to investigate and make recommendations regarding civil rights violations in the United States. Created as part of the Civil Rights Act of 1957, it comprised six members appointed by the president and subject to Senate approval. Their duties were to investigate charges of denial of the right to vote because of color, race, religion, or national origin; to study the laws and policies of the federal government regarding equal protection of the law under the U.S. CONSTITUTION; and to report their findings to the president and Congress.

In response to legislation in the late 1950's designed to increase minority participation in the electoral process, the commission conducted studies in 1960 and 1963 on black voters in the South. Not surprisingly, its efforts faced opposition in conservative states such as Alabama, Mississippi, and Louisiana.

In the 1960 case of *Hannah v. Larche*, opponents challenged the commission's right to guard the identity of complainants and witnesses. At stake was the possibility of reprisals and violence against African Americans who were willing to fight deeply entrenched RACISM. The U.S. Supreme Court upheld the commission's procedures, noting that it was only an investigative body and was incapable of depriving citizens of life, liberty, or property.

The 1960 Civil Rights Act strengthened the commission's powers, and in the following years the commission studied the impact of blacks in the military, school DESEGREGATION, and DISCRIMINATION on the basis of gender, age, physical disability, and ETHNICITY.

A second major challenge came in the 1980's. In 1981, the commission issued a policy statement called *Affirmative Action in the 1980's,* calling for quotas in employment. The newly elected President Ronald Reagan favored a less active approach. In an effort to form a more acquiescent commission, Reagan fired three members and replaced them with his own appointees. The move led to a lawsuit, and in 1983 the Washington, D.C., district court ordered Reagan to reinstate the fired commissioners.

At the same time, the commission's reauthorization, which had been routinely undertaken every five years, was being considered in Congress. Reagan reserved the power to veto the reauthorization bill, and the commission became a heated issue in partisan politics. Ultimately, a compromise was reached, and the commission was reorganized to consist of eight members chosen by the president and congressional leaders along party lines.

After the reorganization, the commission was criticized for submitting to political pressures and wavering in the struggle against racism. During the 1980's, it was constantly in danger of extinction, with opposition from many African American, women's, and civil rights groups and controversy surrounding chairmen Clarence Pendleton and William Allen. In the early 1990's, under President Bush's appointee Arthur Fletcher, the commission returned to a more independent and active stance.

SUGGESTED READINGS. An account of the commission's early years is found in *The Civil Rights Commission, 1957-1965* (1968) by Foster Rhea Dulles. Thomas Sowell's *Civil Rights: Rhetoric or Reality* (1984) and Morroe Berger's *Equality by Statute* (1967) chronicle the Civil Rights movement in general. *Civil Rights and the Reagan Administration* (1988) by Norman C. Amaker explores the controversies of the early 1980's.

Communist Party: Political party formed in Russia in 1918 by the Bolsheviks, who had toppled the czarist regime in 1917. Communists sought to end capitalism and replace it with a system under which all property and businesses would be owned communally. In the United States, the early Communist Party, formed in 1919, had a predominantly foreign-born membership. Therefore, a general American distrust of Communism led to certain distrust of Eastern European immigrants.

In the early twentieth century, Communism vied with the concepts of anarchism, democratic socialism, unionism, and liberalism as possible ways to improve the lot of the downtrodden. American Communism was probably most influential during the GREAT DEPRESSION, when the Communist Party agitated for civil rights, unemployment relief, and unions. Anti-Communist feeling has always been strong in the United States, however, and during and after WORLD WAR II the Communist Party's influence decreased markedly. Partly because of the persecution of alleged Communists under MCCARTHYISM in the 1950's, the COLD WAR, and finally the crumbling of Communism internationally, the party's influence in the United States since the 1950's has been negligible.

Comparable worth: Controversial concept that certain traditional "women's" jobs and traditional "men's" jobs can be measured to determine their relative worth to society. The idea emerged in the late 1970's when feminist leaders protested the low pay assigned to conven-

This female firefighter takes the same risks as her male counterparts. (Don Franklin)

tional "pink collar" jobs usually done by women, such as working as secretaries, nurses, and teachers. The state of Washington was the first to do a comparative study of male- and female-dominated jobs, assigning points

In 1976, Maureen LaVettre was fired from a bank in Hollywood, Fla., after she filed a sexual discrimination suit. (AP/Wide World Photos)

for the job qualifications needed. It concluded that at every comparison level, men's wages were higher. In a decision that was later reversed, the state agreed to pay $482 million in raises to thirty-five thousand government workers. Though Minnesota and Wisconsin have also attempted comparable worth policies, the concept is disputed by critics who believe the laws of "supply and demand" should determine workers' pay and that no point system of comparable worth could be fair. As more women have risen through the ranks of the working world, attention has shifted from comparable worth per se to the consistently lower earnings of women who hold the same positions as men in a two-tiered wage system.

Composers. *See* **Musicians and composers**

Comprehensive Employment and Training Act of 1973: Provided "job training and EMPLOYMENT opportunities for economically disadvantaged, unemployed, and underemployed persons" to help them achieve their potential and become self-sufficient. It created jobs,

gave special hiring incentives to private companies, and provided services such as health care and CHILD CARE. Special provisions were made for those with limited English-speaking ability, VETERANS serving in Indochina or Korea after 1964, American Indians, native Alaskans, "youth offenders," and MIGRANT WORKERS. This act established the Job Corps, a program of education, vocational training, work experience, and counseling for people between the ages of fourteen and twenty-two.

Confederate States of America: Government created by eleven states that withdrew from the United States in 1860-1861 following President Abraham Lincoln's election. The Confederacy, formally called the Confederate States of America, was organized at Montgomery, Alabama, on February 9, 1861, when seven seceded states adopted a provisional constitution. In May, 1861, after Virginia, Arkansas, Tennessee, and North Carolina joined the Confederacy, its capital was moved to Richmond, Virginia. With Jefferson Davis as its only president, the Confederacy pursued war against the Union, finally collapsing in April, 1865.

The CIVIL WAR profoundly affected the society of the Confederate states, especially in bringing to an end the institution of black SLAVERY. Of the population of nine million, more than three and a half million were slaves; 165,000 were free blacks.

President Abraham Lincoln's EMANCIPATION PROCLAMATION declared all slaves behind the Confederate lines on January 1, 1863, to be free; this had practical effect only when that territory was actually occupied by Union forces. Meanwhile, the institution was weakened by internal events: When masters were absent or slaves were under control of business or government authorities, discipline became uncertain, and passive resistance more common. The widespread slave uprisings feared by white Southerners did not occur, but the slaves increasingly anticipated the possibility of emancipation. The rate of escapes by slaves rose, especially as Union armies drew nearer.

In 1864, debate developed over the use of slaves as combat soldiers, under the assumption that they would thereby earn their freedom. For most of the war the government had relied upon recruiting white males for military service. The demand for soldiers depleted workplaces of white laborers and plantations of their overseers. Slaves were increasingly used in the workforce and in support of the military. A law in March, 1865, authorized drafting slaves, but no slave units were ready for combat at the war's end. In March, 1865, Davis sent an emissary to France and Britain to promise that all slaves would be emancipated if those powers recognized the Confederacy; the Europeans declined. Thus, in its final days the Confederate government had been forced to contemplate the end of the very institution it sought to defend.

Although southern society had not been influenced by immigration as much as that of the North, it still held significant elements of the foreign-born and their descendants: German groups in western Virginia and

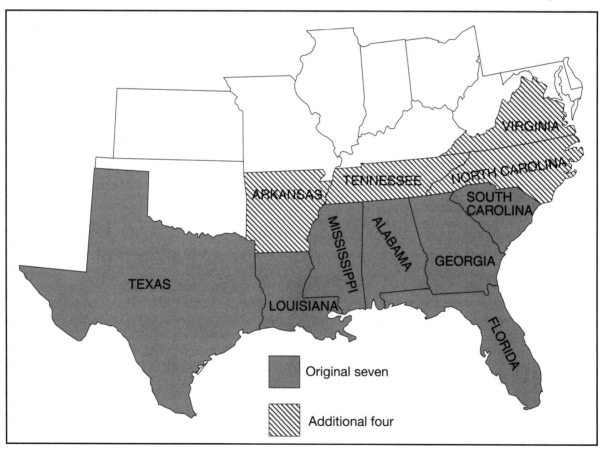

CONFEDERATE STATES OF AMERICA

Texas, Irish laborers in the cities, and a cosmopolitan mixture in the principal ports. The Confederate government placed immigrants in significant military and civilian posts. The army organized a variety of units among the foreign-born, some developing from previous state militia companies. Many more immigrants served throughout the army's ranks, recruited either by the Confederacy's conscription laws or by more stringent state laws which enrolled them in the militia.

SUGGESTED READINGS. The impact of the war on southern society is surveyed in Emory M. Thomas' *The Confederacy as a Revolutionary Experience* (1971). On the black experience, see Bell I. Wiley's *Southern Negroes, 1861-1865* (1938); Robert Durden's *The Gray and the Black* (1972); and Leon Litwack's *Been in the Storm So Long* (1979). Ella Lonn's study, *Foreigners in the Confederacy* (1940), is exhaustive.

Conference of Americans of Hispanic Origin: Meeting first held in Washington, D.C., in 1971, to bring together members of various Latino ethnic groups for the common good of all Latinos. The conference focused on the possibility of exerting greater social and political influence through united effort. Such an approach proved successful in attracting approximately a thousand people from around the nation.

Confucian tradition: Derived from a Chinese philosophy of life based on the ideas of Confucius (551-479 B.C.E.). Confucianism is primarily a guide to moral behavior which stresses the need to develop moral character and social responsibility in the individual and in governmental systems. Social order in China was based on Confucian beliefs that emphasized the importance of a patriarchal family structure, respect for elders, the value of education, and respect and obedience for authority, including the absolute rule by the emperor. Confucianism is still influential not only in China but also in Japan, Vietnam, and other countries in Southeast Asia as well as with overseas Chinese throughout the world.

A basic principle of Confucianism is that wisdom and good government begin at home. A person must start by being honest and brave and learn how to behave courteously and truthfully. If the head of the family follows these principles, he could administer his family wisely and if every family were well-managed, orderly, and moral, the government would also be well-ordered. This stress on families has been one of the most enduring features of the Confucian tradition.

The Confucian tradition includes the five virtues of benevolent love, righteousness, propriety, wisdom, and faithfulness. These values were supplemented by Confucius' views on learning. "Be familiar with the ancient wisdom and become acquainted with the modern; then you may become a teacher"; on society, "What you do not wish others to put on you, do not wish to put on others"; on the good, "Goodness is never far away. You have only to wish for it and you will find that it is with you"; on truth, "A man whose words cannot be trusted is of no use to anybody"; on self, "It is bad enough to have faults but worse not to want to correct them"; and on government, "Govern merely by statute, and people will be evasive. Govern by using the virtue of morality and they will come to you voluntarily."

The Confucian tradition among Asian Americans has had both positive and negative results. Confucian beliefs were in harmony with many established American values—a strong work ethic, a strong sense of family, frugality, and respect for elders—which helped them adapt and succeed in American society. The proportion of adults who live with their parents is five times greater among Asian Americans than in the general population, teenage pregnancies are relatively rare, many children have achieved extraordinary educational results, and family income exceeds the national average.

The Confucian tradition has also presented Asian Americans with difficulties in adjusting to life in the United States. Females have often found employment more easily than males and have been less likely to accept male control, an attitude which has caused friction within families. Children often rebel against traditional parental authority and display independence rarely shown in Asia. Lack of active political involvement has left Asian Americans out of the governmental decision making process.

Although it has lost some of its influence, especially among children born in the United States and with those who have come here without their parents, Confucianism continues to be a powerful force within the Asian American community.

SUGGESTED READINGS. For a background on Confucianism, two excellent, but somewhat dated accounts are James K. Feibleman's *Understanding Oriental Philosophy* (1976) and John K. Fairbank's *Chinese Thought and Institutions* (1957). A more recent account is provided in Patricia Buckley Ebrey's *Confu-*

cianism and Family Rituals in Imperial China (1991). An excellent account of Asian American life in the United States is provided in Stanley Karnow and Nancy Yoshihara's *Asian Americans in Transition* (1992) and Ronald Takaki's *Strangers from a Different Shore: A History of Asian Americans* (1989).

Congregationalists: Members of a Protestant denomination that developed from the religious philosophies of sixteenth century English clerics Robert Browne and Henry Barrowe. Browne is generally considered to have established the first Congregationalist church in 1580 in Norwich.

Browne opposed the controlling aspects of the Anglican church, and central to Congregationalist philosophy is the idea that each individual church should be independent—self-sufficient, self-governing, and self-explicating—although there should be cooperation and fellowship among the churches. Furthermore, equality should exist among all church members in managing the affairs of the church. In order to maintain a strict code of conduct, Browne espoused a process whereby church members would police one another's behavior.

Overzealous adherence to this principle led to bitter divisions that destroyed Browne's own church. His teachings, however (dubbed "Brownism"), survived and were revived by Henry Barrowe. Barrowe kept the idea of the independence of each church but disagreed with the concept of the equality of all members. He believed that elders were necessary to lead the local flock.

Congregationalists were important in America from the colonial period. The PURITANS who established the Massachusetts Bay Company in 1629 and sailed for America the following year were Congregationalists. The so-called GREAT AWAKENING of the 1730's and 1740's, a period of renewed religious fervor in colonial America, was essentially a Congregationalist movement. New England Congregationalist preacher Jonathan Edwards preached powerful sermons such as the famous "Sinners in the Hands of an Angry God."

During the nineteenth century, Congregationalism continued to expand, despite the fact that the nineteenth century United States was not a particularly churchgoing nation. Congregationalists expanded into the new territories of the West. The first Congregationalist churches in Oregon and California were established in 1844. Congregationalists are strong proponents of mass EDUCATION, and they were instrumental in establishing many nonsectarian institutions of learning. Among such institutions are Harvard, Yale, and Dartmouth universities and Amherst College.

SUGGESTED READINGS. Valuable general sources include Martin E. Marty's *Protestantism: Its Churches and Cultures, Rituals and Doctrines* (1974) and J. Gordon Melton's *The Encyclopedia of American Religions* (1987). For the Great Awakening, see Edwin Scott Gaustad's *The Great Awakening in New England* (1965). *The New Schaff-Herzog Encyclopedia of Religious Knowledge* (1908-1914, rev. ed. 1951-1957) also contains a good study of Congregationalism.

Congress of Industrial Organizations (CIO): Formed in 1935 to organize semiskilled and unskilled workers in mass production industries, who were unprotected by the AMERICAN FEDERATION OF LABOR (AFL). CIO membership rose to nearly four million by 1937. It successfully developed a political movement that emphasized a social reform program. Following World War II, the two labor organizations (AFL and CIO) became more similar in structure and composition, leading to a merger as the AFL-CIO in 1955 in order to ensure political and economic strength.

Congress of Racial Equality (CORE): Civil rights organization. CORE was founded and organized by James Farmer in Chicago, Illinois, in 1942. The group believed in using methods of nonviolent direct action to desegregate public facilities and challenge discrimination. In the 1950's, CORE extended its efforts to fight against job discrimination by picketing and boycotting businesses that failed to hire blacks. In the 1960's, CORE played an even greater role in the CIVIL RIGHTS MOVEMENT by sponsoring the FREEDOM RIDES to challenge segregation in interstate bus transportation and conducting voter education and registration drives in the South. When Floyd B. McKissick took over as national director from 1966 to 1968, the group struggled to maintain its interracial membership in the face of McKissick's support of the militant BLACK POWER MOVEMENT.

Congressional caucuses: Organizations of members of Congress devoted to advancing particular interests. Originally caucuses were secret meetings of party leaders to create policy. The membership of each party in the Senate and the House of Representatives still meets in closed caucuses to elect leaders and, on occasion, to determine party legislative agendas.

The Congressional Black Caucus, a political group, defines the promotion of affirmative action as one of its goals. (Library of Congress)

Political lexicographer William Safire notes that the term "caucus" is derived from an American Indian word meaning "elder" or "counselor." In an increasingly diverse society, all types of associations and organizations may have caucuses of membership subgroups, such as women, students, or African Americans. But in Congress, especially in the House of Representatives, caucuses serve to represent various constituent groups, trade interests, and geographic regions. There were more than 130 officially recognized caucuses in the 102nd Congress. The number was growing with each succeeding Congress, as each new class of entering members forms a caucus and as new interests arise.

Besides acting on behalf of interest groups, some caucuses are recognized as "legislative service organizations," which provide information on pending bills to both members and the public and provide congressional testimony. Perhaps the best known is the Congressional Black Caucus, formed in the 1970's by African American members of Congress. With the election of thirteen new African Americans to the House and one to the Senate in 1992, the Black Caucus increased by more than 50 percent to forty members. Among its important functions is presenting an "alternative federal budget" geared to the needs of African Americans every year.

Most of the caucuses, however, are narrowly focused and are funded by sharing the costs of staff and stationery among the members. Some of the larger bicameral (House and Senate) caucuses are the Congressional Arts Caucus, the Congressional Caucus for Women's Issues, the Friends of Ireland (a result of longtime Irish influence in American politics), and the International AIDS Task Force. Large Senate-only caucuses include the Northeast-Midwest Senate Coalition, the Senate Beef Caucus, and the Senate Children's Caucus. Large House-only caucuses include the Congressional Human Rights Caucus, the Northeast-Midwest Congressional Coalition, and the Congressional Urban Caucus.

Despite failure in the early 1980's to extend the deadline for ratification of an EQUAL RIGHTS AMENDMENT to the U.S. CONSTITUTION, the women's caucus has been successful in winning passage of legislation to allow "family leave" for workers with health emergencies at home and to crack down on divorced fathers who ignore court orders to pay child support. The women's caucus has also helped increase the number of female members of Congress and to raise public consciousness of sexual harassment, particularly as the result of Senate confirmation of Clarence THOMAS to the Supreme Court.

SUGGESTED READINGS. The importance of caucuses and other interest groups in shaping legislation is a theme of Hedrick Smith's *The Power Game* (1988). *From the Ward to the White House: The Irish in American Politics* (1991) by George E. Reedy, a former presidential aide, is an entertaining and historical account of IRISH AMERICAN influence. Other continuously published public sources on the composition of various caucuses include *The Congressional Yellow Book, Congressional Quarterly Weekly Report, Congressional Quarterly Guide to Current American Government*, and *The Congressional Staff Directory*.

Conservative Jews. *See* **Jews—Conservative**

Conservatives: Those who support limited central government and reliance on individualism. Conservatism is both a philosophy and a political force that reached its contemporary zenith during the administration of President Ronald Reagan (1981-1989). Modern conservatives believe strongly in less government, lower taxes, more individual responsibility, and stronger national defense. They also uphold the notion of morality and religion as important components of public policy; judicial restraint; free trade; states' rights; and a return to the values of the Founding Fathers.

Historically, conservatism traces its roots to the free-market, laissez-faire capitalism of Adam Smith paired with the views of eighteenth century British parliamentarian Edmund Burke, who favored traditional and legal rights against encroachment by government and opposed new social orders.

In American politics, conservatism has served as a counterweight to liberalism, which flourished between 1933 and 1980 through big spending by Congresses controlled by the DEMOCRATIC PARTY and through the Democratic administrations of Franklin D. Roosevelt, Harry S Truman, John F. Kennedy, Lyndon B. Johnson, and Jimmy Carter. Republican administrations of Dwight D. Eisenhower, Richard M. Nixon, and Gerald Ford, while more fiscally restrained, did not appreciably reverse the progressive social programs of LIBERALS.

Modern American conservatism grew after WORLD WAR II with internal struggles within the REPUBLICAN PARTY between the "Eastern Establishment," controlled by fiscally conservative but socially progressive Wall Street lawyers, and the populist purists, who traced their ideology directly back to Burke. Among the leaders of modern conservatism who rose to prominence in the 1950's were Ohio Senator Robert Taft, Wisconsin Senator Joseph McCarthy, author Russell Kirk, and magazine publisher William F. Buckley, Jr. Buckley's publication, *The National Review,* became an influential forum for conservative political debate.

Conservatives took control of the Republican Party in 1964, nominating Arizona Senator Barry M. Goldwater as the presidential candidate. His landslide defeat was only a temporary setback as his campaign spawned a new generation of conservatives. These included former actor Ronald Reagan, who went on to become governor of California for two terms and then president for two terms, espousing the Goldwater brand of conservatism.

The "Reagan Revolution" in U.S. politics succeeded largely because he wooed "lunchbucket" Democrats—typically Roman Catholic men of Irish, Italian, and eastern European descent—from the liberal ideology of Roosevelt and his political heirs. The Reagan Administration also gave prominence to a number of African American intellectuals who espoused conservative views on the economy—based on entrepreneurship and self-help—and on race, opposing affirmative action in hiring. Among notable black conservatives are economist Thomas Sowell, low-income housing specialist Robert Woodson, and Supreme Court Justice Clarence THOMAS.

Despite the fact that most Americans align themselves with the Democratic Party, polls after the 1992 election of moderate Democrat Bill Clinton indicated that 60 percent of voters considered themselves conservative and 34 percent liberal.

SUGGESTED READINGS. The philosophical underpinnings of conservatism are traced in Robert J. Nagle's *American Conservatism: An Illustrated History* (1989). Historian Garry Wills's autobiographical *Confessions of a Conservative* (1979) is an account of his meeting with and work for William F. Buckley, Jr. In *The Rise of the Counter-Establishment: From Conservative Ideology to Political Power* (1986) liberal columnist Sidney Blumenthal provides a balanced history of the post-World War II rise of conservatism.

Constitution, U.S.: The United States Constitution, written in 1787, established a government dedicated rhetorically to justice and liberty, but it was not until the twentieth century that minorities and women secured the same constitutional rights long enjoyed by white males.

Race: 1787 to the Civil War. The principle of white supremacy was integral to the U.S. Constitution from its inception. SLAVERY had existed in America for more than one hundred years prior to the writing of the Constitution in 1787, and the men who wrote it fully understood slavery's importance to the southern economy. Although some of these leaders did express moral objections to slavery, their concerns were overridden by their primary interest in creating a govern-

In the first half of the nineteenth century, respect for states' rights and a fear of southern secession combined to ensure that white supremacy remained entrenched constitutionally. Southern states held tenaciously to the institution of slavery, while northern politicians sought to prevent the spread of slavery to new states without antagonizing southerners. In 1842, the Supreme Court upheld the FUGITIVE SLAVE ACT and thereby sacrificed the constitutional rights of blacks to the interest of national unity. White supremacy was resoundingly affirmed in *Dred SCOTT v. SANDFORD* (1857) as the Supreme Court held that blacks were not citizens of the United States, and thus were not entitled to enjoy constitutional rights.

The U.S. Constitution is housed in the Rotunda of the National Archives, Washington, D.C., along with the Declaration of Independence. (National Archives)

ment that would protect property rights and join the independent states into a federal union. The document they created contained a fugitive slave clause and a provision that a slave would count as only three-fifths of a person for purposes of determining the number of legislators each state would send to the House of Representatives.

Race: Post-Civil War to 1954. Soon after the CIVIL WAR, amendments to the U.S. Constitution proclaimed an end to slavery and the beginning of equal voting rights without regard to "race, color, or previous condition of servitude." The FOURTEENTH AMENDMENT, ratified in 1868, extended citizenship to African Americans and provided that the federal government

The Preamble of the Constitution of the United States begins with a phrase that is strongly indicative of a democratic government. (National Archives)

would protect the rights of blacks against discriminatory state laws. During this period of RECONSTRUCTION, the promise of racial equality seemed close to fulfillment.

Unfortunately, the South's persistent efforts to reestablish white supremacy were rewarded in the 1870's and 1880's with several favorable Supreme Court decisions that limited the effectiveness of the Civil War amendments. These Court decisions culminated in *PLESSY V. FERGUSON* (1896), which declared that the principle of "separate but equal" was not a violation of the Constitution. This decision forced African Americans to remain second-class citizens by allowing the South to continue to enforce segregation by law in schools, housing, jobs, transportation, public parks, and public hospitals. After *Plessy,* the rights of blacks were placed at the mercy of state governments for the next fifty years.

1954 and Beyond. In *BROWN V. BOARD OF EDUCATION* (1954), the Supreme Court ruled that legal separation of the races in public schools was a violation of the equal protection guarantees in the U.S. Constitution. This decision marked the beginning of the end of officially authorized race segregation in the United States. Southern resistance to this Court ruling and the agitation generated by the CIVIL RIGHTS movement caused the federal government to assume an active role in pursuit of equal protection of the law. Although racial separation and discrimination remain a social and economic fact of life in the United States, the Constitution is understood to require legal equality regardless of race.

Since the 1960's, the Supreme Court has expanded the equal protection guarantee of the Fourteenth Amendment beyond race discrimination. The Court now affords varying degrees of protection to women and members of such nonracial minority groups as aliens, illegitimate children, OLDER AMERICANS, and people with mental disabilities from laws that discriminate unreasonably against them or that impinge on their exercise of such fundamental constitutional rights as the right to vote. Some minorities, notably homosexuals, children, and the poor, enjoy significantly less constitutional protection. The Court has generally upheld AFFIRMATIVE ACTION programs as a means to increase opportunities for minorities and women in education and employment.

Gender and the U.S. Constitution. Once an obstacle to equality, the Constitution has evolved to be an important instrument in the ongoing struggle of women to achieve equal rights. The Constitution, drafted in 1787, made no specific mention of women, though it was generally understood at the time that women would count fully in determining representation in Congress. In the nineteenth century and well into the twentieth century, the political and legal rights of women were defined by state law. In 1873, for example, the Supreme Court upheld an Illinois law that denied women lawyers a license to practice law in state courts. In 1874, the Supreme Court held that the denial of voting rights to women by the state of Missouri was constitutional. The Court, in 1908, allowed the state of Oregon to limit the working hours of women while regularly striking down similar limits on male workers. Decisions such as this affirmed the prevailing view that women were not the legal equals of men.

Voting rights for women were secured with the passage of the NINETEENTH AMENDMENT, but it was not until 1971 that the Supreme Court interpreted the Constitution to prohibit state laws which unreasonably treated women differently from men. The Fourteenth Amendment's equal protection provision, originally understood to be inapplicable to women, is today the primary tool for challenging sexually-discriminatory state laws. In 1975, for example, the Court struck down a Utah law which specified a higher age of majority for males than for females. In 1981, a Louisiana law giving a husband the right to dispose of jointly owned property without his wife's consent was found unconstitutional by the Court. In general, state and federal laws may treat people differently on the basis of gender only if an important governmental objective is present.

SUGGESTED READINGS. Many excellent studies of the Constitution and minorities exist, such as Donald Nieman's *Promises to Keep* (1991) and H. N. Hirsh's *A Theory of Liberty: The Constitution and Minorities* (1992). The constitutional rights of women are explored by Deborah L. Rhode in "Equal Protection: Gender and Justice," in *Judging the Constitution* (1989), edited by Michael McCann.—*Philip Zampini*

Cooking. *See* **Food and cooking**

Coolies: Derogatory term referring to Chinese laborers recruited by trickery or force and employed in involuntary labor in Latin America and the Caribbean. The coolie trade developed in the nineteenth century after Great Britain and other European nations ended their involvement in the slave trade. Like African slaves

Artist's sketch of Chinese men at work on a sugar plantation in Louisiana. (Library of Congress)

before them, coolies were transported by ship under very poor conditions and were treated brutally once they reached their destination. Many of the coolies who were recruited to work in Cuba and Peru died as a result of mistreatment, provoking protests by the Chinese government.

The term "coolie" is sometimes misapplied to the Chinese immigrants who worked in the mines and railroads in North America. While these Chinese workers had to contend with racial prejudice (and sometimes violent abuse) as well as difficult working conditions, for the most part they were voluntary immigrants, not forced laborers.

Corridos: Mexican and MEXICAN AMERICAN narrative ballads in which the lyrical structure is blended with musical elements to comment on legendary, historical, or topical events. The corrido first developed in Mexico in the middle of the nineteenth century, influenced by the Spanish romance form. The corrido served to measure Mexican workers' attitudes toward events affecting their lives; they expressed public values as well as commentary on historical episodes. As such, corridos are important ethnohistorical documents.

The corrido encompasses three forms: the epic, which captures the exploits of the hero; the lyrical, which provides affective overtones; and the narrative, which tells a story in the first or third person. The structure of the corrido has six parts: the initial call of the singer to the public; the place, date, and name of the protagonist; a formula preceding the protagonist's arguments; the main message; the protagonist's farewell; and the singer's farewell.

A review of corridos over time reveals diverse themes ranging from personal tragedies to political critiques, from the coming of the railroads to bank heists. One of the earliest documented corridos, from 1808, is a critique of King Carlos IV. In 1824, "El Corrido de los Tulares" documented an Indian uprising against the Spaniards in Santa Barbara, California. The period from 1836 to 1936 is known as the corrido century, reflecting the experience on the Texas-

Mexican border. Early border corridos dealt with Indian raids, the U.S.-Mexico border conflict, the Mexican revolution of 1910, and the first cattle drives to Kansas in the 1860's. During WORLD WAR II, the Mexican American experience was documented in corridos such as "Las Islas Hawaiianas" and "El Corrido de Douglas MacArthur."

In the second half of the 1900's, the corrido tradition continued to evolve. In the 1960's, the ethnic and political consciousness of the Chicano movement and the sentiments of striking farmworkers were heard in songs such as "Los Rinches de Tejas" and "El Corrido de César Chávez." Another interesting example are the corridos written about John F. Kennedy, which portray him as a hero of the Mexican American community because of shared religious values, respect for his strength and bravery, as well as support for his liberal democratic values. Even the 1989 San Francisco earthquake was documented in a corrido.

SUGGESTED READINGS. See *With a Pistol in His Hand* (1958) by folklorist Americo Paredes for a pioneering analysis of a famous border corrido. Also see, by the same author, *A Texas-Mexican Cancionero* (1976), a songbook of corridos from the border region from Mexico's colonial era through the twentieth century. For studies of the Mexican corrido, consult *The Mexican Corrido as a Source for Interpretive Study of Modern Mexico, 1870 - 1950* (1957) by Merle Simmons, and Maria Herrera Sobek's *The Mexican Corrido: A Feminist Analysis* (1992).

Cosby, Bill [William Henry] (b. July 12, 1937, Germantown, Pa.): African American entertainer and highly successful public personality. Cosby's career began in the 1960's at clubs in his native Philadelphia and New York's Greenwich Village. He became the first black star of a prime time television series, *I Spy* (1965-1968). He has won three Emmy Awards for his television work and five Grammy Awards for his record albums. His long-running *Cosby Show*, various books, and highly paid public appearances and commercials have brought fame and wealth: By 1989 he was earning some $57 million a year. Along the way, Cosby earned an M.A. and Ph.D. (1977). He and his wife have given $20 million to Spelman College in Atlanta and aided other black community causes.

Cosmetics: Substances intended to beautify, enhance, or condition one's appearance. Throughout history, and in virtually all cultures, human beings have been char-

acterized by the need to ornament themselves and the world they inhabit. One of the oldest methods of human ornamentation is the use of cosmetics; cosmetics undoubtedly were first used in prehistoric times. Ironically, although cosmetics were developed by different racial and cultural groups all over the world, in the twentieth century United States the cosmetic industry for many years concentrated almost exclusively on creating cosmetics for white Americans.

History and Multicultural Influences. The word "cosmetics" comes from the Greek *kosmetikos*, meaning "skilled in adornment," but the use of cosmetic adornment has a rich, culturally diverse history predating the Greeks. The earliest forms, used by men as well as women, were produced from herbs, roots, berries, nuts, animal fat, and animal hair. These substances were used for religious purposes and in other ritual practices.

As ancient peoples developed, so did the sophistication of their cosmetics. The function of cosmetics also evolved: Rather than serving primarily as ceremonial or medicinal accouterments, cosmetics became more ornamental in nature.

Archaeological finds in Middle Eastern cultures reveal artifacts intended for cosmetic storage and application: mirrors, cosmetic jars, and applicators. One of the major cosmetics used throughout the region in an-

By 1993, Bill Cosby had won three Emmy awards for his television work and five Grammys for his record albums. (AP/Wide World Photos)

cient times was kohl, made from antimony (sulfide), soot, or galena (an ore of lead). Kohl was used by women to darken their eyelashes and brows. The eyes received considerable attention in these cultures, particularly in Egypt, since the cosmetics served to protect the wearer from flies and the sun.

Both men and women of the upper classes were fond of rouges, lipsticks, bath oils, and body fragrances. Substances such as frankincense and myrrh were treasured perfumes. So too was spikenard, a root obtainable only from the remote valleys of the Himalayas. Almond and olive oil were used as well. The Egyptians mixed animal fat and balsams to make skin creams. The Babylonian, Sumerian, and Hittite cultures contributed to the range of natural substances used to beautify the face: blue eye shadow from lapis lazuli, red lip color from cochineal (dried insects), and rouge from cinnabar.

Asian civilizations were equally concerned with enhancement of the physical appearance. Chinese women used powder, lip color, and rouge, as did the Japanese. Hindus indicated caste with facial marks and colored their bodies with almond paste. They also colored their eyelids with kohl, stained their face and arms with saffron powder, and used henna to redden their feet.

American Indian peoples painted their faces as well as other parts of the body, and they used animal fats and oils for ornamental purposes and to protect themselves against insects and the cold. In traditional Navajo culture, individuals involved in ceremonial rites were decorated with colored sand mixed with herb medicine. Mineral pigments were also used, as were red grease paint, burned charcoal, cornmeal, pollen, and herbal lotions. The Delaware people applied grease, marrow, or sap to their hair; both males and females colored the central part along the crown of the head. Colors used included black made from charcoal and red from red ocher or bloodroot.

Some South American peoples, such as the Oyanas, decorated their faces with plant juices possessing a permanence similar to that of India ink. The Mayans painted corpses red for burial purposes, and the Incas used face paint and other forms of personal ornamentation to indicate social class.

Neither the Greeks nor the Romans used cosmetics as extensively. Early Romans considered cosmetic use effeminate, but by 54 C.E., the empire had adopted the habits of many of the conquered eastern peoples. Major cosmetics included kohl for the eyes; white lead and chalk to lighten the skin; rouge for cheeks and lips; hair dye; and perfumes of almond, rose, quince, olive, and sesame oil.

Many traditional African peoples painted their bodies for ceremonial and ornamental purposes, using red earth mixed with oil or grease, ashes, and white chalk. Turkana men used clay to create intricate hairstyles, such as small plaits shaped into buns. The Samburu warrior wore finely executed facial makeup to create an almost feminine appearance. Rendille women of Kenya fashioned hair pieces made of mud, animal fat, and ocher to signal that they had given birth to their first son. Dinka men decorated their bodies with ashes and stained their hair red with a plaster of ash and cow's urine.

In medieval Europe, highly influenced by Roman culture and the Catholic church, cosmetic use was minimal. A woman who used cosmetics to enhance her appearance risked being branded a witch and burned at the stake. With the end of the Crusades, however, cosmetic use became more acceptable, particularly among the nobility, reaching its peak in the eighteenth century. During this period, both men and women used lotions, facial masks, and powders to achieve a whitened look. They also etched their faces with blue to accentuate the vein lines. Those with blemishes caused by smallpox covered the marks with elaborate beauty patches of silk and velvet.

By the late nineteenth century, in both Europe and the United States, cosmetic use had again fallen into ill repute. Men had virtually given up cosmetics, and respectable middle-class women, particularly in Puritan New England, relied only upon such discreet substances as white rice powder, cucumber cream, lemon juice, and a touch of cologne. With the beginning of the twentieth century, however, European and American styles were transformed by the rapid development of technology and the mass media.

Modern Cosmetics. The rise of technology, coupled with the growing political and economic emancipation of women in the United States, led to the formation of the American cosmetic industry, dominated by such companies as Revlon, Elizabeth Arden, Estée Lauder, and Avon. Modern cosmetics utilize a variety of substances, such as resins, alcohol, lanolin, spermaceti, oil, wax, chalk, hormones, and natural products including aloe, rose petals, and herbs. The Food and Drug Administration (FDA) regulates cosmetics use in the United States, requiring that they be safe and properly labeled.

The U.S. cosmetic industry had developed into a $17 billion-a-year business by 1990. In the first half of the century, growth was attributed to the development of modern methods of mass production and packaging. Since World War II, several additional trends have emerged: a larger population, the growing number of working women, and extensive advertising. The industry has targeted several distinct markets: women entering the work force, older women, ethnic populations, and men.

Working Women and Older Women. Women constitute more than one-half of the U.S. population. Working women, generally between the ages of twenty-five and sixty-five, use cosmetics more regularly and tend to spend more on cosmetics than do nonworking women, purchasing the more expensive franchise lines of cosmetics and toiletries featured in department stores. Younger women tend to purchase less expensive brands available in supermarkets and drugstores or buy through direct sales.

As the generation of children born after World War II has aged, females between the ages of thirty-five and fifty-four have become one of the fastest-growing segments of the population. This group tends to be sophisticated and affluent enough to buy products they believe useful. The cosmetic industry has begun to address this specific population's need to retain a youthful appearance while recognizing that the aging process is natural. Cosmetics for this group include wrinkle preventers, moisturizers, astringents, masks, sunscreens, sunblocks, and hair dyes.

Ethnic Groups. Ever since the invention of the hair straightener for blacks more than a hundred years ago, some cosmetics designed specifically for ethnic groups have been available. The types and variety of ethnic products have been very limited, however, especially in foundation colors, which have traditionally been developed specifically for white skin. In the 1960's and 1970's, the industry began to create new products for African Americans. With the growth of the Latino and Asian populations in the 1980's and 1990's, the cosmetic industry expanded its vision to address the needs of these diverse groups.

Hair and skin care products are the major product lines targeted at ethnic populations. Companies have concentrated on developing foundation colors specifically for the ARICAN AMERICAN, JAPANESE, CHINESE, LATINO, AMERICAN INDIAN, and Caribbean markets. Hair and skin moisturizers that are light and oil free have been developed to facilitate hair styling and to avoid clogging pores. Companies such as Avon have also specifically targeted the Latino female market, creating Spanish-language catalogs and brochures to sell their products.

The example of hair preparations for African Americans illustrates some of the issues and dilemmas faced by members of minority groups regarding cosmetic use. In the early twentieth century, an African American woman, Madame C. J. Walker, developed a product that would straighten hair. An adept businesswoman, she built a hugely profitable business. Yet even in the beginning, hair straightening was debated by African Americans—was it truly desirable, some asked, to try to "look white"?

The issue became hotter in the late 1960's with the rise of the BLACK POWER MOVEMENT and the slogan "Black is beautiful." Full, curly hair—the Afro style—became an emblem of black pride. In the 1970's, emphasizing the new variety of hairstyles being worn by African Americans, one hair preparation was advertised with the slogan "rows, 'fros, anything goes." In many ways, the choice of which hair preparations or cosmetics to use (as well as more radical procedures such as lightening the skin with bleach or undergoing surgery) echoes personal decisions that members of minorities must make in all aspects of their lives: whether to assert their own ethnic heritage or to adopt the images put forward by the dominant Anglo culture.

Men. Cosmetics entered the men's market in the 1950's when French fashion designers began to create fragrances solely for men. By the 1970's, the U.S. cosmetic industry also began to target the men's market, creating what has become a more than $1 billion-a-year business. Men have begun to respond to the growing concern about health, fitness, and aging, as well as to cultural redefinitions of masculinity and femininity; consequently, they have started to use more cosmetics. Until the 1970's, men's products were restricted to shaving creams and colognes carrying brisk, masculine scents. The 1970's saw the expansion of this market to include moisturizers, night creams, eye creams, hair care products, and sunscreens. Many of these products are directed at the man between thirty-five and fifty-five with sufficient income to purchase products intended to combat the effects of aging on skin and hair.

SUGGESTED READINGS. For a thorough review of the history of makeup in western culture, see *Fashions in Makeup* (1972) by Richard Carson. The development of the ethnic cosmetics market is discussed in *Ethnic*

Haircare, Skincare, and Cosmetics Market (1988), compiled by Packaged Facts. The issue of men's cosmetics is dealt with succinctly in the November, 1987, issue of *Health*. The cosmetic industry is detailed in *The Business of Beauty: Cosmetics Retailing* (1989) by Debbie Purvis. *Africa Adorned* (1984) by Angela Fisher presents stunning photographs and a clearly written text on traditional African practices of ornamentation.—*Nancy M. Grace*

Cosmopolitan magazine: Women's magazine founded in 1886. Helen Gurley BROWN, the author of *Sex and the Single Girl* (1962), became its editor in 1965. She guided the magazine to a new format and a new market: young, single, working women. The magazine identified its new readers as attractive and seeking relationships with men yet also as having ambitions to create their own identities and pursue careers. *Cosmopolitan*'s portrayal of modern women drew strong criticism from feminists because the magazine depicted women as eager to look sexually attractive and to please men. Nevertheless, Brown forged an alternative role model to the housewife of the 1950's with her magazine's glossy image of the "Cosmo girl."

Helen Gurley Brown served as editor of Cosmopolitan *magazine since 1965.* (AP/Wide World Photos)

Cotton Club, The: A nightclub that opened in 1923 at 142nd Street and Lenox Avenue in Harlem. Owned and controlled by bootleggers, the nightclub was known for its floor shows, called "Cotton Club Parades," which featured black performers. No African Americans were admitted as club guests. The club featured leading black artists such as Duke ELLINGTON, Cab Calloway, Bill Robinson, and Ethel Waters, and it launched the career of Lena HORNE. At first, the GREAT DEPRESSION affected business only slightly, because wealthy white patrons continued to come. The Cotton Club's owners tried to alleviate Harlem's woes by distributing Christmas baskets to needy local residents. Eventually the end of Prohibition and the long-term effects of the Depression forced Harlem's Cotton Club to close on February 16, 1936. The club reopened outside Harlem but closed permanently at that location in 1940.

Council of Energy Resource Tribes (CERT): Organization founded in 1975 by a number of American Indian tribes in the West and Southwest to protect mineral and energy resources on Indian land from exploitation by non-Indian corporations. Because of the energy crisis and Arab oil embargo of the early 1970's, American corporations were looking for domestic sources of energy. CERT was founded by tribes with significant resources in order to avoid depletion of their holdings and to guard against possible loss of Indian land. CERT also seeks to ensure just compensation for the mining that does occur on tribal lands. Another CERT goal is the training of Indian professionals to become independent producers of energy resources. By 1928 CERT had expanded into a tribal energy coalition with thirty-seven members.

Country and western music: Form of popular American music that blends European and African American influences to celebrate "the simple life." Traditionally this music reflected the values of the dominant folk culture in early American history, giving voice to a largely white, rural, southern population that was comfortably excluded from the mainstream of American life. It is a music so deeply embedded in its rural roots that even when it was urbanized and commercialized during the 1950's, it remained faithful to its traditional values, merely transposing the "country" sound to city situations.

The roots of country music stem directly from the Scottish and Irish settlers who established the folk tradition of colonial America. The music consisted of plaintive ballads sung in a simple style—often with Anglo-Celtic religious overtones—accompanied by instruments such as the dulcimer, the fiddle, and the banjo, which were often homemade. The banjo, which was played by blacks and may be related to African instruments, has been called "America's only native instrument." The fiddle, too, "taken up by Negro musicians who played for white social gatherings . . . finally made its way into the hands of lower-class whites in the hinterlands," according to country music historian Bill C. Malone.

Country and western music is not limited to the FOLK and bluegrass sound of mountain "hillbilly" music. With its historical isolation and its resistance to industrialization, the South provided fertile ground for the development of a distinctively rural style that celebrates simplicity and a resistance to cultural change. Other styles include honky-tonk, a country blues-based sound incorporating some electronic instruments, especially pedal-steel guitar; cowboy songs with a Spanish flair and stories derived from life on the prairie; and western swing, essentially a big-band sound with a Texas accent. Most famous of all is the Nashville sound, centered in the Tennessee home of the Grand Ole Opry, a veritable matrix of traditional music and modern commercialism that has transformed country music from a limited backwoods cultural phenomenon to a multimillion-dollar mainstream show business venture.

It is ironic that a predominantly white music—often associated with white supremacy and segregation—owes such an immense debt to African American musical heritage. Even though many musicologists suggest that country and western music remains closer in style to the folk songs of Western Europe, its harmonies, instruments, and rhythms are derived from African American styles such as ragtime, JAZZ, BLUES, and GOSPEL. Many of the most accomplished country and western musicians have borrowed heavily from African American blues performers such as Robert Johnson, Muddy Waters, and Lightnin' Hopkins.

Perhaps no other form of music blends so dramatically two such distinct styles—the Western European folk ballad and the African American country blues.

SUGGESTED READINGS. For a look at the impact of African American folk and blues on country and western music, refer to Bill C. Malone's *Country Music USA* (1968) and *The Country Blues* (1959) by Samuel Charters. A classic work on the western sound is *Cowboy Songs and Other Frontier Ballads* (1910) by John Lomax. Wilbur Cash has written a study of the cultural influences on country and western music, *The Mind of the South* (1941), and Robert Shelton provides a comprehensive overview in his book *The Country Music Story* (1966).

Cowboys: From the 1850's to the 1910's, the American cowboy was a man hired by a frontier rancher to round up cattle for branding and counting or to drive them across great open lands on the way to market. Along the way, he had to protect the herd from poachers and wild animals. His tools for this job were his horse, saddle, lariat, and gun; his hat, boots, and leather pants offered protection from the sometimes harsh climate. From this modest beginning, the cowboy ascended in the popular imagination to assume a powerful role as an American folk hero.

The image of a lone man driving his herd across a formidable plain with no one to talk to but his horse and his herd has come to symbolize the hardy spirit of American individualism. The cowboy represents the days gone by when the frontier spirit and belief in MANIFEST DESTINY gripped the nation. Although his existence in reality was short-lived, the cowboy lives on in numerous aspects of American culture and society.

The cowboy gave rise to a rich tradition of recited and sung cowboy poetry, as well as prolific literary output beginning with the works of James Fenimore Cooper and continuing with such writers as Zane Grey. The cowboy's heroic image inspired artists and songwriters. He also became a favorite character in films and television programs, as personified by John Wayne, Gene Autry, and others. The cowboy often stood for truth and justice, the pillars of American society. He became a symbol that many Americans revered.

This myth, however, was not entirely faithful to the realities of life in the western United States. The cowboy led a lonely and dangerous life on the American plains. He sometimes went for months with no companionship. When he did stumble upon a frontier town, he often drank to excess and frequented brothels. Because of this wild behavior, cowboys quickly earned the reputation for causing trouble.

The cowboy is commonly remembered as an Anglo-Saxon male riding into the sunset or roping a steer. In fact, a significant number of cowboys were African Americans and Mexican Americans as well as American Indians who could not find other work in the oppressive American society of the time. To them, the freedom of the plains could not be rivaled. Mexican herding traditions had a considerable impact on American cowboy techniques and culture. Though they were rare and unpublicized, some women even met the challenges of the cowboy's life.

SUGGESTED READINGS. Those interested in the life of a woman cowboy should read Agnes Morley Cleaveland's *No Life for a Lady* (1941). *The Negro Cowboys* (1965) by Philip Durham and Everett L. Jones examines African Americans as cowboys. Jack Weston's *The Real American Cowboy* (1985) also includes a chapter on minority cowboys, as well as general information on the cowboy. More general information can be found in Richard W. Slatta's *Cowboys of the Americas* (1990).

Coyote: Spanish slang for a smuggler who brings illegal Mexican workers across the U.S.-Mexican border. At one time, coyotes took workers to labor contractors who organized crews of cotton and vegetable pickers for American growers. Border guards were often bribed by the coyote or labor contractor to assure a constant supply of labor. Coyotes also take high fees to escort people across the border, often under dangerous conditions, and then leave them to fend for themselves. Though they make border crossings possible for some, coyotes are often associated with extortion and exploitation.

Crazy Horse [Tashunka Witko] (1842?, Black Hills of S.Dak.—Sept. 5, 1877, Fort Robinson, Neb.): Chief of the Oglala Sioux Indians revered by the Sioux as their greatest leader. Crazy Horse resisted the encroachment of the white invaders in the sacred, gold-rich Black Hills of South Dakota and led a serious defense against United States troops. He joined SITTING BULL and GALL to defeat George Armstrong CUSTER at LITTLE BIGHORN in 1876. Following the massacre of Custer and his troops, Crazy Horse and his one thousand followers were relentlessly pursued, and they finally surrendered. He was stabbed to death on September 5, 1877, ostensibly trying to escape from prison.

Creation myths—American Indian: Creation myths recount the origin of the world or the universe, and innumerable cultures throughout the world have evolved their own mythical accounts of how existence began. Some scholars have argued that the native peoples of North America do not seem to have evolved true creation myths. In other words, there are many types of myths concerning how a particular people or knowledge of a particular activity came into being, but there are few stories that explain the beginning of existence. It is not known, however, whether the scarcity of such myths reflects the fact that they never existed or is instead the result of European and, later, white American efforts to suppress them.

Contact with Europeans had a strong negative impact on native myths. Christian missionaries actively tried to eliminate "heathen" beliefs among Indians. Moreover, because of the strenuous attempts of missionaries to Christianize the Indians, many myths subtly became combined with biblical elements, and their original forms became lost.

The closest thing to a creation myth in North America may be the Alaskan story of the Crow Father, probably imported from Siberia but widely circulated as far as the northeastern coast. This cycle begins with the emergence of Tulungusaq into the darkened, dead silver sky. There he finds Swallow, who teaches him to make wings and beak out of clay and to assume the image of the Crow. In that disguise he buries clay in the earth, from which spring vegetation, animals, and eventually men. Crow himself creates women to be the companions of men. Eventually Crow has to add material to expand the earth sufficiently to house the population. Again aided by the Swallow, Crow brings light to the world, separates night from day, and fashions sun and moon. As a culture hero, Crow is thought to have taught humans how to build houses and boats and how to hunt and fish. This story has been discredited as a "pure" myth, however, as it seems fairly obviously to have been contaminated by material from the book of Genesis. In later versions Crow punishes greedy mankind by taking the sun back, but his elder brother forces him to return it, after which his descendants become mere common crows. This modification suggests an adaptation and dilution of myth for use in children's stories.

Several tribes, especially in the Northwest, have legends of a totemic animal god, frequently the Raven, who puts the world in order. Typically the god gains control over fire, wind, rain, and snow or other elements by deceiving the existing powers, notably the Sun. Often a natural feature on which the livelihood of the tribe depends is imprisoned in a cave or mountain, and creation cannot proceed until the Raven liberates it. These totemic gods then divide into various tribes; rivalry between them requires the invention of Death as a means of controlling surplus population.

SUGGESTED READINGS. The most thorough treatment of American Indian mythology for the general reader is Pierre Grimal's *Larousse World Mythology* (1965), translated by Patricia Beardsworth. Cottie Burland's *North American Indian Mythology* (rev. ed., 1985) in the series Library of the World's Myths and Legends, is excellent but may be difficult to find. Alice Marriott and Carol K. Rachlin's *American Indian Mythology* (1968) includes a good collection of tales, although they are often of uncertain authenticity. William Brandon's *The Magic World: American Indian Songs and*

1850's through the 1870's. Under this system, a man who wished to emigrate would find a broker in his local area. The would-be traveler could borrow money from a broker for passage, with the understanding that the cost of the ticket—plus substantial interest—would be repaid from the wages earned in the United States. Brokers under this system made large profits from their investments. Because of hard economic conditions in China, the laborers were willing to work and give back most of their wages rather than remain in China and earn no wages at all.

After fighting the Creek War, Andrew Jackson led troops in the Battle of New Orleans in 1815, seen in this engraving. (National Portrait Gallery, Smithsonian Institution)

Poems (1971) rightly emphasizes the literary rather than mythological character of much of the collected material. *Sun Songs: Creation Myths from Around the World* by Raymond Van Over (1980) offers a variety of stories, even though many are of doubtful authenticity.

Credit-ticket system: Way for poor Chinese people to obtain tickets for passage to the United States from the

Creek War (1813-1814): Conflict between Creek Indians and a Tennessee army during the War of 1812 on the American frontier. Prior to the United States' war with England, the remarkable Shawnee TECUMSEH traveled north and south trying to organize an American Indian confederation that would attack the land-greedy white Americans and drive them back across the ocean. Few southern Indians joined Tecumseh except the Red Sticks (named after their painted war clubs) from the Creek

Nation. By 1813 the Red Sticks were attacking various areas in the Mississippi Territory, which included present-day Alabama. On August 30, 1813, they killed and scalped four hundred people at Fort Mims, to which white settlers in the region had fled after being chased from their homes.

News of the massacre at Fort Mims spread rapidly. The Tennessee legislature decided to raise an army to find and suppress those Creeks who had committed the violence. Tennessee governor Willie Blount placed General Andrew Jackson in charge and directed him to take punitive measures. As Jackson moved south and penetrated Indian Country, he led a widespread, vicious assault against innocent Creeks as well as the Red Sticks. After his attack on the Creek town of Talluschatches, many Creeks and members of the other "FIVE CIVILIZED TRIBES" declared their support for Jackson and informally joined his army. The Red Sticks' Chief Red Eagle (also known as William Weatherford) continued to fight. Indeed, upon learning that Talladega had "gone over" to Jackson, Red Eagle attacked the town, but Jackson managed to surround the Red Sticks, killing three hundred Creeks while losing only fifteen men.

A Creek attack on Jackson's camp in January of 1814 while Jackson was training a new group of recruits proved to be a mistake. Jackson's scouts were able to follow the Creek retreat and to learn the location of a new Red Stick fort on the Tallapoosa River at Horseshoe Bend, where the Creeks had put up log breastworks on a small peninsula. After cannon fire had reduced part of the breastworks, Jackson ordered his men to charge. More carnage took place, with the soldiers killing at least 557 Red Sticks.

With the Red Sticks died much of the power of the Creek Nation; Jackson forced surviving chiefs to sign away more Indian lands. Although Jackson won fame and glory in the Creek War, his actions illustrated the lengths to which white Americans would go to obtain land from the American Indians.

SUGGESTED READINGS. Robert Remini's *Andrew Jackson* (1966) gives a brief summary of the war, and Ray Allen Billington and Martin Ridge's *Westward Expansion: A History of the American Frontier* (1982) provides more detailed coverage. Two interesting articles are Frank Owsley's "The Fort Mims Massacre," in *Alabama Review* 24, no. 3 (July, 1971), pp. 192-204, and James W. Holland's "Andrew Jackson and the Creek War: Victory at Horseshoe Bend," in *Alabama Review* 21, no. 4 (October, 1968), pp. 243-275.

Creole culture and African Americans: As a result of both forced and voluntary interaction with Europeans, American Indians, and other groups, African Americans have long been participants in culturally mixed societies. One such society came into being in the parts of Louisiana where Creole culture predominated. The designation "Creole" originally referred, in the sixteenth and seventeenth centuries, to a white person born in Spanish America (of Spanish parents), as opposed to having been born in Spain. In colonial Louisiana, the term gradually came to mean a person of French or Spanish ancestry born in Louisiana. The term tends to defy strict definition, however, being used differently in different contexts.

Creole culture first emerged with the mingling of French, Spanish, West Indian, and African American peoples and customs in French Louisiana in the seventeenth and eighteenth centuries. Many residents of the region spoke Creole, a heavily French-influenced dialect still spoken by some Louisiana natives of mixed descent. Free persons of color from the Caribbean and other parts of the United States were living in French Louisiana territory as early as 1725. These individuals were able to take advantage of virtually all of the rights and privileges of any citizen in French Louisiana territory; some were members of the Creole upper classes. There is controversy, however, among Louisianians over who is a "true" Creole. Some people of mixed descent "passed for white," while others preferred to identify themselves as French-speaking African Americans.

At about the same time as the settlement of French Louisiana, some American Indians of the Southeast, who were being pressured by whites to move west in order to accommodate American expansion, were fleeing to New Orleans. Many hid along with runaway African Americans in underground canals and bayous. Intermarriage between African Americans and American Indians occurred as early as the eighteenth century.

The Creole cultures of African Americans of West Indian descent exploded in the United States when Caribbean immigration increased in the mid-1900's. This diverse group of African descendants transplanted such well-known Afro-Caribbean Creole traditions as Trinidad calypso and Jamaican reggae music, Afro-Cuban and Afro-Brazilian religion (SANTERÍA), and multicultural Caribbean festivals and celebrations.

One profound result of the cultural admixture of the

Creole and African American societies was the development of JAZZ in the early twentieth century. Creole musical traditions, with their French, African, and West Indian influences, were essential to the sound of early jazz. Among the many Creole musicians who were crucial to creating the sound of early jazz were Ferdinand "Jelly Roll" Morton, Edward "Kid" Ory, and Sidney Bechet.

The mid-1900's brought several scholarly works that connected many of the cultures, customs, and language patterns of African Americans to countries in western and central Africa. *Drums and Shadows* (1940) by Guy Johnson was the first to look extensively into the culture of the African American GULLAH communities located in the Sea Islands of South Carolina and Georgia and to record AFRICAN CULTURAL SURVIVALS in that culture. This was quickly followed by *The Myth of the Negro Past* by Melville J. Herskovits (1940), which presented the case for African cultural survivals not only among African Americans but also in mainstream American culture. By the 1990's, Gullah culture was one of the best preserved, most frequently studied African American Creole societies in the United States.

SUGGESTED READINGS. For more information, see *Caribbean Festival Arts* by John W. Nunley and Judith Bettelheim (1988); *Africanisms in American Culture,* edited by Joseph E. Holloway (1990); *African Americans and Creole Culture: From Plantation to Ghetto* by August Meier and Elliott Rudwick (rev. ed., 1966); and *Sea Island Roots,* edited by Mary A. Twining and Keith E. Baird (1991).

Crime and gangs. *See* **Gangs and crime**

Croatian Americans: The Croatians are a South Slavic group closely related to Serbians and Slovenes. They inhabit a crescent-shaped nation in the Balkan peninsula. Croatians have traditionally been ROMAN CATHOLIC, and they use the Latin alphabet. In the late nineteenth century, large numbers of Croatian peasants immigrated to the United States to escape economic hardship and political oppression. Many eventually returned to their homeland.

Early History. During the seventh century, the Byzantine Emperor Heraclius invited the Croatians to migrate into the Balkan peninsula to act as an imperial ally. By the ninth century, most Croatians had converted to Christianity because of the efforts of missionaries from Italy and the Dalmatian coast.

By the tenth century, the Croatians felt confident enough to establish an independent kingdom. This kingdom repelled Bulgar and Magyar invasions, and lasted for more than 150 years. Hungarian kings dominated Croatia from 1102 until the defeat of the Hungarian army by the Turks in 1526.

Ferdinand Habsburg of Austria was proclaimed king of both Hungary and Croatia. For more than a century and a half, the Habsburg armies fought to liberate Hungary and southern Croatia from the Turks. In 1848, Hungarians rose in revolt against the Habsburg dynasty and attempted to force Croatia into their new state. Under the leadership of Croatian Ban Joseph Jelacic, more than forty thousand Croatian troops joined the Austrians in suppressing the rebellion. Croatia was reunited with Dalmatia as an Austrian crown land from 1849 to 1868. During this period, Croatia experienced a great cultural revival generally associated with Bishop Joseph Strossmayer.

When the Habsburg Empire was reorganized in 1868, Croatia was once again placed under Hungarian control. After minor rioting in 1883, Hungarian Count Karl Khuen-Hedervary was put in charge of Croatia. During his twenty year reign, he crushed dissent and pitted Croatians against Serbians by consciously promoting Serbs to official positions and granting concessions to the Serbian Orthodox church.

World War I led to the destruction of the Habsburg Empire. In 1915, a Yugoslav (South Slav) Committee was formed in Paris with the support of notable Croatian leaders. After meeting with representatives of the committee, Serbian King Alexander Karadjordjevic took the title King of Serbs, Croats, and Slovenes.

Yugoslavian Era. Croatians remained a discontented minority within Yugoslavia. The first decade of the Yugoslav state was dominated by a personality struggle between Prime Minister Nikola Pasic, a Serb, and Stjepan Radic, the leader of the Croatian Peasant Party. On June 20, 1928, a politician from Montenegro shot five members of the party in the Yugoslavian parliament, killing Radic. The following year, King Alexander suspended the constitution and established a dictatorship.

During World War II, Germany and Italy created a Croatian puppet state headed by Ante Pavelic. Known as the Ustase, the Pavelic regime persecuted Serbs, Communists, and Jews. Plagued by corruption, the Ustase never gained widespread support and many Croatians joined Josip Broz Tito's Communist partisans.

After the war, Tito established a Communist federated state. In spite of Yugoslavia's relative prosperity during the Tito era, Croatian nationalists remained discontented. In January, 1990, the Communist Party ended its political monopoly and a renewal of nation-

as ten thousand people had been killed, nearly 600,000 others made refugees in the fighting. In March, 1992, a force of fourteen thousand U.N. peacekeepers was sent to Croatia to help end the fighting.

CROATIA

alist sentiment followed. The Croatian Parliament declared independence on June 25, 1991.

In July, fighting broke out between Croatian forces and Serbians aided by the Yugoslav army. By January 3, 1992, the United Nations estimated that as many

Immigration. During the colonial period of American history, sailors from Dalmatia and Catholic missionaries from Croatia had some impact on the European settlement of the New World. Two Croatian Jesuits, Baron Ivan Ratkaj (or Ratkay) and Ferdinand

Konsak (Consago Gonzales), worked among the Indians of the American Southwest. Konsak authored an important history of the Spanish missions in California.

During the early nineteenth century, Croatians from Dalmatia settled in significant numbers in southern Louisiana and California. Croatians in California, such as Mateo Arnerich, helped to develop that state's grape industry. Joe Martinac and John Rados became prominent shipbuilders on the West Coast.

Most Croatian immigrants left their homeland between 1883 and 1924. During this period as many as a half a million Croatians may have entered the United States. Nearly half, however, returned to Croatia. Most were young males from poor families who took jobs as unskilled laborers. Their massive migration was stimulated by economic conditions, political oppression, and improvements in transportation.

During the 1860's, Croatian peasants were given the right to subdivide their land. As a result, land holdings became smaller as the population grew. By 1900, Croatian farms were too small to support the number of people dependent on the land. Along the coastal region, phylloxera infestation devasted the grape vines and forced many from the land. In addition to their economic problems, many Croatians resented the oppressive nature of the Hungarian regime. Taxes were heavy and young Croatians were drafted into an army to which they felt little loyalty.

With the advent of the railroad and the steamship, transportation to the United States became relatively cheap. The rapid industrialization of the United States created a surplus of jobs in American industry. Most of the Croatians who migrated to the United States during this era found work in the industrialized areas of Ohio, Pennsylvania, Illinois, and Michigan.

Within a short period of time, institutions such as banks, insurance companies, newspapers, and churches were established to serve the needs of Croatian immigrants. The Croatian Bank of Pittsburg, California, was founded in 1866. In 1894, the Croatian Fraternal Union was organized to meet the insurance needs of the immigrants and to offer cultural opportunities. Croatian newspapers allowed immigrants to stay abreast of developments in their native land and helped them to adjust to their new home.

World War I and the National Origins Act of 1924 stemmed the tide of immigration from Croatia to the United States. A small number of Croatian political refugees arrived after the establishment of the Communist regime in Yugoslavia.

Cultural Contributions. In addition to their economic activities, Croatian Americans have made significant contributions to the United States in the areas of politics, the arts, education, and sports. Hundreds of others served with distinction in the armed forces of the United States during the twentieth century.

Two Croatian Americans have served as governors. Mike Stepovich became the first governor of Alaska in 1959. Rudolph (Rudy) Perpich was the dominant figure in Minnesota politics for two decades. A member of a large political family from the iron mining region of the state, Perpich was elected lieutenant governor in 1970. In 1976, he became governor upon the resignation of Wendell Anderson. He was defeated in his bid to retain the post in 1978, but ran successfully for the office in 1982 and 1986.

The best-known Croatian artist of the twentieth century is sculptor Ivan Mestrovic. Born in 1883 to a poor family in Croatia, Mestrovic tended sheep until his father apprenticed him to a marble carver in Split. At the age of seventeen, he was sent to study at the Vienna Academy and his talent quickly gained international recognition for his work. Mestrovic was strongly influenced by French sculptor Auguste Rodin and by the artists of ancient Greece. In 1946, he fled Yugoslavia for the United States in order to gain artistic freedom. He taught at Syracuse University and Notre Dame.

Notable painters include Vlaho Bukovac and Maksimilijan Vanka. The latter came to the United States during the 1930's and soon gained fame with his frescoes. His best-known work is the interior of St. Nicholas Church in Millvale, Pennsylvania.

Croatians have contributed outstanding sopranos to New York's Metropolitan Opera. Milka Ternina sang nine years with the company before returning to Zagreb. She discovered and trained Zinka Milanov, who later became a star performer at the same opera. American-born Irene Kramarich also gained fame as a soprano.

In the realm of folk culture, the Croatian tamburitsa bands have entertained large numbers of Americans. The bands are made up of plunked string instruments of various sizes that accompany fast-tempo folk dances and Italian-influenced popular songs. Tamburitsa bands frequently perform at ethnic picnics and folk festivals throughout the United States, and many young Croatian Americans learn about their heritage through playing or dancing to tamburitsa music.

Croatian Americans have had a significant impact on education in the United States. In 1949, there were nineteen Croatian parochial schools containing five thousand students. Most closed as Croatian children integrated into the American mainstream. Dr. Henry Suzzallo gained recognition as one of the United States' leading educators in the early twentieth century. He served as president of the University of Washington (1915-1926) and then as the head of the Carnegie Foundation for the Advancement of Teaching (1930-1933).

Large numbers of Croatian Americans have distinguished themselves in the world of sports. Drazen Petrovic emerged as a star of the National Basketball Association's New Jersey Nets. During the 1991-1992 season, he averaged 20.6 points per game. He led the Croatian basketball team to a Silver Medal in the 1992 Summer Olympics. Bill Belichick was the youngest head coach in the National Football League when he assumed the helm of the Cleveland Browns in 1991. Boxer Fritzie Zivic was Welterweight Champion from 1940 to 1941.

SUGGESTED READINGS. The best general history of the Croatian people remains Stephen Gazi's *A History of Croatia* (1973). *A Short History of Yugoslavia: From Early Times to 1966* (1966), edited by Stephen Clissold, contains essays on Croatia and Dalmatia by H. C. Darby. Edward Ifkovic's *The Yugoslavs in America* (1977) is written in a popular style. Frances Kraljic's *Croatian Migration To and From the United States, 1900-1914* (1978) studies the impact of the Great Migration on Croatia.—*Thomas D. Matijasic*

Crummell, Alexander (Mar. 3, 1819, New York, N.Y.—Sept. 9, 1898, Point Pleasant, N.J.): African American clergyman and educator. A forceful speaker and literate scholar, Crummell was the tenth black American ordained as an Episcopalian minister (1844). He earned a B.A. at Queen's College, Cambridge, in England (1853), and then served as president of Liberia College in Africa for almost twenty years. From 1872 to 1894, Crummell used the forum of his ministry at St. Luke's Church in Washington, D.C., to advocate "black liberation" in Africa and the United States. He founded the American Negro Academy, which promoted scholarship and intellectualism among blacks.

Crusade for Justice: One of the most successful Mexican American civil rights organizations, founded by Rodolfo "Corky" Gonzales in Denver, Colorado, in 1966. The newspaper *El Gallo: La Voz de la Justicia* reported Crusade activities. In 1968 the group opened a center providing the Mexican American community with social services, cultural programs, and leadership classes. The Crusade hosted the first national Chicano Youth Liberation Conference in March, 1969, which was attended by fifteen hundred youths representing many organizations. In the late 1970's the national political importance of the Crusade for Justice declined.

Cruz, Celia (b. Oct. 21, 1925-1930?, Havana, Cuba): Cuban American singer. In the mid-1940's, Cruz studied at the Havana Conservatory of Music and won a radio talent show. In 1950, she became soloist for La Sonora Matancera, a popular orchestra, with whom she toured the Americas through the next decade. After the Cuban revolution, Cruz emigrated with her band to Mexico in 1960 and to the United States in 1961. She recorded more than thirty albums on the Seeco and Tico labels during the 1960's. Her brand of salsa music, incorporating sacred songs from the Caribbean, made her a favorite among Puerto Ricans and Dominicans in New York City. Cruz was named *Billboard*'s Best Female Vocalist in 1978, and she performed a tribute concert at Madison Square Garden in 1982.

Cuban-American Legal Defense and Education Fund (CALDEF): National advocacy organization founded in 1980. Although among Latinos, CUBAN AMERICANS are known for having the best educations and the highest incomes, they, too, have been the victims of PREJUDICE, DISCRIMINATION, and media STEREOTYPES, especially in certain regions of the United States. CALDEF seeks to help Cubans and other Latinos gain equal opportunities in employment, education, and other areas while informing the public about the problems of their community.

Cuban Americans: While many have become so completely assimilated into American society that their presence is sometimes overlooked, Cuban Americans have made significant contributions and have earned well-deserved recognition for their accomplishments in a variety of social, political, and cultural pursuits. Some of the most prominent Cuban American men include the late Cuban bandleader and actor Desi ARNAZ, Pulitzer Prize-winning novelist Oscar Hijuelos, American Ballet Theater dancer Fernando BUJONES, and Coca-Cola chief executive officer Roberto C. GOIZUETA. In the sport of baseball, notable Cuban-born players include Tony

Cuban American singer and actress Celia Cruz arrives for the screening of The Mambo Kings, *in which she had a cameo role.* (AP/Wide World Photos)

Oliva, Tony Perez, and José Canseco, as well as pitcher Rene Arocha, who defected from the Cuban national baseball team in July of 1991. Notable Cuban American women include salsa musician Celia CRUZ, pop singer Gloria ESTEFAN, actress Maria Conchita Alonso, and talk show host Cristina Saralegui. A Florida-born son of Cuban immigrants, Bob Martinez served as an educator before becoming mayor of Tampa, governor of Florida, and then director of drug control policy under President George Bush. A woman, Ileana Ros-Lehtinen, became the first Cuban American representative to serve in the U.S. Congress in 1989. The accomplishments of these individuals are perhaps even more astonishing because the majority of Cuban immigrants arrived in the United States during the last half of the twentieth century.

Historical Background. Originally inhabited by Ciboney and Arawak Indians, the island of Cuba was claimed and secured for Spain by Diego de Velázquez in 1511. As the island's self-proclaimed independent governor, Velázquez helped colonize and found the principal towns. The Indians were vulnerable to European diseases such as smallpox and influenza; most

died off rapidly within the first six years of colonization. Since laborers were needed to replace the diminishing Indian population, African slaves were brought to the island to work on the *latifundios* (large estates). The Spanish believed that the slaves would be more easily managed than the Indians; further, slaves could be traded for various goods at great profit. After establishing a thriving agricultural economy in Cuba, the Spanish ruled the island for almost four hundred years.

As early as 1868, Cuban separatists plotted to free their island from Spanish rule. The resulting conflict, known as the Ten Years' War, was put down by the Spanish military in 1878. The impulse for independence surged again in 1895, when Antonio Maceo, a young mule driver, took command of a rebel army and led machete attacks against the Spanish. Maceo and his army were unsuccessful. José Julian Martí, the great Cuban poet, writer, lawyer, and revolutionary, lived in the United States from 1880 until 1895, when he returned to Cuba and became a martyr in an unsuccessful revolution against Spain.

The Spanish-American War was precipitated in

January of 1898 by an incident in Havana's harbor. The American battleship U.S.S. *Maine* was blown up, and the explosion was blamed on the Spanish. American troops arrived in Cuba in mid-April of 1898. After a few months of fighting on land, the U.S. Navy blockaded and destroyed the Spanish fleet in Cuba, thus ending the war. The Treaty of Paris, signed on December 10, 1898, declared Cuba, Puerto Rico, Guam, and the Philippines to be U.S. territories. With

rains brought malaria, and impoverished Cubans had no money for medical care.

Seeds of Discontent. Cubans who suffered from disease, poverty, and illiteracy grew to resent the country's powerful elite, led by dictators who lived in grand style on the proceeds of graft and corruption. Many Cubans also resented the United States because it allowed and in some cases encouraged their country's political and economic dependence. These griev-

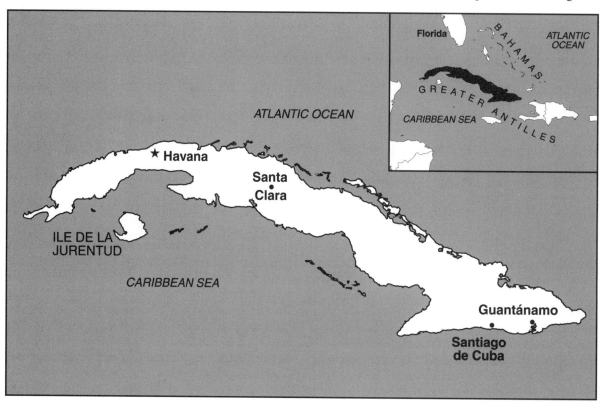

Cuba

this treaty, the Spanish empire lost its final possessions in the Americas. American troops occupied Cuba from 1898 until 1902, when Cuba was declared to be a republic.

Cuba, the largest island in the Caribbean, has a subtropical climate especially suited to agriculture. Sugar has been the country's chief crop and main export product since the eighteenth century. Although the land was rich, many Cubans lived in poverty. Since the sugar crop required only seasonal labor, Cuban peasants were often unemployed for eight months of the year. In 1935, an American commission found that most Cuban peasants were reduced to begging and picking up their food "as best they can." The seasonal

ances finally sparked an uprising against the Cuban government of dictator Fulgencio Batista in 1958. The uprising was led by Fidel Castro, a bearded guerrilla leader who commanded an army of peasants and intellectual rebels. The uprising not only marked a turning point for Cuban government and society but also increased Cold War tensions between the United States and the Soviet Union. With local peasant support, Castro's forces ambushed the national army in muddy Cuban jungles and eventually captured several key Cuban cities. Realizing that his defeat was imminent, Batista fled the island on January 1, 1959.

Upon taking control of Cuba, the Castro government instituted land reform by seizing large estates and breaking them into smaller parcels for distribution to landless families. Roads, schools, and health clinics were built. Fears of Communist influence grew after Castro signed an economic agreement with the Soviet Union in January of 1960 in which Cuban sugar was to be exchanged for Soviet loans, machinery, and technical assistance. This agreement prompted President Dwight Eisenhower to halt all American sugar pur-

problems resulting from a U.S. trade embargo, and Soviet-style central planning, combined with mounting Cold War tensions between the United States and the Soviet Union over Cuba, eventually prompted the immigration of nearly one million Cubans to the United States in the wake of Castro's takeover.

Immigration. Many early Cuban emigrants had taken refuge in the United States during the turmoil

Cuban Americans attend a Cuban Independence Day event in New York City. (Richard B. Levine)

chases in July of 1960. Castro simultaneously accused the United States of economic aggression and began taking over American companies and their holdings in Cuba. Relations between the two countries deteriorated and by October of 1960, Eisenhower broke off diplomatic relations with Cuba.

To shore up the Cuban economy, Castro became more dependent on the Soviet Union. In 1961, he announced his political conversion to Marxism and instituted centralized planning, the closure of newspapers and private schools, and the rationing of food supplies. The loss of political freedoms, the economic

of the Ten Years' War between Cuban separatists and the Spanish military from 1868 to 1878. Warring factions had devastated many tobacco plantations, prompting some Cuban cigar manufacturers to open factories to produce cigars in Key West and Tampa, Florida, as well as in New York City. While some of these emigrants returned to Cuba once it became a republic, many remained. From the turn of the century until Castro's takeover, immigration fluctuated in response to the changing socioeconomic conditions in Cuba.

Cuban immigration swelled in the initial years fol-

Cuban refugee is welcomed by a family member at a Miami terminal. (National Archives)

lowing Castro's rise to power, then waxed and waned according to changes in Cuban and U.S. policies. Many Batista supporters, government officials, and military personnel were among the first to flee to the United States in order to avoid imprisonment or death. Massive migration did not begin until after Castro declared his intention to transform Cuban society along Marxist lines. Between 1959 and 1962, more than 155,000 Cubans left their homeland for the United

States. The Cuban government prohibited immigration to the United States following the Missile Crisis of 1962. In 1965, a special airlift program was agreed to by the Cuban and U.S. governments; during the following eight years, some 260,000 Cubans were reunited with family members in the United States.

The first arrivals to American shores were highly educated, middle- and upper-class professionals and business entrepreneurs who opposed the new revolutionary government. Because they were seen as political refugees fleeing the first Communist regime in the Americas, these Cuban exiles were warmly received. Most Cubans settled in Miami and New York, where they made rapid economic progress and were easily assimilated into mainstream society as well as established enclaves of Cuban-born residents. While many middle-class Cubans were able to find the financial resources to establish restaurants, nightclubs, and retail businesses, others were forced to accept whatever jobs were available and work their way into more suitable employment.

months. As the number of arrivals escalated, it became apparent that Castro had used this opportunity to rid his regime of many unwanted citizens, including convicts and the mentally disturbed. This second wave of Cubans, known as the Marielitos, was the greatest influx of Cuban immigrants to the United States.

Unlike the first wave of Cuban immigrants, the Marielitos had modest job skills and educational backgrounds. During the 1960's and 1970's, nearly 60 percent of the Cuban immigrants who participated in the airlift program were female; more than 70 percent of the Marielitos were male. There was greater ethnic

Hermenegildo and Estrella Rodriguez and their seven children escaped to the U.S. from Cuba in a twenty-foot fishing boat because they wanted their "children to be free." (National Archives)

In May of 1980, Cuban refugees arrived on crowded boats in Key West, Florida, seeking asylum in the United States. Reflecting continued American hostility toward Castro's communist regime, President Jimmy Carter welcomed the new Cuban arrivals with open arms. In the MARIEL BOAT LIFT, an armada of small craft carried 125,000 immigrants from the Cuban port of Mariel to the United States in just a few

diversity than in the previous waves of immigration, since more than 20 percent of the Marielitos were of black Cuban descent. Although the majority were neither marginal to the Cuban economy nor social deviants, the negative label of undesirables was quickly applied to them all. A Coast Guard blockade was hastily mounted to stop the influx, but not before the Cuban population of southern Florida had swollen significantly. Nationally, the Marielitos brought the total number of Cubans to 928,000 (125,000 above the 1982 census figure of 803,000).

Cultural Contributions. Although those who fled Cuba were sometimes forced to give up their life's savings, the immigrants of the first wave were generally well educated and had professional or managerial backgrounds. As a result of these immigrants' economic success, there were 10,000 Cuban-owned businesses in the Miami area in the early 1990's, compared with fewer than 1,000 in 1970. One-third of all construction, including Miami's tallest building, has been financed by the city's Cuban residents.

Cubans have begun to move into suburban areas, and Cuban American family income has been increasing at a faster rate than the average American family income; in addition, their crime rate is well below the norm. Their presence can be felt most in American urban centers. Nowhere is this presence more evident than in the Miami area, where more than half of all Cuban Americans live. An estimated 90,000 (72 percent) of the Marielitos settled in Miami. (Cubans make up 70 percent of all Latinos in the Miami area, attracted by the climate and proximity to Cuba.)

The Cuban impact on Miami has been enormous. Cubans have often settled in blighted areas of the inner city, but their motivation, education, and entrepreneurial skills enabled them to revitalize and stabilize declining neighborhoods. Longtime residents of areas heavily populated by Cubans often credit them with restoring the beauty and vigor of the community. Many Cuban-owned retail businesses are located in the area of Miami known as "Little Havana." The Cuban influence has transformed Miami from a resort town to a year-round commercial center with linkages throughout Latin America. Cubans have also made the city a leading bilingual cultural center, with frequent Cuban festivals and popular music groups such as Gloria Estefan and the Miami Sound Machine. Many non-Cuban Floridians believe that Castro's revolution was the best thing that ever happened to south Florida.

The second largest concentration of Cubans in the United States may be found in and around New York City. More than 80,000 Cubans resided there in the early 1990's, usually close to other Latino groups such as the PUERTO RICANS. Because Cubans have enjoyed high social status throughout the Caribbean for many years, their presence in Latino neighborhoods has brought a new level of leadership and cooperation. As the Cubans began to organize within their new communities, their efforts also helped other Latinos. In one New York neighborhood, for example, an alliance of Latino groups exerted political pressure to improve local schools and increase police protection, while a Cuban bank and the local Latin American Chamber of Commerce worked to encourage successful small business entrepreneurs.

The prospects for a successful future for Cuban Americans is good. In the past, many Cuban immigrants expressed a strong desire to return to their homeland in the event that Castro fell from power. As time has passed and their prosperity has increased, many Cuban Americans probably would not return to Cuba even if the Castro government were overthrown. This is particularly true of the younger generation reared or born in the United States. The desire of most Cubans to become American citizens shows their commitment to live permanently in the United States. The Cuban American population has become a significant political power, particularly in Florida, where the Republican Party counts on the Cuban vote.

SUGGESTED READINGS. For an excellent detailed historical and cultural survey, see Thomas D. Boswell and James R. Curtis' *The Cuban-American Experience: Culture, Images, and Perspectives* (1984). Jose Llanes, a Havana-born social scientist, takes an optimistic view of the Cuban American community and its prospects in *Cuban Americans: Masters of Survival* (1982). For a brief look at the history of Cuban immigration as well as contemporary Cuban American social institutions, see Richard T. Schaefer's *Racial and Ethnic Groups* (1990). *Latinos in the United States* (1980), edited by Carlos E. Cortes, is a rich anthology with useful overviews of Latinos in Florida—*M. L. Miranda*

Cuban cigar making: By the time European explorers of the fifteenth and sixteenth centuries encountered tribal people of the Americas smoking tobacco that had been rolled and twisted into cigars, the tradition was already centuries old. The smoking of cigars soon became a sign of wealth in Spain, then spread to other European countries. Although cigar tobacco is grown in other places (such as Sumatra), it is fitting that what many consider the supreme techniques of cigar making were developed and perfected in Cuba, one of the places where Europeans first encountered people smoking tobacco.

Master cigar makers have spent years learning the subtleties of their craft. It is because of this knowledge that cigar connoisseurs consider Cuban cigar makers to be artists. A master Cuban cigar maker can roll up to 225 cigars a day. When making cigars, or "working up" the tobacco, a cigar maker must first select a binder leaf, then take the long filler leaves in the palm of the hand. Adding tobacco to the bunch, the expert cigar maker can "feel" how much tobacco is needed. The tips of the filler leaves, considered more tender and sweet, must all be at the lighting end of the cigar so the first puff holds the finest flavor. The shape of the cigar must be carefully maintained, and the cigar cannot be packed either too loosely or too tightly. The smoke must travel at just the right pace—not so quickly as to be harsh or burning.

Cigar making was one of Florida's major industries in the last quarter of the 1800's. It made Florida an early industrial center in the South and continued to bring prosperity to the state into the early twentieth century. The heyday of the Cuban-rolled cigar came in the 1920's, when Americans smoked 8.5 billion cigars a year. Florida's cigar industry went into decline with the coming of the Great Depression of the 1930's, the mechanization of cigar making, and intense competition from the cigarette industry.

More Cuban cigar makers came to Florida after Castro's Communist takeover of Cuba in 1959. Some, after first settling in Miami and Tampa, migrated to other major American cities where they established cigar companies to manufacture, sell, and ship cigars to customers from Fairbanks, Alaska, to Paris, France.

SUGGESTED READINGS. For a further look into Cuban cigar making and the development of the cigar industry in Cuba and Florida see L. Glenn Westfall's *Don Vicente Martinez Ybor: The Man and His Empire* (1987). "Reminiscences of a *Lector*: Cuban Cigar Workers in Tampa," in *The Florida Historical Quarterly* 54 (Apr. 1975), by Louis Perez gives an excellent description of Cuban cigar makers. Another good account of cigar making in Tampa, Florida, is *The Cigar Industry of Tampa, Florida* (1939) by Stuart Campbell et al.

Cuban Refugee Center: Established in Miami by President John F. Kennedy in 1961 to help large numbers of refugees from Cuba reestablish themselves in the United States. The Cubans were given food and $100 per month until they could find employment and support themselves. The program was changed somewhat by President Lyndon Johnson to include the resettlement of some Cubans to other parts of the United States.

Cuffee, Paul (Jan. 17, 1759, Cuttyhunk Island, Mass.—Sept. 9, 1817, Westport, Mass.): African American navigator and philanthropist. Cuffee (also spelled Cuffe) was a free black who went to sea as a young man and by 1806 owned considerable property. He used his wealth in various ways to support education and civil rights for blacks. Long before Henry David Thoreau used the technique, Cuffee once refused to pay taxes to protest his lack of the full rights of citizenship; a court eventually upheld his decision. In 1815 Cuffee began a project to resettle black Americans in Sierra Leone, but his health failed and the plan gradually lost favor as the ABOLITIONIST MOVEMENT grew in New England.

Cult of True Womanhood: Set of ideas that defined middle-class women's roles in Victorian America. A "true woman" aspired to be pious, pure in body and mind, submissive, and totally engaged in domestic life. These ideas firmly situated women's place within the home and elevated women's efforts as homemakers and mothers. The prescription obviously excluded many women, particularly those who were poor, enslaved, or wage-earners. Ironically, these same values led some middle-class women into the public arena to promote moral reform, education, temperance, and the abolition of slavery.

Cultural democracy: The idea that people should not be required to give up their ethnic and cultural traditions in order to become a part of mainstream American society. The term is frequently applied to education. Under the concept of cultural democracy, students from different backgrounds (Latino, for example) are not forced to learn only about the mainstream Anglo American culture. Cultural democracy assumes that people have the right, both legal and moral, to maintain knowledge of and identification with their own ethnic values, traditions, and language. It recognizes that people's culturally determined value systems affect the ways they communicate, learn, seek recognition, and ask for assistance. The term "cultural democracy" is often said to have been coined by sociologist Julius Drachsler in the 1920's.

Cultural feminism. *See* **Feminism—cultural**

Cultural pluralism: Interpretation of American cultural diversity that stresses intergroup tolerance and the maintenance of cultural distinctions between groups rather than ASSIMILATION within a common society.

Instead of being viewed as a melting pot in which group differences disappear, American society is considered a cultural mosaic or tossed salad, which preserves the separate identities of various American peoples. Cultural pluralism arose in the early 1900's among social workers such as Jane ADDAMS and sociologists such as Horace Kallen in a reaction against both the melting pot theory and Anglo-conformity (Americanization). MULTICULTURALISM is a late twentieth century outgrowth of cultural pluralism.

Cultural relativism: View that cultural beliefs or traditions are valuable and valid in their original context, regardless of what those outside the culture might believe. Values and beliefs are not inherently true or good; rather, they grow out of the needs of a particular society. Cultural relativists believe that it is not possible for a member of one strong culture to become a member of another while retaining the traditions of the original. Thus, they reject the melting pot theory of cultural blending and the imposition of Anglo-conformity. They argue instead for toleration between groups and for cultural pluralism.

Culture of poverty thesis: Idea that people who live in poverty form a separate culture that cuts across ethnic, religious, and geographic lines. As with other cultures, those who live in the culture of poverty share certain values, family structures, and behaviors in common, and pass them down from generation to generation. Anthropologist Oscar Lewis, who coined the term "culture of poverty," identified some seventy social, economic, and psychological traits shared by the poor. This thesis is challenged by many who believe that it simply replaces older STEREOTYPES about POVERTY with a newer one.

Curanderas: Mexican and MEXICAN AMERICAN folk healers who treat physical and psychological problems with the use of herbs, massages, diet regulation, religious rituals, and prayers. Male *curanderos* or female *curanderas* are believed to have special healing powers from God. Many undergo a period of apprenticeship to an established healer, during which time they learn to identify and treat illnesses, some of which are not recognized by Western medicine. Indian and European beliefs in the natural and preternatural causes of illness are combined with Catholicism to provide a combination of cures used by curanderos and curanderas.

Curtis, Edward Sheriff (Feb. 19, 1868, Madison, Wis.—Oct. 19, 1952, Los Angeles, Calif.): Photographer and writer. Curtis' work documenting the lives of American Indians spanned thirty years, covered eighty tribes, and produced forty thousand photographs. His publications include *The North American Indian* (1907-1911), a twenty-volume set containing fifteen hundred pictures; *Indian Days of the Long Ago* (1914); and *In the Land of the Head Hunters* (1915), a film re-creating the life of the Indians on the Pacific Northwest coast.

Custer, George Armstrong (Dec. 5, 1839, New Rumley, Ohio—June 25, 1876, Little Bighorn River, Mon-

While fighting the Sioux in South Dakota in 1876, George Custer and his entire detachment of more than 200 U.S. soldiers were killed. (Library of Congress)

tana Territory.): Youngest general in the Union army in the Civil War and commander of the Seventh Cavalry in vicious campaigns against Indians. While fighting the Sioux in South Dakota in 1876, Custer and his entire detachment of more than two hundred men were killed by Indians led by Chief CRAZY HORSE at what is now known as the Battle of the LITTLE BIGHORN. This spectacular confrontation is probably the best-known Indian battle in American history.

Czech Americans: The Czech Republic lies in the heart of Europe, east of Germany, north of Austria, and south of Poland. Because it is in the center of Europe, it has often been dominated by other countries, especially the Germanic Austro-Hungarian Empire.

Before World War I, the land that is now the Czech Republic was known as Bohemia and Moravia. Bo-

a rebellion against corruption in the Catholic church. He was executed as a heretic in 1415. This event set off a struggle between Germanic Catholics and Czech Protestants that lasted until World War I.

In 1618, the Czechs ejected their fervently Catholic Habsburg ruler, Ferdinand II. In 1620, the Austro-Hungarian Habsburgs exacted revenge. They routed the Bohemian rulers and forced the Czech people to revert to Catholicism. The entire Czech intelligentsia emigrated to Protestant countries to avoid this fate. Some of those émigrés landed in America by the 1630's.

Young Czech girls present Soviet soldiers with flowers after a bloodless coup in 1989, in which the Czechs overthrew the Communist government. (AP/Wide World Photos)

hemian fortunes peaked in the fourteenth century when the kingdom was ruled by the Holy Roman Emperor Charles IV. He established the first university in Europe, the University of Prague, in 1348. Half a century later, a religious reformer named Jan Hus incited

Czech immigration to the United States continued at a slow and steady trickle until the middle of the nineteenth century. The Revolution of 1848 against the Habsburgs freed the Czech peasants and allowed them to emigrate. Bad economic times in the home-

CZECHOSLOVAKIA

land and promises of open farmland in the United States lured hundreds of thousands of Czechs across the Atlantic.

Nineteenth century urban Czech immigrants settled mainly in Chicago, as well as in New York and Cleveland. Czech farmers settled in Texas, Iowa, Nebraska, Minnesota, and Wisconsin. These immigrants were accustomed to maintaining their ethnic identity under foreign rule. Yet, over the generations, these immigrants and their descendants slowly and reluctantly assimilated into the dominant American culture.

The Czech people are individualistic and contentious. In the United States, Czech immigrants were divided between the Catholics and the anticlerical Freethinkers, for whom Catholicism represented state oppression. It took the establishment of a free Czech state after World War I to unite these two camps. Their rivalry lost its meaning when the struggle between Germanic Catholic forces and the rebellious Czech Protestants finally ended.

After World War I, Czechs gained an independent homeland when they combined with the Slovaks to form Czechoslovakia. This slowed Czech immigration to the United States for a time. Then the Communist coup in 1948 caused many Czech professionals to flee to the United States, as did Soviet repression in 1968. One of these immigrants was Miloš Forman, the director of such films as *One Flew over the Cuckoo's Nest* (1975) and *Amadeus* (1984), who came to the United States in 1969.

In 1989, the Czech people overthrew their Communist government in a bloodless coup that was called the "Velvet Revolution." On the first of January, 1993, the Czech Republic separated from its sister state, Slovakia, in what was known as the "Velvet Divorce."

Meanwhile, in the United States, Czech Americans have seen a revival of ethnic pride. In Nebraska and Texas, they celebrate "Czech Days," when they eat their favorite traditional foods: pork and dumplings with sauerkraut and beer.

D

Dance: There are many different types of dance in the multicultural United States. Some folk or ethnic types are particular to certain groups while others, such as ballroom or rock dancing, are shared by Americans of diverse background. Some uniquely American categories of dance include American Indian traditional dance, African American-inspired tap dance and break dance, and square dance. A rich mixture of the dance steps and styles of many different countries and cultures, American dance is recognized as so unique that it has its own category in international ballroom dance competitions. This essay traces the development of some of these uniquely American dance forms and the influence of ethnic groups on American dance style.

American Indian Dances. Indigenous American Indian dances were not influenced by European FOLK DANCES or imported dancing masters, as were later forms. They were often performed in a circle by males, though females added accompaniment with their voices. American Indian dances reflected traditional life and beliefs, such as celebrating the harvest and the hunt. Ceremonial dances were often performed around tribal totems and had ritual functions. One such dance, the SUN DANCE of the Plains Indians, traditionally involved piercing the skin on the chests of male dancers. Outlawed by the United States government for a period, the Sun Dance regained its popularity in the late twentieth century.

One very important Indian dance was the GHOST DANCE, the basis of a religion founded by the Paiute Messiah WOVOKA in the 1890's. The Ghost Dance sustained the Sioux in their grief over the assassination of their beloved leader, SITTING BULL. Because those who participated in the dance believed so devoutly

At Indianfest in Milwaukee, Wis., Indians teach ceremonial dances to European Americans. (James L. Shaffer)

that the white men would not only disappear from the face of the earth but that their own dead relatives would rise again to rejoin the tribes, the dancers made no retaliatory attacks on the U.S. Army after Sitting Bull's assassination. They believed that those who did the Ghost Dance would be suspended in the air while a new earth was being formed, then set back down among the ghosts of their ancestors on Earth, which would be populated only by Indians. The dancers be-

Scandinavian Americans perform traditional folk dances in America's Midwest. (James L. Shaffer)

lieved that if they wore the sacred garments of the Messiah, which were Ghost shirts painted with magic symbols, no harm would befall them, not even death caused by soldiers' bullets. They danced every day from dawn into the night, even in winter. Army officers considered the dance a disturbance and a provocation. Soldiers attacked Indians merely because they continued to perform the Ghost Dance, leading to the most infamous army massacre in the history of the American Indians, the massacre at WOUNDED KNEE.

Dance remains a central part of contemporary Indian community life. Intertribal POWWOWS feature social dances in circle form that reinforce social relationships. Young people compete in elaborately costumed "fancy dances." Veterans and others have special war dances that only they can do. Though the steps of some Indian dances may appear simple and repetitive, they often have subtle variations in their dignified style.

Early European American Dance. Dance often is not only a reflection of a culture and its religious beliefs but also a reaction to the social climate of its era. In the New England colonies, for example, dance was frowned upon if it was not employed to glorify God. Despite religious prohibitions and sanctions, however, social dance flourished. Wealthy families hired dance instructors from Europe to instruct them in the latest steps, thus planting European dances on American soil. President George Washington was an avid dancer, and he and his wife, Martha, held many balls. Classical ballet, influenced by the French, arrived in America in 1735 in Charleston, South Carolina, and delighted its elite audience. Social dancing became so popular that the military academy at West Point instituted an official course in dance in 1823. Influential dance teacher Allen Dodworth published his *Dancing and Its Relation to Education and Social Life* in 1885, ensuring that the new dances were made respectable for American society.

The waltz, imported from Germany, arrived in America in 1827 and was promptly transformed into its American version. Eventually this was simplified into the popular two-step, influenced by music of American band composer John Philip Sousa. The cotillion, originally a French *contredanse* whose name derives from the French word for petticoat, started out as a dance for four couples and was a precursor of the modern square dance. It was considered more acceptable than the waltz since its partners were required to join together no more than their hands. The faster quadrille traveled west with the pioneers and contributed to the growth of the square dance. A French import and fusion of Scottish lilt, Irish jig, and Bohemian waltz, the polka was a round dance that created more controversy than the waltz, requiring, as it did, that the partners hold each other rather closely.

Early African American Dance. Traditional African animal dances, such as the mosquito dance, the camel walk, and the fish tail, were kept alive in the United States for quite some time with the ongoing arrival of new slaves from Africa. In these dances, the slaves imitated the gait and mannerisms of the animals whose name the dance honored. Later animal dances were performed with furiously fast, grinding motions to ragtime music. Early African Americans also had wedding dances, holiday dances, "crop-over" (harvest) dances, and funeral dances. Such dances intrigued the white masters, who often used the slave dances as entertainment for themselves.

In some early forms of African American dance, the dancers slapped their feet on floorboards or hardened earth, making rhythmic sounds. Later, this rhythmic slapping of the feet was joined with elements of Irish jig dancing, in which the dancer concentrates on blackened faces, were popular entertainment in the early 1800's. They usually ended with a sort of strutting walk for gorgeously dressed couples, with the prize cake going to those with the most inventive steps. The cakewalk, as this dance was called, may have been adopted by African Americans from dances originating with the Seminole Indians. The cakewalk

An African dance company performing in Brooklyn, New York City. (Hazel Hankin)

leg and foot action, keeping the upper body still. This combination became one of the most notable African American dance forms—tap dancing. Born circa 1825, William Henry Lane, or Master Juba, as he preferred to call himself, was one of the originators of what would become modern tap dancing. During his time, Juba was considered one of the best dancers in the country with his syncopated, percussive beat and improvised steps. African American Bill "Bojangles" Robinson would later combine his famous Stair Dance, done on a portable staircase and with a different rhythm for each step, with tap dancing, investing the dance with his own particular style.

As African American ragtime and JAZZ MUSIC became more popular, so did the dances that were inspired by them. Minstrel shows, with white actors in became so popular that it eventually entered European ballrooms, inspiring composers such as Claude Debussy.

Black and Latino Influence on Popular Dances. As African Americans and Latinos became more numerous and visible in American society, they shaped the popular dances of the 1900's. Performed by African American dock workers in Charleston, South Carolina, the Charleston came to the notice of the American public through the Ziegfeld Follies show in 1923. African American Elida Webb claimed to have invented the dance; she choreographed it in the successful stage show *Runnin' Wild*. Dance teachers quickly offered the new dance rage to their students. A fast dance with forward and backward kicking steps, the Charleston included slapping the hands on the body, especially on the knees, while the dancers were in a knock-kneed position. A combination of the two-step and the fox-trot, the Charleston's speed, exuberance, rhythm, and energy was excitingly American. It was so popular that dance halls had to post notices that read P.C.Q. (Please Charleston Quietly), and dancers appeared wearing bandages and braces on their knees from overly exuberant kicking. The dance came to symbolize the Jazz Age of the 1920's and the liberated young American women of that period known as "flappers." African American Josephine BAKER acquired fame and fortune in Europe partly because of her legendary talent with the Charleston.

Dance marathons also marked this period with days- or weeks-long contests in which dancers danced to exhaustion and collapse for prizes. Likened to the Roman gladiatorial contests, the longest marathon on record (listed in the *Guinness Book of Records*) lasted twenty-four weeks and five days before being halted by authorities. The practice was declared illegal in 1933 after a young male participant died after forty-eight days and nights of nonstop dancing.

In 1928, a multiracial marathon featuring Harlem's Savoy Ballroom's champion dancer, George "Shorty" Snowden, started a new dance craze when Shorty decided to fling his partner out and improvise a few solo steps of his own. When asked by a reporter what he was doing, Shorty replied, "the lindy." Swing music, combining popular tunes with jazz rhythms, created new forms of dance such as the jitterbug, also called the lindy or lindy hopping. Consisting of vigorous, frenzied movements to swing music, it broke onto the national scene in 1936. The jitterbug contained what appeared to be two major dance innovations: the "breakaway" or solo part, usually for a male, which was derived from African American dancing and popularized by "Shorty" Snowden; and the "air steps," in which the partners took off from the floor. In addition to the jitterbug, animal dances, and ballroom dances, the 1930's offered novelty dances, many of which returned to the communal round dance. Line dances and circle dances such as the "hokey-pokey," where dancers followed the movements of a leader, and the "boomps-a-daisy," where partners vigorously bumped each other's hips, became popular in nightclubs.

Many Latin American-inspired dances appeared during the same time period. The rumba was a flamboyant, erotic Cuban dance performed to a combined African and Caribbean beat. The conga was the most enduring of the Cuban dances; its participants snaked their way around to a fierce Latin rhythm while performing a one-two-three-kick step. The samba was the Brazilian name for dances originally performed by African slaves as a group dance. In the United States, it was transformed into a couples dance with a distinctive bouncing or dropping action, caused by dramatically bending and straightening the knees. The mambo was a Cuban dance based on African rhythms and invented by black Cuban bandleader Pérez Prado, who syncopated the rhythm of the dances done by sugarcane cutters. The cha-cha was a Latin American dance consisting of two slow steps, three quick ones, and "cha-cha-cha" uttered by both dancers and musicians: It became very popular with the young, who inserted sexy, wiggling variations into the steps. The merengue supposedly came from the Dominican Republic and was a very lively dance with plenty of knee action; it was characterized by the dragging of one foot on each step. Because the Latin American dances were "improved" and taught by formal ballroom dancing instructors such as Arthur Murray, a student of famous American dancer Vernon Castle, these dances stayed in the American social dance repertoire much longer than any of the novelty dances of the same period. Since the mid-1900's, Puerto Rican Americans and large numbers of Latino immigrants have infused the American dance scene with SALSA MUSIC and dance, and a distinctively Latin flair in so-called American social dancing.

Rock and Roll Dances. Once ROCK AND ROLL music took over the country in the 1950's and 1960's, the dances associated with swing, JAZZ, and Latin music disappeared from the youthful crowds frequenting dance halls. Line and circle dances returned in new variations, along with individual dances not requiring partners. Group dancing, as opposed to couple dancing, became one of the hallmarks of the rock and roll age.

Popularized by African American Chubby Checker, who appeared on the television show *American Bandstand* in 1960, the twist became the dance that symbolized an era, much as the Charleston had done for the American 1920's. Its movement was simple: Dancers, with variations such as deep knee-bends, twisted back and forth as if toweling off after a bath. The twist emphasized individual style and skill, though it was done in large groups. Initially condemned by many parents as lewd, the dance quickly spread to all age groups. Dance instructor Arthur Murray com-

During "Semana de la Raza" in Los Angeles, Mexican Americans perform folklórico dances. (Martin A. Hutner)

plained that the twist was not really a dance since it contained no steps at all, only "swivel," but he quickly began offering "six easy lessons for $25."

After the twist, many other rock dances arose that did not involve any steps. In these, the dancers moved various parts of their body, sometimes imitating other, well-known actions. The pony, the locomotion, the swim, the monkey, and the skate were some of these dances. Some movements from dances of the 1920's were reintroduced, as in the discotheque dance called the bump, perhaps a descendent of the earlier boomps-a-daisy. Other dances of the era returned to the communal dances of earlier civilization, as well as to the round dance and the chain dance. DISCO MUSIC AND

siderable acrobatic skill, originated in the Harlem and South Bronx neighborhoods of New York. Its roots could be found in the African American tradition of public competition to show off physical strength and skill. Break dancing began as an accompaniment to RAP MUSIC with its rhythmic, rhyming speech and heavy electronically generated beat. Techniques include lofting, where the dancer dove into the air and landed on his hand with his body and legs still high in the air; the bridge, a backward handstand; and the backspin, where the dancer spun on the floor, using his back as a fulcrum. African American pop singer Michael Jackson and various films helped spread the popularity of break dancing, which became part of the

At a traditional New Year's celebration, Cambodian American children testify to the diversity of dance in modern American culture. (Claire Rydell)

DANCE in the 1970's stressed spectacular couple dancing to loud, fast music with a repetitive beat in elaborately decorated discotheques. Made popular in films such as *Saturday Night Fever*, disco dancing combined steps from Latin American dances with acrobatics.

Break dancing, another type of dance requiring con-

HIP-HOP CULTURE of the 1980's and 1990's.

Square Dancing. Square dances involve four couples in a set whose movements through a variety of formations and maneuvers are led by a caller. The dance most likely to be associated with the United States, square dancing is a mingling and refinement of old French *contredanse* (where dancers faced each other in "contrary" or opposing lines), the quadrille, (where each set of dancers was comprised of four couples), the cotillion (whose steps were called by a leader), and the Appalachian mountain dance, which in turn was derived from Irish, English, and German FOLK DANCES. This unique combination of steps, formations, and "calling" became the American western square dance. The names of the calls clearly announce their European origins: allemande, a counter-clockwise move in which the partners circle one another; the promenade, where the male and female dancers join crossed hands and circle the set; and the do-sa-do, from the French *dos à dos*, meaning "back to back," where two dancers walk toward each other, passing right shoulders, then pass back to back, and walk backward to their original positions.

Square dance callers developed a variety of ways to call the steps, from humorous patter calls to singing calls using the tunes of well-known songs. As square dancing gained in popularity, callers shared their innovations and patterns with each other, spreading their original dances across the country. "Calling" gave the leaders of the dance much initiative and originality. European-trained dance masters, who had once been mandatory for learning dances properly, became unnecessary in American square dancing once the pupils had mastered the basic steps. Because of its options for creativity and mastery, square dancing became a vital and flexible mode of dance that outlasted its predecessors with many regional variations. It remains a popular American pastime and is often associated with senior citizens or rural life and culture.

Ethnic Folk Dance. Virtually every immigrant group that came to the United States brought with it a particular form of FOLK DANCE. Some of these dances, such as the Greek *syrto* or the Serbian *kolo*, are still done in a communal, participatory manner at family and community celebrations, much as they were in the homeland. Other folk dances have been adapted and somewhat packaged for the organized folk dance ensembles that are typically sponsored by ethnic social clubs or religious organizations. These troupes often represent ethnic communities at multicultural festivals. They may range from children performing solo renditions of Irish step dancing to lushly costumed young adults in lively programs of choreographed Mexican folklorico to Jewish students at a Hebrew school who have learned some Israeli folkdances. The ETHNIC HERITAGE REVIVAL of the 1970's inspired many second- and third-generation immigrants to take a renewed interest in the dances of their ancestors.

There is also international folk dancing, which is done by Americans of various backgrounds for social and recreational purposes. It is available on college campuses or in adult education and recreation programs. The origins of these dances are primarily European, with an emphasis on the Balkans. A number of professionally trained troupes perform suites of such dances in major cities.

Ballet, Modern, and Postmodern Dance. Immigrants and ethnic cultures have also played important roles in the development of ballet and modern dance. In the twentieth century, ballet first began to take on a purely American form thanks to Russian-born George Balanchine, who transformed Russian ballet into American idiom when he founded the New York City Ballet and its corresponding school. Balanchine's fusion of Russian classicism and American speed and agility redefined American ballet, influencing dancers and choreographers worldwide. In addition to promoting and transforming the dance styles of many cultures into a style of dance that reflects American manners and character, the New York City Ballet has promoted the careers of many choreographers. For example, ballet master Jerome Robbins choreographed such legendary musicals as *Fiddler on the Roof* (1964), *Gypsy* (1959), and *West Side Story* (1957), all of which identify American dance with showmanship, emotional intensity, explosive power, and agility. Robbins' choreography in *West Side Story*, a musical and film about interracial love, presented male dancing as athletic and powerful, changing the popular American view of male dance.

Arthur Mitchell joined the New York City Ballet in 1955 as the first African American permanent member of a major ballet company. After the death of Martin Luther KING, Jr., in 1968, Mitchell returned to his native Harlem and taught free classes at the Harlem School of the Arts. Mitchell demonstrated that ballet could be a proud, strong, vigorous form of dancing. In 1969, he formed the DANCE THEATRE OF HARLEM to feature a corps of black dancers and artistic interpretations influenced by African American heritage. The free pelvis and back movements of Caribbean and African dance were combined with the elaborate footwork of Balanchine to mark the company's style.

The contribution of modern dance to world culture is distinctly American. African American dance styles and rhythms have been the basis not only for virtually all American popular dance innovations but also for this form of American concert dance. Isadora DUNCAN brought ethnic dance forms to American ballet; to Europeans, she was the "incarnation of pagan America." Duncan came to symbolize the twentieth century's restless creative energy while blazing the trail for continued ethnic exploration and development in modern American dance. Katherine DUNHAM was an anthropologist and dancer who introduced Caribbean forms into the range of modern dance possibilities. Modern dance pioneer Martha GRAHAM drew on diverse cultures for her revolutionary style. Graham's long-time association with Japanese American sculptor Isamu Noguchi inspired her to use nontraditional backdrops in dance performances. In *American Document* (1938), her dances were interspersed with spoken texts from the Declaration of Independence, the Gettysburg Address, and other American writings, forming a new type of dance-drama. Postmodern dance leader Twyla Tharp also seeks uniquely American references, as in her 1972 *Raggedy Dances*, which fused ballet, jazz, and soft-shoe in a new kind of contemporary classicism.

SUGGESTED READINGS. For an in-depth analysis of American ballet, see Robert Coe's *Dance in America* (1985). James Haskins' *Black Dance in America: A History Through Its People* (1990) gives portraits of African American dancers not found in many other sources. On other forms of American dance, consult Peter Buckman's *Let's Dance: Social, Ballroom, and Folk Dancing* (1978), Reginald Laubin and Gladys Laubin's *Indian Dances of North America* (1977), and Hank Greene's *Square and Folk Dancing: A Complete Guide for Students, Teachers, and Callers* (1984).— *Sherri Szeman*

Dance, folk. *See* **Folk dance**

Dance Theatre of Harlem: African American ballet company. Beginning with a primarily African American troupe of dancers with little or no previous training, the Dance Theatre of Harlem evolved into one of the major dance companies in the world.

During the 1950's and 1960's, as a principal dancer with the New York City Ballet under George Balanchine, Arthur Mitchell was one of the few black performers with a major ballet company. In 1968, the assassination of Martin Luther KING, Jr., inspired Mitchell to commit his talents more directly to the betterment of the African American community. With

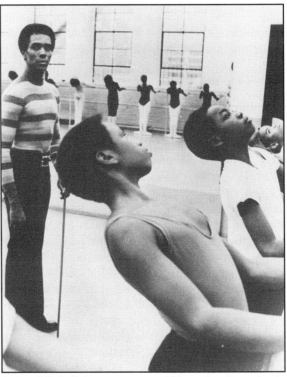

Arthur Mitchell instructs young African Americans in the rudiments of ballet at the Dance Theatre of Harlem's school. (AP/Wide World Photos)

Karel Shook, a former ballet master and choreographer with the Netherlands National Ballet, Mitchell began teaching summer classes in classical ballet at the Harlem School of the Arts. His purpose was to give disadvantaged youths a sense of structure and discipline in their lives. As its enrollment grew from thirty to eight hundred students by the end of the season, Mitchell and Shook recognized the opportunity for establishing a school as a training vehicle for a first-rate black ballet company—only the second known attempt at such an endeavor since the short-lived First Negro Classical Ballet Company of the 1940's.

In 1969, with the initiation of Dance Theatre of Harlem as a nonprofit organization, the school offered classes not only in classical ballet but also modern, ethnic, tap, and jazz dance in the basement of a Harlem church. In 1971, the company moved to a large facility—a renovated garage—and its fledgling professional company of black performers made its debut at the Guggenheim Museum. By the end of the decade, the Dance Theatre of Harlem silenced skeptics by developing into a ballet troupe of international renown.

Each year, the company's school has drawn more than one thousand students of various ages and ethnic groups from across the United States and at least twenty foreign countries. Course offerings have been expanded to include instruction in playing musical instruments, dance notation, music appreciation and theory, sewing, costume design, and stage management. Its multicultural staff has included acclaimed choreographers and dancers such as Istvan Rabovsky, a former star of the Budapest State Ballet, and Tanaquil LeClercq, a former dancer with the New York City Ballet.

The professional troupe remains predominately African American, although it is open to performers of all ethnic groups. Its repertoire includes works from the George Balanchine and Ballet Russe traditions, dances inspired by the cultural traditions of people of African ancestry, modernist revival pieces, and dance drama. The classical work *Giselle*, with its setting relocated to 19th century Louisiana, and a new staging of Stravinsky's *Firebird* remain as two of the company's most acclaimed productions.

The Dance Theatre of Harlem continues to enrich the cultural life of Harlem as well as the rest of the world. It tours internationally more than any other major company with much-publicized excursions to the former Soviet Union, Europe, South America, and South Africa. The success of the company inspired many more African Americans to seek a career in classical ballet than had been possible before the troupe's initiation.

SUGGESTED READINGS. For a comprehensive account of the history of the company, see Ralph Backlund's article, "From a Garage on West 152d Street, a Ballet Company Soars to Moscow," in *Smithsonian* 19 (July, 1988), pp. 28-39. Informative discussions on Mitchell and his company can also be found in Richard Long's *The Black Tradition in American Dance* (1989) and Lynn Emery's *Black Dance in the United States from 1617 to 1970* (1972).

Dancing Rabbit Creek, Treaty of (1830): Treaty between the U.S. government and the CHOCTAW Indians that established the pattern for the removal of whole

After signing the Treaty of Dancing Rabbit Creek in 1830, the Choctaws were forced to walk the Trail of Tears to new lands in Oklahoma—an event commemorated by these Choctaw descendants in 1992. (Elaine S. Querry)

tribes from their homelands to new and distant territories or "reservations" in the nineteenth century. This practice eventually affected the existence of virtually every Indian nation in the United States.

Precontact Choctaws inhabited what is today Mississippi, western Alabama, and eastern Louisiana. By 1830, they had already signed several treaties that federal representatives "negotiated" through bribery, intimidation, and threats. For example, at Doak's Stand in 1820, the Choctaws reluctantly bowed to threats by Andrew Jackson and agreed to exchange more than 5 million acres in the Southeast for 13 million acres in present-day Oklahoma, only to see the U.S. government take back 2 million acres five years later. Stung by what they recognized as deceit on the part of the federal agents, Choctaw leadership adopted a stance of firm opposition to the sale of any of their remaining 10.5 million acres in Mississippi and Alabama. The territory inhabited by the Choctaws was rich and fertile farmland, however, and the government was besieged by white settlers' demands to get rid of the Indians.

The pressures exerted by the federal government to induce the Indians to move west were largely unsuccessful, as few removed of their own accord. The state of Mississippi resorted to enacting a law that made it a crime to hold tribal office and provided for imprisonment of any Indian who attempted to direct, advise, or influence his fellow Indians. Federal agents informed the Indians that all their affairs henceforth would be subject to the regulation of the states. The only federal protection that might still be afforded them was the assurance of permanent possession of and self-government in the new lands offered them in INDIAN TERRITORY.

In the fall of 1830, U.S. government representatives reportedly met with some five to six thousand "Mingoes [Choctaw for "headmen"], Chiefs, Captains, and Warriors of the Choctaw nation" at Dancing Rabbit Creek in Mississippi. The treaty that was presented delineated the plan that the federal agents had held forth as the only possible alternative to state control of Indian affairs. Specifically, the treaty promised that "no state or territory shall ever have a right to pass laws for the government of the Choctaw nation of red people and their descendants; and that no part of the land granted them shall ever be embraced in any territory or state."

Many, if not most, of the Choctaws present at the negotiations flatly rejected the terms of the proposed treaty because they opposed removal from their homes to a distant and, as they viewed it, hostile land. Records reveal that some fifty prominent Indian representatives—those whom the federal commissioners regarded as most disposed to "listen to reason,"—were offered bribes of money and land in exchange for their support. Eventually, 172 Choctaw leaders signed or put their marks to the document on September 27, 1830, and the treaty was formally ratified by the U.S. Senate on February 25, 1831.

In order to maintain the fiction that the removal of the Choctaws (and later the CHEROKEE, Creek, Chickasaw, and Seminole tribes) was not forced, Article 14 of the treaty stipulated that any Choctaw head of a household might remain in Mississippi and receive a "reservation" of 640 acres as long as he or she became a citizen of the state (and thus the United States) and relinquished Choctaw citizenship and the protection it guaranteed.

As a result of the treaty, the Choctaw Indians became the first victims of what was clearly forced removal. The federal government determined that, because the Choctaws were a large tribe, loosely organized politically, and located at a shorter migration distance than the other tribes targeted for removal, the Choctaws should be the first to travel what has come to be known as the TRAIL OF TEARS. The Choctaws were selected from among the FIVE CIVILIZED TRIBES for initial removal precisely because they were most like the whites; they were considered the most "civilized" and amenable to negotiation with the whites. The federal government determined that they were the most susceptible to the bribery, threats, insulting language, propaganda, and military force that were destined to be employed against the Indians in order to take away their lands and resettle them beyond the frontier.

The ultimate effect of the treaty—specifically, the removal of the Choctaws to Indian Territory—was a disgrace to the U.S. government and a catastrophe for the Indians.

SUGGESTED READINGS. A full discussion of the treaty, including its entire text, can be found in *The Removal of the Choctaw Indians* (1970), by Arthur H. De Rosier, Jr. The biography of a Choctaw leader who played an important role in tribal affairs and negotiations of the treaty is *Peter Pitchlynn: Chief of the Choctaws* (1972) by W. David Baird. For further information on this and similar treaties and their continuing ramifications, see Angie Debo's *And Still the Waters Run: The*

Betrayal of the Five Civilized Tribes (1940, repr. 1984) and *The Rise and Fall of the Choctaw Republic* (2nd ed., 1961); Grant Foreman's *Indian Removal* (1932, repr. 1976); James D. Morrison's *The Social History of the Choctaw Nation: 1865-1907* (1987); and Sharon O'Brien's *American Indian Tribal Governments* (1989).—*Ronald Burns Querry*

Danish Americans: In the Middle Ages, Denmark was one of the most powerful empires in Europe. Today, it

Munk led an expedition to Hudson Bay in the early 1600's. In the early 1700's, Vitus Bering, sailing for the Russian czar, explored Alaska and the Bering Sea. Danish immigrants first arrived in the early seventeenth century, when more than a hundred migrated to the Dutch New Netherlands colony. Among them was Jonas Bronck from the Danish-owned Faeroe Islands in the North Atlantic; the Bronx in New York City is named after him.

Immigration and Settlement. There have never been

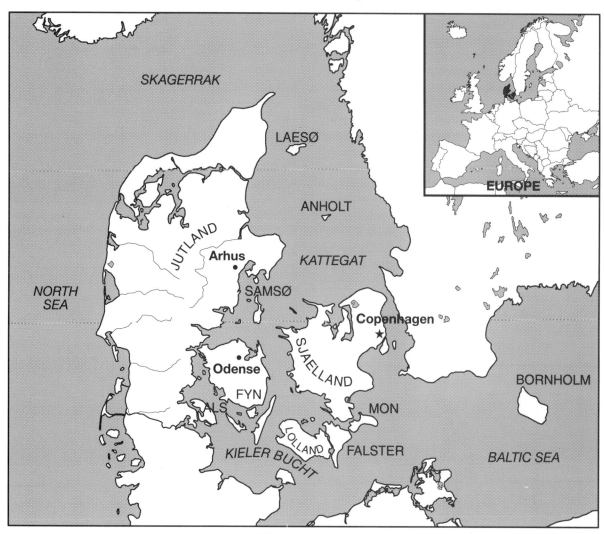

DENMARK

is one of Europe's smallest nations. Because of its high standard of living, its social welfare system, and its valiant conduct during World War II, however, it has a reputation greater than its size.

Two Danes helped explore North America. Jens

great numbers of Danish immigrants in the United States. Denmark is small and has usually had a relatively higher standard of living than most of Europe. With the exception of those in the southern province under German rule, modern Danes have not suffered the upheavals of religious and political persecution that drove many people out of other European countries. Despite their small numbers, however, Danish immigrants and their descendants achieved fame and fortune in the United States.

Before the 1850's, most Danish immigrants were individualists and adventurers. Hans Christian Febiger, called "Old Denmark," was a staff officer to George Washington. Peter Lassen led wagon trains to California and was the first non-Indian to explore much of Northern California; Lassen Peak volcano is named after him. Charles Zanco created the Lone Star Flag of Texas and fought for Texas independence. Chris Madsen served in the INDIAN WARS, as a U.S. Marshal on the western frontier, and a Rough Rider during the SPANISH-AMERICAN WAR.

After the 1840's, Mormon missionaries went to Europe to win converts and bring them to the United States. Denmark then had a new constitution guaranteeing religious freedom, so the MORMONS were not arrested or deported, as they often were elsewhere. Many poorer rural Danes became Mormons and trekked all the way to Utah. By 1900, almost seventeen thousand Danish Mormons had arrived. Because of great distances and poor communications, they often lost contact with home. Mormons of Danish ancestry still predominate in many rural communities of northern Utah and southern Idaho. The majority of Danish Americans, however, are LUTHERANS.

Most Danish immigrants came during the period from 1870 through 1930. By the end of the nineteenth century, almost a quarter million Danes, or about 10

Gutzon Borglum, a Nevada-born Danish American, sculpted some of the United States' most famous monuments, including the presidential heads of Mount Rushmore. (National Park Service)

percent of Denmark's 1900 population, had come to North America. The opening of land in the West, advertisements by railroad and steamship companies, and most important, letters from relatives and friends who had already settled there, attracted thousands of Danes. A large portion of them (listed as German immigrants in the U.S. Census) came from the southern province of Schleswig, which was annexed to Germany in 1864. They resented the enforced use of German language and customs and, most of all, the German military draft. Economic conditions in rural Denmark deteriorated in the late 1800's because of larger families and changes in agricultural exports. This led to the growth of a landless class eager to find new opportunities abroad.

Danish settlements in the United States are scattered throughout the country. Farmers settled in some of the midwestern states, notably Iowa, Minnesota, Nebraska, and Wisconsin. Tradespeople came to the cities, especially Chicago, Milwaukee, Minneapolis, and Omaha. Racine, Wisconsin, has the highest percentage of Danish Americans of any American city. California

While Danish Americans have experienced a high rate of assimilation, they remain proud of their heritage, as these board members of the Danish Brotherhood in America can attest. (Danish Brotherhood in America)

also attracted many Danes; it has the greatest Danish American population of any state. There are also many Danish Americans in Texas, in the New York City area, and in the Pacific Northwest. A few small communities are almost entirely Danish, such as Elk Horn-Kimballton, Iowa; Solvang, California; Askov, Minnesota; Dannebrog, Nebraska; and Danevang, Texas. The Bay Ridge neighborhood of Brooklyn, New York, was once largely Danish and Norwegian.

Community Life and Cultural Contributions. Danish Americans have one of the highest rates of ASSIMILATION and INTERMARRIAGE of any immigrant group, and few speak Danish beyond the first generation. Yet many financially successful immigrants have maintained close ties with Denmark, frequently visiting and in some cases even retiring there. Danish American Max Henius established the Rebild National Park in Denmark and organized its annual Fourth of July celebration, in 1912, the largest such observance outside the United States.

Many Danish Americans have contributed to American society. Gutzon Borglum, born in Nevada of Danish parents, sculpted many public monuments, including Mount Rushmore, which he carved with his son, Lincoln. Sociologist and photographer Jacob A. Riis exposed the problems of slum life in New York City in his book *How the Other Half Lives: Studies Among the Tenements of New York* (1890). Lieutenant General William S. Knudsen came to the United States as a bicycle mechanic, worked with Henry Ford, and became president of General Motors and director of the military's War Production Management Department during World War II. Third generation Danish American Lloyd M. Bentsen, Jr., became a U.S. senator from Texas, candidate for vice president, and Secretary of the Treasury. One of the United States' favorite comedians and pianists is Victor Borge, who arrived as a refugee during World War II.

Despite many Danish Americans' loss of ethnic heritage, most express pride in their ancestry. Some belong to ethnic BENEVOLENT AND FRATERNAL ORGANIZATIONS, such as the Danish Brotherhood in America and Dansk Samvirke. Since the 1970's, a resurgence of ethnic pride and the availability of charter flights has reestablished many Danish Americans' ties to their land of origin.

SUGGESTED READINGS. Dorothy Skårdal's *The Divided Heart* (1964) surveys Scandinavian American immigrant culture. Kristian Hvidt's *Flight to America* (1975) is a detailed sociological study of the immi-

grants, and his *Danes Go West* (1976) is a readable history. John L. Davis' *The Danish Texans* (1979), Ulrik Fries's *From Copenhagen to Okanogan* (1972), and T. Vogel-Jrgensen's *Peter Lassen of California* (1967) describe Danes in the American West.—*Jens Lund*

Daughters of the American Revolution (DAR): Organization founded in 1890 composed of women who are descendants of people who fought in or aided the AMERICAN REVOLUTION. Its objectives are to perpetuate the memory and spirit of those who achieved American independence; to develop an "enlightened public opinion" (in line with George Washington's injunction); to cherish and extend the institutions of American freedom; and to foster patriotism. The DAR has been criticized for its tradition of being an elite WHITE ANGLO-SAXON PROTESTANT (WASP) organization that in the past followed racist policies such as the infamous barring of African American singer Marian ANDERSON from performing in its Constitution Hall in 1939.

Davis, Benjamin O., Sr. (July 1, 1887, Washington, D.C.—Nov. 26, 1970, Chicago, Ill.): African American military pioneer. After serving as a lieutenant in the

Benjamin O. Davis, Sr., the first African American to become a U.S. Army General. (AP/Wide World Photos)

Spanish-American War and joining the regular army as a private (1899), Davis became the first black general in the United States Army (1940). During World War II he returned to duty in the Inspector General's office to work on problems of racial SEGREGATION and DISCRIMINATION in the military. Though critics thought his approach was too conciliatory, Davis helped to accomplish partial INTEGRATION of American combat forces before his retirement in 1948.

Davis, Benjamin O., Jr. (b. Dec. 18, 1912, Washington, D.C.): African American military leader. Davis was the first black graduate of the U.S. Military Academy at West Point (1936) and the first black general in the U.S. Air Force (1965). Shunned by white West Point cadets, he was graduated thirty-fifth in his class. He was a decorated pilot and squadron commander in the Air Force during World War II and in 1965 earned the rank of lieutenant general before becoming a general. After military retirement, Davis served briefly in the city government of Cleveland under Mayor Carl Stokes and on numerous public boards and commissions.

Davis, Sammy, Jr. (Dec. 8, 1925, New York, N.Y.— May 16, 1990, Los Angeles, Calif.): African American singer, dancer, and actor. Often called "the world's greatest entertainer," the versatile, talented Davis began his career in vaudeville, performing in the Will Mastin Trio during the 1930's. After his army service (1943-1945), the trio gained notice in Hollywood clubs and Davis' career rocketed. He recorded hit songs in the 1940's and 1950's such as "Hey There," "Mr. Wonderful," and "Too Close for Comfort." Davis was also successful in nightclub acts; in films, including *Porgy and Bess* (1959); and on Broadway. He had his own television show and appeared in numerous specials. His autobiography, *Yes, I Can*, (1965) was a best-seller.

Dawes Act (1887): Liquidated Indian reservations and replaced them with private property for American Indi-

Assistant Secretary of Transportation Benjamin O. Davis, Jr., speaking before airline officials in 1972, urges resistance to hijackers. (AP/Wide World Photos)

The versatile Sammy Davis, Jr., was often called "the world's greatest entertainer." (AP/Wide World Photos)

ans in the form of individual allotments. Supporters of the act, also know as the Severalty Act, believed that it would hasten the transformation of Indians into civilized members of American society. By dissolving reservations and the wardship status of the tribes, allotment would force an end to the dependence of Indians on the Indian office. As director of the Bureau of American Ethnology John Wesley Powell saw it at the time, little "progress" could be expected until Indians were forced to give up their communal practices. "No measure could be devised more efficient for the ultimate civilization of the Indians," he wrote, "than one by which they could successfully and rapidly obtain lands in severalty."

The act authorized the president to survey reservations, or parts of them, and to assign individual allotments to tribal members who showed sufficient progress toward civilizing themselves. Standard allotments were 180 acres for heads of households; dependents, minors, orphans, and others were to get lots ranging in size from 40 to 160 acres. Lands left over would be thrown open to purchase and settlement by whites. Revenues from those sales would be reserved for the exclusive use of allotted tribes to purchase tools, seeds, and implements; to provide for improvements; and to support civilizing programs. All allottees were granted citizenship at the time they received their land. Finally, in order to prevent alienation of title, a twenty-five-year trust period would keep title to allotments in the hands of the Indian bureau. During that period allottees could not sell, lease, or otherwise dispose of their lands without the approval of the government.

Implementation was swift. Between 1887 and 1921, 117,000 allotments totalling 17.5 million acres were made. Some 48 million surplus acres were opened to whites, and the Indian domain was reduced by more than 50 percent. By 1934, 118 of the nation's 213 reservations had been allotted in whole or part, and 75 percent of all Indians had been affected. While proponents announced that the act was a success, a closer examination reveals serious shortcomings.

Especially critical were the decisions to lower barriers to leasing and selling during the trust period. The first leasing laws were enacted in 1891. By 1925 the Indian office was approving forty thousand leases a year. In 1902 Congress allowed Indians to sell inherited land. The Noncompetent Indian Act of 1907 authorized Indians declared as noncompetent in handling the complexities of severalty (individual ownership) to sell portions of allotments nevertheless. The Burke Act deferred citizenship until the end of the twenty-five-year trust period but lowered barriers to competency, thus encouraging thousands of Indians to claim title long before they could adequately protect themselves against losing their land.

Lowering the Dawes Act's protective barriers proved disastrous. In many communities 70 to 90 percent of allotments were lost. On the Omaha Reservation, 95 percent of those who received title under the provisions of these modifications lost their land. By 1934, two-thirds of all allotted Indians were landless or had too little land on which to make a living. Clearly, the act's original intent had been lost and the incentive to encourage private ownership was largely gone.

By the early 1930's critics launched attacks against the Dawes Act. Describing it as the single greatest disaster in Indian history, reformers demanded its end. Commissioner of Indian Affairs John Collier successfully ended the practice as part of his landmark Indian Reorganization Act of 1934. This act forbade further allotments and authorized the secretary of the interior to buy back parcels of land for tribes. "One becomes a little breathless," said Collier, "when one realized that the allotment law—the agony and ruin of the Indians—has been repealed."

SUGGESTED READINGS. The best general account of allotment is Janet McDonnell's *The Dispossession of the American Indian, 1887-1934* (1991). Fred Hoxie's *A Final Promise: The Campaign To Assimilate The Indians: 1880-1920* (1984) has a brilliant analysis of allotment's failure. Francis Paul Prucha's *The Great Father,* two volumes (1984), remains the best source for understanding policy. Particularly good accounts of tribal experiences under allotment may be found in William Hagan's *United States-Comanche Relations: The Reservation Years* (1976), and Donald Berthrong's *The Cheyenne and Arapaho Ordeal: Reservation and Agency Life in the Indian Territory, 1875-1907* (1976).

Day, Dorothy (Nov. 8, 1897, Brooklyn, N.Y.—Nov. 29, 1980, New York, N.Y.): Cofounder of the Catholic Workers Movement. After college, Day worked as a journalist, later writing for Marxist newspapers such as *The Call, The Liberator,* and *The Masses* (1917-1921), and spending time with progressive thinkers in Greenwich Village in New York City. In 1933, she and Peter Maurin began the Catholic Workers Movement, devoted to helping the poor and pursuing social justice, along with *The Catholic Worker* newspaper. In 1939, they founded St. Joseph's

Cofounder of the Catholic Workers Movement Dorothy Day. (AP/Wide World Photos)

House of Hospitality to aid people who had been hurt by the Depression. Later she fought against U.S. involvement in Vietnam, nuclear war, and fascism. Her books include *On Pilgrimage* (1948), *Loaves and Fishes* (1963), and *On Pilgrimage: The Sixties* (1972).

Day labor. *See* **Migrant workers**

Day of the Dead: Folk celebration of the Catholic holiday All Soul's Day on November 2 to remember one's dead relatives. In Mexico and Mexican American communities, this celebration is known as Dia de los Muertos and is often celebrated with food for the spirits of the dead placed on graves and on specially constructed home altars with candles, flowers, and decorations using skull or skeleton motifs. Far from being macabre, the holiday involves much humor, irony, and joy, recognizing death as an integral part of life. Many Chicano organizations have arranged public activities around the holiday such as parades, art exhibits, and school programs.

Dayal, Har (1884, Delhi, India—1939): Indian revolutionary. A Sikh intellectual educated at the University of Oxford, Dayal became interested in Indian independence and renounced his scholarship. After traveling in Europe, he came to the United States in 1911 to study Buddhism at Harvard University but was soon drawn to California to address the injustices suffered by Indian Americans, particularly agricultural workers and student activists. Dayal organized meetings and raised funds for Indian independence and reform of restrictive U.S. immigration laws. In 1913, he purchased a building in San Francisco where he could publish an Indian language newspaper called *Ghadar*, a word meaning revolt in the Urdu language. Deported from the United States in 1914 as an undesirable alien, Dayal continued his work abroad before retiring to Sweden in 1919.

Declaration of Independence: Founding document of the U.S. government and a central statement of the principles of modern democracy. The Declaration of Independence emerged from the political discontent of England's thirteen American colonies in the 1760's and 1770's. The burgeoning colonial population, angry over taxation without representation, deprivation of liberties, trade restraints, and British military buildup, was ready for separation from the oppressive and exploitive government policies of England's King George.

On June 7, 1776, the Second Continental Congress in Philadelphia considered a Resolution of Independence introduced by Richard Henry Lee of Virginia. Virginia and the New England colonies were supportive; South Carolina and the middle Atlantic colonies were more hesitant. Debate raged among the fifty-five white male delegates over the basic question of revolution, the colonies' interdependence, and the specific form of the declaration that would be issued.

Congress appointed a drafting committee, consisting of Thomas Jefferson of Virginia, John Adams of Massachusetts, Benjamin Franklin of Pennsylvania, Roger Sherman of Connecticut, and Robert Livingston of New York. Jefferson, the second youngest delegate at age thirty-three, was chosen to write the declaration. While showing the influence of such political philosophers as John Locke, the final document is believed to be Jefferson's original composition.

On July 4, 1776, the Declaration of Independence was approved by the Continental Congress, with its president John Hancock of Massachusetts the first signatory. The declaration was publicly proclaimed four days later. Though directed at King George and the English Parliament, it was also clearly a statement of principle to the American people and the rest of the world.

The Declaration of Independence consists of four

sections. First is Lee's resolution, stating the colonies' intent to separate from England. Next is a theoretical discussion of the circumstances under which a people have the right to revolt. These premises are followed by a confirmation that such circumstances exist in the current situation. This is the document's largest section, including eighteen specific charges against King George III. Last is a declaration that the right to revolt is being duly exercised.

Thomas Jefferson, considered the primary author of the United States Declaration of Independence. (White House Historical Society)

Certain concepts and phrases in the declaration have become central to the political philosophy of the United States. The statement that "all men are created equal" posits an incontrovertible natural law; the "right to life, liberty, and the pursuit of happiness" is the cornerstone for American individual liberty. Also articulated are the functions of a government with regard to its citizenry, both as a whole and as individuals. Conversely, a plank that would have censured England for policies encouraging the slave trade was ultimately deleted; while SLAVERY was an important issue, its abolition would have to wait nearly a century. Nevertheless, the libertarian and democratic impulses reflected in the declaration helped spark the French

Revolution in 1789, and inspired the leaders of Latin American independence movements during the 1800's as well as American civil rights leaders in the 1960's.

SUGGESTED READINGS. For a dramatized account of the declaration's origins, see Jim Bishop's *The Birth of the United States* (1976). Carl Becker's 1922 classic *The Declaration of Independence: A Study in the History of Political Ideas* and Garry Wills's *Inventing America* (1979) explore the document's political philosophy. A survey of those involved in framing the declaration is found in C. Edward Quinn's *The Signers of the Declaration of Independence* (1988).

Declaration of Rights of Women (1876): Document prepared by the NATIONAL WOMAN SUFFRAGE ASSOCIATION. The group met at the country's first centennial celebration in Philadelphia, Pennsylvania, to plan an event to publicize the inequitable political status of women. They created a three-foot-long scroll which listed the rights overdue to women. These included no taxation without representation and the repeal of the word "male" in the Constitution. The women were officially denied the opportunity to present the document, but on July 4, five women led by Susan B. ANTHONY and Matilda Joslyn Gage mounted the platform and presented the scroll to the presiding official, who accepted it without comment.

Del Amo Foundation: Established in California by Dr. Gregorio del Amo in 1929 to promote cultural relations between Spain and Southern California. To accomplish this goal, the foundation grants scholarships to American students who wish to study in Spain. The foundation also provides facilities for Spanish people who wish to increase and broaden their knowledge in the United States.

Delano grape strike (1965-1970): Strike begun by Filipinos of the Agricultural Workers Organizing Committee (AWOC) in the San Joaquin Valley, who demanded the same wages as Mexican workers in the BRACERO PROGRAM. On September 16, 1965, members of the National Farm Workers Association joined the strike, led by César CHÁVEZ. The strikers used a red flag with a thunderbird as their symbol, together with a banner of the Mexican Catholic image of La Virgen de Guadalupe. The AWOC and NFWA merged into the United Farm Workers Organizing Committee (UFWOC). Farm workers voted to be represented by UFWOC rather than the Teamsters union. The strike ended in 1970 with growers signing agreements with the new UFWOC. The pro-

Labor leader César Chávez helped spearhead the effort to organize a consumer boycott of table grapes in support of the Delano grape strike waged by farm workers from 1965 to 1970. (AP/Wide World Photos)

longed strike raised Americans' awareness of farm workers' needs and paved the way for gains made by the UNITED FARM WORKERS in the 1970's.

Delany, Martin Robison (May 6, 1812, Charles Town, Va. [now W. Va.]—Jan. 24, 1885, Xenia, Ohio): African American leader. Born a free black, Delaney studied medicine at Harvard University. He advocated practical solutions to the "Negro problem" such as education, job training, and ownership of property and businesses. In the 1850's he supported repatriating blacks to the Niger valley in Africa. He became an army doctor in the Civil War and then a Republican official and judge in Charleston, South Carolina, where he lost the race for lieutenant governor of the state in 1874. Author of *Principia of Ethnology: The Origin of Races and Color* (1879), Delany is known for calling American Negroes "a nation within a nation"—an idea that was to inspire later black nationalist movements.

De la Renta, Oscar (b. July 22, 1932, Santo Domingo, Dominican Republic): Dominican American fashion designer. After studying at Santo Domingo University and in Madrid, de la Renta began his fashion career with Balenciaga in Madrid and at Lanvin in Paris. He came to New York in the early 1960's, and was successively a partner at Jane Derby, Inc., and a designer with Eliza-

Dominican-born Oscar de la Renta, a leading figure in fashion. (AP/Wide World Photos)

beth Arden before establishing his own lines and company in 1969. Considered a leading figure in the international fashion world, de la Renta's numerous honors include the Nieman-Marcus Award in 1968, election to the Coty Hall of Fame in 1973, the Jack Dempsey Award for Humanitarianism in 1988, and a Lifetime Achievement Award in 1990 from the Council of Fashion Designers of America.

Deloria, Ella Cara (Anpetu Wate Win, "Beautiful Day Woman"; Jan. 30, 1888, Yankton Indian Reservation, S. Dak.—Feb. 12, 1971, Tripp, S. Dak.): American Indian linguist and anthropologist. Deloria attended the Dakota reservation's mission school as a child and later earned a scholarship to OBERLIN COLLEGE in Ohio. In 1932 she published *Dakota Texts,* a collection of traditional myths and stories compiled through interviews with her people. In 1941 she and anthropologist Franz Boas published a book on Dakota grammar; in 1944 she wrote another linguistic study, *Speaking of Indians.* Much of her work illuminated Dakota culture from a woman's perspective.

Deloria, Vine, Jr.: (b. Mar. 26, 1933, Martin, S. Dak.) American Indian political scientist, author, and leader. Born in a border town on the Pine Ridge Indian Reservation, South Dakota, Deloria, a Standing Red Rock Sioux, is descended from a distinguished family of scholars, clergy, and warrior chiefs. A political science educator and writer, his best-known book is *Custer Died for Your Sins: An Indian Manifesto* (1969). Some of his other publications are *Behind the Trail of Broken Treaties: An Indian Declaration of Independence* (1974), *The Metaphysics of Modern Existence* (1979), and *American Indians, American Justice* (1983). The former Executive Director of the National Congress of American Indians, he heads the Institute for Development of Indian Law and has been instrumental in shaping the direction of American Indians in the twentieth century.

De Mille, Agnes (Sept. 18, 1905, New York, N.Y.—Oct. 7, 1993, Greenwich Village, N.Y.): Choreographer. Using dance and music as an integral part of dramatic action, de Mille changed the face of American musicals. Among the musicals and ballets she choreographed were *Oklahoma!* (1943), *Carousel* (1945), *Brigadoon* (1947), the influential *Rodeo* (1942, to Aaron Copland's score) and *Fall River Legend* (1948), the story of Lizzie Borden. As a member of the National Advisory Council of Performing Arts and the Committee for the National Endowment of the Arts, she helped increase federal aid for the performing arts.

Democratic Party: One of the two major political parties in the United States, first established by Thomas Jefferson as an antimonarchist popular government and ironically called "republican." Not until 1829, with the election of Andrew Jackson to the White House, did the various political factions that joined to elect him agree on the name Democrat and adopt the donkey as their national symbol.

Agrarian, conservative, and antiprotectionist, the Democrats lost only two presidential elections be-

tween 1829 and 1860. The split in the party over slavery, however, and the debacle of the CIVIL WAR seriously damaged the Democrats, and from 1860 to 1900 they held the White House only twice. Even so, their political strength was solid in the South, where most Southerners associated the Republicans with Radical RECONSTRUCTION and blamed them for the war itself.

The unbridled economic expansion of the 1920's, the Republicans' failure to impose government regulations on banking and industry, and the resultant GREAT DEPRESSION led to new support for the party. The Democrats recaptured the White House under the leadership of Franklin Delano Roosevelt, whose NEW DEAL policies basically defined the modern Democratic Party. Roosevelt's administration also established a new, larger role for the federal government itself by establishing social programs such as Social Security.

Representing organized labor, African Americans, and other minorities, as well as liberals and social reformers, the party accepted the role of federal intervention to alleviate economic inequalities and to protect the rights of individuals (and minorities) against the prejudicial policies often enacted by states.

During the 1970's and 1980's, there was a growing

Choreographer Agnes de Mille changed the face of the American musical. (AP/Wide World Photos)

Franklin D. Roosevelt (shown here with Eleanor Roosevelt and TVA Director A. E. Morgan) instituted New Deal policies that helped define the modern Democratic party. (Tennessee Valley Authority)

conservative movement in the United States, exemplified by the religious right, antitax movements, and the politics of "Reaganism." The Democrats were portrayed by REPUBLICANS as a party that was held hostage by special interest groups and that was on the fringes of mainstream American society. In the late 1980's and early 1990's the Democratic Party concentrated on trying to rid itself of its image (fostered by the Republicans) of favoring high taxes to pay for spending on social programs without alienating its core ethnic and minority constituencies. By representing the rights of racial and ethnic minorities, women, gays, and lesbians, the Democrats tried to rally under concepts such as Jesse JACKSON'S RAINBOW COALITION, but with limited success. It was not until 1992 that voters elected a Democrat (Arkansas governor Bill Clinton) to the presidency for the first time since 1976. Despite its evolving policies through the years, the Democratic Party has maintained its inclusive philosophy as a party that accepts diversity and promotes tolerance and civil rights.

SUGGESTED READINGS. For a history of the modern Democratic Party, see David Sarasohn's *The Party of Reform: Democrats in the Progressive Era* (1989). William J. Cooper, Jr.'s *The South and the Politics of Slavery, 1828-1856* (1978) provides a good overview of the party's antebellum philosophy, while *Search for Consensus: The Story of the Democratic Party* (1979) by Ralph M. Goldman offers a general history. For a more reformist view, see Caroline Arden's *Getting the Donkey out of the Ditch: The Democratic Party in Search of Itself* (1988) and Barney Frank's *Frankly Speaking: What's Wrong With the Democrats and How to Fix It* (1992).

Depression of the 1930's. *See* **Great Depression**

De Rivera, José: (b. Sept. 18, 1904, West Baton Rouge, La.—Mar. 19, 1985, New York, N.Y.): Latino sculptor. Born José A. Ruiz, de Rivera adopted his maternal grandmother's surname. He worked in a steel plant for eight years before executing his first sculptures, small geometric human and animal shapes in highly polished metal, in 1930. That same year, he began formal studies at the Studio School in Chicago. Among de Rivera's notable commissions were his 1938 *Flight* for New Jersey's Newark Airport and a piece for the U.S. Pavilion at the 1958 Brussels World Fair. His first one-man show was in 1946, and significant retrospectives of his work were exhibited at the Whitney Museum in 1961 and 1972.

Desegregation. *See* **Segregation, desegregation, and integration**

Desfile Puerto Ricano: Parade in New York City which takes place on the second Sunday of June each year. Although the parade, which began in 1959, originally focused on Puerto Ricans, over the years it has grown and developed into a more cosmopolitan and multicultural event. The parade features floats and marching bands representing many diverse segments of the city.

Detroit, Mich. (founded July 24, 1701): Dubbed the "Motor City" because of its extensive automobile industry, it stretches for 11 miles along the Detroit River in southeastern Michigan. It is directly across the river from Windsor, Ontario, in Canada. Two politically independent communities, Highland Park and Hamtramck, exist within Detroit's city limits.

The city received its name from the French word *détroit* ("strait" or "narrows") when, in 1701, the early French settlers presumed that the Detroit River was a strait on the Great Lakes. During the nineteenth century, the city attracted large numbers of English, Irish, Canadian, German, and French immigrants, giving the city a 34-percent foreign population by 1900. In the next two decades, as the automotive industry grew, Russians, Poles, Austrians, and Hungarians joined the migration to the city, but restrictive immigration laws during the 1920's stemmed the flow of foreigners.

During World Wars I and II, Detroit's technological prowess made it a major center of the defense industry. In the period from 1915 to 1920, many southern blacks migrated to the city to work in arms factories. More came between 1940 and 1945, this time joined by substantial numbers of Latinos. Many of these mi-

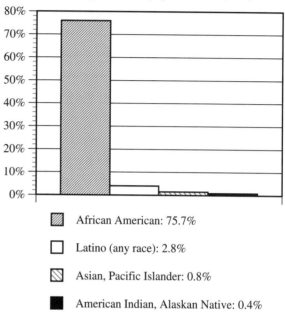

Detroit Minority Population: 1990

Percentages of total population of 1,028,000

African American: 75.7%

Latino (any race): 2.8%

Asian, Pacific Islander: 0.8%

American Indian, Alaskan Native: 0.4%

Source: Data are from *Statistical Abstract of the United States, 1992.* Table 38. Washington, D.C.: U.S. Government Printing Office, 1992.

norities remained in Detroit after the wars. Racial tensions became intense in 1943 and again in 1967, when full-scale racial riots broke out and resulted in the deaths of many people.

Detroit originally appealed to people who wanted economic security. Jobs were plentiful, and salaries were attractive. Those who held jobs usually could count on working steadily until retirement. Some 80 percent of the houses in the city are single dwellings, with 75 percent of these owner occupied until recently. Declines in the automotive industry beginning in the 1980's, however, have threatened job security. Detroit's residential areas have deteriorated. The city's population in the 1990 census was reported to be 1,027,974, down 14.6 percent from the 1980 population of 1,203,368.

The downturn in the automobile industry has not only depopulated Detroit but also exacerbated some of the racial tensions that have been smoldering for decades. As many unemployed members of minorities have moved from the city, whole neighborhoods have been virtually abandoned, severely scarring a city that boasts dozens of extraordinary skyscrapers and the

Workers at the Ford assembly plant in Dearborn, outside Detroit. (Jim West)

world-class Renaissance Convention Center.

SUGGESTED READINGS. An interesting assessment of contemporary Detroit is Donald Finlay Davis' *Conspicuous Production: Automobiles and Elites in Detroit, 1899-1933* (1988). Thomas James Ticknor reviews the effects of the automobile industry in *Motor City: The Impact of the Automobile Industry upon Detroit, 1900-1975* (1978). A sociological approach with strong ethnic overtones is *Metropolitan Detroit: An Anatomy of Change* (1977) by Robert Sinclair and Bryan Thompson. Steve Babson's *Working Detroit: The Making of a Union Town* (1984) is a thoughtful study of the impact of labor unions on the automobile industry, the city, and the state of Michigan. Dominic J. Capeci, Jr., focuses on racial unrest in his *Race Relations in Wartime Detroit* (1984).

Detroit riots (July 23-28, 1967): Worst riots in modern American history until that time in terms of death and destruction. Detroit, the fifth largest city in the United States, was thought to be insulated from civil unrest. The city's African Americans, however, faced with displacement, alienation, and POVERTY, had grown increas-

ingly frustrated with their living conditions. Problems were exacerbated by the lack of minority representation on the police force: only 227 African American officers on a force of 4,356.

The United Community League for Civic Action was an after-hours drinking establishment in the Virginia Park section on the west side of Detroit. On the morning of July 23, a police sergeant led a raid on the club, acting on a tip from an informant. More than eighty African Americans, celebrating the return of two Vietnam veterans, were arrested. A mob gathered, which grew in number and began breaking windows and looting stores. By daybreak, the police commissioner had ordered a full mobilization of the department and called on the African American community leaders to help quell the disturbance.

As reports of looting spread, residents began arming themselves to defend their homes. African American business owners placed signs saying "Soul Brother" in the windows of their shops to discourage potential looters. Restrictions were placed on the sale of gasoline to private citizens to prevent fires.

By mid-afternoon, Mayor Jerome Cavanaugh contacted Governor George Romney and requested that he send in the Michigan National Guard. The total mobilization would reach fifteen thousand people, including federal troops, before peace was restored. Romney declared a state of emergency and imposed a 9:00 P.M. curfew. Both Cavanaugh and Romney had previously verbalized their belief that what had happened in the WATTS RIOTS of 1965 could not happen in Detroit.

Ultimately the rioting covered 14 square miles and triggered minor uprisings in other Michigan cities. The most tragic events occurred during the third day of violence when police, responding to reports of sniper fire, converged on the area around the Algiers Motel and killed three African American teenagers. Although police reports stated that they were killed during a gun battle with police, motel residents claimed that the unarmed youths had been murdered. Officers tried for one of the murders and charged with violating the victims' civil rights were later acquitted.

Statistics portray the grim reality of the riot's toll. Forty-one people were killed, including seventeen looters, two of them white. Of the 347 people who reported injuries, eighty-five were police officers. More than four thousand arrests were made. More than five thousand residents, mostly African American, were left homeless. Fire damage to more than thirteen hundred buildings and destruction of twenty-seven hundred businesses resulted in a total property loss of $500 million.

The special commission appointed by President Johnson to study the riot, the KERNER COMMISSION, issued a report which concluded that "the nation was moving toward two societies—black and white—separate and unequal."

SUGGESTED READINGS. For more information on the Detroit riots see *Voices of Freedom: An Oral History of the Civil Rights Movement from the 1950's Through the 1980's* (1990) by Henry Hampton and Steve Fayer, *The Detroit Riot of 1967* (1969) by Hubert G. Locke, and *Layered Violence* (1991) by Dominic J. Capeci, Jr., and Martha Wilkerson.

DeWitt, John Lesesne (Jan. 9, 1880, Fort Sidney, Neb.—June 20, 1962, Washington, D.C.): Military leader. DeWitt fought in the SPANISH-AMERICAN WAR in 1898 and over the next four decades amassed an impressive list of credentials as an army bureaucrat specializing in logistics. In 1941, two days after the Japanese attack on Pearl Harbor, Lieutenant General

DeWitt was appointed Western Defense Commander. The following year, President Franklin Roosevelt's Executive Order 9066 to protect military installations from enemy aliens gave DeWitt wide latitude for enforcement. He went far beyond designating restricted zones and established systematic procedures for the exclusion, evacuation, and relocation of thousands of Japanese Americans to INTERNMENT camps in California, Utah, Arizona, Idaho, Arkansas and elsewhere for the duration of World War II.

Dewson, Molly: (Mary Williams Dewson, Feb. 18, 1874, Quincy, Mass.—Oct. 21, 1962, Castine, Maine): Social reformer. Influenced by WELLESLEY COLLEGE professor and reformer Emily BALCH, Dewson was active in social services committees just after college. Concerned with the treatment of young female prisoners, she wrote "The Delinquent Girl on Parole" (1911). Her research as secretary of the National Consumer's League led to the first MINIMUM WAGE act in 1912. In 1930 she helped pass the New York law which limited women's working hours. In 1933, with the help of Eleanor ROOSEVELT, she organized the Women's Division, a group dedicated to getting women elected to government positions.

Emily Dickinson as a child. (Library of Congress)

Dickinson, Emily (Dec. 10, 1830, Amherst, Mass.—May 15, 1886, Amherst, Mass.): Poet. Emily Dickinson was a nonconformist from a strong religious and academic background. She eventually moved into isolation, rarely leaving the upstairs rooms of her Amherst home. She wrote close to 1,775 poems, two of which were published in her lifetime without her consent. Her poems are secretive, locked quatrains, the insides of which contain absolute freedom through a use of inner harmonics, unexpected emphasis, and slant rhyme. She corresponded regularly with Thomas Wentworth Higgins, who helped publish her works after her death, despite her wish to have them burned.

Dillingham Commission: Established by Congress in 1907 to examine issues related to immigration. The commission presented a theory that "new" immigrants (those coming after 1883 or so) were different—and less desirable—than the "old" immigrants. The "new" immigrants, according to the commission, were more likely to be single males, unskilled, illiterate, and transient. Even though the commission's own data did not support these claims, this view shaped official U.S. policy and unofficial attitudes for decades. The commission believed itself to be concerned primarily with economic considerations, but many have seen racist motives in its recommendations.

Ding, Loni: Chinese American documentary filmmaker. After producing films such as *Bean Sprouts* and *How We Got Here* about the Chinese experience in America, Ding turned her attention to the experiences of Japanese Americans during World War II. Ding's *Nisei Soldier: Standard Bearer For an Exiled People* (1983) explores the segregation of Japanese American soldiers during World War II, focusing on the 100th Battalion from Hawaii and the 442ND REGIMENTAL COMBAT TEAM. With the support of the National Japanese American Historical Society, she wrote, produced, and directed *The Color of Honor* (1987), a frank examination of the INTERNMENT of Japanese Americans during the war, which was broadcast on public television in 1989.

Dinkins, David N. (b. July 10, 1927, Trenton, N.J.): African American lawyer and politician. After earning a B.S. degree at HOWARD UNIVERSITY (1950) and attending Brooklyn Law School (1956), Dinkins became a partner in a New York law firm (1956-1975). He gradually rose in the world of politics by serving as a district leader in the DEMOCRATIC PARTY (1967) and a state assemblyman (1966) before assuming roles in city government after 1972. In 1986 he was elected mayor of New York City.

Disability rights movement: Organized efforts to promote the human and civil rights of people with physical, mental, and emotional disabilities. Like many social change movements of the 1960's and 1970's, the disability rights movement was inspired by the African American CIVIL RIGHTS MOVEMENT. Advocates believed that people with physical and mental impairments had long been treated as second-class citizens. They were the victims of widespread PREJUDICE, STEREOTYPES, and DISCRIMINATION. They were often kept segregated and hidden from the rest of society and had difficulty gaining equal opportunities in education, employment, and housing, as well as access to public buildings, accommodations, and transportation.

There are an estimated forty-three million people with disabilities in the United States, including about one-tenth of all children and one-fifth of all adults. Part of the struggle of the disability rights movement has been to gain recognition for these people as dignified human beings with the same human rights as able-bodied persons. Activists have discarded pejorative labels such as "crippled" and "handicapped"; many also do not like to be labeled as "disabled," which puts the emphasis on what they cannot do rather than on their many abilities. They prefer to be known

In 1986, David Dinkins became the first African American to be elected mayor of New York City. (AP/Wide World Photos)

Approximately one-tenth of all U.S. children have a disability. (Jim West)

as people with disabilities or the "differently abled." Over the years, the movement has helped to educate Americans about disabilities and to make public attitudes more tolerant. The movement also brought about important legislation to promote the rights of people with disabilities, beginning in the late 1960's and culminating in the landmark AMERICANS WITH DISABILITIES ACT (ADA) of 1990. Enforcement of such laws, however, has lagged, continuing to deprive people with disabilities of certain basic rights.

Historical Background. The roots of the movement date to the end of World War II, when persons with disabilities and their families and allies began to advocate on behalf of disability rights. Prior to that time, public opinion and common practice relegated most persons with disabilities to lifetime stays in large, institutional settings. There, a medical model prevailed that prescribed brief, intensive, introductory periods of therapy. Those who failed to recover quickly found themselves consigned to neglected back wards where their return to mainstream activities remained doubtful, if not impossible.

Following World War II, the upsurge in numbers of VETERANS with disabilities led to major investments in hospitals to accommodate their needs. Yet there was little difference in the treatment offered to veterans with physical and mental disabilities, who were often lumped together. At the same time there was large-scale construction of institutions to house children and adolescents with physical or mental disabilities, whose numbers had also increased.

Many children died from the ravages of severe childhood illnesses prior to the development of antibiotics and sulfa drugs. With the newer treatments and the development of effective vaccines, most children survived. Others, however, suffered brain damage or physical breakdown of a permanent nature, such as paralysis or palsy. Meanwhile, the increase in instrument-assisted births resulted in an increase in brain injury resulting from lack of oxygen. Few families were equipped to care for these children at home, and community services for affected families were nonexistent. Education and rehabilitation of children with

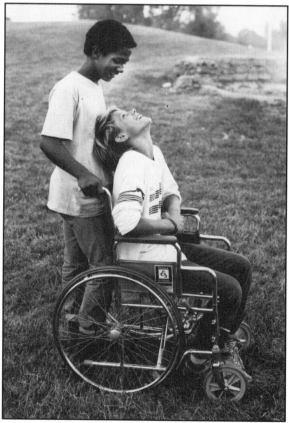

People with disabilities are not "disabled"—they are "differently abled." (Jim and Mary Whitmer)

Persons with Disabilities in the United States by Age Group

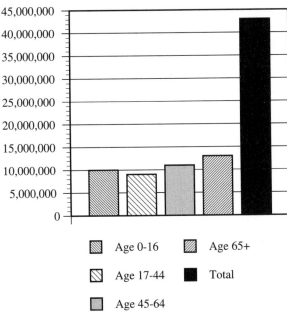

Age 0-16 ▨   Age 65+ ▧

Age 17-44 ◨   Total ■

Age 45-64 ▦

Source: From Gregory J. Walters, *Equal Access: Safeguarding Disability Rights.* Human Rights series, p. 3. Vero Beach, Fla.: Rourke Corp., 1992.

disabilities occurred only in a few enlightened private settings and were not available to middle-class and poor families. Community public policy dictated that all children with disabilties be educated privately or in state institutions for the mentally or physically handicapped, far removed from their home communities.

Following the Korean War and the Vietnam War, the number of VETERANS with disabilities increased exponentially, owing to improved battleground medical care and the policy of immediate medical rotation of the wounded to high technology, intensive care facilities. Theoretically, advances in prosthetic design allowed the returning veterans access to the community, but architectural barriers encountered there made community access virtually impossible. Attitudinal barriers, moreover, intensified the alienation, depression, and anger these veterans experienced after participating in an unpopular war. Mental illness among returning Vietnam veterans soared together with posttraumatic shock syndrome (shell shock), resulting in the overcrowding of psychiatric facilities.

Vietnam War veterans with disabilities, in particu-

lar, raised their voices to protest their exclusion from mainstream society because of architectural and attitudinal barriers. Borrowing techniques from the Civil Rights movement and peace activism and joining the already active parent advocacy groups on behalf of people with disabilities, the disability rights movement was born.

The Move Away from Institutions. Meanwhile, parents and families of severely mentally, emotionally, or intellectually impaired children and adults had begun to resist the SEGREGATION of their offspring and siblings in institutions, where they were neither educated nor treated for their ailments.

Desiring to keep their family members at home, they began to promote public, community-based education for people with disabilities. Advocacy for services and programs that would make it possible for persons with disabilities to remain in their communities also increased. Public attitudes that viewed people with mental or emotional disabilities as outsiders to American society and a threat to the nondisabled population, however, made and continue to make the integration of the mentally or intellectually impaired difficult. It took the movement that began in the 1950's nearly two decades to see the first state laws passed that guaranteed children with disabilities the right to education at public expense. The federal REHABILITATION ACT of 1973 established rehabilitation commissions in the states and territories to provide access to education and training for persons with physical disabilities who were deemed employable. This was followed by the establishment of disabilities councils in 1974 to provide for and educate the public about developmental disabilities (with onset before age eighteen).

The public acknowledgment of the disabilities of their mentally impaired children by famous American families, such as the Robert Kennedys and the Hubert Humphreys, in the 1960's began to break down misconceptions about mental disabilities. The founding of the SPECIAL OLYMPICS by Eunice Shriver and other efforts at MAINSTREAMING persons with retardation bolstered the decision of many families to rear their sons and daughters with mental disabilities at home.

This was followed, in the 1970's and 1980's, by a nationwide deinstitutionalization movement, propelled by advances in psychopharmacology and education. Thousands of people with mental disabilities were released from mental hospitals and left to fend for themselves. Because of the lack of preparation and community services for these deinstitutionalized persons, however, the result was often tragic. Large numbers of them became homeless persons who wandered the streets of urban areas, at great risk to their safety. Public fear of people with mental disabilities seemed particularly entrenched; efforts to establish community residences for them met with particularly vicious response from local communities. So-called snob zoning, restricting the numbers of unrelated persons who could occupy the same dwelling, as well as other artificial, unconstitutional barriers were raised in an effort to discourage groups of persons with disabilities from establishing residences. These NIMBY ("not in my backyard") laws were found unconstitutional by the courts in numerous decisions in the 1980's and 1990's based on the Fair Housing Act of 1984.

Legislation and Public Policy. Meanwhile, people with physical disabilities were increasingly using tactics borrowed from the CIVIL RIGHTS MOVEMENT and other social change organizations. They wrote letters to government officials and staged "wheel-ins" (modeled on lunch counter SIT-INS) blocking the entrance to government buildings to protest public facilities that were not accessible to people with physical disabilities. They formed organizations such as the American Coalition of Citizens with Disabilities to work for changes in government and social policy. They began to be heard more in the media and in public forums on an issue that had previously been prominent only within their own families and communities.

The attention and pressure paid off in new legislation. The ARCHITECTURAL BARRIERS ACT (ABA) of 1968 required all public buildings using federal funds to be accessible, setting new standards, but it was not

Braille typewriters and services have become increasingly available. (James L. Shaffer)

Children with hearing impairments learn with the help of American Sign Language. (James L. Shaffer)

enforced. The stronger REHABILITATION ACT of 1973, patterned after the CIVIL RIGHTS ACT OF 1964, banned discrimination against "handicapped" individuals in all programs that received federal funding, such as schools, hospitals, and transportation systems. Unfortunately, this act was poorly enforced, leading activists to agitate for more legislation and stronger enforcement mechanisms. Families of persons with disabilities had long been concerned about the inadequate, segregated education available to them, often at exorbitant cost. They had a landmark victory in the Education of All the Handicapped Act (EHA) in 1978, which guaranteed a free and appropriate education, from birth to age twenty-one, for all citizens with disabilities. Many concerns of the movement came together in the AMERICANS WITH DISABILITIES ACT OF 1990, which has been called the Emancipation Proclamation for those with disabilities. It protects the rights of this population in employment, government

services, public accommodations, transportation, and telephone services. This was followed by the Civil Rights Act of 1991, which extended the 1978 Civil Rights Act to include persons with disabilities.

Another important achievement of the movement was the growth of independent living programs that allow persons with disabilities to live with dignity and self-sufficiency in appropriate housing and supportive communities. Activists Edward Roberts and Judy Heumann founded the Center for Independent Living in Berkeley, California, in 1972. The center's provision of peer counseling, legal aid, transportation, personal attendant referrals, and many other services drew many young adults with disabilities to Berkeley. The INDEPENDENT LIVING MOVEMENT spread to other cities with both private and publicly funded programs.

The disability rights movement continues to educate the public and push for better enforcement of protective legislation. Many people with disabilities serve on public and private accessibility advisory councils across the United States. Debate continues on controversies in disability rights, such as the MAINSTREAMING of children with disabilities into regular schools and classrooms. People with disabilities are an increasingly visible minority in multicultural American society whose needs and views can no longer be ignored.

SUGGESTED READINGS. A summary of the topic for younger readers can be found in *Equal Access: Safeguarding Disability Rights* (1992) by Gregory J. Walters. For background on the early disability rights movement, see *The Quiet Revolution: The Struggle for the Rights of Disabled Americans* (1979) by James Haskins with J. M. Stifle. Edward D. Berkowitz's *Disabled Policy: America's Programs for the Handicapped* (1987) offers a history of protective legislation. For a view of what movement activists promote, see Charles Goldman's *Disability Rights Guide: Practical Solutions to Problems Affecting People with Disabilities* (2d ed., 1991).—*Barbara Miliaras*

Disco music and dance: A style that originated in the Latino neighborhoods of New York City, especially those in the South Bronx, in the early 1970's. Like its later South Bronx cousin, HIP-HOP CULTURE (RAP MUSIC, breakdancing, and the like), disco began as both a group dance and music, emphasizing synchronized steps, repetitive rhythms, and a bragging-rights contest of individual skills and showmanship. Unlike the political implications of hip-hop, the blatant hedonism of disco made it simply yet another commodity for consumption. Disco's only "social" dimension was its naïve faith in the power of dance music to transcend social conflict, a faith that has characterized American popular music since the 1920's.

In its formative years, 1973-1975, disco was largely confined to the East Coast and, in particular, urban ethnic and gay nightclubs. With the success of Van McCoy's "The Hustle," the Bee Gees' "Jive Talkin'" and K.C. and the Sunshine Band's "Get Down Tonight" in mid-1975, the music and dance exploded into a national multicultural phenomenon. Two years later, the film *"Saturday Night Fever"* and its soundtrack, composed and performed largely by the Bee Gees, became smash hits, propelling disco to international fame.

Disco encompassed more than just rhythmically predictable music, which was frequently written to promote specific dances. It also included codes of

dress, types of nightclubs (discotheques), unselfconscious hedonism, and a certain live-and-let-live attitude. The music, like disco dancing, combined Latin SALSA with Philly soul to create a hybrid genre that was at once formulaic and cross-cultural. As the popularity of disco music and the dances it spawned spread both westward across the United States and eastward across the Atlantic from New York, refinements occurred. In terms of music, there was club disco, Eurodisco, technodisco, and disco rock. In terms of dance, there was the watergate, the shuffle, and various modes of the hustle: American hustle, Latin hustle,

Gloria Gaynor's 1979 recording "I Will Survive" became an enormous hit on the disco music scene. (AP/Wide World Photos)

and California hustle. Given the discotheque format of continuous music and dancing under swirling colored lights and flashing strobe lights, clothes had to be loose and comfortable, yet dressy and stylish; dancers favored colorful shirts and pants, short dresses, and platform shoes whose exaggerated elevation underscored the importance of dexterity.

A representative sample of disco recording stars suggests that disco was the first multicultural pop music. Among the biggest hits from roughly 1975 to 1979 were recordings by African Americans: Donna Summer's sexy send-up, "Love to Love You, Baby," the

Trammps' ferocious "Disco Inferno," and Thelma Houston's "Don't Leave Me This Way." White Americans who scored with disco included the members of such groups as Wild Cherry ("Play That Funky Music, White Boy") and the racially mixed K. C. and the Sunshine Band ("That's The Way I Like It"). Also hitting it big were French, Australian, Caribbean, Hawaiian, and German disco stars.

SUGGESTED READINGS. The most informative books on disco music and dance are Albert Golman's *Disco* (1978), Brian Sherratt's *Disco Chic* (1979), and Jack Villari's *The Official Guide to Disco Dance Steps* (1978).

Discrimination—business and employment: During most of the past three and a half centuries, WHITE ANGLO-SAXON PROTESTANTS (WASPs) composed an official majority of the American population. WASP males largely determined the laws, dominant values, and business practices of both colonial America and the nation. During much of this period women, African American slaves and freedmen, American Indians, members of minority religious sects, immigrants, homosexuals, the poor, children, and the aged, among others, were victimized by overt forms of discrimination that became the norm. The tide began to turn with reform movements of the late 1800's and especially the civil rights struggles of the 1960's. By the 1990's, subtle discrimination still pervaded some parts of the American workplace, particularly at higher managerial levels. Yet this discrimination ran counter to basic tenets of American liberal individualism, popular democratic tendencies, a general egalitarian spirit, and the prevailing understanding of what constitutes legitimate personal rights.

Historical Background. The assertion of the Declaration of Independence that "all men are created equal" and were "endowed with . . . certain unalienable rights," along with Abraham Lincoln's call at Gettysburg in 1863 for "a new birth of freedom," set the tone for American democracy. For many years, however, equality and freedom were not accorded to women and minorities; indeed, laws and institutions such as slavery were put in place specifically to curtail the rights of some Americans.

Appeals, movements, and measures aimed against various types of discrimination and inequality were symbolized late in the eighteenth century in the federal BILL OF RIGHTS (the first ten amendments to the U.S. CONSTITUTION) and in nearly identical state documents. General expansion in American conceptions of individual and collective "rights" continued through the nineteenth century. Notable examples were the ABOLITIONIST MOVEMENT, the growth of the women's SUFFRAGE MOVEMENT after the mid-1800's, the broad implementation of free public education in the 1850's, the emancipation of African American slaves after the Civil War, and RECONSTRUCTION reforms such as ratification of the THIRTEENTH, FOURTEENTH, and FIFTEENTH AMENDMENTS and federal legislation intended to extend civil rights to free African Americans.

African Americans and other racial and ethnic minorities have historically been relegated to unskilled, low-paying jobs; government charwoman c. 1940. (Library of Congress)

The transformation of American society from one that was predominantly agricultural and commercial to one that was overwhelmingly industrial and financial during the late nineteenth century altered the perceptions and the criteria defining discrimination in business as well as other quarters. Early labor unions attacked the individualistic, "hands off" (or laissez-faire) practices of the nation's business world, which was increasingly under the control of large corporations after 1890. There were many demands from within the labor movement beginning in the late

1860's and continuing to the end of the Progressive Era in 1917, for equal pay for women and African Americans, for "a living wage," for shorter hours, for improved working conditions, for the right of all workers to organize and to strike. There were outcries, too, against the exploitation of women and children in the workplace.

A realization of many of these objectives was signalled during the 1930's by passage of important leg-

President Lyndon B. Johnson signs the Civil Rights Bill of 1964, a sweeping bill that outlawed discriminatory practices in employment, among many forms of discrimination. (AP/Wide World Photos)

islation such as the Norris-LaGuardia Act (1930), the National Labor Relations Act (Wagner Act, 1935), and the FAIR LABOR STANDARDS ACT (1938), as well as efforts to make permanent the FAIR EMPLOYMENT PRACTICES ACT between 1941 and 1952. Such legislation paved the way for increases in labor's power over conditions of employment and job security that touched the lives of fifteen million union members, as well as the millions more who made up their families. In addition, these laws established precedents for both more sweeping and more specific assaults on employment discrimination affecting women, African

Americans, and other ethnic minority groups.

American public opinion began to shift increasingly in favor of legislation against employment and job discrimination after World War II. New outlooks were encouraged by wartime labor shortages, the opening of thousands of jobs to women and to minorities, and wide recognition of the contradictions between the American values being fought for abroad and the unconscionable discrimination suffered by Americans at home. It was not until the 1960's, however, that federal sanctions against discriminatory employment and job practices (supplemented by state laws) began to affect nearly every business and job in the country.

Federal policies, along with constitutional amendments and U.S. Supreme Court decisions, exemplify the variety of direct and indirect approaches invoked against discrimination in employment and jobs. Examples include the EQUAL PAY ACT OF 1963, the CIVIL RIGHTS ACT OF 1964, President Lyndon B. Johnson's Executive Order 11245, President Richard M. Nixon's Executive Order 11375, the creation of the EQUAL EMPLOYMENT OPPORTUNITY COMMISSION (EEOC), Supreme Court interpretations of the "due process" and the "equal protection" clauses of the FOURTEENTH AMENDMENT, the Court's decision in *BROWN V. BOARD OF EDUCATION* (1954), and the Age Discrimination Act (1967). Taken collectively these laws, amendments, and judicial rulings afforded all genders, races, and ethnic groups substantive redress from many commonplace discriminatory practices.

Women and Discrimination. In 1973, the AMERICAN CIVIL LIBERTIES UNION (ACLU) reported a consistent pattern of business discrimination against women. Since more than 90 percent of jobs customarily held by women had rarely been occupied by men—housekeepers, nurses, babysitters, maids, receptionists, seamstresses, secretaries, and typists—not only had there been no equal pay for these normally low-paying, repetitive jobs but also there were few comparisons on which to base progress toward wage equity. Women seldom held such relatively high-paying jobs as electricians, long-haul truck drivers, mechanics, plumbers, or construction workers. Moreover, where comparisons could be made, as was true with teachers, professionals, and managers, women were invariably paid less than their male counterparts for comparable tasks and responsibilities—problems that continue in the TWO-TIERED WAGE SYSTEM.

The nation's jobs, in short, were segregated by sex. Women were commonly asked by prospective employers whether they were or intended to be pregnant or whether their household duties required time away from work, questions not asked of men. Furthermore, through the 1960's, many state laws "protectively" regulated women's work, not men's, by prohibiting heavy lifting, overtime, night work, bartending, mine labor, and other jobs during and after pregnancy.

lower federal court decisions broadened the range of such advances by applying new substantive interpretations of the Fourteenth Amendment's "due process" and "equal protection" clauses. Rulings confirming this by 1971 included *Griggs v. Duke Power Co., Phillips v. Martin Marietta Corporation*, and *Rosenfeld v. Southern Pacific Railroad Company*.

In the 1950's and 1960's, desegregation of schools began to open the way to new job opportunities; James Meredith was the first African American to enroll at the previously all-white University of Mississippi. (Library of Congress)

Many companies that never intended discrimination nevertheless discriminated in practice. Requiring college degrees as a condition of employment or promotion excluded many women, particularly ethnic minority women, from jobs and promotions. Having enjoyed fewer educational opportunities than men, fewer women had secured higher educations.

Government took action to provide remedies to this situation. The CIVIL RIGHTS ACT OF 1964, especially its Title VII, struck massively at the discriminatory practices cited above. This included remedies to what lawyers termed the "neutral doctrine"—discriminations that stemmed neither from company policies nor intentions, but which nevertheless resulted in sex discrimination. A number of U.S. Supreme Court and

African Americans and Job Discrimination. Attempts to remedy discrimination against African Americans resulted in two national, so-called Black Reconstructions, the first from 1865 to 1877 and the second from the mid-1950's through the mid-1970's. Pervasive RACISM adversely affected the lives and self-esteem of black Americans. Until it was torn apart, employment and job discrimination would remain only one vital issue on the agenda of the CIVIL RIGHTS MOVEMENT.

By the 1950's, some detectable progress had been made, and by 1980 positive results were apparent. Without appropriate educational qualifications, African Americans in particular found that decent jobs were nonexistent. Since educational qualifications by the mid-twentieth century demonstrably affected people's earnings, BROWN V. BOARD OF EDUCATION and subsequent court decisions desegregating the schools proved vitally important. Public schools were gradually desegregated (at least in law) and colleges and universities, including graduate and professional schools, were opened to African Americans. Partly as a result of desegregation, in the 1960's and 1970's nearly three-quarters of a million African Americans each decade rose economically and entered the middle classes. African American managers such as Yale's Levi Jackson, Cornell's Burke Pierce, and Harvard's Fred Wilkerson became early role models of educational success. Other blacks earned prominence in federal, state, and local civil service and political positions, just as they did in the arts, television, sports, and the military. It is unlikely that these opportunities would have been available without the mobilization of the Civil Rights movement, whose political pressure and clout raised public awareness of the moral, economic, and social costs of discrimination and prompted reforms.

Anti-discrimination actions by the EEOC, Supreme Court reinterpretations of the FOURTEENTH AMENDMENT, the 1964 CIVIL RIGHTS ACT (and revisions of it in 1965 and 1968), the 1965 VOTING RIGHTS ACT, and governmental initiation of effectual hiring, seniority, and promotion quotas all proved valuable agents of change.

Another aspect of government strategy was AFFIRMATIVE ACTION programs, which carried financial penalties for noncompliance where federal funding was involved. By 1990, pertinent American law banned or provided legal redress for employment and job discrimination based on race, sex, or age.

The antidiscrimination struggles of women and African Americans—numerically the country's largest disadvantaged groups—reflected those of Latinos and Asian Americans, as well as homosexuals, older Americans and other minorities. Each group faced unique challenges; many Chicanos, for example, charged that the employer sanctions of the IMMIGRATION REFORM AND CONTROL ACT OF 1986, which forbade hiring undocumented immigrants, led to widespread mistreatment of all Latinos, including the American-born. Homosexuals continue to protest patterns of job discrimination in the health professions, education, and the military, among other arenas.

By 1990, the American workplace was a microcosm of a multicultural society underpinned by a political and legal structure that, while leaving millions uncompensated for past or future losses, outlawed many types of discrimination and weakened manifestations of others. Continuing forms of work-related discrimination such as sexual harassment were still being exposed in the media and defined by the courts in the early 1990's, while women, blacks, and Latinos generally remained underrepresented and underpaid in business and the professions, and subtle types of institutional RACISM persisted.

SUGGESTED READINGS. Of the general works dealing with discrimination, race, class, and ethnicity, one of the best is Richard Polenberg's *One Nation Divisible* (1980). Two balanced studies by William H. Chafe, *The American Woman* (1971) and *Women and Equality* (1977), may be supplemented by Juanita Kreps's *Women and the American Economy* (1977) and Susan C. Ross's *The Rights of Women* (1973); all provide informative, accurate pictures of their subjects and have much to report on employment and job discrimination. Franklin Frazier's *The Black Bourgeoisie* (1965) depicts early experiences and attitudes of African Americans who succeeded in the face of discrimination, while Floyd and Jacqueline Dickens' *The Black Manager* (1982) and George Davis and Gregg Watson's *Black Life in Corporate America* (1982) furnish many examples of the rage, frustration, and bafflement of African Americans who have "made it" in the corporate world yet still deal with attitudes and standards that are residues of discrimination. Studs Terkel's *Working* (1974) is a refreshing collation of multicultural interviews about the affirmations people found in their work.—*Clifton K. Yearley*

Discrimination—ethnic: Practice of applying negative treatment toward individuals of distinct race, color, religion, or national origin. Although ethnic discrimination is related to PREJUDICE, these two terms should not be used synonymously or interchangeably. Whereas ethnic discrimination refers to negative actions or behavior, prejudice refers to negative attitudes toward ethnic groups. Ethnic discrimination in American society occurs in both subtle and overt ways, and it generally involves the belief that ethnic and minority groups and their individual members may be regarded as inferior beings.

Ethnic and Minority Groups. Ethnic groups are composed of members who share a unique social and cultural heritage passed from one generation to another. These groups are frequently identified by distinctive customs and patterns of family life, language, recreation, customs, and values that differentiate them from others. Typically, members of such groups share some sense of identity with fellow members. This ethnic identity may include the perception of differences among ethnic groups; the feelings of belonging to and taking pride in one's distinct ethnic group and cultural heritage; and the perception of prejudice and discrimination against one's own ethnic group. Thus ethnic identity involves both cultural awareness and ethnic loyalty to the group.

One of America's greatest ironies—and hypocrisies—is its belief that it is the land of "justice for all" while ethnic discrimination persists. (Library of Congress)

A related concept is that of MINORITY GROUPS. Sociologists use this term to refer to those groups whose members share various racial, cultural, ethnic, or other similarities that are considered different from or inferior to the traits or characteristics of the majority group (the DOMINANT CULTURE) and, as such, suffer from discrimination. Ethnic discrimination, then, applies to both ethnic and minority groups.

Discrimination takes place at both the individual and group level. Within ethnic and minority groups, there is a wide variation in the degree to which individuals face discrimination. Although ethnic discrimination, like other types of discrimination, is prohibited under state and federal laws, city and county ordi-

nances, and university policies, ethnic groups and their individual members may experience discrimination through overt or subtle actions and behavior.

HATE CRIMES against minorities such as African Americans or Jews may be considered an overt form of ethnic discrimination. Other overt discriminatory actions by the dominant group may also lead to general violence and destruction. For example, in May, 1991, in Washington, D.C., residents and police officers confronted each other during a protest by Latin American immigrants against discrimination. This incident left numerous people injured and much property destroyed. The LOS ANGELES RIOTS of 1992, which participants significantly called a rebellion, were another response to social injustice and unfair treatment of minority and ethnic groups.

Because ethnic and minority groups historically have been perceived as inferior and thus in some way unworthy of holding power in society, these groups have unequal access to various kinds of power. Ethnic discrimination may also produce exclusion or restriction from educational opportunities, jobs, franchise, citizenship, or even specific neighborhoods. In other words, discrimination sets up political, economic, and social barriers for members of ethnic and minority groups.

Political Barriers. These obstacles result from biased laws that deprive certain ethnic and minority groups of services and opportunities, as well as misapplications or violations of the law when directed against these social groups. Since the passage of major CIVIL RIGHTS LEGISLATION in the 1960's, most political discrimination in the United States has taken the form of misapplication or violation of the law, rather than the passage of discriminatory laws per se. Such discrimination may occur, for example, when minorities are prevented from exercising their right to vote, when law enforcement fails to give equal protection to minorities during RACE RIOTS, or when public officials such as judges show partiality and favoritism in applying the law without officially violating it.

Economic Barriers. Creating economic barriers for ethnic groups is another way in which ethnic discrimination in put into effect. This involves any activity or lack of activity that prevents a group of people or its individual members from earning a decent living or attaining other material benefits from society because of their race or ethnicity rather than their lack of training or ability. Such economic barriers are present, for example, when new immigrants are channeled into minimum wage jobs, when employers fail to promote qualified minority members into higher-level positions, and when banks or other financial institutions refuse to lend money to potential entrepreneurs of color who have adequate ability and security to start a business. Certain economic barriers remain very much present in American society even when discrimination appears in more subtle forms. Lack of economic power, some believe, is at the root of many of the social problems that plague some minority communities.

clubs; making it difficult or impossible for members of minority groups to reside in neighborhoods where persons of the majority group live; and behaving in ways that suggest attitudes of superiority and suspicion of minorities, as in assuming that all young black males are dangerous.

Affirmative Action and Other Remedies. Various measures have been taken to eliminate or at least lessen the presence of ethnic discrimination in American society. Policymakers have used categories such as ethnicity to determine the different resources and

The growing number of neo-Nazi groups attests to the fact that ethnic discrimination and racial prejudice remain both strong and dangerous. (AP/Wide World Photos)

Social Barriers. Perhaps nothing does more permanent damage than the social barriers erected against ethnic and MINORITY GROUPS. Such barriers may separate members of an ethnic group from each other as well as from members of the dominant group; indeed, they have the effect of creating a socially underprivileged group. This treatment is closely related to regarding ethnic groups as inferior and is a clear manifestation of PREJUDICE. Examples include denying minorities access to public accommodations or private

needs within a population. Policies aimed at benefiting particular ethnic groups by redressing past injustices are referred to as AFFIRMATIVE ACTION. This concept first appeared in the CIVIL RIGHTS ACT OF 1964, and in 1965, President Lyndon Johnson incorporated it in Executive Order 11246. Under this order, government contractors were not only prohibited from practicing discrimination but also compelled to take the initiative to recruit and hire more minority workers and give them equal treatment on the job without regard to their race, religion, color, or national origin. Since 1965, the concept of affirmative action has been incorporated into legislative acts, executive orders, and court decisions pertaining to equal opportunities in education and employment for all ethnic and minority groups. By the 1990's, affirmative action was a pervasive force in American society. Pro-minority policies were in effect in public housing, private and public employment, higher education, the military, and numerous other contexts.

Courts and government agencies have used various other remedies to end discrimination. For example, injunctions have been issued ordering employers to keep records to ensure nondiscriminatory hiring practices. Furthermore, employers have been ordered to provide back pay and punitive damages for those individuals against whom they have discriminated. They have also been made to provide training programs for minority employees to prompt advancement. Some courts have even ruled that in order to enforce equal employment opportunity where there has been a long record of discrimination, some forms of preferential remedy are needed and mandated.

Preferential remedies have taken a number of forms. For example, courts have required employers to hire on the basis of ratios of minority to majority employees. Employers may be asked to use this ratio until a certain percentage of the total work force consists of minority employees or until a specified number of minority workers are hired. These preferential remedies apply to admission to college and universities as well.

Preferential forms of affirmative action, especially quotas, are the subject of intense debate and controversy. Debate mainly focuses on whether governmental intervention in favor of ethnic groups and minorities should be aimed at equalizing the opportunities for achievement and advancement of members of these groups, or whether those efforts should continue in ways that instead will ensure the equality of achievement itself for the groups, as compared with the majority or dominant group in society. This controversy and all such issues are determined in the Supreme Court, where the constitutional rights of all groups and individuals involved are decided.

If ethnic discrimination is to be eliminated or at least lessened in the United States, all its citizens and residents must come to embrace some form of MULTICULTURALISM with understanding and respect for the "differentness" of each ethnic and minority group. Tragic ethnic clashes and destructive actions, whether overt or subtle, will not cease to occur until the civil rights of all ethnic groups and minorities are fully respected and protected.

SUGGESTED READINGS. For a detailed account of how ethnic awareness has had some healthy consequences but has had its price as well, consult Arthur M. Schlesinger's *The Disuniting of America: Reflections on a Multicultural Society* (1992). *Ethnic Families in America: Patterns and Variations* (2d ed., 1981), edited by Charles H. Mindel and Robert W. Habenstein, offers a collection of essays examining ethnicity, the various liberation movements that have had an impact on ethnic groups, and the problems that come with ethnic diversity in the United States. The fifth edition of George Eaton Simpson and J. Milton Yinger's *Racial and Cultural Minorities: An Analysis of Prejudice and Discrimination* (1985), Lawrence H. Fuch's *The American Kaleidoscope: Race, Ethnicity, and the Civic Culture* (1990), and Ronald Takaki's *A Different Mirror: The Making of a Multicultural America* (1993) offer more complete reviews of racial, cultural, and ethnic issues (including discrimination and its multiple impacts on society) in the United States.—*Maria Isabel B. Villaseñor*

Discrimination—housing: Until well into the second half of the twentieth century, African Americans were denied the right to vote, attend integrated schools, ride in the front of the bus, and buy or rent a home where they wished. For hundreds of years not only African Americans but more than one-sixth of the U.S. population was segregated into limited residential areas. To eradicate this problem minorities have resorted to protest and even violence, sometimes meeting with violence when they integrated a neighborhood. Until 1968 there was no major legislation created to prevent discrimination in housing. Change in housing patterns has been slow and often painful for all Americans.

Historical Background. The basis for housing integration for African Americans started with the passage of the THIRTEENTH AMENDMENT of the U.S. CONSTITUTION, which abolished slavery; the FOURTEENTH AMENDMENT, which guaranteed equal protection under the law to all citizens; and the FIFTEENTH AMENDMENT, which gave African American men the right to vote. During RECONSTRUCTION after the CIVIL WAR, Congress passed a series of landmark Civil Rights Acts to fight racial discrimination. These laws, however, lacked any force because the U.S. Supreme Court decided in virtually all civil rights cases that the decision belonged to the state and that these rights were not protected under federal law.

In 1896 the Supreme Court ruled in PLESSY V. FERGUSON that "separate but equal" was constitutional. This resulted in JIM CROW LAWS that created an atmosphere of open, legal SEGREGATION in every walk of life. The "separate but equal" doctrine was rejected, however, as a defense for residential segregation. In *Buchanan v. Warley* (1917) the Supreme Court ruled that a Louisville, Kentucky, city ordinance that did not allow African Americans to live on any block where the majority of the residents were white or allow whites to reside where the majority of residents were African Americans, was unconstitutional and inherently unequal. The Court also struck down another ordinance barring African Americans from white communities and whites from black communities.

In spite of these favorable rulings, the Court left the door ajar for discrimination by ruling that RESTRICTIVE COVENANTS were legal. Restrictive covenants are portions of the deed that state that the property can never be owned by a member of a minority group. These covenants went with the land; therefore, anyone who bought the property had to abide by the covenant or the violator would be enjoined from selling the

In spite of antidiscrimination laws, many minorities are forced to live in poorly maintained, overcrowded dwellings like these Bronx tenements. (Robert Maust, Photo Agora)

property. In 1926 the Supreme Court reasoned in *Corrigan v. Buckley* that the sale of a house was a private matter that did not involve the state, and therefore, was not protected under the Fourteenth Amendment. Rulings such as this allowed for legal private discrimination, while in discrimination cases in which the state was clearly involved the "separate but equal" doctrine was sanctioned. It was not until 1947 that the Supreme Court ruled that these restrictive covenants were unconstitutional.

The CIVIL RIGHTS ACT OF 1964 prohibited the exclusion of anyone on the basis of race, color, or religion from any program receiving federal financial assistance. This act, however, only fought discrimination in housing that was federally assisted. Other federal statutes followed to help minorities gain equal access to housing.

While the Supreme Court and the federal government were virtually at a standstill on housing discrimination, many individual states and towns took an aggressive stand. In 1950 New York was the first state to pass a comprehensive antibias housing law stating housing discrimination was a form of discrimination. In 1957 New York passed the nation's first law barring discrimination in private housing. This barred religious and racial discrimination in rentals and sales involving all apartment houses of ten or more units. In 1959 Massachusetts, Connecticut, Oregon, and Colorado passed similar antibias laws covering private housing, while California, New Jersey, New York, Washington, Minnesota, and Rhode Island prohibited discrimination in all publicly aided housing. By 1959 fourteen states and thirty-two cities had passed laws or resolutions to combat discrimination in housing.

Then, in 1968, the Civil Rights Act took an affirmative stand on housing discrimination, stating, "It is the policy of the United States to provide, within Constitutional limitations for fair housing throughout the United States." This act outlawed discrimination because of race, color, religion, or national origin in most private real estate actions, whether sale or rental and regardless of whether federal funding was involved. The Secretary of Housing and Urban Development (HUD) was to administer programs to further this purpose and investigate all complaints of residential discrimination, according to Title VII of the act.

Victims and Effects of Discrimination. There was an anti-Asian campaign in the United States that attempted to restrict housing of Asians to certain areas. In 1880 a California statute was passed requiring local authorities to compel the removal of Chinese people to prescribed areas, resulting in compulsory residential segregation.

There were also anti-Jewish barriers found throughout the United States that resulted in many American residential communities being closed to Jews. PUERTO RICANS, MEXICAN AMERICANS, and many other minorities have suffered heavily from housing discrimination.

In the 1950's more than 60 percent of African Americans and Latinos were living in substandard housing because of discrimination. People who were forced to live there suffered from overcrowding, unhealthy conditions, and crime. In the early 1990's Mexican Americans, Puerto Ricans, and African Americans composed more than one-sixth of the U.S. population; in spite of numerous antidiscrimination laws, a large portion of the population was still living in inferior housing. Minorities still live in poorly maintained dwellings plagued by overcrowding.

Some white real estate agents foster the continuation of segregated housing by actively promoting separate housing markets for whites and minorities. They tell white sellers, for example, that the presence of minorities in the neighborhood will lower property values. Even more unscrupulous agents have been known to induce white homeowners to sell by instilling fear in them that their neighborhood is turning into a racially mixed or all-minority neighborhood and will therefore be less desirable. Such techniques can lead to panic selling and can, indeed, lead to the creation of ghettos.

All of society pays a price for the detrimental effects of discrimination in housing. Residential discrimination tends to bring about segregated schools, churches, hospitals, public accommodations, recreation facilities, and civic activities. The victims of housing discrimination suffer from public indignity and humiliation. Some studies have shown that discriminatory practices "have direct and indirect detrimental influences upon the formation and functioning of personalities among individuals subjected to such practices."

Large-scale migration of middle-class African Americans to suburban areas did not occur until well after the advances of the Civil Rights movement in the 1960's. African Americans did not integrate suburban areas until after laws banning housing discrimination came into existence in 1968. Housing patterns depend on factors other than racial discrimination;

among them are economic constraints that restrict the quality and the quantity of housing, as well as individual taste and preference.

The Persistence of Housing Discrimination. Even though minorities are legally able to live anywhere, housing discrimination persists. For example, the Fair Housing Council (FHC) was formed in northern New Jersey in the 1960's to fight housing discrimination, but in the 1980's the area was still plagued by inequality in the sale and rental of housing. In northern New Jersey alone, the FHC investigates approximately two hundred complaints a year and files about twenty law-

This Washington, D.C., rooming house symbolizes the standards of housing segregation before 1968, when the Civil Rights Act provided for fair housing. (Library of Congress)

suits annually. It has found that real estate agents have consistently steered African American clients away from some communities while allowing other areas to integrate steadily.

Another reason that housing or residential discrimination still exists is that middle-class suburbanites often reject the presence of federally subsidized low-income housing in their communities. Many people still harbor the old belief that if minorities move into the area the property values will go down.

Even with laws on the books, many people of color continue to experience discrimination when attempting to buy a home. The NATIONAL ASSOCIATION FOR THE ADVANCEMENT OF COLORED PEOPLE (NAACP) receives daily complaints about housing discrimination. Even in the 1980's and 1990's, whites considering selling their homes to blacks have backed down when threatened with violence by white neighbors; real estate agents have been told in RACIST language to take away black clients; and African American families who moved to integrated neighborhoods have found such things as bags of excrement along with racist messages at their door.

The complete elimination of housing discrimination and segregation in the United States is still unaccomplished, in spite of all the legislation and Supreme Court rulings that have occurred over the years. The goal of the U.S. Department of Housing and Urban Development (HUD) when the Civil Rights Act was passed in 1968 was to create equal housing opportunity, meaning that all individuals of similar income levels in the same market area would have a similar range in the housing market regardless of color, race, religion, or national origin. This has been achieved in part, but discrimination has continued in more subtle ways. The result has been a move from outright segregation to limited de facto segregation in certain areas.

SUGGESTED READINGS. See *Clear and Convincing Evidence: Measurement of Discrimination in America* (1992), edited by Michael Fix and Raymond J. Struyk, and *Combatting Housing Discrimination* (1991) by Michal R. Belknap. *Housing in America* (1973) by Daniel R. Mandelker and Roger Montgomery discusses the growth of substandard housing and ghettos. Two works that examine housing discrimination before the 1960's are *Discrimination, U.S.A.* (1960) by Jacob A. Javits and *Residence and Race* (1960) by Davis McEntire.—*Valerie S. Hartman*

Discrimination—laws: The FOURTEENTH AMENDMENT to the U.S. CONSTITUTION is the legal basis for protection of citizens against the harmful effects of discrimination. According to the amendment, "All persons born or naturalized in the United States and subject to the jurisdiction thereof, are citizens of the United States and of the State wherein they reside." In essence the amendment forbids any state from making or enforc-

ing laws that would abridge the privileges or immunities of citizens of the United States or deprive any person of life, liberty, or property without due process of the law, or deny to any person within its jurisdiction the equal protection of the law.

The guarantee of equal protection of the law is the

NEGRO EXPULSION FROM RAILWAY CAR, PHILADELPHIA.

Discriminatory Jim Crow laws allowed many African Americans to be evicted from first-class accommodations on trains and other forms of public transportation. (Library of Congress)

tool by which the Constitution prohibits arbitrary discrimination, such as laws that seek to restrict people's rights to travel, vote, or marry whom they please. Although the Constitution does not explicitly require the federal government to ensure equal protection of its laws against arbitrary discrimination, the U.S. Supreme Court has held that the Fifth Amendment's guarantee of due process of the law ensures the citizens of the United States equal protection of the law with respect to the federal government.

Historical Background. Before the 1960's, the Supreme Court's standard for measuring whether statutes regulating a particular group or classification of people (such as a particular racial, religious, gender, or marital status group) violated the equal protection guarantee was largely limited to a review of state court decisions. Generally, laws aimed at any particular group or classification were upheld as long as the state could show that the state had a reasonable basis for its classifications.

The development of the equal protection standard began after Congress passed the CIVIL RIGHTS ACT OF 1964, which prohibited discrimination on the basis of race, color, national origin, or religion in most public facilities such as buses or restrooms and in privately owned public accommodations, such as hotels and restaurants. The VOTING RIGHTS ACT OF 1965 authorized federal action to enforce the rights of African Americans to vote. In addition, in 1968 Congress passed legislation that barred discrimination in the sale and rental of housing.

Citizenship and Racial Discrimination. In *Strauder v. West Virginia* (1880), the Supreme Court held that the Fourteenth Amendment assured African Americans all the civil rights and federal government protections that were enjoyed by white persons under the law. The Court emphasized that the amendment not only gave citizenship and its privileges to African Americans but also denied to any state the power to withhold from them the equal protection of the laws; it also authorized Congress to enforce the amendment's provisions. Previously, however, in 1873, the Court had held in the *Slaughterhouse Cases* that there were two distinct types of citizenship, one state and one federal. In the 1873 cases, the court held that the Fourteenth Amendment protected a person only from state infringement on the privileges and immunities of national citizenship such as the right to petition the federal government and the right to vote in federal elections. Thus the Court reasoned that the privileges and immunities conferred by state citizenship were outside the protection of the Fourteenth Amendment.

Education. BROWN V. BOARD OF EDUCATION in 1954 set the stage for the Supreme Court to decide whether public school segregation was per se unconstitutional. A federal district court had found the segregation policies of the school board of Topeka, Kansas, detrimen-

Bella Abzug and other women activists demonstrate in favor of the Equal Rights Amendment—a proposed amendment to the Constitution that was intended to outlaw discrimination based on gender. (AP/Wide World Photos)

tal to black children, although it ruled there was no constitutional violation because black and white primary schools were substantially equal with respect to buildings, curricula, transportation, and teachers. The case *PLESSY V. FERGUSON* (1896) had held that "separate but equal" public facilities for blacks and whites did not violate the equal protection clause of the Fourteenth Amendment. The U.S. Supreme Court, on hearing the *Brown* case, however concluded that in the field of public education, the doctrine of "separate but equal" as set forth in *Plessy* had no place in the United States, for separate educational facilities are inherently unequal.

In *LAU V. NICHOLS* (1974) the Supreme Court held that public schools must make some effort to ensure that its non-English speaking students are equipped with language skills necessary to profit from their attendance at school. The Court based its ruling on the Civil Rights Act of 1964, which forbade discrimination based on national origin, race, or color in any program receiving federal aid. The Court struck down racially discriminatory policies in private education in 1976 in deciding the cases of *Runyon v. McCrary* and *Fairfax-Brewster School v. Gonzalez* (1976).

Travel and Accommodations. The Civil Rights Act of 1875 declared that all persons within the jurisdiction of the United States were entitled to the full and equal enjoyment of the accommodations of inns, public conveyances on land or water, theaters, and other places of public amusement. This was subject only to the conditions and limitations established by law and applicable alike to citizens of every race and color.

Beginning with *Muir v. Louisville Park Theatrical Assn.* (1954), the Court declared that state-imposed segregation in public accommodations and transportation was unconstitutional. An end to state-imposed segregation on public beaches, municipal golf courses, and vehicles of interstate transportation, and in public parks, municipal auditoriums, athletic contests, and seating in traffic court, as well as prisons and jails, was ordered. The freedom to associate with persons of one's own choosing, however, is protected by the First Amendment, up to a certain point. Thus private clubs with racially discriminatory admissions policies are generally considered beyond the reach of the Fourteenth Amendment as long as there is no substantial state involvement in providing essentials such as police protection, electricity, and water to private individuals who discriminate.

Employment. Before 1964 there were so few legal

protections available to prevent employment discrimination that such cases rarely reached the Supreme Court. In 1938, the Court decided in *New Negro Alliance v. Sanitary Grocery Co.* that picketing to force the hiring of blacks was a labor objective within the meaning of the law. In *Steele v. Louisville and Nashville Railroad* (1944), the Court, although it carefully avoided any constitutional issues, compelled the exclusive bargaining agent for a class of employees to represent all those employees fairly without hostile discrimination against any of them. In *Colorado Anti-Discrimination Commission v. Continental Airlines* (1963), the Supreme Court reversed the trial court in holding that Colorado's antidiscrimination law did not conflict with a federal law that might also regulate employment discrimination by airlines.

Title VII of the Civil Rights Act of 1964 prohibited employers of more than twenty-five workers; union hiring halls; and employment agencies from discriminating on the grounds of race, color, religion, gender, or national origin in the hiring, classification, training, or promotion of employees. In 1972 coverage of the act was extended to employers and unions with fifteen or more employees or members, state and local governments, and educational institutions. The act also created the EQUAL EMPLOYMENT OPPORTUNITY COMMISSION (EEOC) to hear complaints about discrimination in employment and seek compliance with the law.

Since the 1970's, the Supreme Court has handed down decisions regarding AFFIRMATIVE ACTION programs, both in employment and in education. In *REGENTS OF THE UNIVERSITY OF CALIFORNIA V. BAKKE* (1978), the Court agreed with Bakke that an affirmative action admissions policy at the University of California, Berkeley, medical school had discriminated against him. In *United Steelworkers of America v. Weber* (1979), however, the Court upheld the legality of a voluntary affirmative action program of Kaiser Aluminum and Chemical Company against a suit by a white employee claiming that it had discriminated against him. The Court's decisions on affirmative action, therefore, have been mixed.

Alienage and National Origin. Congress has the exclusive authority to determine who may enter the country, but once an alien is admitted that person has a right to the equal protection of the laws. In *Yick Wo v. Hopkins* (1886) the Supreme Court held that although a law itself may appear fair and impartial, if it is applied and administered by public authority with an unequal hand, so as to make unjust and illegal discriminations between persons in similar circumstances, the denial of equal justice is still within the prohibition of the Constitution.

During the early 1900's, however, the United States was growing more suspicious of aliens. In response, Congress passed laws requiring the deportation of aliens convicted of crimes and subversive activity. Immigration quotas were established based on national origin, which heavily favored immigrants from northern Europe and eventually barred most immigration from Asia.

The Court used a "public interest test" established in 1877 to forbid aliens to shoot wild game and, thus, to possess shotguns and rifles. (The public interest test, established in *McCready v. Virginia*, provided that the privilege and immunity clause did not invest the citizens of one state with any interest in the common property of the citizens of another state.) Thus the Court condoned state laws that explicitly excluded aliens from enjoying certain activities and from the ability to work in certain jobs and professions. In *Patsone v. Pennsylvania* (1914), the Court held that a state could make laws that discriminated against certain classes of people if the class discriminated against is or reasonably might be considered a group from whom wrongdoing is particularly to be feared. The Court also used this special public interest test in *Heim v. McCall* (1915) and *Crane v. New York* (1915) to uphold the right of a state to confine hiring on state public projects to United States citizens and thus to protect its citizens from the "evil" of competition in the job market. In *Ozawa v. United States* (1922) the court interpreted the federal laws restricting citizenship as allowing only whites and blacks of African descent to become citizens, thus excluding Japanese Americans from citizenship.

With the onset of WORLD WAR II the Court in *Hirabayashi v. United States* (1943) and *Korematsu v. United States* (1944) held that discrimination against Japanese citizens was justified by the necessities of war and the need to protect the country from the possibility that some disloyal JAPANESE AMERICANS might collaborate with the Japanese enemy.

Later, in *Graham v. Richardson* (1971) the court asserted that classifications based on alienage, like those based on nationality or race, are inherently suspect and subject to close judicial scrutiny. The Court found that aliens as a class are a prime example of a discrete and insular minority for whom such heightened judicial solicitude is appropriate.

In *Plyler v. Doe* and *Texas v. Certain Named and Unnamed Undocumented Alien Children* (two cases decided together in 1982), the Court held that illegal aliens present in the United States must be accorded the full protection of the equal protection clause regardless of their legal status. Moreover, the Court decreed, they are clearly persons and may not be denied the right to public education by any policy or state interest.

Sex Discrimination. The Supreme Court's attitude toward women and their role in the political and economic life of the nation generally reflected the prevailing societal attitudes of the times. Relying on this view in *Bradwell v. Illinois* (1873), the Court upheld a state's refusal to admit a woman to the practice of law. In *Minor v. Happersett* (1875), the Court held that although women were citizens, the right to vote was not a privilege or immunity of national citizenship before adoption of the Fourteenth Amendment, nor did the adoption of that amendment add SUFFRAGE to the privileges and immunities of national citizenship; thus, the national government could not require states to permit women to vote or to serve on a jury.

Congress began to act to remedy some of the more obvious inequities based on gender with passage of the EQUAL PAY ACT OF 1963. Title VII of the CIVIL RIGHTS ACT OF 1964 also prohibited employment discrimination on the basis of gender.

In *Griswold v. State of Connecticut* (1965), the Court held as an unconstitutional interference with personal privacy a law that prohibited married couples from using contraceptives. Then in *Loving v. Virginia* (1967), the Court struck down a law that punished persons who entered interracial marriages as violative of the equal protection clause that denied those it affected due process.

In 1972 Congress barred gender-based discrimination in all education programs that received federal support. The following year it approved a bill prohibiting lenders from denying credit on the basis of gender or marital status. In *Frontiero v. Richardson* (1973), the Court observed that a person's gender was a noncontrollable and immutable characteristic. The Court reasoned that what makes gender a suspect criteria for discrimination is that the sex characteristic frequently bears no relation to the ability to perform a job or contribute to society. Statutory distinctions between the sexes often have the effect of invidiously relegating the entire class of women to inferior legal status without regard to the actual capabilities of individual women; thus, such classifications may be justified only by a compelling governmental interest.

The most controversial legal decision of the 1970's vastly enlarged a woman's right to privacy, striking down all state laws banning ABORTION. In *ROE v. WADE* (1973), the Court extended the right of personal privacy to embrace the right of a woman to terminate a pregnancy.

Other Forms of Discrimination. Although discrimination based on relative wealth has not been declared inherently unconstitutional, the Court has found that classifications based on wealth in violation of the equal protection clause work to deprive poor people of certain fundamental rights and interests such as access to justice, right to an appeal, and right to legal counsel based on an inability to pay costs. Regarding discrimination against homosexuals, the Court had no decisive stand by the early 1990's, although some local and state laws were passed to provide protection to gays and lesbians.

SUGGESTED READINGS. For a detailed discussion of the impact of the judicial system upon the rights of individuals, see *The Supreme Court and Individual Rights* (2d ed., 1988) by Elder Witt. *The American Constitution: Its Origins and Development* (6th ed., 1982) by Alfred H. Kelly and Winfred A. Harbison analyzes the document that is the foundation of the American legal system. See *Civil Liberties and the Constitution: Cases and Commentaries* (5th ed., 1986) by Lucius J. Barker for additional details on the refining of the Constitution by case law. For a comprehensive view of the workings of the Supreme Court, see *The Oxford Companion to the Supreme Court of the United States* (1992), edited by Kermit L. Hall. Richard Kluger's *Simple Justice: The History of Brown v. Board of Education and Black America's Struggle for Equality* (1977) analyzes the famous case and its legacy. John Hope Franklin's *From Slavery to Freedom: A History of Negro Americans* (1987) provides additional insight into the legal, political, and social struggle of African Americans to obtain equality.—*Cherri N. Allison*

Discrimination—public education: The denial of equal opportunity in public education because of race, ETHNICITY, religion, language, or gender. Educational discrimination generally takes one of three primary forms: Students may be denied the opportunity to enter a school or program; they may be separated into a program offered only to students of specified racial, ethnic, or other groups; or they may be given lesser or greater opportunities or different treatment within a program.

Discrimination in education can range from the very obvious to the nearly invisible. Blatant examples include SEGREGATED schools; more subtle forms include questions on standardized tests that assume certain cultural assumptions or knowledge that people of one group have but those of another group do not share. The latter is an example of institutional RACISM (or discrimination), which until the late 1960's was not even recognized as a serious and pervasive problem.

In the 1950's and 1960's, the focus of attempts to end discrimination was on discrimination against African Americans. In following decades, however, it expanded to include examination of other biases in the educational system, many of which mirror biases and discriminatory practices in society as a whole. Among these are the STEREOTYPING of gender roles and a lack of equal opportunity for students with disabilities or students for whom English is a second language.

School Segregation. For years—in fact, since the founding of the United States—segregation was simply a fact of life, especially in the South, where African American children were required to attend separate schools. White state and local governments gave their primary attention and the vast majority of their funds to white schools, so schools for black students were far inferior. Even basic necessities such as textbooks could be impossible for African American schools to come by. In 1954, this injustice was finally declared unconstitutional by the U.S. Supreme Court. In *BROWN v. BOARD OF EDUCATION* of Topeka, Kansas, the Court unanimously rejected the earlier principle found in *PLESSY v. FERGUSON* (1896) that "separate but equal" schooling was permissible. In *Brown*, the NATIONAL ASSOCIATION FOR THE ADVANCEMENT OF COLORED PEOPLE (NAACP) successfully argued that separate schooling for African Americans is inherently unequal.

What this decision did not address was the problem that segregation in education could continue, even after desegregation, because of segregated housing. That is, if people of different races live in different neighborhoods (either because of overt racism in housing practices or because of economic disparities between groups), their children will attend different neighborhood schools. Economic segregation is an example of de facto segregation, and its effect on education was not addressed by the Supreme Court until 1973.

The Coleman Report. Ten years after the Supreme Court's *Brown v. Board* decision, the federal government commissioned a research study to see how well desegregated education was working. The results were published in 1966 under the title *Equality of Educational Opportunity*, often referred to as the "Coleman Report" because Professor James Coleman of the Uni-

school if they were from middle-income or higher-income families. They did poorly if their families were in POVERTY. Because of bias in employment or past schooling practices, African American and Latino families are often in poverty.

Diplomas, degrees, and other educational credentials are required for many good jobs and career fields.

In the South, segregated schools for African Americans, such as this one in 1939, often lacked the funds to provide basic necessities. (Library of Congress)

versity of Chicago headed the research group. Their main finding was that the income level or socioeconomic status of the student's family was much more important in predicting school success than race or culture. That is, Caucasian, African American, and other students were generally found to do well in

If schools make it hard for students of one race to get the needed credentials, discrimination in education can lead to discrimination in employment, leading in turn to discrimination in economic matters generally.

Language and gender biases. Non-English speakers and students for whom English is a second language have long been at a disadvantage in educational systems in the United States. Grades have been given without consideration of the possibility that students may know the material but be unable to understand a question or express their knowledge effectively in English. Studies have shown that when test questions are translated into their native languages, such students are able to score much higher. Historically, the use of languages other than English in schools was strongly discouraged. The BILINGUAL EDUCATION ACT OF 1968 attempted to provide equal educational opportunity for students with limited English proficiency. Even into the 1970's, however, school districts in parts of Texas maintained a "no Spanish" rule; the use of Spanish by Latino students was considered a social problem.

Bilingual programs have been developed to provide additional services to students who do not speak English well. Bilingual educators teach in a student's native language while also teaching the English language. One of the most heated debates regarding educational policy in the 1980's was between advocates of bilingual (or multilingual) education and those favoring an "English-only" policy. Those opposed to strictly English-language education called it discriminatory against many intelligent and capable students; defenders of such policies insisted that students should learn English in order to score well on tests as well as to be successful later in life.

Women and girls are another group that has suffered discrimination in public education. One example is in the area of varsity sports, where much larger amounts are spent for boys' teams than for girls' teams. Another example of gender bias is in guidance counseling; boys who do well in biology, for example, might be encouraged to become medical doctors, whereas girls traditionally would most likely be "guided" toward nursing as a profession.

American Indians and educational discrimination. Historically, American Indian students have endured a number of affronts and discriminatory practices. Speaking their native languages was prohibited at reservation schools by the 1880's. Many Indian children were sent to be educated at boarding schools, which attempted the forcible ASSIMILATION of students into American society. Teachers were often either openly or subtly PREJUDICED against Indian students. Indian students also formed one of the groups that was urged by the American educational system into a "track" of vocational education, which would prepare them for

Lacking access to public schooling on their reservations, many American Indian children were sent to boarding schools, as were these Sioux students at the Carlisle School. (Library of Congress)

manual jobs but detour them from the possibility of academic excellence and advancement into professional work.

American Indians were in a unique situation because schools on reservations are under federal control; until the last quarter of the twentieth century, the voices of Indian leaders themselves went largely unheeded in Washington. A 1969 federal report entitled *Indian Education: A National Tragedy—A National Challenge* gained wide attention. It declared that racism and poverty plagued American Indian education; condemned the education policy of the BUREAU OF INDIAN AFFAIRS (BIA); and called for adding Indian history, culture, and language to the school curricula. It was in 1978 that the Education Amendments Act finally gave controlling authority over American Indian schools to local communities.

Another way American Indians have been discriminated against in education is in the way U.S. history courses have been taught. Textbooks often described the westward expansion of the United States as a heroic struggle against bloodthirsty savages. They ignored the fact that, from the American Indian point of view, the advance of the European settlers was a hostile invasion and occupation of their homeland.

Horizontal and Vertical Equity. Various attempts have been made to ameliorate some of the disadvantages of students who have been victims of present or past discrimination. AFFIRMATIVE ACTION programs, for example, may give preference in school enrollment to members of a minority in order to make a school's enrollment racially balanced. People opposed to such practices have used the term "REVERSE DISCRIMINATION" to indicate that they believe it is unfair. Those who favor the use of QUOTAS and affirmation action to give racial balance to enrollments appeal to a dis-

keep students of one race from having appropriate opportunities. Sometimes the additional argument is made that students of a race which has been discriminated against in the past will come into the admissions competition with a deficit because of the effects of past discrimination and should be given a compensating advantage in order to make the process fairer and to hasten the time when quotas and compensatory advantages will be no longer necessary. Bilingual education is one example of an educational program with a vertical equity approach.

To accommodate the diverse cultural backgrounds of schoolchildren in the 1990's, educators have adopted textbooks and instructional materials that incorporate a multicultural perspective. (Hazel Hankin)

tinction between two different kinds of equity: horizontal and vertical. Horizontal equity is equal treatment of equals and is clearly violated by the practice of admitting one student but denying admission to another with equal test scores and other admissions criteria.

Under the vertical equity concept, it is thought to be fair to treat unequals in appropriately unequal ways. The argument is that the racial difference between the two students justifies treating them differently because strict adherence to test scores would

In-School Discrimination. "In-school segregation" can occur if students of one race are assigned to separate programs or ability-level tracks within the school or if preferential treatment is given to one race in regard to participation in curricular and extracurricular activities. Schools have been accused of institutional racism, under which their procedures help students of one race or culture to be more successful than others. For example, if Caucasian children are given the opportunity to participate in after-school extracurricular activities while African American children who have been bused into that school are denied such opportunities because their buses leave promptly after school, the school has a structural feature which gives preference to one race over another.

Closely related to the idea of institutional racism is bias in curricular or evaluation materials. Test questions and textbooks may be written in ways which make it easier for students of one race or culture to understand and use these materials. For example, a book for beginning readers with many pictures of Caucasians and no pictures of African Americans may lead young black students to wonder whether the school program is intended to include people like themselves. Some federal courts have found widely used intelligence tests whose results are used to classify students to be unconstitutionally biased (as in *Larry P. v. Riles*, 1984), while others (*PASE v. Hannon*, 1980) have not.

Teacher expectations can also make a significant difference in student achievement. Some teachers expect more from a student of one race than from one of a different race; some expect more from one gender than the other. Thus, even if a teacher treats all students with respect, there is educational discrimination if the student receives a message that he or she is not expected to do very well.

SUGGESTED READINGS. The effect of teacher expectations is discussed by Robert Rosenthal and Lenore Jacobson in *Pygmalion in the Classroom* (1968). For a teacher's view of how educational discrimination can work against African American students in a school system administered by Caucasians, see Jonathan Kozol's *Death at an Early Age* (1967). For an African American educator's view of the school needs of young African American males, see Jawanza Kunjufu, "Should We Create Separate Classrooms for Black Males?," in *American Teacher*, April, 1990, pp. 74-76. The film *Stand and Deliver* (1987) is a dramatization of the success of a Latino teacher in helping urban Latino students achieve advanced placement credit in mathematics. For a political and philosophical analysis of educational discrimination, see *Education for Whom?* (1974) by Charles Tesconi and Emanuel L. Hurwitz.—*Ward Weldon*

Discrimination—religious: In 1979, the United States COMMISSION ON CIVIL RIGHTS sponsored a consultation entitled "Religious Discrimination: A Neglected Issue"; the title indicates the fact that religious discrimination tends to be less prominent in the national consciousness than ethnic, racial, and gender discrimination are. Nevertheless, religious discrimination is a complicated issue that has affected—and continues to affect—millions of Americans.

It is a paradox that some religious people do hurtful, even vicious, things in the name of religion. Frequently such people have distorted the teachings of their own religion; moreover, people who practice religious discrimination are usually ignorant of other faiths. The existence of religious discrimination in the United States is particularly ironic because many of the founders of the original American colonies, as well as later arrivals to American shores, were fleeing religious persecution. Yet even from the beginning, those groups fleeing persecution sometimes showed little tolerance of others.

Religious Bigotry in the United States. A nineteenth century organization officially called the American Party but usually referred to as the Know-Nothing Party was strongly anti-Catholic and anti-alien. The Know-Nothing Party was most prominent in the 1850's. In the 1890's, another group, the AMERICAN PROTECTIVE ASSOCIATION, was also bitterly anti-foreigner and anti-Catholic. The KU KLUX KLAN, in its post-WORLD WAR I phase, was anti-Catholic and anti-Jewish as well as antiblack.

In 1922, Oregon passed an initiative that required public school enrollment of all children between the ages of eight and sixteen. The statute was pushed by groups, including the Ku Klux Klan, that feared the effects of allowing children to be educated in private religious schools. In 1925 the U.S. Supreme Court, in *Pierce v. Society of Sisters*, unanimously struck down the statute. It said that the state could require school attendance but could not specify which school children had to attend. The Court also invalidated Hawaii's restrictions on foreign-language schools, which were at least partly intended to control Japanese Buddhist schools.

When Democrat Al Smith ran for president in 1928, the fact that he was Catholic stirred deep controversy; anti-Catholic rhetoric flew during the campaign, and Smith lost the election to Herbert Hoover. As late as 1960, there was still enough anti-Catholic feeling in the United States to cause many people to wonder whether Catholic Democratic candidate John F. Kennedy had a chance of being elected. In the 1960's, Pope John XXIII's opening of the Catholic church to the modern world created an era of increased interfaith cooperation and amity. Yet the question remains open when the United States would be ready to accept a

JEWISH, MORMON, or agnostic president.

In colonial America, although religious freedom was held to be the ideal, there was an implicit understanding that the religion in question was a branch of Christianity. The Maryland Act of Religious Toleration (1649) provided freedom to practice any religion that included a belief in Jesus Christ; it also provided the death penalty for anyone who denied that Jesus Christ was the son of God. In 1658, a Jewish doctor was charged under Maryland's blasphemy laws; however, he was not convicted. In Massachusetts, Jews were not allowed to hold public office until 1828. ANTI-SEMITISM existed centuries before the founding of the United States, and it persists into the twentieth century. A poll taken during WORLD WAR II found that twice as many Americans considered Jews to be a "menace to America" as believed that Germany and Japan were. For years, there were limits on the number of Jews admitted to some educational institutions, and Jews were completely excluded from many social clubs and corporate hierarchies.

Religious Discrimination and the Supreme Court. Sunday closing laws, often called "blue laws," began in the colonial era. They prohibit labor or business on Sunday, the traditional weekly Christian holy day. Because many religions (Jews, MUSLIMS, and SEVENTH-DAY ADVENTISTS, for example) do not observe Sunday as the sabbath, these laws have been challenged in court on the basis that they are discriminatory. The Supreme Court upheld such laws in 1961, stating that they do serve a secular purpose—to provide a common day of rest for the community—and do not cause undue hardship on businesses forced to close on Sunday. Nevertheless, since the 1960's, blue laws have become relatively unimportant, as they are very rarely enforced.

Religion in public schools has been an ongoing and emotional issue. Until the 1930's, the governmental and educational systems of the United States (in fact, nearly all American public life) showed a distinct bias toward Protestant Christianity, a slant that has been called a "de facto Protestant" bias. In *Everson v. Board of Education* (1947), the Supreme Court in a sense ruled against that bias when it held that boards of education could reimburse parents for their children's bus transportation to school even if the school was a parochial school. Arguments that the reciting of Protestant-based prayers in public school, once a common practice, discriminated against children of many faiths (and against atheists) ultimately sent this•issue to the

Supreme Court as well. In *Engel v. Vitale* (1962) the Court held that the state could not compose an official prayer, even a "nonsectarian" prayer, to be said in school. A year later, in *Abington School District v. Schempp*, the Court decided that it was unconstitutional to begin the school day with a prayer or biblical meditation. Ever since, the Supreme Court has been strong in its refusal to allow prayer in school. Regardless, however, there are still school districts where sectarian prayers, Bible readings, and religious songs are routine.

Another issue concerning religion and education was decided by the Court in 1972 in the case *Wisconsin v. Yoder*. Wisconsin sought to force AMISH children to attend high school. The Court, however, agreed with the Amish and held that such compulsory education violated the Amish community's rights. Central was the recognition that Amish beliefs that secular education beyond the eighth grade would endanger their young peoples' religious convictions were sincerely and deeply held.

Among the American religious groups that have been subject to persecution and discrimination are the Mormons and the JEHOVAH'S WITNESSES. In 1836, the governor of Missouri publicly declared that the Mormons must be "exterminated or driven from the state." Thousands fled, and an estimated $2 million in property was confiscated without compensation. Joseph Smith, the founder of Mormonism, was killed by an angry mob in Illinois in 1844. The Supreme Court, in two cases in the nineteenth century, refused to uphold the Mormons' rights. As late as 1950, in fact, the Court refused to overturn a state decision depriving fundamentalist Mormons of the custody of their children.

In the 1930's and 1940's, the Jehovah's Witnesses were confronted with compulsory flag-salute rules (which went against Jehovah's Witnesses' belief that such saluting constitutes serving a God other than Jehovah) and bans on solicitations. In *Minersville School District v. Gobitis* (1940), the Supreme Court held that Jehovah's Witness children could be expelled from public school for not saluting the flag. In the two years following this decision, years during which World War II was raging and patriotic feelings were high, there were numerous acts of violence and persecution directed at the Witnesses. In 1943, the Court reversed its decision in *West Virginia Board of Education v. Barnette*.

Legislative Protection. A number of states have established machinery to monitor and punish religious

8 THE DEARBORN INDEPENDENT

Jewish Power and America's Money Famine

The Warburg Federal Reserve Sucks Money to New York, Leaving Productive Sections of the Country in Disastrous Need

THE international Jewish banker who has no country but plays them all against one another, and the international Jewish proletariat that roams from land to land in search of a peculiar type of economic opportunity, are not figments of the imagination except to the non-Jew who prefers a lazy laxity of mind.

Of these classes of Jews, one or both are at the heart of the problems that disturb the world today. The immigration problem is Jewish. The money question is Jewish. The tie-up of world politics is Jewish. The terms of the Peace Treaty are Jewish. The diplomacy of the world is Jewish. The moral question in movies and theaters is Jewish. The mystery of the illicit liquor business is Jewish.

These facts are unfortunate as well as unpleasant for the Jew, and it is squarely up to him to deal with the facts, and not waste time in trying to destroy those who define the facts. These facts are interpreted by the Jew and the anti-Semite with strange extremes of blindness. The Jew never gets the world's point of view at all; he always gets the anti-Semite's point of view; and the anti-Semite is equally at fault in always getting the Jew's point of view. What both need is to get society's point of view, which is the one being set forth in this present series of articles.

Jews Must Try to Find Solution

TO SAY that the immigration problem is Jewish does not mean that Jews must be prohibited entry to any country; it means that they must become rooted to a country in loyal citizenship, as no doubt some are, and as no doubt most are not. To say that the money question is Jewish does not mean that Jews must get out of finance; it means that they must rid finance of the Jewish idea which has always been to use money to get a strangle-hold on men and business concerns, instead of using finance to help general business. To say that the tie-up of world politics is Jewish does not mean that Jews, as human beings, are to be denied a voice in affairs; it means that they must give up trying to make the world revolve around the Jewish nation as its axis. To describe the influence of the Jew on the theater is not to demand that he leave the theater, but it is to demand that he rid the theater of his idea that sensualism is entertaining.

The Jewish Question is first for the Jews to solve; if not, the world will have to solve it for them. They may stay in business, say the theater, for example, if they will cease spoiling the theater; if they do not cease, the theater will be taken away from them just as certainly as that day follows night. The world has been patient and the world will be fair, but the world knows the limit of imposition.

It is not the true Jewishness of the Jew, nor yet the nationalism of the Jew that is on trial, but his anti-national internationalism. A true Mosaic Jew—not a Talmud Jew—would be a good citizen. A nationalist Jew would at least be logical. But an international Jew has proved an abomination, because his internationalism is focused on his own racial nationalism which in turn is founded on his ingrained belief that the rest of humanity is inferior to him and by right his prey. Jewish leaders may indulge in all the platitudes they possess, the fact which they cannot deny is that the Jew has for centuries regarded the "goyim" as beneath him and legitimately his spoil.

International Jewish Banker Confesses

THE internationalism of the Jew is confessed everywhere by him. Listen to a German banker: imagine the slow, oily voice in which he said:

"We are international bankers. Germany lost the war?—what of it?—that is an affair of the army. We are international bankers."

And that was the attitude of every international Jewish banker during the war. The nations were in strife? What of it? It was like a Dempsey-Carpentier bout in New Jersey, or a base ball game in Chicago—an affair of the fighters—"we are international bankers."

A nation is being hamstrung by artificial exchange rates; another by the sucking of money out of its channels of trade; what of it to the international banker? —he has his own game to play. Hard times bring more plums tumbling off the tree into the baskets of the international bankers than does any other kind of times. Wars and panics are the Jewish international bankers' harvests.

Citizens wake up with a start to find that even the white nations are hardly allowed to see each other nowadays except through Jewish eyes. When the United States supposedly speaks to France, through whom does she speak? All that France sees is Otto H. Kahn! Why must a Jew represent the United States of America to France? When France supposedly speaks to the United States, through whom is it done? Through Viviani, Jewish in every thought and method. Now they are talking of sending Millerand over, another Jew. Britain sends Lord Reading. Germany sent Dr. Dernberg. And to other countries the United States sent Morgenthau, Strauss, Warburg, and lesser Jewlings.

VOLUME two of this series of Jewish Studies is now off the press. It is entitled "Jewish Activities in the United States," being the second volume of "The International Jew," twenty-two articles, 256 pages. Sent to any address at the cost of printing and mailing, which is 25 cents.

It comes with something of a shock to learn that Foch is coming to the United States. We have not seen a Frenchman since Joffre visited us. It is good to see men of the white race come across the sea as if to reassure us that white men still live in those countries. The business of the Peace Conference was done by Jews—has it come to a point where international diplomacy is to become a Jewish monopoly also? Must the special conversations between France, Britain and the United States be held through Jewish interpreters, while Anglo-Saxons and true Frenchmen do the routine embassy work—or shall it be possible for the non-Jewish nations to see one another occasionally through non-Jewish representatives?

Internationalism is not a Jewish conviction but a Jewish business device. It is most profitable. In diplomacy and at the immigrant station, internationalism pays. Jews interpret nation to nation in the high rites of special conversations between governments; Jewish interpreters swarm at the ports of every country also, where the poor swarm in. It was stated in the House of Lords the other day that most of the trouble in Palestine was caused by Jewish interpreters. It was charged that the Jewish administration added an extra language to the official list in order to make Jewish interpreters indispensable.

"A Jew Let You Into This Country"

GO THROUGH the government of the United States, where the income tax secrets are kept, where the Federal Reserve secrets are kept, where the State Department secrets are kept—and you will find Jews sitting at the very spot where International Jewry desires them to sit, and where nothing is kept from their knowledge.

Go abroad and come back to your country, and a Jew will open the gate to let you in, or close it to keep you out—as he chooses.

"Will you be going to Detroit while you are here?" asked a Jewish government agent of a gentleman entering the country on a visit a few weeks ago.

"I may go to Detroit," was the reply.

"Well, you go to the damned DEARBORN INDEPENDENT and tell them a Jew let you into this country," said the government agent.

What the visitor replied is known, but had better not be quoted. The American Jewish Committee might shriek that the people were being incited to pogroms.

The incident, however, is but a sample of what is occurring every day. The truth about the Jewish Question in the United States is perhaps the one form of truth that cannot be indiscriminately told.

The international Jewish bankers regard themselves as in similar fashion "letting" the nations do this or that, regarding the nations not as fatherlands but as customers—and as customers in the Jewish sense. If an army wins or loses, if a government succeeds or fails, what of it?—that is their affair—"we are international bankers," and we win, whoever loses.

For international Jewish bankers the war is not over. The period of actual hostilities and the emergencies of the nations were but the opening of the trade. The ready cash was skimmed in then—all the cash the world had. True, some of it had to be distributed among the people as war wages and bonuses, in order to keep the struggle going, but this was soon recovered through the means of high prices, artificial scarcities and the orgy of extravagance deliberately organized and stimulated among the people. That phase over, and money disappeared.

Is there any more tragic joke than that diligently disseminated in this country—"The United States has more gold than any other country in the world." Where is it? How long since you have seen a piece of gold? Where is all this gold—is it locked up in the Treasury of the United States Government? Why, that government is in debt, desperately trying to economize, cannot pay a soldier bonus because the finances of the country cannot stand it! Where is that gold? It may be *in* the United States, but it does not belong *to* the United States.

The American farmer, and those American industries which were not "wise" to the tricks of international Jewish bankers, and who were nipped by small loans, are wondering where all this money is. Furthermore, Europe, suffering from every possible lack, is looking to us and wondering where the money is.

Jewish Political and Financial Headquarters

THIS dispatch in a London paper may throw light on the matter: (italics are ours)

"It is learned today that new gold shipments aggregating $2,800,000 are consigned to Kuhn, Loeb & Company, New York, making nearly $129,000,000 imported by that firm since the movement started. In responsible banking circles the belief is expressed that some of the *German* coin recently imported by the firm *is from Russia, instead of Germany*, as generally supposed."

This dispatch, coupled with one printed in a former article which showed Warburg & Company of Germany arranging with Kuhn, Loeb & Company of New York for a $5,000,000 loan to Norway, is not devoid of light on the question—*Where is the money?*

The Jewish international banking system may be easily described. First, there is the international Jewish headquarters. This was in Germany. It had ramifications in Russia, Italy, France, Great Britain and the South American states. (South American Jewry is very menacing.) Germany and Russia were the two countries scheduled for punishment by the International Jewish bankers because these two countries were most aware of the Jew. They have been punished; that job is done.

Jewish political headquarters, as related to the internal affairs of the Jews, was also located in Germany, but the headquarters dealing with the "goyim" was in France. Statements have been made that the political center of Jewry has been transplanted to the United States. But these statements have been made by American Jews whose wish may have been father to the thought. During the Wilson Administration it was possible for a Jew to think and to hope this, but affairs have slightly changed. The ousting of American Jews from the Zionist movement at the behest of Eastern Jews indicates that if the political center of world Jewry has shifted to the United States, the *power* is still in the hands of *aliens* resident here. The center is still in Jewry; the United States is merely a square on Jewry's world checker-board.

Fine for War: Helpless in Peace

BUT, wherever the financial and political world centers may be, each country is separately handled. In every country—the United States, Mexico and the republics of South America; in France, England, Italy, Germany, Austria—yes, and in Japan—there is an international Jewish banking firm which stands at the head of the group for that country. Thus, the chief Jewish firm in the United States is Kuhn, Loeb & Company, of which one of the members is Paul M. Warburg, brother of M. Warburg & Company, of Hamburg; and another member of which is Otto H. Kahn, resident successively of Germany, Great Britain and the United States, and self-appointed financial spokesman for the United States to France and Great Britain. Great Britain and France seldom see a special American spokesman who is not a Jew. That may be the reason why they reciprocate by sending Jews to us, thinking perhaps that we prefer them.

Paul M. Warburg was the inventor, perfector and director of the Federal Reserve System of the United States. He is not the only Jew in the Federal Reserve System, but he was the chief Jew there. His mind counted for a great deal. There were others in the war government, of course; Bernard M. Baruch; Eugene Meyer, Jr.; Hoover's regiment of Jews; Felix Frankfurter; Julius Rosenwald—hundreds of them, and everywhere; but the financial group alone is receiving

This article in an old issue of a Michigan newspaper attests to deep-seated prejudice against the stereotyped Jewish banker during much of America's history. (Library of Congress)

discrimination. The federal CIVIL RIGHTS ACT OF 1964 included religion in its list of proscribed discriminations. Employers are expected to make reasonable accommodation for the religious needs of their employees. Congress passed the American Indian Religious Freedom Act in 1978. American Indians have been among those religious groups discriminated against in prisons and have had their SUN DANCE and PEYOTE religions (such as the NATIVE AMERICAN CHURCH) banned.

SUGGESTED READINGS. See Richard E. Wentz's *Why Do People Do Bad Things in the Name of Religion?* (1987), Robert N. Bellah and Frederick E. Greenspahn's edited volume *Uncivil Religion: Interreligious Hostility in America* (1987), Leo Pfeffer's *Church, State, and Freedom* (1967), William Seward Salisbury's *Religion in American Culture: A Sociological Interpretation* (1964), and Winthrop S. Hudson's *Religion in America* (3d ed., 1984). The U.S. Commission on Civil Rights published its 1979 consultation on *Religious Discrimination: A Neglected Issue*. Rodney K. Smith's *Public Prayer and the Constitution* (1987) looks specifically at the prayer issue.—*Martin Gruberg*

Discrimination, reverse. *See* **Reverse discrimination**

Discrimination, Supreme Court rulings on. *See* **Supreme Court rulings—discrimination and minority status**

Disfranchisement: Loss of certain legal rights, especially the right to vote. Many segments of American society are without effective political power because they cannot or do not vote. For example, it is difficult for homeless people to register to vote because they do not have permanent addresses. Rural poor people find it difficult to travel to the polls on election day. Historically, minority groups were denied the vote by law. Without the vote, people cannot make their voices heard, and their problems and concerns tend to receive low priority. Many of the social change movements of the nineteenth and twentieth century were efforts to combat disfranchisement.

Displaced Persons Act (1948): Enabled the Displaced Persons Commission to issue up to 202,000 immigration visas to Europeans displaced by World War II without regard for previously established quotas. "Displaced persons"—including war refugees identified by the International Refugee Organization as well as those who had entered Germany, Austria, and Italy between December 22, 1945 and January 1, 1948, or fled from Czechoslovakia after that date—were given preference, particularly those the Nazis persecuted. They had to show that they could find employment and housing without displacing American citizens.

Divorce: More than a million couples in the United States divorce each year. The divorce rate for 1990 was 4.7 per thousand persons, down from 5.8 per thousand persons in 1979. The marriage rate for 1990 was 9.8 per thousand. Only about one-tenth of American adults were divorced or separated in 1988. According to a 1989 article in the journal *Demography*, however, two-thirds of current marriages were likely to end in separation or divorce. A marriage was also more likely to break up if one or both partners had been married before.

Divorce has become an acceptable solution to an unhappy marriage. The stigma and social ostracism once associated with divorce have become relatively uncommon. Marriage has been transformed into a voluntary, perhaps temporary partnership, a contract dissolvable at the will of either partner. These changes in attitudes and the law only came about in the latter half of the twentieth century. The South was the region most resistant to divorce; South Carolina, for example, outlawed divorce completely until 1949. New England treated divorce as a civil matter. Only in the West with its sparse, mobile society, was divorce historically easy to obtain.

Religious and Political Constraints. Ending a marriage has been considered at least as much a concern of one's church as oneself, one's mate, and one's state. Under ROMAN CATHOLIC canon law, divorce is forbidden. An annulment may be possible, however, if certain conditions can be proven, such as impotence, refusal to have children, coercion of one of the partners into wedlock, or close blood ties. Catholics generally have lower divorce rates than non-Catholics.

Among Protestants, EPISCOPALIANS have the highest divorce rates and LUTHERANS the lowest. Some mainstream Protestant churches have liberalized their positions on divorce and remarriage (previously, only the "innocent party" in the case of desertion or adultery could remarry). The more conservative faiths, however, regard a Christian marriage as an indissoluble union.

Under ORTHODOX JEWISH law, a marriage cannot be dissolved without the consent of both partners.

Those receiving civil divorces remain unable to remarry if their mate is unwilling to grant them traditional Jewish divorces. REFORM JUDAISM considers civil divorce sufficient, while in CONSERVATIVE JUDA-

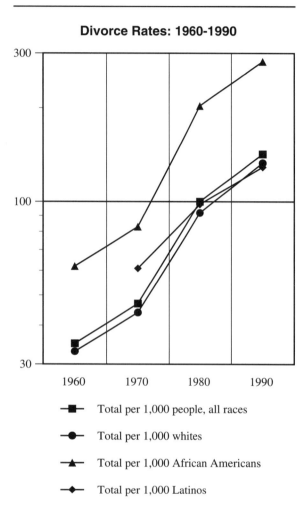

Divorce Rates: 1960-1990

- ■ Total per 1,000 people, all races
- ● Total per 1,000 whites
- ▲ Total per 1,000 African Americans
- ◆ Total per 1,000 Latinos

Source: Data are from Carol Foster, ed., *Women's Changing Role.* Tables 1.5 and 1.7. Wylie, Tex.: Information Plus, 1992.
Note: Data for Latinos not available for 1960.

ISM, a special rabbinical court can issue the divorce decree if a wife presents proof of serious attempts to get the religious divorce.

In traditional Islam, divorce is the prerogative of the husband. Divorces and divorce settlements have been matters of MUSLIM personal law, out of the range of civil courts. It is likely that this will change among American Muslims as it has in Muslim countries such as Egypt.

American states varied in the conditions under which divorce was permissible. Grounds for divorce included adultery, insanity, alcoholism, extreme physical or mental cruelty, desertion, conviction of a felony, irretrievable breakdown of the marriage, and mutual consent. (The emphasis upon fault was an inheritance from English ecclesiastical law.) Desertion (without a formal, legal end to the marriage) has been called the poor man's divorce. A substantially higher proportion of nonwhite than of white persons were reported as separated. For many years, the only grounds for obtaining a divorce in New York was adultery. Persons seeking an end to their marriage in that state sometimes had to use fraud, perjury, and collusion to simulate the evidence of adultery (usually done by the male because of the greater stigma placed on a woman for the deed).

The grounds for divorce were interpreted differently according to gender. Husbands charged with cruelty were often alleged to have caused their wives bodily harm, while wives under that charge were more typically accused of neglecting their husbands, homes, or wifely duties. Desertion by the wife consisted of withdrawal of affection, refusal to do housework, or attention to outside duties. Desertion by the husband included failure to support his wife financially. In many states if both parties were at fault, neither could obtain a divorce.

Persons seeking a divorce moved to states with favorable divorce laws. Out-of-state divorces were usually recognized as a matter of convenience, though "quickie" Mexican divorces were sometimes overturned as not bona fide, especially if obtained by only one spouse. For example, in the 1945 decision of *Williams v. North Carolina*, the U.S. Supreme Court sustained the right of a North Carolina jury to determine that a six-week sojourn in Nevada had not made state residents out of two erstwhile North Carolinians. They were therefore not legally divorced from their former spouses or legally married to each other. (North Carolina had brought bigamy charges against the couple.) On the other hand, in *Sherrer v. Sherrer* (1948), the Court overruled a Massachusetts court that had voided the Florida divorce of a wife who went from her Massachusetts home to Florida and sued for divorce after the ninety-day period of residence required by Florida law. Since her husband had been a party to the contested divorce years earlier, he could not later challenge the matter of his wife's domicile. (Florida later changed its residence requirement from ninety days to six months.)

Alimony and Child Support. Traditional divorce laws assumed a gender-based division of labor. The wife had her domestic responsibilities while the husband's obligation was to provide financial support. This also applied with regard to children: The father was responsible for their economic support and the mother for their care in their tender years. Paternalism sometimes resulted in judicial decisions favorable to women. As the spouse who was usually the dependent one, the wife's economic status had to be protected. Women did not participate in the management of family income and may not have known how it was spent or invested. In the era of divorce for cause, a husband's obligations to support his wife and children extended beyond divorce and could be discharged through alimony or property division.

In practice, however, alimony awards tended to be extremely rare, and child support awards were usually low and not monitored. (The Supreme Court in 1979 struck down an Alabama law which permitted only women to seek alimony upon divorce.) The extent and rationale for maintenance payments varied. When a couple had been married for many years, some people believed that the wife should receive financial support because of her contribution to the marriage, her previous absence from the work force, and her inability to earn a living in her old age. In the event of a divorce of a couple whose marriage was of short duration, at most it was assumed that the wife would need some transitional support until she was able to fend for herself; the shortness of the marriage did not prevent her from competing in the job market and her time in marriage had not resulted in that great a contribution to the family's finances. The exception to this case was when the wife had been the breadwinner while her husband was completing his education.

Class and Race. The divorce rate is higher among Americans with less income, less education, and fewer skills; the rate becomes lower as income rises. The reason is partly economic: a comfortable economic merger makes many personal irritations tolerable. Also, upper-class women are aware that their living standards as divorcées will be impaired. This is true even where there is an equal division of the marital property, that is, in those states with community property rights and in other states such as Wisconsin that have enacted legislation similar to the Uniform Marriage and Divorce Act.

The likelihood of divorce varies among racial groups. The divorce rates for African Americans are

Single parenthood is the common aftermath of many divorces and separations. (James L. Shaffer)

the highest; in some states, they have been found to be more than twice as high as rates for whites. In the South, however, African Americans traditionally had lower divorce rates than white persons. Among the factors that may contribute to the greater instability of black marriages are vestigial traumas from the SLAVERY experience and the many effects of RACISM, such as the denigration of the black male, the separation strains experienced by families seeking housing or employment, and the opportunities available to African American women that are not available to men.

Other races (to the extent that they can be determined from the official records) had lower divorce rates than those for either whites or blacks. Religious and cultural factors, such as the tradition of a close-knit family unit and the stigma attached to a divorced person, may account for these lower divorce rates among Asians and Latinos (who are of various races). The descendants of the foreign-born are less influenced by Old World customs and more likely to divorce. Some immigrant groups, such as Southeast Asian refugees, who rarely divorced in their homelands, have experienced an alarming increase in divorce under the stresses of war, displacement, and re-settlement in the United States.

No-Fault Divorce. By 1984, all states except South Dakota had adopted some form of no-fault divorce. California pioneered no-fault divorce legislation in 1970, eliminating the concept of a guilty party. This approach is an effort to reduce the acrimony and bitterness of the divorce process. Either spouse can seek the divorce by alleging irretrievable breakdown of the marriage.

Critics assert that no-fault divorce tends to decrease the bargaining power of the economically dependent spouse. The rules that treat the wife as equal serve to deprive her of the financial support she needs. Statistics suggest that divorce is economically advantageous for men but often disastrous for women and children. As a result of divorce, many single-parent families headed by women have become part of the new American poor. Child support payments are often inadequate or inconsistent. Some women are forced to accept unfavorable or inadequate child support arrangements under threat that their husbands will contest the custody of the children. A 1992 position paper of the Communitarian Network, a group that advocates balance between individual rights and community needs, observed: "A parent should be able to divorce a spouse if a marriage has irretrievably broken down, but a parent should never be allowed to divorce a child."

Many divorced fathers fail to pay child support. Default may arise from anger at the former spouse or from irresponsibility, particularly if and when the noncustodial parent moves on to a relationship with another family.

While dysfunctional marriages are often kept going "for the sake of the children," many children may be better off after the divorce than during a marriage of unremitting hatred, unhappiness, and parental rivalry. In the early 1990's there were a few court cases in which children were allowed to "divorce" themselves from their parents when there were irreconcilable differences between them.

The "best interest of the child" was historically understood to mean "mother custody," that is, favoring the parent who typically provided the day-to-day care and nurturing. Since the 1980's, partly in response to feminism and the men's movement, more couples have arranged joint custody—a sharing of parenting that recognizes men's responsibility for and interest in nurturing.

Despite its greater frequency and the greater ease of obtaining it, divorce remains a major life crisis, especially for women. They tend to suffer both a greater economic loss and a harsher stigma attached to their divorced status than men. As the party who most often has child custody, the woman must make arrangements to support her family and find adequate, affordable child care for preschoolers and after-school programs for older children. Psychologically, divorced people of all genders, classes, races, and ages must come to terms with their sense of loss or new identity.

SUGGESTED READINGS. See Glenda Riley's *Divorce: An American Tradition* (1992); Martha Albertson Fineman's *The Illusion of Equality: The Rhetoric and Reality of Divorce Reform* (1991); Lenore J. Weitzman's *The Divorce Revolution: The Unexpected Social and Economic Consequences for Women and Children in America* (1985); and Hugh Carter and Paul C. Glick's *Marriage and Divorce: A Social and Economic Study* (1976). For a discussion of religious views, see Richard L. Morgan's *Is There Life After Divorce in the Church?* (1985).—*Martin Gruberg*

Dix, Dorothea Lynde (Apr. 4, 1802, Hampden, Maine—July 18, 1887, Trenton, N.J.): Nurse, social reformer, and advocate of rights for the mentally ill. Dix

Social reformer Dorothea Dix advocated rights for the mentally ill. (AP/Wide World Photos)

was responsible for reforms in insane asylums world-wide. In 1841 she taught Sunday school at The House of Correction in East Cambridge, Massachusetts, and was appalled at the existing conditions for mentally ill women. In 1844 she presented a survey of prisons and

dominant group need not make up the majority of the population, as a minority group need not be a numerical minority. In the United States, for example, WASPs compose only about one-third of the population. The critical difference is power, not numbers.

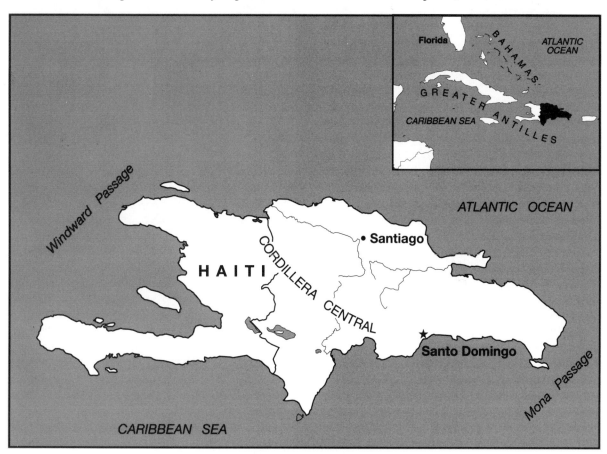

DOMINICAN REPUBLIC

asylums to the Massachusetts Legislature, which alerted the world to the subhuman conditions she had witnessed. Dix founded thirty-two mental hospitals, and partly because of her influence, the United States increased the number of existing hospitals from 13 in 1843 to 123 in 1880.

Dominant culture: Culture of the dominant group within a society—that is, of the group that holds primary economic and political power. In the United States, people of Anglo-European ancestry—the white Anglo-Saxon Protestant (WASP) ethnic group—form the dominant group. Members of a subordinate group, or minority group, have traditionally had to acculturate to the culture of the dominant group to be successful in society. A

Dominican Americans: The Dominican Republic lies on the island of Hispaniola, south of Cuba, at the eastern edge of the Caribbean Sea. It shares Hispaniola with the country of Haiti.

Hispaniola was originally inhabited by aboriginal people called the Tainos. Christopher Columbus encountered them when he landed on Hispaniola in December, 1492, on his first voyage to the New World. Fifty years later, the Tainos had been completely decimated, both by a war with the Spanish over control of their island and by European diseases. The Spanish exploited the island for gold. When that ran out, Spain gradually allowed Dutch, British, and French entrepreneurs to develop Hispaniola for their own purposes. An English explorer named Sir John Hawkins brought

In 1965, after the Dominican Republic exploded in a popular revolution, Dominican Americans in New York City staged a protest against the United States' intervention in the fighting. (National Archives)

African slaves to the island in 1563.

The nation of Haiti was established on the eastern section of the island in 1801. In 1844, Ramón Mella, Juan Pablo Duarte, and Francisco del Rosario rebelled against the Haitians and declared the independence of the Dominican Republic.

The Dominican political situation was mostly in turmoil until dictator Rafael Leónidas Trujillo Molina came to power in 1930. Under his strong-arm rule, the Dominican Republic prospered. Sixty years after his reign began, the population of the Dominican Republic had grown nearly fivefold.

Trujillo tightly controlled emigration from his tiny country. When he was assassinated in 1961, the floodgates opened and Dominicans began streaming into the United States, mostly to NEW YORK CITY. Hispaniola is only eighty miles from Puerto Rico, and Dominicans often take advantage of PUERTO RICANS' right of unrestricted access in order to enter the United States illegally.

In the 1980's, the Dominican Republic supplied more immigrants to New York City than any other country. These newcomers were often unskilled peasants from the Dominican countryside who migrated to the United States to improve their economic prospects. The Dominicans maintain strong family ties and value education. As a result, some Dominicans have been able to move into the middle class by operating small businesses or moving into white-collar professions. Prominent Dominican Americans have included fashion designer Oscar DE LA RENTA and baseball players Juan Marichal and Pedro Guerrero.

Douglass, Frederick (Feb., 1817, Tuckahoe, Md.— Feb. 20, 1895, Washington, D.C.): African American writer, orator, and politician. Born a slave, Frederick Douglass escaped in 1838, at the age of twenty-one. Eventually he made his way to Massachusetts, then the center of the ABOLITION MOVEMENT. There he first read William Lloyd Garrison's antislavery journal, *The Liberator*. Accepting its principles and philosophies, Douglass attended abolitionist meetings, gradually becoming a leader among the New Bedford abolitionists.

In August, 1841, Douglass met Garrison, who urged him to become a public spokesman for abolition. Agreeing, he traveled widely, lecturing on the evils of

SLAVERY. His personal experiences and fine oratory moved audiences to pity and roused much anger against the slave system. Yet Douglass also pointed out to his listeners that RACISM was strong in the North and that his was a dual fight: against southern slavery and northern PREJUDICE.

Douglass' autobiography enhanced his strength and credibility as an abolitionist. *The Narrative of the Life of Frederick Douglass*, published in 1845, became a best-seller; by 1848 it had gone through nine editions and was as popular abroad as in America. Douglass became the living symbol of what black people could be and accomplish once they were free.

In the 1850's, Douglass and Garrison separated because of differences over how to end slavery. Garrison condemned the U.S. CONSTITUTION as a "Covenant with death and an agreement with hell," urging dissolution of the Union. Douglass disagreed, and the two quarreled enough to split the abolitionists.

At the onset of the CIVIL WAR in 1861, Douglass stressed two goals: an emancipation proclamation and recruitment of African Americans into the Union Army, policies he saw as helping the North to victory. President Abraham Lincoln finally agreed with Douglass and other abolitionists when he issued the EMANCIPATION PROCLAMATION to take effect on January 1, 1863, and also authorized acceptance of black volunteers into Union forces.

At the war's end, Douglass' work was far from over. The Reconstruction Era (1865-1877) had not brought full rights for African Americans. Angered and frustrated by President Andrew Johnson's policies, which seemed "soft" on the South and lax on rights for blacks, Douglass rejoiced when Ulysses S. Grant was elected president. He took some comfort in passage of the FOURTEENTH and FIFTEENTH AMENDMENTS, which gave citizenship and the vote to black males, but firmly believed that a friendly federal government was needed to enforce the laws. President Rutherford Hayes's administration saw the end of RECONSTRUCTION; neither the party nor the Constitution could be relied on to protect blacks.

In 1889, President William Harrison appointed Douglass minister-resident and consul-general to the Republic of Haiti. Haitians received him warmly, but in July, 1891, Douglas resigned, citing personal reasons. During his last years, he continued writing and speaking on behalf of full rights for African Americans.

SUGGESTED READINGS. Philip S. Foner's *Frederick Douglass* (1950) quotes extensively from Douglass' speeches and writings. An intellectual biography, David W. Blight's *Frederick Douglass' Civil War* (1989) explores Douglass' contribution to American political and religious thought before and after the Civil War. See also William F. McFeely's *Frederick Douglass* (1991) and Robert B. Stepto's *From Behind the Veil: A Study of Afro-American Narrative* (1979).

Draft riots (1863): Antiblack, antidraft disturbances started by white workers in NEW YORK CITY during the CIVIL WAR. The incident is a revealing case of white racism in the North.

For some time prior to the riots, northern newspapermen had launched scathing attacks charging that President Abraham Lincoln had plunged the country into a war in which all whites would suffer to help the "undeserving Negro." The *Philadelphia Age* charged that abolitionists had caused the war and had blindly ignored the interests of the free white northern population. Not surprisingly, northern white hostility toward African Americans increased as the war continued to consume more white men and material.

White workers were among those showing the most hatred for African Americans, as the workers feared that a mass exodus of southern blacks to the North would cause competition with whites for both jobs and housing. Striking white workers also resented the use of African American strike breakers (or "scabs") by white employers. In 1862, a white mob assaulted a group of African American women and children who worked at a New York tobacco factory. White longshoremen in New York often beat blacks who were brought on the job and later played a central part in the draft riots of 1863.

That year, three thousand white longshoremen went on strike for better pay. Helped by the local police, African American "scabs" took their place. At the same time, the Lincoln government started drafting unemployed whites into the union armies. The white workers' view was that first their jobs had been taken by blacks, and then they were taken south to fight. Further angering white workers were provisions of the Union's conscription act which allowed a white man to escape the draft by paying $300 to draft authorities. To many workers, the Civil War seemed like a "rich man's war" but a "poor man's fight."

In July, 1863, after the great twin Union victories at the Battle of Gettysburg and the Battle of Vicksburg, full-scale riots broke out. Beginning on July 11, and continuing for four days, whites attacked African Americans, killing many and burning their homes and businesses, while also storming and destroying draft offices. The rioters in general acted like revolutionaries in four continuous days of destruction, which prompted the Lincoln Administration to send in detachments of combat troops from the Army of the Potomac to help local police. By the time peace was restored, thousands of civilians, blacks and whites, had been killed or wounded, and property damage mounted to $1.5 million. Such disturbances demonstrated deep divisions about the war among white northerners and also continuing widespread racism even in the free North.

SUGGESTED READINGS. One dated but useful survey of the Draft Riots is Emerson D. Fite's *Social and Industrial Conditions in the North During the Civil War* (1910); other volumes which cover the topic are Bruce Catton's *The Civil War* (1971), Benjamin Quarles' *The Negro in the Civil War* (1953), and James McPherson's *The Negro's Civil War* (1965).

Dramatists and drama: Although Broadway is often seen as synonymous with American drama, American writing for the stage encompasses far more than is generally seen in mainstream theaters. While Broadway theater paid scant attention for years to American cultural diversity, American drama has been enlivened by the voices of minority playwrights since the production of the first African American play early in the twentieth century. Midcentury political, social, and cultural changes contributed to the flowering of new kinds of American theater—regional, local, ethnic, and multicultural. David Henry HWANG's 1988 Tony Award for *M. Butterfly* proved that American drama had finally come to reflect the country's diverse cultural climate.

African American Drama. The first play written and performed by African Americans in the twentieth century was *Rachel*, by Angelina Grimké, sponsored by the NATIONAL ASSOCIATION FOR THE ADVANCEMENT OF COLORED PEOPLE (NAACP). Presented on March 3, 1916, the play was intended to educate Americans on racial issues. Willis Richardson's *The Chip Woman's Fortune* (1923), first performed at the Lafayette Theater in Harlem, became the first serious play by a black writer to be performed on Broadway. Other Broadway plays by African Americans followed: Garland Anderson's *Appearances* (1925); Hall Johnson's *Run, Little Chillun* (1933); and Langston HUGHES's *Mulatto* (1935), which for years remained

Ellen Stewart began the Off-Off-Broadway Café La Mama Theater in the 1950's, which has encouraged multicultural playwrights ever since. (Hazel Hankin)

the most successful Broadway play by a black writer.

Even earlier than the Broadway triumphs were two other important types of African American drama: propaganda plays and folk plays. Difficult social and political questions inform the work of the propaganda dramatists. Alice Dunbar Nelson's *Mine Eyes Have Seen* (1918) asks whether blacks should fight for freedom in Europe during World War I when they have none at home; Mary Burrill's *They That Sit in Darkness* (1919) addresses women's need for birth control education; Marita Bonner's *The Purple Flower* (1928) argues for revolution. The folk plays use black culture for inspiration. Among those who wrote folk drama were Thelma Duncan, Zora Neale HURSTON, and Willis Richardson.

During the 1930's, folk and propaganda elements combined in the work of Georgia Douglas Johnson, whose plays used black dialect and folkways to dramatize the violence against African Americans. That decade also saw the flourishing of the Federal

Theatre Project (an arm of the Works Progress Administration, one of the NEW DEAL programs), which staged the commercially successful *The Black Macbeth* (1936) and *Swing Mikado* (1938), as well as two new plays by black writers, William Dubois' *Haiti* (1932) and Theodore White's *Big White Fog* (1938).

Attempts to organize African American theater companies began as early as 1917 with the Lafayette Players and 1919 with the Howard Players, directed by Montgomery Gregory. Other groups followed in the 1920's such as The Kwigwa Players (organized by

units of the Federal Theatre Project. These companies faced the same problem of financing that plagued all American theaters during those decades. Even more serious for the emerging African American drama were the twin problems of discovering black playwrights and developing a black theater audience in a cultural milieu that did not recognize African Americans.

Although the Harlem-based American Negro Theatre (ANT) was established to provide opportunities for African Americans, it was not a completely black

Theater not only reflects multicultural America but also provides a forum for expressing and responding to issues surrounding race and ethnicity, as in this rehearsal of a high school play. (Cleo Freelance Photo)

W. E. B. DU BOIS), the Harlem Experimental Theatre, and the Negro Art Theatre. The 1930's and 1940's saw a proliferation of short-lived black theater groups: Langston Hughes's Harlem Suitcase Theater, the Rose McClendon Players, the American Negro Theatre, the black Playwrights Company, and the twenty-two black

venture. The theater hired white actors and technicians and after 1945 produced only white-written plays. Nevertheless, the ANT provided the American stage with major performers such as Ruby Dee, Sidney POITIER, and Harry Belafonte. The ANT closed after nine years, victim of a lack of grant money and performing space as well as the departure of the best performers, who moved on to larger companies.

Broadway's 1959 season introduced Lorraine HANSBERRY's *Raisin in the Sun,* the first play by a woman or an African American playwright to win the prestigious New York Drama Critics Circle Award. The play's success enabled other black playwrights to find support in the American theater, and helped black performers get opportunities to work with serious drama on mainstream stages. Although Hansberry remains the most recognizable name from the 1950's, other important black dramatists of the period were William Branch, Alice Childress, Loften Mitchell, and Beah Richards.

The 1960's brought another significant wave of African American theater groups. In New Orleans in 1963, Gilbert Moses and John O'Neal organized the Free Southern Theater, a part of the CIVIL RIGHTS MOVEMENT that brought theater to small towns where blacks were denied entrance to motion picture houses. In 1966, Douglas Turner Ward founded the Negro Ensemble Company on New York's Lower East Side. The most important development of the 1960's was the black theater movement, which opened Black Arts theaters. Its efforts began with LeRoi Jones (who later took the name Amiri BARAKA) and the Black Arts Repertory Theatre, a Harlem venture that turned white audiences away from highly successful productions including Jones's *Dutchman* (1964) and *The Slave* (1964). Other similar theaters included Spirit House (also organized by LeRoi Jones) in Newark; Concept East in Detroit; and the New Lafayette in Harlem, as well as Black Arts/West and Aldridge Players/West on the West Coast. In 1968 Barbara Ann Teer began the National Black Theater.

Among the other African American dramatists whose careers developed through the black theater movement of the 1960's and 1970's are Ray Aranha, Ed Bullins, Ben Caldwell, Steve Carter, Gus Edwards, Lonnie Elder III, Adrienne Kennedy, Leslie Lee, Sonia Sanchez, Ntozake SHANGE, Joseph A. Walker, and Edgar White. These playwrights include some whose work is overtly political and militant, as well as others whose plays are more personal explorations of the black experience.

Today African American playwrights are diverse, and their contributions to American drama are noteworthy for their portrayals of the complex concerns, conflicts, roles, and identities of modern African Americans. Although August Wilson, recipient of two Pulitzer Prizes for drama, is the most visible of these writers, the 1980's and 1990's have produced a whole new generation of African American dramatists: Elizabeth Brown-Guillory, Kathleen Collins, California Cooper, Marsha Jackson, Samm-Art Williams, and George C. Wolfe. Contributing to the American musical are Vinette Carroll, Micki Grant, Vy Higginson, and Saundra Sharp. Working in different forms and genres—comedy, revue, one-person play, performance art, musical theater, theatrical sketch, serious drama—these writers and others provide audiences with dramatizations of modern African American life.

Asian American Drama. Historical records show that Chinese theaters flourished in nineteenth century California; however, formal Asian American theater began in 1965 with the formation of the East West Players in Los Angeles. Composed of actors of Asian ancestry, and directed by Mako, a successful screen and stage actor, the company initially performed traditional Western plays and dramatizations of fiction by Asian authors.

In 1973, Frank CHIN, with Janis Chan and Jeffrey Chin, started the Asian-American Theatre Workshop (later called the Asian-American Theatre Company) in San Francisco with the help of the American Conservatory Theater. Chin's *Chickencoop Chinaman* (1972) was the first major play by an Asian American playwright. Portraying the widespread ethnic stereotyping in American media and popular culture, the production toured college campuses for more than a year, making possible a production of Chin's *The Year of the Dragon* (1974) by the American Place Theater in New York.

Other Asian American theater groups that started in the 1970's include the Northwest Asian American Theatre Company (originally the Asian Exclusion Act), founded through Seattle's Asian Multi Media; the Pan Asian Repertory Theatre, founded by actress Tisa Chang in New York; and the Toronto-based Canadian Artists Group.

The best-known Asian American playwright is David Henry Hwang, whose first play, *F.O.B.,* won an Obie Award in 1979. In 1981, Hwang wrote *The Dance and the Railroad* and *Family Devotions,* creating what is called his "Chinese American trilogy"; in 1988 he won the Tony Award for *M. Butterfly,* a Broadway success that went on to be produced all over the United States.

A list of notable Asian American playwrights also includes the avant-garde Ping Chong, Philip Kan Gotanda, Jessica Hagedorn, and Wakako Yamauchi. Other important playwrights include Ernest Abuba, Rosanna Yamagiwa Alfaro, Velina Houston, Momoko Iko, Warren Kubota, Dom Magwili, and R. A. Shiomi.

Asian American drama, because it is created by Americans who trace their ancestries to Japan, China, the Philippines, Korea, and other Asian countries, is varied in style, genre, focus, and point of view, but a familiar yet alien culture.

Latino Drama. The most dominant form of Latino theater is Chicano theater, which originated in 1965 with EL TEATRO CAMPESINO. The company was founded by Luis VALDEZ to perform *The Conscience of a Scab* in support of the union-led struggle of migrant laborers during the DELANO GRAPE STRIKE in Delano, California. Initially performing on flatbed

The multiethnic San Francisco Mime Troupe is well known for its street theater productions. (Hazel Hankin)

common themes are evident in many of the plays. They reveal the writers' concerns about their dual identities and sense of otherness and the tensions of living simultaneously in two worlds: an ancestral homeland and the United States of their birth or coming of age. The plays address racial and ethnic issues as well as conflicts between generations with different cultural values. They depict journeys toward identity and self-definition in what many Asian Americans find

trucks, El Teatro Campesino dramatized labor problems through short improvisations called *actos*. The company eventually severed its ties to the UNITED FARM WORKERS and evolved into a theater collective. The *actos* developed into longer plays on a wider variety of issues of concern to Chicanos.

Many of El Teatro Campesino's plays were inspired by traditional Mexican entertainment such as the *carpa* (a traveling tent show), *pastorella* (sacred drama), *corrido* (a narrative ballad), and *mito* (recited myth). The plays were improvised and revised through intense group work combining traditional forms with political commentary, social satire, verbal acrobatics, broad gestures and movement, and bawdy humor. Their purpose was to portray real Chicano life, illuminate problems, and offer solutions, thereby creating unity. Until the early 1980's, El Teatro Campesino was the cultural and spiritual center of Chicano theater; the company toured the United States and Europe with the well-received *La gran carpa de los Rasquachies* (1973-1978) and *Fin del mundo* (1974-1980).

Some Chicano theater scholars cite 1980 as the end of the company's first phase as a collective, as many of its ensemble members then went their separate ways into other theaters. In 1981, Valdez acquired property near San Juan Bautista, including a produce-packing building that now houses El Teatro Campesino. After a twelve-year hiatus during which Valdez became a successful filmmaker, the company resumed touring in 1992 with *How Else Am I Supposed to Know I'm Alive* by Evelina Fernandez and *Simply Maria* by Josefina Lopez.

Other West Coast developments in Latino theater since the 1960's include El Teatro de la Esperanza, started in Santa Barbara, California, and later transferred to a San Francisco church; the Bilingual Foundation of the Arts in Los Angeles; the Hispanic Playwrights Project in Orange County, California; Brava! for Women in the Arts in San Francisco; and the Latino Theater Lab in Los Angeles.

On the East Coast, in 1978, the Puerto Rican Traveling Theater began a playwriting workshop, inviting several writers from Spanish-speaking backgrounds to participate. In 1984, the Theater Communications Group sponsored the Hispanic Translation Project to bring Spanish plays to American audiences.

Aside from Valdez, the most influential Latino playwright is Maria Irene Fornes, a Cuban-born dramatist. A well-regarded writer, teacher, and director, Fornes has won many awards and fellowships and written more than two dozen plays, which have been widely produced and anthologized.

Other significant Latino playwrights include Lynne Alvarez, John Jesurun, Eduardo Machado, Cherrie Moraga, José de Rivera, and Milcha Sanchez Scott. Lesser-known playwrights deserving recognition include Barbara Brinson-Pineda, Cara Hill de Castañon, Arthur Giron, Josefina Lopez, Edgar Poma, Estela Portillo Trambley, and Rene Yanez. Their plays address the reality of being an "other" in American society and illuminate the complexities of being bicultural and bilingual, attempting both to escape and to acknowledge ethnic roots, and of being both part of and apart from mainstream America.

American Indian Drama. Lynn Rigg's *The Cherokee Night*, the first professionally staged play by a full-blooded American Indian, played in 1930 at the Hedgerow Theatre. Indian drama has developed more slowly than Indian poetry or fiction, perhaps because there is no strong native tradition of formal scripted drama, although there is a rich heritage of ritual performance. Nevertheless, there are a few American Indian dramatists.

Hanay Geiogamah is a Kiowa whose most active period of playwriting spanned the early 1970's. *Body Indian* (1972), produced at La Mama Experimental Theatre Club in New York, subtly reveals how white culture has defined American Indian life, creating despair and self-inflicted degradation. *Foghorn* (1973), which premiered in Germany, explores white-scripted Indian history by juxtaposing white culture, electronic music, readings of broken treaties, and reenactments of historical events. The play *49* (1975), first performed at the University of Oklahoma by the Native American Theater Ensemble, refers to a ceremony that highlights "Indianness" and intertribal bonds. As in his other plays, Geiogamah blends music, dancing, ritual, legend, and poetry.

Two American Indian women playwrights have met with success: Le Anne Rowe, a Choctaw journalist for *The Dallas Morning News* and *U.S.A. Today,* collaborated with Roxy Gordon on *The Big Powwow,* performed in Fort Worth, Texas; and Sharon French, writer and performance artist, is the author of *Anasazi: The Ancient Ones,* an outdoor drama performed every summer at Lions Wilderness Park near Farmington, New Mexico.

SUGGESTED READINGS. A comprehensive introduction to multiculturalism in American drama is included in C. W. E. Bigsby's four-volume *A Critical Introduction to Twentieth-Century American Drama* (1982); the fourth volume has informative chapters on El Teatro Campesino, American Indian theater, and African American theater. Ruby Cohn discusses the work of Fornes, Hwang, and Valdez in *New American Dramatists 1960-1990* (1991). *Contemporary American Theatre* (1991), edited by Bruce King, includes Holly Hill's "Black Theatre into the Mainstream" and Gerald Rabkin's "The Sound of a Voice: David Hwang."

African American drama and dramatists are analyzed in Doris E. Abramson's *Negro Playwrights in the American Theatre, 1925-1959* (1969); Genevieve Fabre's *Drumbeats, Masks, and Metaphors* (1953); *The Theatre of Black Americans* (1980), edited by Errol Hill; and Loften Mitchell's *Voices of the Black Theatre* (1975). Regarding Asian American dramatists, some scholars include David Hwang in their discussions of contemporary American theater. Misha Berson's introduction to her edited volume *Between Worlds* (1990), an anthology of Asian American plays, outlines the development of Asian American drama.

Latino drama is treated in M. Elizabeth Osborn's preface to *On New Ground* (1987), an anthology she edited of plays by writers of Spanish-speaking heritage. More wide-ranging are Roberto J. Garza's *Contemporary Chicano Theatre* (1976), Jorge Huerta's *Chicano Theater: Themes and Forms* (1982), Nicolas Kanellos' *Hispanic Theatre in the United States* (1984), and Kanellos' edited volume, *Mexican American Theatre Then and Now* (1983). For a bibliography on Chicano theater, see *Literatura Chicana: Creative and Critical Writings Through 1984* (1985), compiled by Roberto Trujillo and Andres Rodriguez.—*E. D. Huntley*

Dred Scott decision. *See* **Scott v. Sandford**

Dress reform for women—nineteenth century: A reform movement spearheaded by health reformers, liberal educators, and campaigners for women's rights that insisted that women's clothing was unhealthy and should be changed. Politically minded dress reformers pointed to a correlation between social customs, morals, and the legal position of women as analogies to the heavy, restrictive clothing that women wore. These reformers argued that women's clothing—tight corsets, multiple-layered petticoats, and long, trailing skirts made up of at least twenty yards of fabric—was not only unhealthy and restrictive in itself, but effectively prevented women's freedom of movement just as customs and laws prevented women's social freedoms.

Many nineteenth century feminists proposed the necessity of dress reform for women, and several campaigned for the necessity of "rational dress" for women. Amelia Bloomer promoted the "Bloomer costume," which consisted of loose trousers gathered at the ankle and worn under a skirt that reached about five inches below the knee. Adopted by suffragists such as Elizabeth Cady STANTON and Susan B. AN-

Amelia Bloomer's recommended uniform for women included the loose trousers that now bear her name. (Library of Congress)

THONY, the Bloomer costume was regarded as the symbol of the WOMEN'S MOVEMENT. It was preached against from the pulpit and ridiculed in the press, particularly in newspaper and magazine cartoons that portrayed the "Bloomer girl" as Amazonian and "unsexed." In a short time, both to escape constant jokes and criticism and because they became convinced that the costume's notoriety was diverting attention from more important issues, many women went back to traditional, restrictive clothing.

By the 1890's, a second wave of the dress reform movement emerged when large numbers of women began publicly to express their desire to be rid of the "bondage of skirts." In large measure, this change in attitude can be attributed to changing ideas of social class. In the 1840's, corsets, hoops, and bustles had

A page from Godey's magazine displays the more traditional, restrictive clothing that dominated women's attire by 1875. (Library of Congress)

indicated middle-class female status in contrast to working women and the wives of laborers or farmers, whose shapeless bodies and simple clothes were consequences of poverty and hard work. By the late nineteenth century, however, simplicity in women's dress had come to be associated with exciting new possibilities for female activities, especially female participation in sports, such as bicycling. Change notwithstanding, skirts remained the standard until long after World War I, although even moderate women's magazines began to espouse the notion of lighter, more comfortable clothes. Immigrant women tended to retain more traditional styles of female dress, and most American women wore some form of corset until the 1920's.

SUGGESTED READINGS. Charles Neilson Gattey's *The Bloomer Girls* (1968) discusses the bloomer controversy. Other sources on dress reform include Ellen Carol DuBois' *Feminism and Suffrage: The Emergence of an Independent Women's Movement in America, 1848-1869* (1978); David Kunzle's *Fashion and Fetishism: A Social History of the Corset, Tightlacing, and Other Forms of Body Sculpture in the West* (1982); and William Leach's *True Love and Perfect Union: The Feminist Reform of Sex and Society* (1980).

Drew, Charles Richard (June 3, 1904, Washington, D.C.—Apr. 1, 1950, Burlington, N.C.): African American physician and medical researcher. A distinguished student and athlete at Amherst College, Drew took his M.D. at McGill University (1933) and became the first African American to earn the doctor of science degree (Columbia University, 1940). In Washington, D.C., he practiced surgery and taught at HOWARD UNIVERSITY. A pioneering expert on "banked blood," Drew set up the

African American physician Charles Drew was the first director of the American Red Cross blood bank. (AP/Wide World Photos)

first blood bank in England and directed the American Red Cross blood donor project during World War II. He worked to train young black physicians to a level of excellence that he hoped would overcome racial bias.

Drug abuse. *See* **Alcoholism and drug abuse**

Dual-wage system. *See* **Two-tiered wage system**

Du Bois, W. E. B. [William Edward Burghardt] (Feb. 23, 1868, Great Barrington, Mass.—Aug. 27, 1963, Accra, Ghana): African American sociologist, historian, editor, and racial activist. W. E. B. Du Bois was one of the most important advocates for African Americans in the first half of the twentieth century. Through his insistence on the need for political rights for blacks and through his scientific approach to research on blacks, he did much to advance the progress of African Americans to full equality.

Du Bois was the son of Alfred and Mary (Burghardt) Du Bois, who were of African, Dutch, Indian, and French ancestry. He received his A.B. degree from FISK UNIVERSITY (1888) and his Ph.D. from Harvard University (1895). His dissertation, *The Suppression*

of the African Slave Trade to the United States (1896), was published as the first volume of Harvard Historical Studies. His *The Philadelphia Negro: A Social Study* (1899) is considered a pioneering sociological work on African Americans.

From 1897 to 1910, Du Bois taught history and economics at Atlanta University, where he organized conferences concerned with problems of blacks and edited or coedited sixteen annual publications on topics such as family life, business, health, and crime. He also published *The Souls of Black Folk: Essays and Sketches* (1903), an outstanding collection.

As a racial activist, Du Bois was a leader of the PAN-AFRICANISM movement, which supported the rights of blacks everywhere. He spoke out vigorously against racial discrimination and vehemently opposed Booker T. WASHINGTON's advice to African Americans to accept discrimination for the present and improve their lot through hard work. He was one of the founders of the NIAGARA MOVEMENT, a protest group of black scholars and intellectuals. In 1909, he became one of the founders of the NATIONAL ASSOCIATION FOR THE ADVANCEMENT OF COLORED PEOPLE (NAACP), serving as director of publicity and research, board member, and editor of *The Crisis,* its monthly journal, between 1910 and 1934. After a ten-year absence, he worked again for the NAACP from 1944 to 1948.

After 1948, Du Bois became dissatisfied with the slow change in racial relations in the United States. Having considered himself a socialist for years, he saw Communism as a means of solving the problems of blacks. In 1961, he joined the COMMUNIST PARTY of the United States. He moved to Ghana, Africa, in 1961, to work as director of the *Encyclopedia Africana, renouncing his U.S. citizenship a year later.*

SUGGESTED READINGS. *The Autobiography of W. E. B. Du Bois (1968) is a helpful starting point in understanding his life. A critical biography, W. E. B. Du Bois: A Study in Minority Group Leadership* (1960) by Elliott M. Rudwick, offers a balanced account. Two other useful biographies are *W. E. B. Du Bois: Propagandist of the Negro Protest* (2d ed., 1968), also by Rudwick, and Manning Marable's *W. E. B. Du Bois: Black Radical Democrat* (1986).

Duncan, Isadora (May 26, 1877, San Francisco, Calif.—Sept. 14, 1927, Nice, France): Dancer and choreographer. Duncan developed a naturalistic, highly individual style of dance in rebellion against the strictures

Choreographer Isadora Duncan, known for her bare feet and flowing robes, revolutionized dance as well as women's place in the arts. (AP/Wide World Photos)

of ballet. By 1905 she had established the Grunwald dance school in Germany with her sister. Duncan found greater recognition for her art in Europe and Russia than she did in the United States. She was known for her bare feet and flowing robes, her moody and primitive dances in which movement became emotion, and her uninhibited lifestyle. She died as she had lived when her long shawl got caught in her car wheel, strangling her.

Dunham, Katherine (Kaye Dunn; b. June 22, 1910, Chicago, Ill.): African American modern dancer, actor, anthropologist, and writer. After 1931, Dunham taught and directed in her own schools of dance, theater, and cultural arts in Chicago, New York, Stockholm, and

Katherine Dunham, shown here in Haiti with voodoo religious objects, enjoyed a long and distinguished career as a dancer, anthropologist, and educator. (AP/Wide World Photos)

Paris. Thereafter she pursued a long, distinguished career as a dancer, choreographer, and university professor, working particularly in St. Louis, Missouri. She built her career on formal education, including a B.A. from the University of Chicago and a Ph.D. from Northwestern University. Dunham's academic credentials as an anthropologist and ethnologist allowed her to integrate African and West Indian dance forms into her modern dance compositions. She believed that dancers had an obligation to understand the cultural history of the communities from which they borrowed various dance forms and use this knowledge to educate audiences through their activities on and off the stage. Dunham is the much-honored author of poems, plays, and autobiographical books.

Du Sable Museum of African American History (Chicago, Ill.): Founded in 1961 under Margaret T. Burroughs' directorship, the Du Sable Museum is located on Chicago's South Side, a mainly African American community. The museum evolved from an earlier arts center that was established during the Depression by the Works Progress Administration (WPA), one of the NEW DEAL agencies created during the Roosevelt Administration to employ artists. The museum houses several art galleries of both African and American works with an emphasis on the cultural renaissance of the 1960's and the history of blacks in Chicago.

Dutch Americans: The Netherlands is a small country, two-thirds of which is below sea level. The Dutch have a saying, "God created the world but the Dutch created Holland." By draining and pumping out the sea, swamps, and lakes, the Dutch people reclaimed land for farming and settlement. Its wealth allowed it to become a colonial power, bringing some of the first European settlers to North America.

History. Roman civilization dominated the area, with Germanic tribes hovering nearby, until the Middle Ages. The rule of the Catholic Habsburgs began to amalgamate the area in the fifteenth and early sixteenth centuries. Calvinist Protestantism curtailed the Habsburg rule in 1550 and subsequently Charles V abdicated to his son, Philip II of Spain, a militant Catholic. Despite considerable military force against the seven provinces north of the Scheldt River under Protestant rule, Spain was unable to maintain its control and ultimately granted the Dutch people their independence. The independent Dutch republic became Protestant in 1648, with the Dutch Reformed Church in a position of privilege.

The seventeenth century, known as the Golden Age of the Netherlands, saw this little country loom large in becoming a world commercial empire with colonies spanning the globe from Asia to Africa and the Americas. The sciences and the arts flourished; Rembrandt van Rijn, Franz Hals, and Jan Vermeer are only three of the many illustrious painters of the Golden Age. Dutch influence waned in the 1700's, however, as France, England, and Germany overwhelmed The Netherlands, with Napoleon ruling there from 1806 to 1813. The Congress of Vienna (1815) established a free and unified Dutch nation with ten Belgian provinces. In 1830, Belgium rebelled and left the union; the Dutch borders have been fixed since then. The country became and remains a constitutional monarchy, which since 1890 has been ruled by queens.

The Dutch are known to be family-centered, industrious, honest, friendly, and multilingual. During World War II, they aided the Allies against Germany and many Dutch families helped to protect the Jews by hiding them from the Nazis. These qualities and actions have helped to build strong relationships between the Dutch and American people.

Immigration. Unlike the Irish, who immigrated in large numbers to the United States because of the potato famine, and the Germans, who migrated because of libertarian and political ideals, the Dutch, after expelling the Spanish, were primarily contented with life. They enjoyed security of life and property, religious toleration, and a genial lifestyle. They were even more reluctant to emigrate to the New World when they heard about Indian raids, austerity, and loneliness.

The Dutch staked their claim to New World possessions with Henry Hudson's exploration of the Hudson River Valley in 1609. They established the colony of New Netherland in 1621 and established trading posts. Dutch colonists settled New Amsterdam (later NEW YORK CITY) in 1625. To encourage Dutch emigration, the West India Company in 1629 published its "Privileges and Exemptions" charter. Any member of the company attracting fifty adults to settle along the Hudson River would receive a liberal land grant and become a "patroon" or lord of the manor, with hunting and fishing rights and other privileges. The émigrés, in turn, would be exempt from public taxation for ten years, as long as they remained on the manor. Although these were conditions of servitude, many Dutch persisted so that after their tenure expired they could move on to other pursuits. Meanwhile, the patroons prospered since they could buy whatever goods they wished (except furs) and resell them at exorbitant prices.

The era of commercial expansion in the seventeenth century attracted Dutch immigrants of various backgrounds to improve their lot in life. Those sailing to colonial America included teenagers from Dutch poorhouses and orphan asylums; unemployed workers from Amsterdam; and agricultural tenants. Most of them settled along the Hudson and Delaware river valleys and western Long Island. When the Dutch lost New Netherland to the British in 1664, colonization declined until the 1830's and 1840's.

During the eighteenth century, the Dutch colonists in New York multiplied through large families. First- and second-generation Dutch settlers fanned outward along the Pocantico, Mohawk, and Harlem rivers, and some families moved into New Jersey, Pennsylvania, and Kentucky.

Free immigration during the next century encouraged thousands of Dutch immigrants, including 250,000 peasants and artisans, as well as dissenters from the Dutch Reformed Church. A large group settled in Holland, Michigan, and in Pella, Iowa. Located on fertile soil, Pella experienced almost immediate prosperity in the 1840's as a center of intensive farming and of the cattle and dairy industry, with its products of lard, bacon, and ham. Traditionally thrifty and conservative with money, the Dutch settlers were known for their owning of homes, investment in education, and hard work. During the Gold Rush of 1849, some Dutch settlers in California made fortunes overnight by selling provisions to prospectors. Holland's agricultural crisis in the 1880's brought another seventy-five thousand Dutch to the United States. Wisconsin lured the Dutch, especially around Milwaukee. Families from Friesland, Catholics from Brabant, and Dutch Reformed Church believers from Amsterdam settled in Wisconsin to improve their economic lot. Chicago, too, became a magnet for Dutch settlers. In South Chicago, the Dutch became wealthy by working as teamsters and garbage collectors. Even in the early 1990's, in Denver, Dallas, Phoenix, and Chicago, the Dutch dominated the refuse trade.

The third conspicuous phase of Dutch immigration occurred after World War II, when Holland was suffering from economic troubles, overpopulation, and the effects of 500,000 men having been exiled to German labor camps. U.S. Immigration quotas were lifted for Dutch and Indonesians from the Far East, refugees suffering from the displacement of war, and Jews whose families had been killed. There was such overcrowding in the 1950's that the Dutch government provided free air transportation for emigrants to leave for Canada and Australia. It is estimated that some

80,000 Dutch immigrants came to the United States between 1945 and 1965.

The U.S. Bureau of the Census reported that in 1990, people of Dutch ancestry in the United States totaled 6,227,089. Many of these people and their forebears contributed to all facets of American life and culture.

Contributions. The Holland Society of New York, founded in 1855, provides historical information, educational grants, and funds for special Dutch American

EUROPE

NORTH
SEA

West Frisian Islands

Leeuwarden

Groningen

IJsselmeer

Amsterdam

Utrecht

IJssel

The Hague

Rotterdam

Lek

Waal

Rhine

Maas

GERMANY

BELGIUM

NETHERLANDS

projects. Henry Hudson's famous ship, *The Half Moon*, which arrived in New York in 1609, was replicated in 1988 by this society; it is now berthed in Liberty Street Park, New Jersey.

The Dutch have contributed to American education in many ways. Hope College in Holland, Michigan, was founded by the Reformed Churches in the East, as was Rutgers College in New Brunswick, New Jersey, and Union College in Schenectady, New York. To encourage cementing of Dutch-American relations, a chair in Dutch History, Literature, and Art at the University of Chicago was established. The Queen Wilhelmina Lectureship at Columbia University in New York City was founded for visiting Dutch scholars, as well as the Erasmus Lectureship at Harvard University. After World War II, thousands of Americans lived in The Netherlands under Fulbright grants, designed for educators to spend a year teaching the English language; American history, literature, and culture; and pursuing research. All of these universities, fellowships, lectureships, and exchanges have strengthened the bond which was firmly established between the Dutch and the Americans during World War II.

Thousands of well-known Americans in business, politics, the arts, literature, and education claim Dutch heritage. Three American presidents—Martin Van Buren, Theodore Roosevelt, and Franklin D. Roosevelt— were of Dutch ancestry. Eleanor Roosevelt, also of Dutch background, recalled that during her childhood, only Dutch was spoken in her home.

Some Dutch Americans have pursued traditional Dutch horticulture. Jan de Graaff, whose ancestors had grown flowers in Holland since 1611, came to Mt. Hood, Oregon, in the early 1930's and purchased several hundred acres of land. Within a few years, he produced six million daffodils of 1,500 varieties. Another Dutchman, Hendrick Van Dorp, settled in North Carolina and became known as the "Tulip King of America."

Cornelius Vanderbilt, the first American multimillionaire, was a direct descendant of one of the poorest of New Netherland workers. His father, a farmer by day, obtained a second job as ferryman at night.

In arts, in literature, and in motion pictures, Dutch Americans are many. Cecil B. DeMille of Hollywood is known for producing and directing many films, including *The Ten Commandments* (1956) and *The King of Kings* (1927), seen by millions of Americans. Edward Bok, Dutch-born editor of the *Ladies' Home Journal*, is well-known for the Pulitzer Prize-winning

The Americanization of Edward Bok (1921), a paean to the opportunities of the New World. Herman Melville, famed author of *Moby-Dick* (1851), also cherished his Dutch ancestry, as did poet Walt Whitman, whose *Leaves of Grass* (first published in 1855) is an American classic.

One of the most elegant and sophisticated writers of Dutch American ancestry, Van Wyck Brooks, pub-

A tenth-generation American of Dutch descent, John Hasbrouck Van Vleck received the 1977 Nobel Prize in Physics for his research in quantum mechanics and magnetism. (The Nobel Foundation)

lished *The Flowering of New England,* which won the Pulitzer Prize in 1937. Brooks's *The Ordeal of Mark Twain* (1920) received instant acclaim. Jan de Hartog, born in Haarlem, a province of North Holland, came to America and distinguished himself by writing the drama *The Fourposter* (1947), made into a film of the same title and subsequently becoming the inspiration for the Broadway musical *I Do! I Do!* He is also known for his historical novels. Novelist John Updike used his arch-conservative Dutch background for his famous book *Couples* (1968). His novels, known throughout the world, have sold in the millions, among them the Rabbit series and *The Centaur* (1963). Other well-known Dutch Americans include Gladys Swarthout, a diva who sang with the Metropolitan Opera, and Walter Cronkite, radio and television news anchor and commentator.

Many festivals have been organized by Dutch Americans. Two of the most lavish are offered yearly in Pella, Iowa, and Holland, Michigan. The Pella Tulip Festival, begun in 1935, includes street scrubbing, reflecting Dutch cleanliness, wooden shoe dances, tulip lanes, windmills, bands, the singing of Dutch anthems, and parades by children and adults in Dutch costumes from all the regions of Holland.

SUGGESTED READINGS. One of the most comprehensive and well-written books about Holland is Simon Schama's *The Embarrassment of Riches: An Interpretation of Dutch Culture in the Golden Age* (1988). A comprehensive overview of the Dutch can be found in *The Dutch in America, 1609-1970*, edited by Pamela and J. W. Smit (1972). An informative essay on the Dutch by Robert P. Swierenga appears in *The Harvard Encyclopedia of American Ethnic Groups* (1980), edited by Stephan Thernstrom. *The Dutch in America: Immigration, Settlement, and Cultural Change* (1985), edited by Robert P., Swierenga, is another useful source to consult.—*Julia B. Boken*

E

Earhart, Amelia (July 24, 1897, Atchison, Kans.—c. July 2, 1937, near Howland Island, mid-Pacific Ocean): Aviator. In 1928, a year after Charles Lindbergh made the first transatlantic flight, Earhart became the first woman to cross the Atlantic; she kept the log. As a pilot she made the first nonstop flight from Mexico City to Newark, New Jersey, and the first solo trip from Hawaii to California. In 1937 she set out for her round-the-world flight with Fred Noonan as navigator. Their plane, the *President Roosevelt*, disappeared near Howland Island in the Pacific. Throughout her life Amelia Earhart lectured on opportunity for women. She also founded the Ninety-Nines, a women's flying group.

East Indians. *See* **Asian Indian Americans**

East Los Angeles, Calif.: An unincorporated area immediately east of the Los Angeles River, encompassing approximately eight square miles. The area is bounded on the west and north by LOS ANGELES itself and on the east and south by the communities of Monterey Park, Montebello, and Commerce.

Although Los Angeles was settled as early as 1769, the population remained in the low hundreds as a result of the dispersion of residents among the various land-grant ranches that dominated the Southern California landscape. In 1853, a few years after California was admitted into the union, the city's population stood at approximately 3,500. The majority of the city's residents were Californios (Spanish colonists or their descendants); only 300 were Anglo Americans. By 1881, the Californios and immigrants from Mexico had become the minority, constituting approximately 25 percent of the city's population. As the ranchos were subdivided and land developers began to build on city properties, the Spanish-speaking minority was displaced from its original holdings to less desirable lands east of the Los Angeles River.

Within the eastern portion of Los Angeles by 1930, Mexicans constituted more than 90,000 of the city's population of 1 million. The barrios of East Los Angeles became a major center of MEXICAN AMERICANS in the United States, with an estimated Latino population of more than 600,000 by 1971. The barrio attracted new immigrants from Mexico as well as resi-

Amelia Earhart, the first woman to fly across the Atlantic Ocean. (AP/Wide World Photos)

dents from small towns throughout California. While providing a sense of security and community among Spanish-speaking residents, the barrio was too impoverished to provide sufficient EMPLOYMENT opportunities for its residents. Most residents of East Los Angeles had to work as day laborers outside their community in order to benefit from the region's expanding economy.

The concentration of Chicano residents within East Los Angeles, while more than sufficient to constitute a voting bloc, failed to translate into political clout. Portions of East Los Angeles were represented in six U.S. congressional districts, nine state assembly districts, and seven state senate districts—all of which had non-Latino majorities. Poverty and the continuing effects of discrimination prompted many East Los Angeles residents to support the emerging CHICANO MOVEMENT of the 1960's. During the 1970's and 1980's, the area attracted many new Spanish-speaking immigrants, especially people from war-torn areas of Central America.

SUGGESTED READINGS. For a historical overview, consult Ricardo Romo's *East Los Angeles: History of a Barrio* (1983). The postwar growth of East Los Angeles is chronicled in Rodolfo F. Acuña's *A Community Under Siege: A Chronicle of Chicanos East of the Los Angeles River, 1945-1975* (1984). Marguerite V. Marin places the development of the Chicano movement within the urban context of the East Los Angeles barrios in *Social Protest in an Urban Barrio: A Study of the Chicano Movement, 1966-1974* (1991).

Easter: Christian celebration of the resurrection of Jesus Christ from the dead. The oldest and principal festival seasons preceding and following the day itself. Lent, the forty-day period prescribed by the Roman Catholic church, is a period of preparation for candidates for baptism, discipline for sinners, and general renewal for all even to this day, although many of its more severe strictures have been relaxed. Pre-Lenten festivals such as MARDI GRAS (French for "Fat Tuesday"), date from the time when no meat products could be used in the preparation of food during Lent.

The last week of Lent, Holy Week, is especially important. It recalls the final events of Jesus' life and death, sometimes with elaborate ceremony. Maundy Thursday commemorates the Last Supper and Holy Communion. Good Friday is celebrated in remembrance of the Crucifixion. Many customs outside of-

Coloring Easter eggs is a favorite part of the modern Easter celebration. (Robert Fried)

of Christianity, Easter is celebrated on the first Sunday after the first full moon following the vernal equinox. The term "Easter" derives from the Old Norse *Eostur*, for "spring season."

Easter celebrations are always connected with the ficial liturgies have arisen to parallel church services. In Latin communities, elaborate re-creations of the passion and death of Jesus, complete with costumed players, public floggings, and even crucifixions have been a part of the celebration since the Middle Ages.

These two young men take part in Easter Holy Week ceremonies at a Greek Orthodox church in San Francisco, Calif. (Robert Fried)

Some of the most dramatic Holy Week customs are maintained by the PENITENTES sect in rural New Mexico and Colorado.

The liturgical celebration of Easter has varied through the centuries but since at least the fifth century has prominently included symbols of fire, water, and fertility in the context of baptizing new members. In the nineteenth century, American Protestantism added the tradition of the Easter sunrise service. The custom of wearing new clothes at Easter stems from the early Christian practice of dressing all newly baptized people in white robes for Easter and the following week.

Foods have a special place in Easter celebrations. To celebrate the end of the Lenten fasts, Polish Christians prepare a gruel with herring and then bury it, in gratitude for no longer having to refrain from meat. Greek Americans make a round sweet Easter bread with a dyed egg in the middle. Many national groups, especially those with origins in central Europe, bring baskets of food to church to be blessed.

The most widespread Easter symbol is probably the Easter egg, which has nothing to do with Christian scripture. The egg and the Easter bunny—the latter a relatively late addition to Easter from eighteenth century England—express abundant fertility. Ukrainian, Russian, and Polish Americans maintain an 800-year-old tradition of decorating eggs with elaborate designs, rich colors, and ornaments. Easter egg hunts have been an important part of the American celebration of Easter since the nineteenth century. The most famous of these takes place on the White House lawn.

SUGGESTED READINGS. Anscar J. Chupungco's *Shaping the Easter Feast* (1992) discusses the development of the celebration of Easter, especially the computations for the calendar and the relationship between Easter and natural phenomena. *The Folklore of American Holidays* (1987), edited by Hennig Cohen and

Tristram Potter, collects much anecdotal information about the history and practice of American festivals. Venetia Newall's *An Egg at Easter: A Folklore Study* (1971) discusses the rich decorative history of this development, with abundant bibliography. Franz X. Weiser's *The Easter Book* (1954) draws on a wide range of sources to discuss popular customs at Easter.

Eastern European Jews: Eastern European Jews fled in unprecedented numbers from violence and anti-Semitic legislation in Russia, Galicia, and Romania between 1881 and 1914. More than two million arrived in the United States, a phenomenon that changed their new country and the balance of Jewish influence in the world.

The vast majority of the arrivals were poor, Orthodox, non-English speaking, and frightened. They crowded into the Lower East Side of New York, an area of dark, densely crowded tenements. Most of these immigrants found work in the "needle trades" or GARMENT INDUSTRY, working a seventy-hour week in dingy, poorly ventilated rooms. By 1888, 234 out of 241 New York clothing firms were Jewish, and by 1913 the Jewish-dominated garment trade was New York's largest industry.

In the early years of the twentieth century, the submissive workers were transformed into a powerful, Jewish-led LABOR MOVEMENT through a series of dramatic strikes. Many members of the second generation went on to college and became doctors or lawyers. Others became small businessmen in the garment district where their parents labored; some, such as Julius Rosenwald (who created Sears, Roebuck), founded mail-order houses and vast department stores.

The world's largest YIDDISH-LANGUAGE press developed in New York in the early 1900's to serve the area's million Yiddish speakers, and Jews soon became prominent in New York publishing. Arthur H. Sultzberger and Arthur Ochs ran *The New York Times,* Dorothy Schiff and J. David Stern the *New York Post.* Great publishing houses such as Viking Press, Simon & Schuster, Random House, and Alfred A. Knopf were all established by Jews.

In those early years a good portion of the entertainment industry was based in New York, some of it in Jewish hands. The Schubert brothers owned numerous theaters throughout the country. Two Jewish furriers, Marcus Loew and Adolph Zukor, together with the Schenck brothers, started a vaudeville circuit in 1909 and later went on to become powerful figures in Hollywood. Performers such as George Burns, Fanny Brice, and Eddie Cantor received early training on the teeming streets of New York. Eastern European Jews were also notable in some sports such as baseball and basketball.

With the easing of discrimination in education and employment after the 1950's, the majority of eastern European Jews in the United States earned their living through middle-class and occasionally upper-class occupations. Established patterns of social exclusion served to keep all but a handful away from economic power. By the 1980's, however, they were so well integrated into American life that they were no longer considered a minority in some quarters but part of the power structure. They set a pattern of upward mobility that other immigrant groups have tried to follow.

SUGGESTED READINGS. One of the most accessible accounts of this massive migration is found in Irving Howe's *World of Our Fathers* (1976). Its counterpart on the role of women is *The World of Our Mothers: The Lives of Jewish Immigrant Women* (1988) by Sydney Stahl Weinberg. Paul Johnson's *A History of the Jews* (1987) offers a chronicle of the Jews from antiquity to the late twentieth century. An account of their history in the United States is found in Howard M. Sachar's *A History of the Jews in America* (1992). Mary Antin's *The Promised Land,* the second edition of which was issued in 1959 by Princeton University Press, is an autobiography of a young woman who was part of the immigration. For further research, see Moses Rischin's *The Promised City: New York's Jews, 1870-1914* (1962).

Eastern Orthodox churches: Generally known by their national names such as Russian Orthodox, Greek Orthodox, and Syrian Orthodox. The worldwide Orthodox Communion includes fourteen self-governing churches and seven so-called autonomous churches. The Orthodox church developed from the Eastern Roman or Byzantine Empire with its see at Constantinople. Doctrinal frictions with the see at Rome beginning in the ninth century led gradually to schism by 1054.

The first Eastern Orthodox parish in the United States was established in New Orleans in 1866, but real growth took place only in the early twentieth century. Following World War I, Greeks, Serbs, Syrians, Ukrainians, and Albanians all withdrew from the aegis of Russian Orthodoxy and rearranged themselves into separate churches. Assimilation of the three to four million members of Eastern Orthodox churches has been rapid since World War II but has been marked

Greek Orthodox father and son kiss a holy icon as is customary at their church in Astoria, N.Y. (Odette Lupis)

by several complications.

The instability of the institutions in Eastern Europe, the home of Eastern Orthodoxy, has left the Eastern churches in the United States with tenuous ties to their sources. Partly as a consequence of this fact, the various national churches have suffered their own internal schisms. Moreover, Orthodox worshipers have always sensed a close affinity between their church and their regional culture, but this closeness endured tremendous stress in a newly industrializing land with an alien language and a bewildering spectrum of ethnic differences. Finally, the demands of American members for English-language preaching and liturgies have changed some of the aspects of American Orthodoxy since World War II, if not its substance.

Each Orthodox church has a separate synod, or Council of Bishops, so the various churches have no counterpart to the Roman Catholic pope. The Eastern Orthodox and the ROMAN CATHOLIC churches divide on several doctrinal issues: Eastern Orthodoxy rejects the existence of purgatory and the doctrine of the immaculate conception of the Virgin Mary, but both are accepted by Roman Catholicism; Eastern Orthodoxy

teaches that the holy spirit comes only "from the Father," whereas Roman Catholicism says it proceeds "from the Son" as well; Eastern Orthodoxy rejects Roman Catholicism's teaching of the physical assumption of the body of the Virgin Mary; and Eastern Orthodoxy does not accept the saints canonized by the Roman Catholic church since 1054 unless it has also canonized them. The two churches also disagree on aspects of liturgy and many rituals such as communion and baptism. Veneration of two-dimensional icons is important to the Eastern Orthodox, as seen in the decorative environment of their churches. In these churches, EASTER tends to be more important than CHRISTMAS.

Orthodox clergymen may marry before ordination but not after, and married clergymen may not become bishops. Women cannot be ordained; DIVORCE has traditionally been forbidden but is permitted under special circumstances; ABORTION is allowed only when the mother's life is threatened; and homosexuality is absolutely forbidden. Black people and converts are welcomed into the Eastern Orthodox churches, but membership is usually dominated by immigrants from Orthodox homelands.

American Eastern Orthodox churches are vigorous and evolving. The collapse of the totalitarian regimes in Eastern Europe may have important worldwide consequences for Orthodoxy and will probably support its further growth in the United States.

SUGGESTED READINGS. *The Oxford Illustrated History of Christianity* (1990), edited by John McManners, includes a beautifully illustrated essay on "Eastern Christendom" by Kallistos Ware. An excellent overview is given in "Eastern Christianity" by Paul D. Garrett, in *Encyclopedia of the American Religious Experience: Studies of Traditions and Movements* (1988), edited by Charles H. Lippy and Peter W. Williams. Sydney E. Ahlstrom's chapter on "The Ancient Eastern Churches in America," in his *A Religious History of the American People* (1972), sets the subject in an American context. For details on the Greek Orthodox church, see "What Is a Greek Orthodox," in *Religions of America* (1975), edited by Leo Rosten, and Demetrios J. Constantelos's *Understanding the Greek Orthodox Church: Its Faith, History, and Practice* (1982).

Eastern Rite churches: Also known as Eastern, Byzantine, or Greek Catholics, adherents to these faiths belong to churches whose foundations were laid in the

Eastern Roman Empire or the Byzantine Empire. Eastern Rite churches should not be confused with EASTERN ORTHODOX CHURCHES; Eastern Rite churches, unlike Eastern Orthodox churches, give allegiance to Rome. Although these churches joined with the ROMAN CATHOLIC church, some as early as the sixteenth and seventeenth centuries, they have traditionally retained their unique rites and usages, which were guaranteed

There are three major groups of Eastern Rite adherents in the United States. The largest of these, listed as Ruthenians in *The Official Catholic Directory* (1979), includes Carpatho-Rusyns, Croats, Hungarians, and Slovaks. This group joined Rome in 1595. They practice the Byzantine rite, as does the second largest group, the Ukrainians, who joined Rome in 1646. Both groups came to be known as the Greek

Eastern Orthodox churches, like that pictured here, are better known than those of the Eastern Rite. (James L. Shaffer)

them when they joined with Rome. These rites include singing the liturgy in languages other than Latin; an altar separated from the rest of the church by high screens; a married as well as a celibate priesthood; the use of both bread and wine in communion services; the observance of the Julian rather than the Gregorian calendar, resulting in holidays occurring a week or two later; and the representation of the cross as having three bars, the bottom of which is placed diagonally.

Catholic church in the late eighteenth century. At the end of the nineteenth century, large numbers of Greek Catholics immigrated to the United States. By 1907, they had their own bishop. Ethnic and political conflicts, however, caused Roman Catholic authorities to split them into two groups, establishing a Ruthenian diocese in Pittsburgh and a Ukrainian diocese in Philadelphia.

The third-largest group, the Melkites, are descended

from Arab Christians and also practice the Byzantine rite. Originally the Melkites split off with the Eastern Orthodox churches in 1054, but they rejoined Rome in the early eighteenth century. Their administrative center in the United States is established in Newton, Massachusetts.

The fourth-largest group of Eastern Rite adherents, the Maronites, are also Arab Christians; they claim spiritual descent from Maron, a hermit who lived on a mountaintop in Syria in the fifth century. They joined with Rome in the sixteenth century. They practice the Antiochene rite and their diocese is located in Brooklyn, New York.

Other groups include Syrians (Antiochene rite); Armenians (Armenian rite); Belorussians, Albanians, Romanians, and Russians (Byzantine rite); and Assyrians (Chaldean rite). These groups operate under the jurisdiction of local Roman Catholic authorities.

The Melkites have been the most successful at retaining their unique practices against Roman Catholic pressures, but ethnic revival in the late twentieth century has inspired the reintroduction of such practices as vernacular languages in the liturgy.

Eastman, Crystal (June 25, 1881, Marlborough, Mass.—July 8, 1928, Erie, Pa.): Lawyer, industrial reformer, and women's rights advocate. In 1907 Eastman and Paul Kellogg published the "Pittsburgh Survey," a study exploring the effects of industrialism on workers. In 1910 she published *Work Accidents and the Law*, which resulted in improved workers' compensation laws. She was a member of the Political Equality League (later the WOMAN'S PEACE PARTY) and in 1912 founded the Congressional Union for Women's Suffrage. From 1917 to 1921 she and her brother, Max, published the journal *Liberator*.

Ebony magazine: General interest magazine by and for African Americans founded by John H. Johnson's Johnson Publications in Chicago in 1945 during the heyday of the black press in the United States. The magazine's founding came in the wake of the GREAT MIGRATION of southern African Americans to the North and Midwest; efforts to desegregate the military; and tense encounters with discrimination in all areas of American life. *Ebony* challenged the frequent media stereotypes of blacks by portraying those who had been successful in a variety of fields and could serve as role models for other African Americans who wished to be fully integrated into American society. Until late in the

century, these were stories that no mainstream magazine was likely to cover. In the 1980's, *Ebony* was still one of the most popular of about thirty general interest African American periodicals. Its circulation in 1992 was about two million.

Economic conditions: During the second half of the twentieth century, the structure of the American economy has undergone tremendous change. The relocation of businesses outside the country and the increased use of new technologies have contributed to high rates of unemployment and an overall reduction in the standard of living for most Americans. While most Americans suffer as a result of a depressed economy, racial minorities tend to experience far greater economic difficulty than whites, whatever the status of the economy. Minorities are more likely to be marginalized even during periods of moderate economic growth.

Conditions such as these in 1941 Harlem led to legislation and reform in the second half of the twentieth century designed to improve the life of many African American families. (AP/Wide World Photos)

African Americans, Latinos, American Indians, and other minority groups are found in disproportionate numbers below the POVERTY level and more often fall within the lowest income earning sector of the economy. They are far more likely to be seasonally employed, unemployed, or underemployed. Consequently, minorities more frequently hold positions that offer low income, fewer benefits, lack of job security, and low status. A careful examination of the approximately 116 million people in the American work force reveals a decreasing number of people of color in the upper levels of the professional and occupational hierarchy. On the other hand, movement down the professional and occupational hierarchy indicates a work force that increasingly becomes inundated with darker-skinned people.

Economic Status. By any standard of measurement, minority economic status has historically been lower than that of whites. Every year that data on median income has been compiled, minority median income has fallen considerably short of that for whites.

Median Income by Selected Characteristics: 1950–1990

Year	All Races	Whites	Black and other Races	Black Only	Hispanic
1950	$2,990	$3,135	$1,569	NA	NA
1960	$4,960	$5,220	$2,636	NA	NA
1970	$8,335	$8,730	$5,286	$5,136	NA
1980	$21,023	$21,904	NA	$12,674	$14,717
1990	$29,943	$31,231	NA	$18,670	$22,330

Source: Data are from *Current Population Reports*, 1978 and 1990.
NA = Data not available

Census data from 1980 to 1990 show that African American median income also fell below that for Latinos.

Analysis of the rate of poverty for African Americans, Latinos, and whites is quite revealing. It provides some indication of relative economic status among groups. Since 1950, the percentage of African Americans below the poverty line has always been greater than 30 percent, significantly higher than whites and Latinos. For example, in 1990, the Bureau of the Census reported a poverty rate of 31.9 percent for blacks, 12.2 percent for Latinos, and 10.7 percent for whites.

Institutional DISCRIMINATION, more than any other factor, accounts for lower economic achievement among minorities in the United States. Ian Robertson in *Sociology* (1987) describes institutional discrimination as a type of discrimination embedded in social custom. Based solely on group membership, it is characterized by covert patterns of SEGREGATION and sub-

tle forms of discrimination, especially in employment. Caroline Hodges Persell in *Understanding Society* (3d ed., 1990) comments that African Americans with the same level of EDUCATION as whites and Latinos tend to earn less money. This occurs at every level of education.

African Americans. African Americans are the largest minority in the United States with approximately 12 percent of the total population (around thirty million people).

Africans were first brought as slaves to North America in 1619, one year before the arrival of the *Mayflower*. They proved to be an excellent source of labor for the developing European colonies. In its early stages, American slavery was not justified by attitudes about racial superiority or inferiority, but simply by the need for cheap labor. Racial justification for the institution came later as a strategy for maintaining the continued subjugation of blacks. The THIRTEENTH, FOURTEENTH, and FIFTEENTH AMENDMENTS to the U.S. Constitution, the Civil Rights Act of 1866, and the Civil Rights Act of 1875 were designed to provide former slaves with the guarantee of citizenship and the promise of certain inalienable rights.

While African Americans fought against segregationist policies, discrimination, and other pernicious social, political, and economic constraints, it was not until the Supreme Court's 1954 BROWN V. BOARD OF EDUCATION decision that race relations were profoundly changed in the United States. The *Brown* decision legally ended segregation in public facilities, but it did not end social, political, and economic exclusion. Subsequent CIVIL RIGHTS LEGISLATION such as the CIVIL RIGHTS ACT OF 1964, the VOTING RIGHTS ACT OF 1965, AFFIRMATIVE ACTION programs, and a host of initiatives under the auspices of the "WAR ON POVERTY" during the Johnson Administration, contributed more to African American progress than all the previous efforts in the first half of the twentieth century combined.

Yet despite these tremendous changes in society, African Americans still lag conspicuously behind white Americans in all quality-of-life indicators. About one out of every three African Americans lives below the poverty line compared to about one in ten for whites. Forty percent of African Americans in nonmetropolitan areas cannot find full-time employment, are unemployed, or cannot earn enough money to raise themselves above the poverty line. This phenomenon

opportunity were responsible. Its report declared that the United States was moving toward two separate and unequal nations—one black and one white. The same assessment was made by some observers following the LOS ANGELES RIOTS in 1992.

Latinos. The second largest minority group in the

During the 1940's Mexican agricultural workers arrived in California seeking better wages. (Library of Congress)

cannot be totally explained by lack of skills or the high concentration of African Americans in areas with declining industries. Young African American males have an unemployment rate three times that of young white males, a disparity that has continued to increase since 1948.

African Americans still typically reside in segregated neighborhoods, receive a generally inferior education, and generally earn only a fraction of white income. Such conditions often lead to frustration and may be a precursor to violence in some minority communities. The KERNER COMMISSION, following a series of RACE RIOTS in the 1960's, concluded that "white racism," discrimination, and a lack of real economic

United States, Latinos represent 9 percent of the total population, with twenty-two million people in 1990. While there are clear distinctions in economic conditions between Latino groups, as a whole they tend to face less discrimination than African Americans.

Whereas the median family income for whites was $32,274 in 1990, it was $20,306 for Latinos, and $18,000 for African Americans. Latinos earned 63 percent of the median income for white families, while African Americans earned only 56 percent. Latinos also tend to have a higher median income than African Americans for any comparable level of education, but less than whites.

MEXICAN AMERICANS (Chicanos) are found primarily in the western and southwestern United States. They are the largest proportion of the Latino population, with more than thirteen million people. In many urban areas in the Southwest, Mexican Americans are the single largest minority population.

Mexicans have historically served as a convenient source of labor for the U.S. economy. During the building of the railroads and the expansion of industries in the Southwest, Mexicans were encouraged to immigrate for work. During the GREAT DEPRESSION, however, more than 500,000 were deported to Mexico. Again in 1941 (during World War II), they were encouraged to immigrate under the BRACERO PROGRAM. This pattern suggests that during periods of economic expansion they are brought in to work, but when the economy experiences problems they are pushed out, through layoffs, firings, or deportation.

New technology in AGRICULTURE has dramatically reduced the need for MIGRANT WORKERS, who have historically been predominantly Chicano. Consequently, many Chicanos have moved to urban areas seeking work. Chicano males are primarily employed as laborers, machine operators, craftsmen, repairmen, precision-productionists, and fabricators. Females are overwhelmingly represented in service occupations. In 1985, the median family income for Mexican Americans was about 68 percent of that for whites, while approximately 29 percent lived below the poverty line. Like African Americans, Chicanos often experience prejudice and job discrimination. Along with racism, low educational attainment, a lack of English proficiency, and the reluctance to assimilate into mainstream American culture have contributed to their low economic achievement.

PUERTO RICANS, like many Mexican Americans, became American citizens through military conquest. Following the Spanish-American War of 1898, Puerto Rico was ceded to the United States. Puerto Ricans represent a mixed Spanish, Indian, and African ancestry. They have experienced prejudice and discrimination, not only because they are Latino, but also in many instances because of their identifiable African ancestry. As U.S. citizens, Puerto Ricans are free to immigrate at any time. Yet many Puerto Ricans began to return to Puerto Rico in large numbers in the 1970's because of discrimination and lack of economic opportunity. Those who remain in the United States are the most segregated and destitute of any Latino population. Most live in the Northeast, primarily in and around New York, often in their own barrios. In 1985,

their median family income was only 46 percent that of whites, and 43 percent of Puerto Ricans lived below the poverty line and/or in families with a female head of household.

CUBAN AMERICANS are somewhat different than the other Latino populations. More than 700,000 Cubans fled Cuba after the socialist revolution in 1959. Many early Cuban refugees were affluent and educated with marketable skills or business experience. They adapted quickly to American society and as a result have incomes approximating the national average. The estimated 25,000 Cubans who left Cuba during the MARIEL BOAT LIFT of 1980, however, were decidedly poorer and less educated than those who preceded them; several thousand were also criminals or mentally disabled. They have had more of a struggle fitting into American economic life.

Asian Americans. The seven million Asian Americans are represented by more than twenty distinct national and ethnic groups. The largest groups are Chinese, Filipino, and Japanese, followed by significant numbers of Koreans, Vietnamese, and Asian Indians. They are primarily located in California and Hawaii. Sizable populations may also be found in New York, Boston, Washington, D.C., and Chicago. Asian Americans, unlike African Americans and many Latinos, came to the United States voluntarily. Nevertheless, they have still experienced significant levels of prejudice and discrimination. Like Chicanos, Asian Americans have historically been valued as a source of cheap labor. Chinese and Japanese were at various times encouraged to immigrate to the United States to provide labor for railroad construction and the mining industry. They were eventually viewed as a threat to white workers because they were willing to work for lower wages; this had the impact of lowering all wages. Prejudice against Asian Americans became so pronounced that by the 1880's Congress had been pressured to pass the CHINESE EXCLUSION ACT, followed by other restrictionist immigration legislation.

Chinese Americans. The first Chinese immigrants arrived in California in the 1840's to work on the railroads and in the gold mines. From 1850 to 1882, more than 322,000 Chinese entered the United States. They were forced into segregated housing, schools, and public facilities. Racism and anti-Chinese violence forced them to congregate in areas referred to as CHINATOWNS. Here they were free to maintain their own language and culture while operating restaurants, vegetable stands, hotels, and laundries.

Following World War II, Chinese Americans began taking advantage of the blue collar opportunities that opened up in industry. They also began to move into professional and technical occupations. In 1940, only 3 percent were going into the professional and technical ranks, but by 1980 the number had jumped to 30 percent, largely due to increased immigration of

for their relatively high median income. In 1980, FILIPINO AMERICAN median family income was $23,680. Like other minorities, Filipino Americans have experienced considerable prejudice and discrimination.

The Japanese began entering the United States in the latter part of the nineteenth and early part of the twentieth centuries. As a result of financial discrimi-

Three generations of Chinese Americans are witness to the ebb and flow of prosperity in America's Chinatowns. (AP/Wide World Photos)

highly skilled Chinese after 1965. In 1980, the median family income for CHINESE AMERICANS was $22,550.

The United States gained control of the Philippine Islands following the Spanish-American War. From 1899 to 1934, Filipinos freely entered the United States as American subjects. They were not subject to the immigration quotas and restrictions imposed on other Asian populations. Between 1966 and 1976, approximately 250,000 Filipinos entered the United States. Many of these immigrants settled in Los Angeles, Chicago, New York, and Honolulu. Most possessed professional or technical skills. This accounts

nation, JAPANESE AMERICANS started their own mutual aid societies. These operated much like credit unions and provided capital when traditional lending institutions refused to do so. Other Asian Americans such as the Chinese and Koreans have pooled funds in similar ways.

Japanese Americans live primarily in the urban areas of Hawaii, California, Washington, New York, and Illinois. They comprise more than one-third of the population in Hawaii. In 1980, their median family income was $27,350, the highest of any minority population. Nevertheless, Japanese Americans still receive a lower economic return on their educational achievement than do white Americans.

Koreans began entering the United States in substantial numbers following the passage of the IMMIGRATION AND NATIONALITY ACT OF 1965. Most settled in California, primarily in Los Angeles, where more than 150,000 live. In 1980, the median family income was $20,450. Korean families have often pooled their economic resources to start small business enterprises, usually small food markets. Almost one in eight KOREAN AMERICANS owns some type of business, often in a black neighborhood. Their apparent economic success and cultural exclusiveness have sparked confrontations in AFRICAN AMERICAN–KOREAN AMERICAN RELATIONS, most notably in several murder incidents and during the LOS ANGELES RIOTS.

The Vietnamese represent one of the most recent groups of Asians to immigrate to the United States.

Filipino American advertises his business in San Lorenzo, Calif., 1942. (National Archives)

Following the Vietnam War, large numbers of Vietnamese refugees began coming to the United States. Restrictions were relaxed to allow for this large influx of economically diverse people. While the first wave of VIETNAMESE AMERICANS to settle in the United States was made up of mostly more privileged, better skilled, and well-educated refugees, later waves of BOAT PEOPLE were less well positioned to compete in the U.S. economy. Thus, the community has a wide range of incomes, from domestic workers to doctors, with a median family income of $12,840 in 1980.

American Indians. There are approximately 1.9 million Indians in the United States with about a third residing in urban areas. There are more than 170 distinct Indian populations in the United States. About half live on or near RESERVATIONS managed by the Bureau of Indian Affairs. Their current economic conditions can only be understood in light of their history, which included dramatic population losses from war and disease after European contact; a legacy of broken treaties; and Indians' unique status as members of sovereign nations.

Collectively, American Indians suffer from a host of maladies including high rates of disease, suicide, and alcoholism. They have a life expectancy of forty-six years, about thirty years less than the national average. Indian unemployment usually runs around 50 percent and often climbs as high as 80 percent. Almost 60 percent of Indian children do not complete high school. American Indians have the lowest standard of living of any group in the United States. In 1980, their average annual family income was $1,500.

SUGGESTED READINGS. For an unbiased account of the treatment of racial minorities in the United States, see Ian Robertson's *Sociology* (1987). For statistical data on selected characteristics of racial minorities, see government documents such as those of the Bureau of the Census and Current Population Reports. Christopher Jencks's *Rethinking Social Policy: Race, Poverty, and the Underclass* (1992) and William Julius Wilson's *The Truly Disadvantaged: The Inner City, the Underclass, and Public Policy* (1987) focus on economic conditions faced by African Americans as well as other disadvantaged minorities.—*Charles C. Jackson*

Ecuadoran Americans: The Republic of Ecuador is located on the west coast of South America between Colombia and Peru. The cultural heritage of the nation is strongly Indian but includes heavy influence from Spain. This is reflected in a very diverse population that is about 40 percent Indian (particularly Quechua), 40 percent mestizo (Indian and European ancestry), 10 percent African (as a result of colonial slavery), and 10 percent recent immigrants from the Middle East and elsewhere.

Ecuadoran People and Immigration. Like many South American countries, Ecuador has experienced a population explosion in the twentieth century. This is largely traceable to a dramatic increase in birth rates coinciding with a rapid decrease in death rates brought on by the spread of modern health care. The population has also grown as a result of immigration from Lebanon, China, Korea, and Japan, as well as from South American countries such as Colombia and Chile, which have less stable political climates.

The number of Ecuadorans emigrating to the United States has become significant, though it is not equal to the emigration rate from other Central and Latin American countries such as Mexico. A fairly large population of Ecuadorans is concentrated in New York City. The Ecuadoran community there is known for its participation in athletics, especially volleyball.

Immigration. Historically, the immigration of Ecuadorans to the United States has ebbed and flowed according to political, social, and economic conditions in Ecuador. During the early twentieth century, Ecuador enjoyed a succession of moderate presidents who instituted a number of liberal political reforms, and there was little motive for emigration. From 1935 to 1948, however, there was a succession of military juntas whose oppressive policies prompted people to leave at the same time that post-World War II prosperity beckoned them to come to the United States. After a brief time of stable government in Ecuador (1948-1952), military coups and dictatorships again caused many Ecuadorans to look abroad for better lives. The peak period of immigration came between 1963 and 1968, with most Ecuadorans coming to the United States settling in New York City.

According to the 1970 census, there were nearly 50,000 Ecuadorans in the United States. Between 1971 and 1978, another 76,600 Ecuadorans were legally admitted. These figures are low compared to other populations of Central and South American ancestry primarily because of a high rate of return migration to Ecuador. Nevertheless, New York City agencies estimated that an average of 2,200 Ecuadoran residents of the city received green cards each year during the 1980's. The greatest problem to be over-

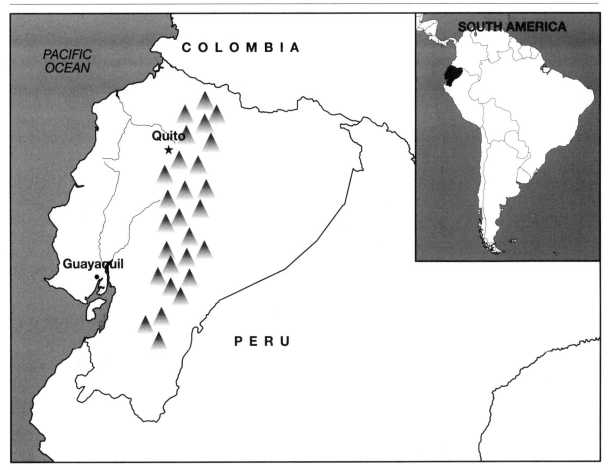

ECUADOR

come by the Ecuadoran immigrants has been that other Americans generally make no differentiation among immigrants from various Latin American cultures. Ecuadorans have been viewed as part of an undifferentiated mass of Latinos with no regard paid to their unique history, strong Indian culture, and outstanding artistic accomplishments. Also, the fact that many Ecuadoran immigrants speak an Indian language rather than Spanish has tended to isolate these groups from the American economy and mainstream culture.

Cultural Contributions. Ecuadoran Americans as a group have generally kept a low profile. In New York, they are known for their participation in athletics and sports, particularly volleyball. Some communities boast Ecuadoran ethnic restaurants. Ecuadoran Indian immigrants have often taken part in musical groups that popularize the pipe, drum, and string-dominated native folk music of the Andean region. Perhaps the greatest Ecuadoran influence in the United States has been exercised not by Ecuadoran immigrants but by

the work of native Ecuadoran artists and writers whose depictions of conditions in their country have aroused interest in the United States. The artist with the largest following and greatest influence in the United States is probably Oswaldo Guayasamin, born in 1919 of an Indian father and a mestizo mother. The poverty and oppression that he witnessed in his own country and among the native peoples of Peru, Chile, Argentina, and Bolivia prompted him to begin a series of paintings called *Huacaynan*, which in the Quechua Indian language means "Road of Tears." This series of 103 paintings was exhibited in Washington, D.C. Guayasamin's commitment to the cause of human rights and the preservation of Ecuador's native peoples and cultures is well known in the United States among those concerned about these issues. Because he has persisted in speaking out about such abuses, he has come to be a hero in the Ecuadoran American community and has been cited for his stands by the United Nations.

Jorge Icaza (1906-1978) is another internationally known and controversial Ecuadoran figure who has influenced people in the United States in their views toward Ecuador. A novelist and playwright, Icaza was censored in the 1930's for his scripts. His most famous novel is *Huasipungo* (1934), which was translated into many languages including Russian, Chinese, and English. The title refers to the plot of land given to Indian laborers in return for work on Ecuadoran plantations. Because of its graphic portrayal of the horrors of In-

Ecuadoran American woman and her daughters demonstrate the techniques of sand art. (Odette Lupis)

dian life on the plantations and because of the unflattering portrayal of the Catholic church, *Huasipungo* caused a great deal of controversy in Ecuador. Icaza's distinctive use of literary realism has made him a major influence for many contemporary Latin American writers and for some authors in the United States. His works have also helped fuel American demands for a foreign policy toward Latin America that emphasizes human rights in those nations.

SUGGESTED READINGS. For a general overview of Ecuador's physical and human diversity, see Martha Murray Sumwalt's *Ecuador in Pictures* (rev. ed., 1987). *Cultural Transformations and Ethnicity in Modern Ecuador* (1981), edited by Norman E. Whitter, Jr., provides more in-depth coverage of various ethnic groups. For a historical perspective, see Betty J. Meggers' *Ecuador* (1966). Jorge Icaza's *Hua-*

sipungo is available in English under the title *The Villagers* (1964), translated by Bernard M. Dulsy. Ann Orlov and Reed Veda's article on "Central and South Americans" in *The Harvard Encyclopedia of American Ethnic Groups* (1980), edited by Stephan Thernstrom, contains some useful material on Ecuadorans in the United States, as do Alan Cullison's *The South Americans* (1991) and L. H. Gann and Peter J. Duignan's *The Hispanics in the United States: A History* (1986).—*Michael R. Bradley*

Eddy, Mary Baker (Mary Morse Baker; July 16, 1821, Bow, N.H.—Dec. 3, 1910, Brookline, Mass.): Founder of Christian Science. Eddy turned to the New Testament when she could not find help for a spinal illness. In 1875 she published *Science and Health with Key to the Scriptures*, the book which became the basis of her religious movement. In 1876 the Christian Science Association was founded to promote the movement's belief in divine healing. Eddy's other works include *Retrospection and Introspection* (1891), *Unity of Good* (1894), and *Rudimental Divine Science* (1908). Eddy was revered by her followers, and her works are still studied by contemporary CHRISTIAN SCIENTISTS.

Edelman, Marian Wright (b. June 6, 1939, Bennettsville, S.C.): African American lawyer and children's advocate. With a law degree from Yale University (1963), she directed the Legal Defense and Education Fund of the NATIONAL ASSOCIATION FOR THE ADVANCEMENT OF COLORED PEOPLE (NAACP), and in other jobs in Washington, D.C., worked with the Southern Center for Public Policy and Harvard's Center for Law and Education. Since 1973, Edelman has made her mark as founding president of the CHILDREN'S DEFENSE FUND in Washington, D.C., lobbying on behalf of deprived children, especially minority children. Recognition for her work includes a MacArthur fellowship (1985) and many honorary degrees. She has published *Families in Peril: An Agenda for Social Change* (1987).

Education: (*See also* **Higher education.**) Education is a chief means by which Americans are integrated into political and socioeconomic life in the United States. While the rhetoric of American nationhood has strongly supported the ideals of social equality and a literate citizenry, educational institutions have implemented the ideal of equality more slowly than the ideal of literacy. The realization of equality of educational opportunity, founded on respect for the dignity and worth of each individual regardless of race, religion, cultural affiliation, ethnicity, national origin, gender, or disability, is a latecomer to American education.

Recognition of cultural diversity and pluralism is a contemporary trend in public education. This awareness largely resulted from the U.S. Supreme Court decision in BROWN v. BOARD OF EDUCATION of May 17, 1954, and the subsequent CIVIL RIGHTS MOVEMENT (1956-1965). These efforts culminated in congressional enactment of the CIVIL RIGHTS ACT OF 1964 and the Elementary and Secondary Education Act of

of the United States: *"E Pluribus Unum"* ("From the Many, One"). "Oneness," or national unity, was defined in American public education ideologically by a process often termed AMERICANIZATION or "pressure cooker assimilation." Generations of American immigrant children were encouraged in public schools to replace the cultures of their birth with a distinctly American culture as rapidly as possible. This was known metaphorically as the MELTING POT THEORY of ACCULTURATION and ASSIMILATION, after the play *The Melting Pot* (1909) by a Russian émigré, Israel Zang-

Edelman speaks at a 1983 press conference decrying proposed budget cuts by the Reagan Administration to the Children's Defense Fund. (AP/Wide World Photos)

1965, two federal laws that recognized the educational implications of the United States being constituted as a pluralistic society—an assumption long denied ideologically and operationally in American public schools.

Ideology of Public Education. After the American Revolution, public education became a chief agent for constructing a new society populated by good citizens. This task was guided by the motto on the Great Seal

will. The ideology of Americanization stressed an exclusive division between what was considered "American" and what was termed "un-American." American public education historically practiced an "exclusivist" policy of expecting children from diverse cultures to "melt" into a unique American culture, characterized by allegiance to capitalism, republicanism, and a secularized Protestantism, all of which was communicated in a uniquely Americanized English.

This ideological perspective has its critics, especially those advocating CULTURAL PLURALISM.

Cultural pluralist ideology, by contrast, replaced the metaphor of the "melting pot" with that of the "tossed salad." It emphasizes public education's support for cultural diversity in which the individual's equal rights and free choices are framed within a common civic culture. This ideology, also referred to as "voluntary pluralism," assumes that Americans willingly enter into what cultural pluralist theorist Horace Kallen called a "national fellowship of cultural diversities." Proponents argue that American public education should adopt this "inclusivist" ideology because it supports a political reality—namely

"Melting pot" or "tossed salad"? either way, most classrooms today are multicultural. (Jim and Mary Whitmer)

that since its founding, pluralism has characterized the United States, a society institutionally committed to recognizing the inalienable right of its citizenry to self-determination. The cultural pluralist ideology has been pivotal in creating multicultural education programs in which the cultural coercion of traditional Americanization is replaced by positive regard for all people. This positive regard for diversity is conspicuously absent in the history of American public education.

Historical Background. American public schools were ideologically committed to "pressure cooker assimilation" until the CIVIL RIGHTS MOVEMENT of the mid-twentieth century and the wealth of equal opportunity judicial opinion (such as *LAU V. NICHOLS*) and new laws that the movement fostered. The Equal Educational Opportunities Act of 1974 made history when it declared that "all children enrolled in public schools are entitled to equal educational opportunity without regard to race, color, sex, or national origin." Prior to

that time, refusal to adopt a cultural pluralist ideology in the American public education movement—historically viewed as the great crucible of American democracy—resulted in a history of exclusionary policy in public, state-supported schools.

Prior to 1900, American public education was characterized by the politics of exclusion. For example, Thomas Jefferson's 1779 "Bill for the More General Diffusion of Knowledge" stated that all free (non-slave) female and male children in Virginia should be taught at commonwealth expense, yet his proposal did not include all youth regardless of race, religion, or socioeconomic status.

The first round of compulsory school attendance legislation in the northern states was an outgrowth of the pre-Civil War common school reform movement. This was led by individuals such as Horace Mann (1796-1859), secretary of the State Board of Education in Massachusetts, the first state to enact compulsory school attendance. The common school reformers pioneered a dual-school system for rich and poor. The common or elementary school and the high or secondary school were to teach all free poor children previously educated in charity schools, while affluent children would be schooled in academies (male) and seminaries (female) governed by self-appointed state-chartered corporations. This common school reform movement was engineered by the Whig political party to enlist government support for educating American children in the ideological triad of capitalism, Protestantism, and republicanism. Although championed by such groups as the New York Workingmen's Party because of their belief that the old privately sponsored charity schools sharpened class differences, the reforms also appealed to and were utilized by the middle and upper classes. Unlike the privately sponsored and state-chartered tuition-charging academies and seminaries, the common schools and high schools were places where upwardly mobile industrial entrepreneurs and shop proprietors could send their children at state expense while keeping them at home.

In the post-Civil War period, there was a second round of compulsory school attendance legislation. The common school movement was transformed into a late nineteenth century bureaucratic school movement. It was accompanied by state efforts to enforce schooling for certain groups of children, especially those males viewed as incorrigible in the regular classroom and children with mental or physical impairments. Following Pennsylvania's passage of a compulsory school attendance law (1897), Philadelphia developed special classes for these children. Stated Baltimore's superintendent of schools after passage of Maryland's 1902 compulsory school attendance law: "[S]ome special provision will need to be made for . . . boys who are unmanageable in the regular schools." That "special provision" consisted of classes variously labeled in the early 1900's as "disciplinary," "mentally handicapped," "prevocational," "subnormal," and "vocational." Pupils subject to this "special provision" were characterized as "irregular attendants,

migrant children as tainted by their national origin and status as members of a religious minority. For example, Roman Catholics felt excluded from state-funded and Protestant-dominated schools sponsored by philanthropic agencies such as the New York Free School (and later Public School) Society. The Third Plenary Council (1884) urged the creation of a system of Catholic parochial schools, a policy that encouraged other religious groups to offset a trend toward secularization in public schools by establishing separate schools.

One-room schools—such as this one in Lancaster County, Pa.—in the Old Order Amish parochial system provide students formal education through the eighth grade. (Pennsylvania Dutch Visitors Bureau)

and neglected children," "incorrigible, backward and otherwise defective pupils," and "unmanageable in the regular schools."

Immigrant children from southeastern and southwestern Europe, were subject to Americanization programs as early as the kindergarten year. Such programs were designed to develop ENGLISH-ONLY language fluency, foster appropriate sanitary conditions, and counter the spread of radical political ideologies. Public school advocates often portrayed im-

Meanwhile, public schools also practiced gender segregation. Women were encouraged to teach in nineteenth century state-supported common schools, yet females were welcome as students only at a small but growing number of privately sponsored female academies, WOMEN'S COLLEGES, and seminaries. Coeducation was infrequent until the twentieth century.

Exclusion and Segregation of Ethnic Minorities. African Americans, Asian Americans, and Latinos were specific targets of exclusionary practices in American

Exclusion and segregation in the eighteenth and early nineteenth centuries made scenes such as this impossible at college graduations. (Frances M. Roberts)

public education prior to World War II. Few free African American children attended colonial reading and writing schools in New England and Virginia. Rhode Island's 1784 Emancipation Bill making the teaching of literacy to African American children compulsory was unenforced. After the American Revolution, African American parents in the North established separate schools for their children. These were accessible only to free African Americans, thus their designation as "African free schools," a rubric resulting from their typical location in or adjacent to an African church. In 1827, the first African American weekly newspaper, *Freedom's Journal*, noted the existence of eleven African free schools operating in northern cities.

Abolitionist David Walker argued that white Americans sought to deprive African Americans of educational opportunity, poignantly illustrated by an 1848 Ohio law stipulating that fewer than twenty African American students in a school district could attend a white school only if no white parent or citizen in the district objected. This exclusion of blacks from public

schools received impetus from the Massachusetts Supreme Court ruling in *Roberts v. City of Boston* (1849) requiring a five-year-old African American child to attend an all-black school further distant from her home than white schools. Massachusetts resolved its segregation issue with an 1855 statute forbidding denial of access to public schools on the basis of race or religion. The "separate but equal" doctrine in public schools, however, was given federal support in 1896 in PLESSY V. FERGUSON by the U.S. Supreme Court.

While the North passed compulsory school attendance legislation prior to the Civil War, the southern states passed compulsory ignorance legislation aimed at their African American populations. South Carolina enacted a 1740 statute making the teaching of writing to slaves illegal. In 1823, Mississippi forbade the gathering for educational purposes of six or more African Americans. Following the Civil War, the FREEDMEN'S BUREAU established schools for former slaves, institutions patterned after the Port Royal experiment of the early 1860's in the Sea Islands located between

Charleston, South Carolina, and Savannah, Georgia, in which African American children and adults were taught by northern teachers. African American education remained segregated from American public education until well into the post-World War II era. In the 1970's, court-mandated busing to achieve school desegregation ordered in the Supreme Court *Brown* decision of 1954 made the inclusion of African Americans in public education again problematic.

AMERICAN INDIAN children faced somewhat different educational barriers and options. Early colonists tried to Christianize American Indian children as in Congregational minister Eleazar Wheelock's Moor's Indian Charity School, founded at Lebanon, Connecticut, in 1754. Later, federal Indian boarding schools, such as twenty built in Sioux country in the early 1890's, attempted to Americanize Indian children. Indian education policy by the mid-1920's favored the total destruction of tribal economy and society.

During and after the Great Depression, Indian children began to attend public schools for the promise of greater achievement; authorities welcomed Indian children for the additional federal monies their attendance would bring because of the Johnson-O'Malley Act (1934). The Indian Reorganization Act of the same year shifted control of Indian education from the federal government to state governments, although a colonial, exclusionary attitude toward Indian children persisted. In the 1970's, Congress provided funds to improve public schools with large numbers of reservation children as clientele. Moreover, Indian adults were encouraged to serve on local advisory boards for these schools as well as for Bureau of Indian Affairs schools. Inclusivist policy is gradually replacing its opposite in American Indian involvement in public education. This trend is exemplified in the 1975 Indian Self-Determination and Educational Assistance Act, which provides for the inclusion of Indian parents on advisory committees in school districts where the school boards of education include a majority of non-Indians.

In the late nineteenth century, exclusion of Asian Americans from public education was blatant. In the early 1880's, the San Francisco Unified School District refused to admit Chinese American children to public schools. The district petitioned the California State Assembly to permit separate school facilities for "Mongolians." Known as the "Oriental School," this facility was replicated by Sacramento in 1893. By 1905 Chinese American parents had successfully

threatened to boycott the elementary school and cost the San Francisco public schools state revenue if segregation did not cease; JAPANESE AMERICANS were as restive. When the federal government found only ninety-three Japanese American students enrolled in San Francisco's public schools, President Theodore Roosevelt persuaded the San Francisco school board to admit more of these students. In return for this concession, he came to an informal understanding with the Japanese government, the so-called GENTLEMEN'S AGREEMENT, not to provide Japanese laborers with passports, thereby stemming their immigration to the

Education is viewed as a right for all people; these New York City college students protest budget cuts and tuition hikes. (Hazel Hankin)

United States and competition with American workers.

By 1920 Chinese American and Japanese American students were attending San Francisco public schools along with their Anglo American counterparts. As was the case with "incorrigibles" of an earlier day, however, exclusion would move from outside to inside the school. Until the 1974 *LAU V. NICHOLS* decision, many

Chinese-speaking students in San Francisco public schools were denied remediation classes in English-language proficiency. Moreover, Asian American students became stereotyped as the "MODEL MINORITY" and singled out for special approbation.

At the peak of their twentieth century immigration to the United States, MEXICAN AMERICANS, as well as other Latinos, were often placed in segregated schools in the American Southwest. Most Latino students left these so-called Mexican schools by the fourth or fifth

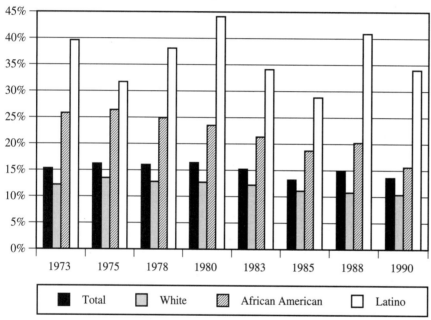

High School Dropout Rates Among 19- and 20-year-olds: 1973-1990, Selected Years

Legend: Total (Total), White (White), African American (African American), Latino (Latino)

Source: Data are from National Center for Educational Statistics, *The Condition of Education: A Statistical Report*, pp. 58-59. Washington, D.C.: Department of Education, 1992.

grade in order to augment family income, a situation these schools did little to change. Curricula focused on domestic and manual industrial education—an agenda that would help Mexicans obtain jobs. Thus, Mexican American children were deprived of general academic training. In the early 1930's, the San Bernardino School District in California decided to solve its "Mexican problem" by establishing a segregated "barrio" school for vocational education. The efforts of some educators—the University of New Mexico's Loyd Spencer Tireman (1896-1959), for example, to introduce bicultural education to rural Latino youth in New Mexico at the San José Demonstration School

and the Nambé Community School—represent an unorthodox policy of inclusion for Latino youth in American public education. BILINGUAL EDUCATION programs have had a profound impact on Latinos, helping some while hindering others; they remain the subject of intense debate among parents and educators.

These examples point to a supreme irony in American public education: Historically, public schools segregated various groups of students rather than serving as centers for the creation of a common, civic culture that was supportive of diversity. The effort to construct a public education system that is accepting of diversity and "voluntary" cultural pluralism occurs in schooling programs that are defined as inclusive.

Inclusive Education. Inclusive education programs are based on a positive regard for CULTURAL PLURALISM in American society and a respect for all forms of racial, religious, ethnic, gender, and other diversity among the American people. Inclusive education seeks to develop this respect by teaching a common civic culture in which each individual possesses intrinsic worth and has equal access to educational opportunity. To implement equality of opportunity, American public schools created desegregation, AFFIRMATIVE ACTION, BILINGUAL EDUCATION, ETHNIC STUDIES, global education, human rights education, peace education, and WOMEN'S STUDIES PROGRAMS. Through congressional legislation such as the AMERICANS WITH DISABILITIES ACT OF 1990, public school sites became more accessible to those with mental and physical impairments. Program development and site accessibility were key components of inclusive education defined as multicultural.

For example, maintenance bilingual education programs for the children of migrant workers in the Rio Grande Valley of Texas became popular public school programs in the 1970's and 1980's. Spanish-speaking migrant workers' children are viewed as contributors to American culture, not mere remnants of preindustrial culture in Mexico. Latino students in Los Angeles, however, are more apt to attend segregated schools than African American students in Alabama or Georgia. Public education for ethnic minority groups in the United States is problematic in the face of an increasing desertion of urban public schools by whites. Proposals for reexamination and reorganization of the public education system often include calls for increased funding for early childhood programs and innovative dropout prevention programs for minority youth.

An alternative approach in Baltimore, Maryland; Detroit, Michigan; Milwaukee, Wisconsin; and Portland, Oregon, has been the creation of all-black schools or academies. The all-black Malcolm X Academy in Detroit is one of six public elementary schools in that city created in the early 1990's as an educational alternative for urban African American boys and—after a federal court order—girls. The academy's 470 students, selected from a citywide lottery with one-fourth of the enrollment reserved for neighborhood children, study an African-centered curriculum that highlights African American achievements. The academy seeks to raise cultural heritage awareness and school success by including, for example, discussion of Mae Jemison, the first female African American astronaut, in fifth-grade science lessons and celebrating the seven days of KWANZAA, Swahili for "first fruits of the harvest." This academy movement, unlike its counterpart prior to the common school reform movement of an earlier day, represents an effort to include a key minority group in American culture on its own terms.

MULTICULTURAL EDUCATION supports cultural pluralism rather than "monoculturalism" or "oneness" as an absolute standard of what is ethically appropriate. As public school classrooms increasingly reflect the full ethnic and racial diversity of the United States, inclusive education is education that is multicultural: School clientele and staffing patterns mirror that diversity; school programs incorporate contributions from minority cultural groups; divergent cultural styles of learning are viewed as different, not deficient; instructional resources present human relations

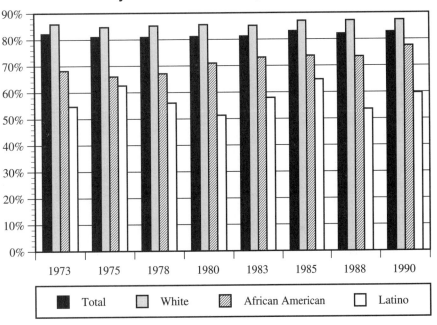

High School Completion Rates Among 19- and 20-year-olds: 1973-1990, Selected Years

Source: Data are from National Center for Educational Statistics, *The Condition of Education: A Statistical Report*, pp. 58-59. Washington, D.C.: Department of Education, 1992.

inclusively, not stereotypically. These public school programs remained controversial in the late twentieth century, fueling much of the debate on multiculturalism. For example, ongoing concerns regarding the multiethnic content of curriculum, mandatory school desegregation policies, and racially discriminatory practices in vocational education programs have been impediments to the realization of inclusive education in American society and equality of educational opportunity for all.

SUGGESTED READINGS. Literature on the transition from exclusive to inclusive American public education is vast. An excellent source for the history of American education prior to the post-Cold War era is Joel Spring's *The American School 1642-1990: Varieties of Historical Interpretation of the Foundations and Development of American Education* (1990). Two especially readable histories of discrimination in public schools are Lawrence H. Fuchs's *The American Kaleidoscope: Race, Ethnicity, and the Civic Culture* (1990) and Meyer Weinberg's *A Chance to Learn: The History of Race and Education in the United States* (1977). Jonathan Kozol's *Savage Inequalities: Children in America's Schools* (1991) offers an analysis of inequality between inner-city and suburban schools.

Jeannie Oakes's *Keeping Track: How Schools Structure Inequality* (1985) provides a useful discussion of how curricular offerings in American public junior high schools discriminate against nonwhite students.

Exhaustive and helpful multicultural resources for building inclusive American education are *Comprehensive Multicultural Education* (1990) by Christine I. Bennett and *Multicultural Nonsexist Education: A Human Relations Approach* (1985), edited by Nicholas Colangelo, Dick Dustin, and Cecelia H. Foxley.— *Malcolm B. Campbell*

Education—American Indian: American Indian education has passed through several phases in the history of the United States. Hostile contacts with European settlers after the eighteenth century brought about the establishment of religious-based "missionary" or boarding schools for Indians, often with the tacit encouragement of the U.S. government. These schools were often the result of treaty agreements to provide the education that tribes requested. Although some aspects of the religious schools were positive, one of their most significant legacies was their role in official government attempts to force the assimilation of American Indian nations into "MAINSTREAM" society. The religious schools saw their task as "civilizing" the students, in part by keeping them separated from native customs, dress, and languages. The schools were set up as boarding schools in order to keep children apart from the "heathen" influences of their families and communities.

Despite these attempts, tribal culture flourished and the American Indian population grew significantly. Of-

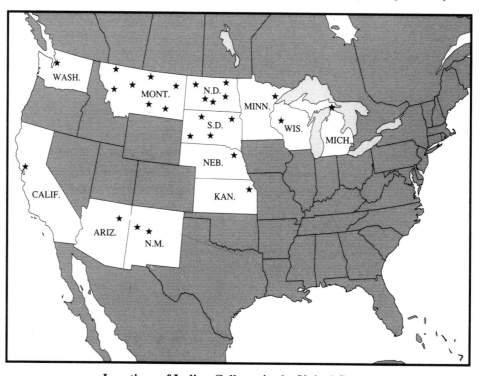

Locations of Indian Colleges in the United States

ficial government policy changed from assimilation to granting the treaty rights of separate "nations" within the borders of the United States. Similarly, changes in the religious attitudes of missionary schools, particularly among the larger Christian denominations such as the Roman Catholic, Presbyterian, Methodist, and Episcopalian churches, have been significant. No longer are native customs or beliefs seen as incompatible with Christianity. Furthermore, in many locations, churches are actually turning over school administration to local communities, such as the former Jesuit schools in St. Francis, South Dakota, on the Rosebud Lakota (Sioux) Reservation.

Sioux boys arrive at the Indian Trade School in Carlisle, Pa., in 1879. (National Archives)

A third stage in American Indian education was heralded in 1968, when Navajo Community College was founded, the first of twenty-three two-year and three four-year tribally based colleges and universities. In 1991, for example, fully 14 percent (13,800) of all American Indian college students were at tribal colleges. Most of these colleges have less than five hundred students, but their popularity is growing, partly because of their cultural adaptation to the unique needs of American Indian students and partly because of their proximity to reservations (all but four are located on reservations). The tribal colleges represent a significant source of hope for the future development of American Indian education.

In general, however, the situation of Indians in American education is bleak. In 1988, the Indian high school dropout rate was 35.5 percent, compared to 28.8 percent nationally. American Indians still account for less than 1 percent of all American higher education students. Nearly one-tenth of American Indians have completed four years of college, compared with a national average of one-fifth. One serious indication of these problems is a strong absence of hope for the benefits of education. In 1990, only 17 percent of Indian eighth graders planned to attend college, compared with 37 percent of Asian Americans, 31 percent of European Americans, and 23 percent of Latinos.

These problems frustrate modern tribal leaders, who express serious concern about educational needs and the future of native peoples. For example, the management of natural resources on Indian lands requires higher degrees in math and the sciences. As a result, one in four of all reservation jobs are held by non-Indians, despite high unemployment among Indians.

SUGGESTED READINGS. Research on American Indian education is growing. *The Journal of American Indian Education*, published by the Center for Indian Education at Arizona State University in Tempe, deals with all levels of American Indian education. See also *Tribal Colleges: Shaping the Future of Native America* by the Carnegie Foundation for the Advancement of Teaching (1989); William Tierney's *Official Encouragement, Institutional Discouragement: Minorities in Academe—The Native American Experience* (1992); M. C. Szasz's *Education and the American Indian* (2d ed., 1977); and numerous publications by the U.S. Department of Education's National Center for Education Studies in Washington D.C.

Education, multicultural. *See* **Multicultural education**

Education and discrimination. *See* **Discrimination—public education**

Egyptian Americans: People of Egyptian ancestry living in the United States make up a relatively small group among Arab Americans. Unlike the more numerous Syrian Americans and Lebanese Americans, who began arriving in significant numbers in the early 1900's, most Egyptian Americans have immigrated since 1965. Their land of origin, however, is better known for its ancient history than for the modern conditions that prompted immigration.

Land, Language, and History. Located on the extreme northeastern tip of the African continent in the Middle East, Egypt contains one million square miles of desert with convenient oases, fertile valleys watered by the Nile River, and fascinating cities. The Mediterranean Sea, the Gulf of Suez, and the Red Sea frame three of Egypt's borders, with Sudan as the fourth.

In ancient times, educated Egyptians employed a

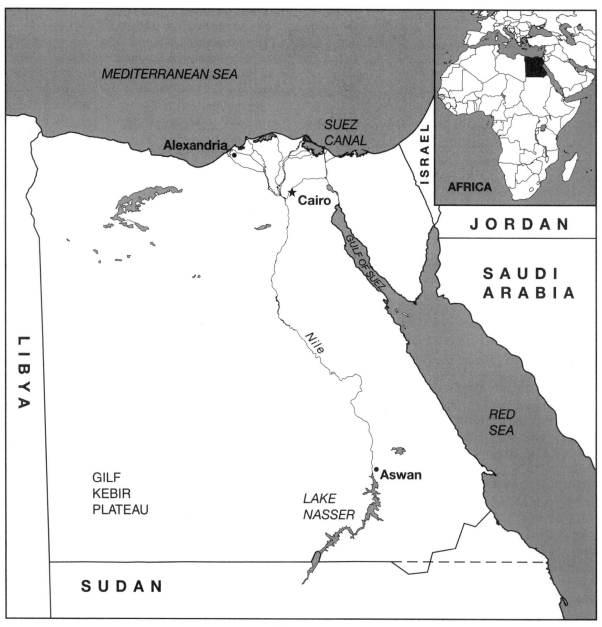

EGYPT

pictographic-ideographic script known as hieroglyphics that could be written vertically or horizontally in both a rounded form and an abbreviated version. In time the language faded into oblivion until scholars found translating hieroglyphics an intriguing challenge. With the discovery of the Rosetta Stone, Thomas Young discerned that hieroglyphics had alphabetic qualities and others were able to crack the code. Since about the eighth century, Arabic has been the official language of Egypt.

Egypt has a rich history stretching back over thousands of years. The ancient world viewed Egypt as the source of all the arts and the sciences. One of Egypt's ancient scientific achievements, the mummification process, still generates speculation and conjecture.

From 3100 B.C.E. to 525 B.C.E., the entire nation served the pharaoh, whom they believed to be a god. The Pharaonic dynasties were marked by the building of the great pyramids, the reunification of Upper and Lower Egypt, and irrigation projects. The country was later conquered by Libya, Ethiopia, Assyria, Babylon, and Persia, followed by Alexander the Great of Greece in 332 B.C.E. In 31 B.C.E. Cleopatra led a revolt in support of Julius Caesar and Egypt became a province of Rome.

In 323 Constantine made Christianity the official religion of Egypt. Present-day Copts are descended from these early Christians, whose beliefs have survived into modern times. Muslim Arabs conquered Egypt in 641 and Islam became the official religion. Most twentieth century Egyptians consider themselves both Arabs and Muslims.

In 1878 Ahmed Arabi, a militant colonel, organized a protest to secure promotions and better pay for the army. His action grew into a full-scale rebellion against the government. Because the British interpreted this as an affront and a threat to peace in Africa, they sent in their troops. After their victory at Tel el Kebir in 1882, the British occupied Egypt. Under British rule, Lord Comer instituted social reforms and gave small land grants to the poor. He improved irrigation methods and built a dam at Aswan.

A 1922 treaty gave the Egyptians their land back, but it also gave England sweeping concessions. The British administered the communication system, controlled the Sudan, guaranteed Egypt protection against foreign aggression, and swore to maintain and preserve foreign business interests. In effect, Britain withheld home rule from the Egyptians. Disenchantment

with the British colonial system led to a military takeover in July, 1952. The British presence ended when Egypt took control of the Suez Canal. Gamal Abdel Nasser became president in 1956, and a new constitution took effect. Egypt joined with Syria to form the United Arab Republic in 1958 but dissolved this tie in 1961.

Egypt took a leading role in fighting Israel during the Arab-Israeli War in 1967 and the Yom Kippur War in 1973. In 1979, however, President Anwar Sadat signed the Camp David peace accords and later made a historic state visit to Israel. In the 1980's and 1990's, Egypt took on the new role of peacemaker in the Middle East while trying to contain Muslim fundamentalists.

Immigration. The migration of Egyptians to the United States was motivated by a combination of "push" factors driving them out of their homeland and "pull" factors drawing them to a new life. Egyptian immigration did not really become significant until the reforms of the IMMIGRATION AND NATIONALITY ACT OF 1965, such as preference for certain types of professionals. Egyptians came in unprecedented numbers seeking educational and economic opportunities. A further impetus was the defeat of Egypt in the Arab-Israeli War in 1967, which brought a wave of fifteen thousand Egyptian immigrants to the United States over the next ten years.

Egyptian Copts, a Christian religious minority, had a special set of reasons for leaving. Since their church broke with Rome in 451, they had grown to become one of the best educated and professionally prominent communities in Egypt, active in medicine, law, education, banking, and commerce. Their interests were threatened after Gamal Abdel Nasser came to power and promoted a pan-Arabist philosophy for Egypt as an Islamic state. Their immigration and resettlement began in 1966, aided by a number of Jewish American organizations. Other Egyptian immigrants, such as Jews and conservative Muslim businessmen, shared the Copts' concern about modern political developments in their homeland.

The Copts, like most Egyptian Americans, settled in urban and suburban areas, especially New York and Los Angeles, with smaller communities in Chicago, San Francisco, Detroit, Philadelphia, Washington, D.C., and Houston. By 1980, there were about twenty Coptic Orthodox churches in the United States, which served as both religious and general community centers. A number of local and national Coptic and Egyptian American organizations were formed, but no distinctive Egyptian neighborhoods developed like the "Little Syrias" of Brooklyn, New York. Rather, the vast majority of Egyptians in the United States have attempted to blend in with their fellow students and professional colleagues. Some have found common cause with other Arab Americans in combating U.S. media stereotypes of Arab culture and aspects of U.S. policy in the Middle East.

Apollo program and has made significant contributions to understanding the geological configuration of the moon. Mohammed Nour and Negil Megaly have garnered honors in the field of medicine. Mona Mikahil and other educators help the nation's students learn more about the Middle East. Other immigrants have started successful retail businesses, both large and small, that offer goods, services, and employment to other Americans.

Egyptian leader Anwar Sadat shakes hands with Israeli leader Menachem Begin, while U.S. president Jimmy Carter looks on during the historic Camp David meetings. (National Archives)

Cultural Contributions. Egyptians have made significant contributions to world culture. The designs of their ancient ancestors have inspired modern artists; academics have used the ancient culture and religion as a springboard for important theories of historical development.

Following their ancient forebears, some Egyptian Americans have made their mark in the arts and sciences. Omar Sharif transferred his successful film career from Egypt to the United States, capturing women's hearts with his commanding, romantic presence. Farouk el Baz worked with the National Aeronautics and Space Administration (NASA) on the

SUGGESTED READINGS. Georgiana G. Stevens' *Egypt Yesterday and Today* (1963) presents a history of Egypt from Pharaonic to modern times. Albert Hourani's *A History of the Arab Peoples* includes Egypt's history in his comprehensive discussion. For information on Egyptians in the United States, see Brent Ashabranner's *An Ancient Heritage: The Arab-American Minority* (1991); Gregory Orfalea's *Before the Flames: A Quest for the History of Arab Americans* (1988), and "The Coptic-Americans: A Current African Contribution" by Gabriel Abdelsayed in *The New Jersey Ethnic Experience* (1977), edited by Barbara Cunningham.—*Maxine S. Theodoulou*

Ellington, Duke [Edward Kennedy] (Apr. 29, 1899, Washington, D.C.—May 24, 1974, New York, N.Y.): African American jazz composer and bandleader. Leader of top bands for fifty years, the self-trained "Duke" had a sophisticated style in harmony, tone, and mood. In the 1920's, when he performed at the COTTON CLUB on Lenox Avenue in Harlem, records and radio brought him fame, enhanced by world tours in the 1930's. Ellington's varied compositions include the classics "Mood Indigo" (1931) and "Don't Get Around Much Anymore" (1942); his suite "Black, Brown, and Beige" (1943) merged jazz with formal concert features. His many awards include the Presidential Medal of Honor (1969).

Ellis Island: Principal port of entry into the United States for European immigrants between the years 1892 and 1943 and the most famous symbol of the legacy of American immigration. Located in upper New York Bay, the roughly 27-acre island is about a mile southwest of Manhattan but only 1,300 feet from the shores of New Jersey, locating it within that state's territorial waters. An 1834 pact between New York and New Jersey, however, placed the island under the jurisdiction of New York.

Italian immigrants on the ferry to Ellis Island in 1905, seeking a home in the new land. (Library of Congress)

The island's initial owner—a butcher/chandler named Samuel Ellis—deeded it to the state of New York, which then sold it for $10,000 to the United States government in 1808. It became a fort, then a powder arsenal. In 1892, it was transformed into an immigration station, which it remained until 1943, when the station itself was moved to New York City. The island then became a detention center for deportees until it was closed in 1954. Eleven years later, Ellis Island became part of the Statue of Liberty National Monument; it was opened to tourists in 1977. Still, the buildings fell into disrepair. In the late 1980's, the center's buildings were refurbished at a cost of more than $150 million, most of which was raised through the donations of hundreds of thousands of private citizens. In September, 1992, Ellis Island was opened to the public as part of a national museum of American immigration.

At the island's peak as the primary immigration center for the United States, more than one million immigrants a year passed through its gates. All told, approximately twenty million immigrants—90 percent of the immigrants entering the United States between 1892 and 1943—came through Ellis Island. Indeed, in 1992 more than 40 percent of the U.S. population could trace roots back to this single immigration center.

Most immigrants arrived at Ellis Island exhausted and penniless after a long passage from Europe. Few knew the English language, and even those who did were usually afraid to speak. All prospective immigrants underwent a rigorous course of medical examinations and questioning by immigration officials determined to reject any sick or politically undesirable people. A typical test administered, for example, was that of asking the immigrant to place pegs in holes. Failure to complete this task successfully would mark that person as feeble-minded and would be grounds for deportation. Those who passed all the tests had their clothes and belongings fumigated while they were given an opportunity to bathe. Even though approximately 10 percent of the immigrants were detained at some point in this process, only 2 percent were denied entry and forced to return to their homelands.

According to oral tradition, many immigrants had their foreign names changed by officials at Ellis Island to sound more "American," but it is not certain just how often this occurred. Tradition also holds that Italians without the necessary documents had W.O.P. ("without papers") written in their files, while Jewish immigrants had their clothes marked with a chalk circle, which they called a "keikel"—the Yiddish word for circle. Perhaps some of the American language of bigotry and racial intolerance in the form of ethnic slurs can be traced to Ellis Island. Thus, the immigration center has both positive connotations of hope and the negative connotations of fear and prejudice for those who went through it.

Asian American children view a display at Ellis Island's Immigration Museum, which opened in 1992. (Mary Pat Shaffer)

SUGGESTED READINGS. For more information about Ellis Island, see Thomas M. Pitkin's *Keepers of the Gate: A History of Ellis Island* (1975), Wilton S. Tifft's *Ellis Island* (1990), and Mary J. Shapiro's *Ellis Island: An Illustrated History of the Immigrant Experience* (1991). Michael C. LeMay's *From Open Door to Dutch Door: An Analysis of U.S. Immigration Policy Since 1820* (1987) is an excellent place to start for information on immigration legislation.

Emancipation Proclamation: On September 22, 1862, at the height of the American CIVIL WAR, President Abraham Lincoln issued a general proclamation to the American people outlining the substance of what would be the third most important document in the history of the United States. It is superseded only by the DECLA-RATION OF INDEPENDENCE and the CONSTITUTION. The Emancipation Proclamation declared that as of January 1, 1863, "all persons held as slaves within any state, or designated part of a State, the people whereof shall then be in rebellion against the United States, shall be then, thenceforward and forever free." Although generally considered the prime example of Lincoln's much-fabled idealism and altruistic spirit, the proclamation was more realistically a strategic move to revitalize the support and morale of the northern states, which were considerably enervated by a series of Confederate victories. Volunteer enlistments in the Union Army had seriously declined, and it became clear to the Lincoln Administration that the preservation of the Union alone was not sufficient cause to effect the kind of enthusiasm and energy necessary for the successful prosecution of the war.

The proclamation was intended primarily to have two effects: to rally the northern abolitionists and to provide additional manpower from the ranks of freed slaves for new enlistments. Since the days immediately following the attack on Fort Sumter in 1861, the abolitionists and radical Republicans in the North had pressed vigorously for the government to declare that the war was being fought not only to preserve the Union but also to abolish forever the abomination of slavery. Lincoln had consistently resisted such pressure, and was determined to maintain the preservation of the Union as the sole issue. Twice in 1862 he proposed a "compensated" emancipation for the southern states but was unsuccessful in gaining congressional support for the measure. Added pressure came from the governors of the northern states, who were becoming increasingly reluctant to supply additional manpower unless emancipation became a declared objective.

Before the preliminary proclamation could be made, however, Lincoln and his cabinet needed a victory. Otherwise, the emancipation issue might be perceived as an act of desperation rather than an action taken on principle. When General George McClellan's Army of the Potomac halted Robert E. Lee's northern advance at the Battle of Antietam on September 17, 1862, Lincoln was given his timely opportunity, but the proclamation continued to be divisive. Lincoln had issued it as a war measure, an action which he considered within the purview of presidential "war powers" delegated to him to effect the prosecution of war. It was not an act of Congress, but a statement of intent by the chief executive, and its constitutional legality

A copy of Abraham Lincoln's Emancipation Proclamation. (Library of Congress)

An Emancipation Day celebration in Richmond, Va. (Library of Congress)

was in doubt. Many in the border states, proslavery supporters of the Union, felt that the president had exceeded his authority. The abolitionists, however, felt that it was insufficient, since it freed only those slaves residing in states that had seceded from the Union, while permitting slavery to continue in states and territories remaining under federal control.

The Emancipation Proclamation ultimately survived its opposition, giving the North the dual objective of liberty and freedom, and resolving contradictions in both the Declaration of Independence and the Constitution concerning the issue of the term "freedom."

SUGGESTED READINGS. Adolescent readers will find Dorothy Sterling's *Forever Free: The Story of the Emancipation Proclamation* (1963) eminently readable and comprehensive. For greater detail and thoroughness, consult John Hope Franklin's *The Emancipation Proclamation* (1963). Hans L. Trefousse's *Lincoln's Decision for Emancipation* (1975) provides background on Lincoln's thoughts about the timing and extent of the proclamation.

Emi, Frank Seishi: Japanese American political activist. An American-born Japanese who was interned during World War II, Emi protested the loyalty questionnaire posed to all arriving internees at the Heart Mountain Relocation Center in Utah. In early 1944, after the Selective Service was reinstated for Japanese Americans, Emi was one of sixty-three draftees arrested for refusing to report to their preinduction physicals. Along with Kiyoshi Okamoto, he was an organizer of the HEART MOUNTAIN FAIR PLAY COMMITTEE, which demanded restoration of constitutional rights before military conscription. One of seven protest leaders convicted of conspiracy to violate the Selective Service Act, Emi spent four years in federal prison at Leavenworth.

Emily's List: Fund-raising group begun in 1985 to support Democratic, pro-choice women candidates in U.S. congressional races. The name Emily is an acronym for Early Money Is Like Yeast, referring to the idea that money in the early stages of a campaign will "make the dough rise" and overcome the barrier of insufficient campaign financing which often plagues women candidates. The organization researches candidates, assesses their stands on issues, and evaluates their ability to succeed. A list of prospective candidates is then sent to donor members who select the candidates of their choice and pledge a sum of money to various campaigns. In 1992, Emily's List was the largest single campaign donor base in the nation.

Emmons, Delos Carleton (Jan. 17, 1888, Huntington, W. Va.—Oct. 3, 1965, Hillsborough, Calif.): Military leader. Born into a military family, Emmons graduated

Brigadier General Emmons, commanding First Wing GH2 Air Force. (AP/Wide World Photos)

from West Point in 1909. He served at posts in California, Alaska, New York, and Texas, and in 1917 entered the young field of army aviation. By 1941, he had achieved the highest rank in the Army Air Force as Chief of the Air Force Control Command. After the bombing of PEARL HARBOR by the Japanese on December 7, 1941, Emmons was appointed commander of the Hawaiian

Department and served as military governor of Hawaii through the end of World War II. Because of Emmons' faith in their loyalty, JAPANESE AMERICANS in Hawaii were not subjected to evacuation and internment.

Employment: Over the course of the nineteenth century, the United States became a nation of wage earners. By the early twentieth century, a majority of male Americans participated in a market economy, not as independent craftsmen, farmers, or contractors, but as the employees of someone else. For native-born and immigrant men and women, finding and retaining work in a wage labor market was one of their most important individual and familial activities. Without work and the monetary compensation it provided, POVERTY and destitution were guaranteed. Even with work, wages were often too low to sustain a family. As a consequence, family members—husbands/fathers, teenage sons and unmarried daughters, and in some cases, married wives/mothers and smaller children—pooled their financial resources, relying upon a familial strategy to ensure basic economic survival.

The search for stable employment has also been a powerful motivation behind immigrants and migrants' decision to undertake often-difficult journeys and to relocate in new places. Although economic deprivation and political and religious persecution constituted important factors behind immigrants' decision to move, the availability or lack of work, as well as the prospect of higher wages, has exerted a strong influence on the timing and direction of labor migration.

The nation's job market has historically been segmented along racial lines. Yet the relationship between race, ethnicity, and employment in the United States has never been a static one; it has undergone dramatic shifts over the past three centuries. Since at least the early nineteenth century, the economic opportunities available to different racial or ethnic groups reflected economic conditions (the demand for labor); the character of the economy and job structure; the level of skills possessed by each group; the cultural, familial, and economic strategies of the migrants; and the response of dominant groups to workers of different races or ethnicities. Of critical importance were the attitudes and approaches of key groups—especially employers and workers—that led them to restrict or encourage employment of specific racial minorities or immigrants.

The Economy and Immigration. The health of the American economy influenced the overall rate and size of immigration, at least until the passage of the IMMIGRATION ACT OF 1924 drastically reduced the numbers of immigrants. The vast expansion in industrial production in the late nineteenth century generated a huge demand for human labor. During periods of economic prosperity, there were expanding job opportunities in meat packing, iron and steel production, and textile and garment manufacturing, as well as in realms of common labor—railroad-track work, mineral extraction, and building construction. Prospective

lower rates of immigration, while periods of economic expansion saw higher rates. For example, immigration from Europe dropped sharply during the depression of 1873 to 1878, the economic downturn from 1882 to 1885, and the 1893-1897 depression, while it reached its highest numbers in boom years such as 1892 and 1910. In the year immediately following the 1907 financial panic, out-migration exceeded immigration for both Italians and Austro-Hungarians. In 1921, when a post-World War I economic downturn

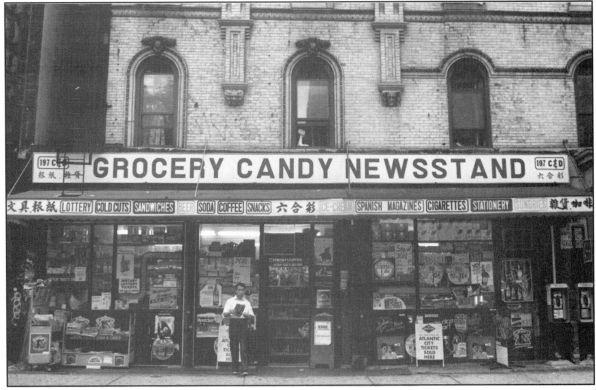

Many Chinese immigrants created Chinatowns and opened businesses, which in turn provided employment opportunities. (Frances M. Roberts)

immigrants learned of employment opportunities from family members, former townsfolk, and friends already in the United States, who wrote back home advertising the possibilities of high wages and available jobs, or from labor brokers and agents/recruiters (such as the Italian *PADRONES*), middlemen who contracted with employers to provide immigrant labor for a particular job.

The availability of jobs directly affected the tempo of immigration into the United States. Given the importance of economic opportunity in the migrants' calculations, it is not surprising that economic depressions and periods of high unemployment witnessed

increased unemployment, some 150,000 Mexican immigrants left the United States.

The INDUSTRIAL REVOLUTION in the United States depended on the labor of large numbers of Europeans in the eastern and midwestern states, and, to a lesser extent, Asians in the West and Mexicans in the Southwest. It served as a magnet, drawing immigrants from industrially less developed or economically impoverished regions abroad. Those immigrants had reason to seek out new opportunities, for many confronted financial uncertainty in the increasingly commercialized economies of and political or religious persecution in Europe, Asia, or Mexico. American work sites in the industrial era were highly segmented, with native-born whites and "old immigrants" from Germany and the British Isles dominating skilled labor positions and newer immigrants and African Americans dominating unskilled labor. Industries relying heavily upon unskilled labor quickly assembled extremely heterogeneous work forces. The U.S. Immigration Commission estimated in 1910 that foreign-born workers (roughly two-thirds of whom came from southern and eastern Europe) in some twenty-one major industries constituted 57.9 percent of the labor force. For any given industry or individual firm, the percentage might be higher or lower. For example, eastern Europeans made up 11,694 out of a total labor force of 14,359 working in steel magnate Andrew Carnegie's Allegheny County, Pennsylvania, factories in 1907.

The Diversifying Work Force. Racial and ethnic diversity characterized the work force in virtually all principal industries by the early twentieth century. In the copper and silver mines in New Mexico and Arizona, white American and Cornish miners worked alongside Italians, Slavs, and Mexicans. Southern Colorado's coal mining communities mixed Italians with Slavs, Poles, Greeks, Irish, Scots, English, and Mexicans. Although native-born whites numerically dominated the West Virginia coal fields in 1900, the industry also provided employment to large numbers of African Americans and smaller numbers of immigrants from Austria-Hungary, Great Britain, Ireland, Italy, Germany, Poland, and Russia. By the early 1890's, the demand for mining labor in West Virginia exceeded the available supply of native-born whites and blacks, leading some of the larger mine operators to solicit immigrants, seemingly without distinction or preference of race, from other mining regions and from labor agencies in New York. New arrivals included Poles, Slovaks, northern Italians, and Hungarians. Similarly, the Alabama coal fields of the Birmingham district employed native-born blacks and whites, including Italian, Scottish, Slovak, French, English, Bulgarian, German, Irish, and Welsh workers by the early twentieth century. During the 1908 coal strike in Alabama, mine operators imported new immigrants as strikebreakers. This move enabled them to crush the United Mine Workers of America in Alabama, a labor organization that had succeeded in uniting blacks and whites, native- and foreign-born miners into a single body.

The experience of female immigrants (and native-born women as well) in the U.S. labor market differed

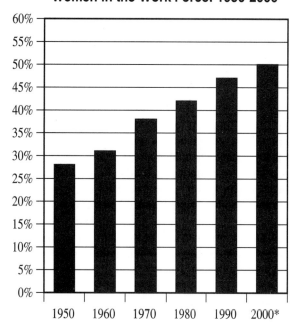

Women in the Work Force: 1950-2000

Source: From Michael R. Bradley, *On the Job: Safeguarding Workers' Rights.* Human Rights series, p. 68. Vero Beach, Fla.: Rourke Corp., 1992.
*Projected for the year 2000

sharply from that of their male counterparts for a number of reasons. These included gender discrimination; prevailing notions of what work was appropriate for men and women to perform; "protective" legislation that limited the hours, conditions, or type of work women could perform; and the values and strategies of women themselves. Some industries or trades—such as the GARMENT INDUSTRY, textiles, tobacco and food processing, commercial laundries, and domestic service—relied heavily upon women's labor. In early twentieth century New York City and Chicago, for example, the garment trade provided employment for young immigrant Jewish women from Russia and young Italian women. For both groups, wage earning tended to be restricted to the years before marriage. After marriage, women often left the paid job market to perform unpaid work in the home or supervised the taking in of boarders to supplement often-inadequate male wages.

During the world wars, a shortage of male labor and sharply rising costs of living both induced employers to hire women in better-paid positions previously reserved for men and led women to seek out actively those new opportunities. Although women lost economic ground by being forced out of many of those jobs after each war, in the post-World War II period the percentage of women (and especially married women) in the paid labor force increased dramatically. The expanding clerical, sales, and service sectors remain heavily dependent upon a female work force.

Race, National Origin, and Employment. Nineteenth and early twentieth century immigrants first and foremost sought employment upon their arrival in the United States. The Italian phrase *"pan e lavoro"*—bread and work—summarized that imperative and desire. Immigrants were attracted by the higher wages that jobs in the United States provided, for those wages allowed them to accumulate funds to enable them to bring over their relatives. Not all immigrants, however, viewed their jobs or residence in the United States as permanent. Some, described as "birds of passage," saw American employment as the vehicle to save funds sufficient to enable them to return home to purchase land. Return migration rates reflected both the state of the U.S. economy—rates increased during depression years—as well as the original desires of the immigrants themselves.

Between 1850 and 1880, more than 300,000 Chinese workers, most of them male, crossed the Pacific to find employment in the United States. At first many of these Chinese migrants worked as independent gold placer miners, despite a discriminatory "foreign miners" license tax levied in 1852. The demand for Chinese labor increased dramatically in the mid-1860's when a shortage of whites forced the managers of the CENTRAL PACIFIC RAILROAD to search for new sources of labor to complete their portion of the transcontinental railroad. Between 1866 and 1869, perhaps twelve thousand Chinese men became railroad laborers, boring tunnels and laying track through the mountains of California and the deserts of Nevada and Utah, while the railroad's white employees found themselves upgraded into skilled and managerial positions. By the 1880's, the Chinese constituted roughly half of California's farm labor population; they also served as the mainstay of the sugar industry of Hawaii. With the increase in white migration from the East after 1870, Chinese workers in the American West found themselves further relegated to the margins of the region's economy, occupying poorly paid, unskilled jobs with little prestige. In western cities such as San Francisco and Seattle, the formation of CHINATOWNS represented the limited economic and social options available to the Chinese, as well as efforts to construct viable, protective communities.

Other workers denounced both the competition from and the very presence of the Chinese in California and other western states, characterizing them as members of an inferior race, as servile contract laborers, or "COOLIES," who could never be assimilated to American norms and standards. Courting the support of political leaders, they campaigned hard to end Chinese immigration to the United States. The result was the CHINESE EXCLUSION ACT of 1882, which barred the arrival of new Chinese laborers for a ten-year period; in 1888, Congress expanded the law to cover "all persons of the Chinese race," and it was not rescinded until 1943. Chinese Americans already in the country were also defined as aliens ineligible for citizenship because of their race.

The first three decades of the twentieth century witnessed a substantial migration of Mexican workers across the U.S.-Mexico border, with as many as half a million seeking work from 1900 to 1910. In the Southwest, where the majority of Mexican immigrants resided, employment could be found in railroad construction and maintenance, mining, and a rapidly expanding agricultural sector (whose development was facilitated by the 1902 Newlands National Reclamation Act, which encouraged irrigation projects). Smaller numbers worked as railroad laborers, sugar beet hands, and meat packers in midwestern cities such as Kansas City and Omaha. Seasonal labor mobility characterized Mexicans' search for employment and wages. Railroad-track gangs were constantly on the move, while the fluctuating demand for miners tended to draw more Mexicans to Colorado's coal communities during the high-fuel-consumption winter months. Sugar beet farming and processing was even more seasonal, and entire families moved from region to region during harvest time.

Mexican labor was essential to the profitable functioning of the economy of the Southwest in the twentieth century. For the most part, impoverished Mexican immigrants performed work that native-born white workers would not. In the words of a 1920 congressional investigating committee, "white men are averse to accepting, and refuse to accept . . . employment as unskilled or common laborers" in the Southwest. Eleven years earlier, the DILLINGHAM COMMISSION characterized the place of Mexicans in the economy of Southern California: "The members of this race

Unemployment Rates: 1980-1990

Percent of each group unemployed

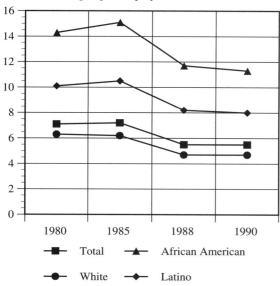

◼ Total   ▲ African American

● White   ◆ Latino

Source: Data are from *Statistical Abstract of the United States,
1992.* Table 612. Washington, D.C.: U.S. Government Printing
Office, 1992.

have always been the hewers of wood and the drawers
of water in Los Angeles."

The vast reduction in European immigration during
World War I exacerbated labor supply problems for
southwestern employers. In response, railroad managers, mine operators, and farmers intensified recruitment efforts in Mexico and lobbied the U.S. government for exemptions for Mexicans from restrictive
provisions of the IMMIGRATION ACT OF 1917. During
the 1920's, Mexicans were far less affected by immigration quotas than other national groups, and almost
500,000 new Mexican immigrants received permanent
visas. The growth of the U.S. economy during and
after World War II again created labor demands that
Mexicans helped to meet. The BRACERO PROGRAM,
launched in 1942, established a system of short-term
contract agricultural labor that brought in hundreds of
thousands of temporary migrants.

If a healthy state of the economy drew increasing
numbers of Mexicans into the United States, the economy's ill health had dramatic and adverse effects.
Shortly after World War I, rising unemployment led
the U.S. government to eliminate immigration exemptions for Mexicans, at least temporarily. The onset of
the GREAT DEPRESSION in 1929 intensified pressures

to remove large numbers of now-surplus Mexican and
even MEXICAN AMERICAN laborers. The Immigration
and Naturalization Service BORDER PATROL grew in
size and vigorously enforced immigration laws. Between 1930 and 1935, some twenty thousand Mexicans and Mexican Americans were expelled from
Colorado; perhaps as many as half a million were re-
patriated forcefully from the entire Southwest and
Midwest. Throughout this period and afterward, discriminatory treatment remained a fact of economic life
for immigrants from Mexico and their descendants.
Subject to dismissal from jobs or removal from states
and the country, they received lower wages than those
paid to native-born whites and were constantly denied
access to more desirable jobs.

Black Workers from Slavery to Freedom. The Africans who arrived on the North American continent
from the early seventeenth through the early nineteenth century differed profoundly from all other
groups of immigrants. Unlike their counterparts from
Europe or Asia, roughly 400,000 Africans came to the
Colonies and later to the United States not in search
of religious freedom or economic opportunity but as
slaves—involuntary laborers who were legally the
property of other human beings. Forcibly imported by
white European settlers, in the seventeenth and eighteenth centuries Africans worked in every American
colony. The majority labored on the farms and plantations of the South, cultivating tobacco, rice, and indigo. Slave labor constituted the foundation of the
southern economy. Yet whites profitably employed
slave labor not only in agriculture but also in urban
centers in both the South and the North. Urban slaves
loaded and unloaded ships, while enslaved teamsters
transported goods within cities and domestic servants
prepared food and cleaned the homes of wealthy
whites. By the late eighteenth century, however, northern states began enacting gradual emancipation laws
that provided for freedom for children born of slaves
after a certain date. These laws were the result of
changes in political and religious sensibilities: Many
white northerners during the Revolutionary era believed that holding slaves violated both natural law
and God's law. The emancipation laws also reflected
SLAVERY's declining importance to the northern economy, based upon commerce, artisan labor, and small
family farming. As the North slowly abandoned its
commitment to slave labor in place of free white labor,
the South increased its commitment. With the invention of the cotton gin by Eli Whitney in the 1790's,

cotton quickly became the dominant crop requiring slave labor.

The presence of slavery and a slave labor economy affected immigrant destinations in the first half of the nineteenth century. The South received relatively few immigrants from Europe, and those who did arrive settled in the wage labor enclaves of port cities, where free white workers sometimes competed with slaves. Even after the Civil War and emancipation, most immigrants avoided the agricultural South, with its relatively undiversified economy and limited job opportunities. Despite southern industrialists' and politicians' efforts to promote white immigrant labor as an alternative to black labor, as much as 80 percent of

CODES" designed to limit sharply the economic opportunities available to freed slaves. In many cases, the codes prohibited African Americans from leasing or purchasing land or urban real estate, and required them to purchase costly licenses to practice certain nonagricultural trades. The laws also included "vagrancy" statues, allowing police to arrest any black person found without visible signs of employment. The codes aimed at forcing blacks to work as plantation hands for their former owners under conditions similar to those that existed under slavery.

The black codes proved to be short-lived. Offensive to some northerners' sensibilities and resembling slavery too closely, the codes were overturned by the fed-

African American women, and particularly the poor, face the most prejudice in finding jobs. (Hazel Hankin)

European immigrants settled in the Northeast, with many of the rest going to the West.

Emancipation brought about an end to slavery but neither eliminated racial DISCRIMINATION in the labor market nor ushered in a free, wage labor society in the post-Civil War South. Employment for southern blacks remained restricted largely to agricultural work under harsh conditions. Immediately after the defeat of the Confederacy in 1865, conservative southern white legislators enacted a series of draconian "BLACK

eral government in late 1865. In their place, the Bureau of Refugees, Freedmen, and Abandoned Land, a federal agency directed by the military, sought to construct a free labor economy based upon the signing of annual contracts that stipulated specific rights and responsibilities for laborers and employers alike. Ultimately, the contracts bound freed men and women to work under penalty of arrest or forfeiture of wages. By ensuring year-round labor, they deprived the former slaves of one of their few weapons in the marketplace: mobility, or the ability to quit their work at any time in search of improved conditions.

A system of SHARECROPPING emerged as the dominant type of agricultural employment for blacks over the course of the late 1860's and 1870's. Families of freedpeople worked small plots of land owned by whites, under far less white supervision and with a smaller degree of employer interference on a daily basis. In exchange for this limited autonomy and for receiving an advance on food, clothing, and tools, the former slaves turned over a substantial portion of their crop to the landowners at the end of each year. Constantly in debt to landholders or merchants (because of both fraud and the declining price of cotton), few former slaves managed to accumulate the economic resources necessary for social mobility. This system of employment thus trapped most southern blacks at the bottom of the agricultural ladder, leaving them economically powerless and impoverished.

Not all African Americans remained landless farmers after the Civil War. A small but growing number of men moved back and forth between agriculture and the new expanding extractive industries of the South. Working as sharecroppers or tenant farmers for part of the year, they also secured seasonal employment in coal mines; timber, lumber, and turpentine camps; common labor crews on the rapidly expanding railroads; and in the small iron industry of Alabama, Tennessee, and Virginia. In the South's growing towns and cities, many black men worked as longshoremen, teamsters, cotton compress operators, warehousemen, and track crewmen, while a smaller number performed skilled work in construction and other trades. African American women also participated heavily in the wage-earning economy, but because of discrimination on the basis of both their race and sex, most were confined to private household service and laundry work. In some parts of the South, they also worked in tobacco and canning factories and in truck farming.

Black Migrations and Work. In the half century following the Civil War, a small stream of southern black migrants made its way to the North. In contrast to the South, northern states had either passed gradual emancipation laws in the late eighteenth or nineteenth centuries or, in the case of newer states, had never known the institution of slavery at all. Yet African Americans in the "free labor" North confronted a wide array of discriminatory practices before and after the Civil War. A small number of blacks were clergymen, doctors, entrepreneurs, lawyers, and teachers, but most secured employment in domestic work, common labor, and service (as hotel and restaurant waiters, janitors, and porters). Black scholar and activist W. E. B. Du Bois noted in an 1899 study that "every one knows that in a city like Philadelphia a Negro does not have the same chance to exercise his ability or secure work according to his talents as a white man." Although a lack of training and skills played some role, of critical importance was the "discrimination against them on account of their race." Their economic rise was hindered by "a widespread inclination to shut against them many doors of advancement open to the talented and efficient of other races." What was true of Philadelphia held for most other northern cities as well.

With the outbreak of war in Europe in 1914, a dramatic if gradual transformation in African American life began. European immigration to the United States virtually halted, depriving industrialists of desperately needed workers during a time of growing war orders. Employers addressed their new labor shortage by tapping two previously ignored sources of labor within the United States: women and African Americans. Roughly 450,000 southern blacks moved to northern industrial centers during the GREAT MIGRATION of 1916 to 1919, while perhaps 700,000 made the northern journey in the 1920's; during the 1940's, black southern migrants numbered 1.5 million, while an additional 2.5 million departed in the two decades after 1950. New economic opportunities in the North and West and deteriorating economic conditions at home, such as the introduction of the mechanical cotton harvester that dramatically reduced the need for agricultural labor, spurred the final collapse of sharecropping and the old racial agricultural order in the South.

During the Great Migration of the WORLD WAR I era, black male wage earners for the first time won limited employment in the modern industrial sector, including the steel mills of Gary, Indiana, as well as Chicago and Pittsburgh; automobile plants in Detroit; and meat-packing houses in Chicago and Kansas City. Black women, too, found new employment opportunities in some cities during the war years. *Crisis,* the journal of the National Association for the Advancement of Colored People (NAACP), assessed the changes in 1918: Few realize, it noted, that at the same time thousands of black men were recruited into the military to fight in Europe, "an army of women is entering mills, factories and all other branches of industry." The list included jobs involving the operation of power sewing machines and work in railroad yards, cigar factories, box factories, and lumber yards. Yet like their male counterparts, black women found most skilled positions closed to them because of entrenched racial discrimination. Many continued to receive piecework remuneration for "industrial homework"— the home-based manufacture of such goods as garments and artificial flowers. The postwar economic downturn saw many black men and most black women lose the new jobs they had obtained. While black women's employment breakthroughs proved especially short-lived, lasting only for the war's duration, black men had at last cracked the employment color bar that kept them out of heavy industry. They remained concentrated in unskilled and unpleasant industrial jobs, however, through World War II and the ensuing decades.

Jobs and Racial/Ethnic Stereotyping. The range of jobs open to workers of different races or nationalities was determined in part by decisions made by those doing the hiring. In the nineteenth through mid-twentieth century, industrialists, personnel managers, and foremen relied upon, and contributed to, racial and ethnic STEREOTYPES in making their decisions about whom to hire and what jobs to assign to members of different groups. In so doing, they attributed broad character traits to entire groups, using those traits to justify their decisions to hire or deny employment to different groups of workers. In response to an informal survey conducted in 1905 by the *Manufacturers' Record,* a southern management periodical, a white proprietor of a foundry and machine company in Valdosta, Georgia, concluded that there "is no stability or efficiency in the negro," who, he concluded, was "certainly retrograding" since the Civil War—an opinion shared by many if not all of the other respondents. Similarly, a northern white plant manager reported in 1918 that the "negro is different physically, temperamentally, and psychologically from any of the white race." Likening the "darky" to "a child," he contended that the use of "firmness is an absolute necessity." The manager's task was to recognize just how blacks were different, issue careful and precise orders, offer more supervision "than the rank and file of whites," and "provide the negro with the foresight of which his ancestors' environment has largely deprived him." In 1923, a personnel manager for a Cleveland, Ohio foundry described recent African American migrants from the South as "temperamentally quite different from the other classes of help that works in our shop." Those differences consisted of the assertion that

the black migrant "is naturally of a sunny disposition, happy, friendly, anxious to please, but inclined at times to overlook minor details which are essential for quality and production." Moreover, if he feels that he is not getting a square deal, the "probabilities are that he will quit."

Many of these stereotypes were self-serving, allowing employers to justify harsh discipline, poor working conditions, and discriminatory treatment toward African Americans. The lens of racism distorted managers' insights into the character and aspirations of their black labor force. What whites saw as indolence or unnecessarily high turnover based on some innate racial characteristics, blacks might see as subtle or overt resistance to brutal and offensive treatment.

African Americans were not the only group to suffer from demeaning racial stereotypes and practices that affected their status in the job market. In different times and places, many newcomers to the United States experienced comparable denigration by employers and white trade unionists alike. A labor union newspaper from El Paso, Texas, denounced Mexicans as "criminals of the most dangerous types." Trade unionists in the railroad industry at the beginning of the twentieth century contended that eastern and southern Europeans constituted "cheap" or "pauper" labor who were content to live in "misery and squalor" by accepting wages and conditions unacceptable to native-born white Americans. Drawing upon a powerful nativist tradition that crossed class lines, white trade unionists argued that these men and women represented a "lower grade of humanity" as well as "human wreckage." Given this definition of the new immigrants, as well as African Americans, as alien or unassimilable, the white railroad unionists saw little need to work in common cause with them. Instead, they joined the larger chorus calling for immigration restrictions.

From employers' perspectives, immigrant or migrant workers were a source of inexpensive labor to be exploited for maximum profitability. As a result, employers often demonstrated little concern for the harsh conditions migrants experienced; expressed little sympathy for their efforts to better their conditions; remained uninformed or uninterested about their culture, goals, and values; and expressed no appreciation for their individual or collective strategies. In assembling a multiracial or multiethnic labor force, managers employed broad, crude stereotypes to classify immigrants, ranking individuals according to the group

This Taos, N. Mex., man represents a large number of Mexican American agricultural experts, many of whom are descendants of early immigrants who came to the United States as farm laborers. (Elaine S. Querry)

to which they belonged. For example, a railroad truckmaster in southern Kansas in 1907 believed Mexicans to be "better than Greeks or Italians, and next to the American 'hobo.'" Given that group preference, his company dispatched an agent each spring to the Rio Grande to "get our men for the summer." In that same year, a government investigator did not hesitate to attribute negative characteristics to all Mexican immigrants: The "Mexican laborer is unambitious, listless, physically weak, irregular, and indolent" at the same time "he is docile, patient . . . orderly . . . fairly intelligent under competent supervision, obedient and cheap." His greatest advantage was "his willingness to work for a low wage."

The coal mining industry of West Virginia offers numerous examples of employer racial/ethnic preferences and stereotypes. Mine operators around 1911 expressed a clear desire to hire English, Scottish, and Polish immigrants instead of either native-born whites or blacks, for the "immigrants were thought to be more attentive to work than the natives, and also more

tractable." In one mining community, operators found English and Scottish immigrants superior to Poles, Magyars, and Italians, who were the "least tractable" and required more supervision. A survey of employers' opinions revealed a wide range of preferences: At one company, Russians, natives, and Italians headed the list; at a second, "native negroes, native whites, and Italians were preferred in the order named," with native whites superior to immigrants in "all positions of authority." Yet a third company found Hungarians the "most useful employees," followed by Italians, while a fourth preferred Englishmen and Scots to Poles and native-born workers. Virtually all respondents who raised the issue of supervisory positions admitted that "native whites" were more desirable than any other group.

The heterogeneity of the mine labor force did not necessarily ensure close collaboration across ethnic or racial lines. In the mining communities of Oklahoma and Kansas, the Immigration Commission found that "it is an almost unheard-of situation to find an American miner and an immigrant from continental Europe working in the same room." Yet during work hours, "relations between Americans and immigrants were pleasant, the foreigner receiving as fair treatment as the native at the hands of the company."

The Modern Era. Since the 1940's, discrimination on the basis of race and sex has come under intense legal attack. During World War II, the Fair Employment Practices Commission (FEPC), a federal investigating body created in response to protests by African Americans, publicized the widespread patterns of discrimination against African Americans, Latinos, and other minorities by both business and labor unions. The FEPC was more successful in exposing and condemning discrimination than in alleviating its consequences.

Court cases from the 1940's onward brought by African American victims of racial discrimination in the railroad industry and building trades in particular generated a series of important Supreme Court rulings on the illegality of employment and union discrimination. Title VII of the CIVIL RIGHTS ACT OF 1964 banned discrimination on the basis of race, sex, religion, and national origin by unions and firms with twenty-five or more members or employees (a figure reduced to fifteen in 1972). An EQUAL EMPLOYMENT OPPORTUNITY COMMISSION was created to oversee the implementation, but in subsequent decades, it investigated only a fraction of the cases filed.

Notwithstanding the illegality of discrimination on the basis of race or ethnicity and the dramatic advances of some women and members of racial and ethnic minorities, employment discrimination (often of a far more subtle sort than in the past) has persisted as a central political, social, and legal problem. The profound restructuring of the American economy since the 1960's has eliminated many of the higher-paying manufacturing jobs and in their place has generated a new "service" economy. While some new jobs require higher education and training (particularly in computers and information processing), much of the new jobs growth has been centered in the very low-skill, low-pay, and no-benefits fast-food and retail sector. Deindustrialization and the rise of the service economy has exacerbated job segmentation along racial, ethnic, and gender lines, as well as the inequities for women and minorities in the two-tiered wage system.

SUGGESTED READINGS. A classic and still important work that describes African American experience in the labor market is *The Black Worker: The Negro and the Labor Movement* (1931) by Sterling D. Spero and Abram L. Harris; a more recent contribution is Peter Gottlieb's *Making Their Own Way: Southern Blacks' Migration to Pittsburgh, 1916-30* (1987). Jewish women immigrants from Russia are analyzed in Susan A. Glenn's *Daughters of the Shtetl: Life and Labor in the Immigrant Generation* (1990), while the experiences of Mexican workers are explored in Mario T. Garcia's *Desert Immigrants: The Mexicans of El Paso, 1880-1920* (1981). For discussions of German, Irish, Sicilian, Czech, Finnish, and other immigrant groups, see *"Struggle a Hard Battle": Essays on Working-Class Immigrants,* edited by Dirk Hoerder (1986).—*Eric Arnesen*

English Americans: Immigrants from England hold a unique place in the array of ethnic groups that compose the American population. Because the United States began as a group of seventeenth century English colonies, the early and continuing English cultural influence was pervasive. A number of nationalities lived in the thirteen American colonies, but English society furnished the majority of the population as well as the colonies' laws, literature, customs, and political thought. The most immediately visible English contribution to life in the United States, however, was and still is the English language, with all its cultural associations. American laws of persons and property also have English origins; the U.S. Constitution and Bill of Rights reflected the ideas behind England's "Glorious Revolution" of 1688.

English contributions to American culture have continued to be so widespread that, ironically, they sometimes seem difficult to delineate clearly. The very facts that the phrase "WHITE ANGLO-SAXON PROTESTANT" (WASP) connotes traditional American wealth and power and that ASSIMILATION into American society has been called "Anglo-conformity" indicate the pervasive nature of the English influence on the United States.

The Colonies and the Revolution. Early English migration to America was part of the exploration and colonization efforts as well as the religious, territorial, and economic rivalry characterizing the expansion of Europe from 1492 to the start of the twentieth century. The founders of England's 1607 Virginia Colony hoped that it would grow to challenge the fabled wealth of Spanish America, and the settlers were overwhelmingly male, single, and youthful; many were indentured servants. In 1619 the first African slaves were brought to Virginia as long-term labor to generate the expected profits.

Religious liberty for sects dissenting from the English state church was a significant motive for the 1620 colony at Plymouth, Massachusetts, and the 1630 Massachusetts Bay Colony. Here entire English family and social units were drawn from the "mother congregation" of an English Puritan church and transplanted to the New World. By 1640, Massachusetts had a population of 20,000. The English Toleration Act of 1689 finally reduced some of the religious reasons for emigration.

In 1690, the American seaboard colonies had a population about 90 percent English by birth or descent. Eighteenth century non-English migration increased the proportion of African slaves and of Germans, French, Scots, and Scots-Irish colonists. The first U.S. Census, in 1790, shows that about 60 percent of the white population (49 percent of the total population) had distinctly English surnames.

The AMERICAN REVOLUTION has been called "a civil war in the British Empire" by which the colonists gained freedom from English control without changing their society. George Washington and the signers of the DECLARATION OF INDEPENDENCE, including Thomas Jefferson, John Adams, and Benjamin Franklin, formed an almost entirely English leadership, and the CONSTITUTION, with its subsequent amendments forming the BILL OF RIGHTS, followed the pattern of the English Bill of Rights of 1689. Colonial era legislation generally continued in force under the new government, and English precedents and legal commentaries were essential supplements to American statute law for some time.

Although only marginally a majority, Anglo Americans dominated the new United States politically and culturally. Other ethnic groups became an increasing part of the population, but they had to struggle for a place, voice, and identity. In contrast, English newcomers were not perceived as "ethnic immigrants" bringing changes, because their language, laws, churches, society, and customs were already the established norms of American life.

Immigration Patterns. From 1775 to 1825, wars and political tensions severely reduced English immigration to the United States. During the War of 1812, male British aliens were forced to register with a U.S. marshal, and some were sent to internment centers. Even long after the war was over, there was significant anti-British feeling in the United States. Such feelings did not often carry over to serious antipathy toward English immigrants themselves, however, unless they proclaimed their affection for the Old Country too boldly. English immigration increased steadily after 1825, except for the Civil War years, and reached its peak in the 1880's.

There were three main waves of nineteenth century English immigration. The first occurred in the late 1840's and early 1850's; the second began in the 1860's and peaked in 1873. The third wave was the largest, beginning in 1879 and ending in the early 1890's. In the peak years of 1882 and 1888, as many as 82,000 English people arrived per year. Throughout, many arrived as part of family units making the trip together, intending to move to the United States permanently. At the same time, the non-English population was increasing rapidly as well, both because of immigration and because the United States annexed territory that had been settled by French and Spanish people.

In the twentieth century, there was a general decline in English immigration. Those who came were more likely than their predecessors to be skilled workers, however, and the percentage of professionals increased dramatically. They were less likely than their predecessors to come with families in tow. In the later twentieth century, although the percentage of English people permanently moving to the United States decreased, the percentage of those visiting or working temporarily in the country increased. People in this group range from academics, scientists, and physicians to actors, musicians, clerical workers, and nannies.

Geographic Dispersion, Religion, and Social Organizations. Geographically, English settlement in the United States has been widely distributed. By the late twentieth century, the rural South, Appalachian Tennessee and Kentucky, northern Maine, and most of Utah showed the highest proportions of people claiming English ancestry. On the other hand, the greatest numbers of first-generation Anglo Americans are

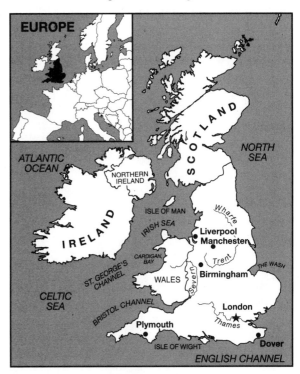

ENGLAND

found in Los Angeles, Orange, and San Diego counties in California and in Harris and Dallas counties in Texas. Hawaii and the Dakotas have the smallest proportions of people of English ancestry. Whatever region they chose, English immigrants did not settle in the linguistic or religious enclaves or ethnic neighborhoods typical of many other groups. Because they spoke English as their first language and because they intermarried widely with other groups, they became nearly invisible as a specific immigrant presence.

In the early nineteenth century, the English immigrant population was particularly significant in the mid-Atlantic states, especially New York and Pennsylvania. There were also early movements to settle in the Midwest. In the second half of the century, patterns shifted; more went further west to farm or ranch, with many settling in Kansas and Iowa. There was a revival of New England as a destination as manufacturing grew in that area. Southern Massachusetts, especially centers of textile manufacturing such as Fall River, New Bedford, Lowell, and Lynn, had a large English population in the nineteenth century.

The Virginia Colony's faith was Anglican, and New England was mostly Puritan, but neither became the established church for the new United States, and neither developed as the primary religious focus for later English immigrants. While Catholicism was a unifying

Re-creations of English-style hunts are popular with English Americans. (James L. Shaffer)

ethnic faith for such immigrant groups as the Irish, Italians, Poles, French, and Latinos, and Lutheranism played a similar role for Scandinavians, English immigrants were distributed into many Protestant churches. Episcopalians, Methodists, Presbyterians, Congregationalists, Baptists, Quakers, and the Salvation Army were all of English origin. The widespread use of the King James translation of the Bible, however, did unify these Protestant faiths and gave them a sense of forming the mainstream of American religious life.

Similar to the way that English immigrants seldom lived in ethnic enclaves, they did not develop the social networks or self-help and benevolent associations that some groups did (one exception to this was in the mill towns of New England). There is no English equivalent, for example, of the Ancient Order of Hibernians or Sons of Italy, and there are no ethnic parades for Saint George like those for Saint Patrick or Christopher Columbus. Chapters of the St. George Society were established in the nineteenth century, but it was essentially a club of the prosperous elite. The more influential Freemasons and International Order of Odd Fellows accepted native-born Americans very early, and so were not truly Anglo American organizations. Perhaps the most significant unifying social element among English immigrants was an emotional connection to the British king or queen. By the late nineteenth century, anti-English sentiment in the United States had become nearly nonexistent, and Americans in general began to be interested in the royal family, an interest that has persisted.

Economic Development. The INDUSTRIAL REVOLUTION in England was quickly duplicated in the United States thanks to British exports of locomotives, rails, machinery, factory equipment, and capital. In the early nineteenth century, English scientists and inventors were too well rewarded in their own land to emigrate. Underpaid technicians did leave, however, lured by American bonuses, despite English prohibitory laws designed to retain skilled workers. Among significant English immigrants were Samuel Slater, the founder of the American cotton industry, and William Colgate, soap manufacturer and philanthropist. Publisher James Scripps was an English immigrant, as was Samuel Gompers, founder of the AMERICAN FEDERATION OF LABOR. Somewhat earlier, English immigrant John Harvard had left his library and his name to the oldest university in the United States, and while James Smithson never saw America, his Smithsonian Institute has become a national treasure.

Twentieth Century Developments. By the late nineteenth century, U.S. industrial production had surpassed that of England; at the same time, an English vogue came to characterize American tastes. English literature and England's playwrights, poets, and novelists had dominated American reading habits since colonial days, and in 1869 novelist Henry James left the United States for England, an example followed in the twentieth century by writers T. S. Eliot and Ezra Pound.

Anglophilia in American society from 1880 to 1914 was more than literary and was not entirely a matter of Tudor-style homes, English butlers, or even the marriages of American wealth to English titles. American finance capitalists and political leaders saw the United States' new role in world markets as linked to the free trade policies of the British Empire against the increasing threat of German industrial competition.

lor, Alfred Hitchcock, Peter Sellers, and Angela Lansbury, has continued to be an asset to the American entertainment industry.

Since 1945, English migration to the United States has been measured by talent rather than numbers. Earlier, a few English-born writers, such as Frances Hodgson Burnett and Ernest Thompson Seton, had made the United States their home. In the 1940's, they

Thousands of Americans of all backgrounds enjoy English traditions at annual English Renaissance Faires held throughout the United States. (Sally Weigand)

Close cooperation between England and the United States during World Wars I and II brought the two countries closer together still. In cooperative scientific and weapons research during World War II, the United States reaped great benefits from British research contributions.

In the 1920's and 1930's, the new, prosperous American society began advertising itself to the world through Hollywood films, with significant contributions from such English-born talents as Charlie Chaplin, Stan Laurel, Cary Grant, and Bob Hope. Ever since, British-born talent, whether rock musicians or film and television performers such as Elizabeth Tay-

were followed by humorist P. G. Wodehouse, poet W. H. Auden, and Christopher Isherwood, whose Berlin stories were dramatized as *Cabaret* (1966). British novelist Aldous Huxley, author of *Brave New World* (1932), settled in California. Between 1952 and 1961, 16 percent of English and Scottish Ph.D.'s left Britain, half of them for the United States. There was a similar migration of medical doctors and nuclear physicists, such as Freeman John Dyson. Worried British leaders termed this emigration a "brain drain."

Increasingly, the American WASP establishment has been criticized as being unrepresentative of the American people. Indeed, the distinctly English lineage in the United States is clearly diminishing. The 90 percent of 1690, 49 percent of 1790, and estimated 45 percent of 1920 has dropped, according to voluntary statements for the 1980 and 1990 censuses, to between 25 and 29 percent. English remains the common language of the United States, but its monopoly is being challenged. English legal precedents, political ideals, and literary traditions are also gradually being modified in the evolution of American culture. The multicultural population of the United States will undoubtedly continue to modify its inherited English traditions in the years ahead.

SUGGESTED READINGS. There are not many general works on British immigrants available, but among the more useful are Shirley Blumenthal's *Coming to America: Immigrants from the British Isles* (1980); Rowland Tappan Berthoff's *British Immigrants in Industrial America, 1790-1950* (1953); Richard C. Robertiello's *The WASP Mystique* (1987); and E. Digby Baltzell's *The Protestant Establishment* (1964). —*K. Fred Gillum*

English as a second language programs (ESL programs): Classes designed to teach English communication skills to students who speak another native language. There are millions of people in the United States who speak English as a second language or are in the process of learning it. Some of these people are immigrants, but many are native-born citizens. Hundreds of languages are represented by this group, but Spanish speakers are by far the largest language minority.

A variety of American public agencies and private community organizations provide ESL classes. The public schools have had the major responsibility for helping school-aged children in this learning process. Some schools even offer ESL classes to the parents of their students to enable better parent-teacher communication. In cities with large Spanish-speaking and new immigrant populations, such as Los Angeles, the need for ESL programs far exceeds the availability.

Language Diversity in the United States. There have always been languages other than English spoken in the United States. The various Indian tribes spoke many different languages, and Spanish-speaking Mexican colonists were in the Southwest long before Jamestown was settled in 1607. Other non-English-speaking European groups such as the French, Germans, Dutch, and Swedish also settled in North America. Acknowledgment of linguistic pluralism was quite common in the early days of American colonial history. Laws in some regions were written bilingually, and the schools provided instruction in languages other than English—for example, French in Louisiana, German in Ohio, and Spanish in New Mexico. By the middle of the nineteenth century, the Cherokees, Creeks, and Seminoles were operating their own schools in their native tongues. While English became the predominant language after the American Revolution, non-English-speaking communities coexisted and were, for the most part, an accepted part of the American landscape. A notable exception was the Africans sold into slavery, who were forbidden to speak their native languages.

With the intense American nationalism engendered by World War I, tolerant sentiments toward linguistic and cultural diversity began to change. Along with this shift came the rise of compulsory public education. This implied that the public schools would be used as an agent of ASSIMILATION into a monolingual, monocultural, English-speaking society. Between World War I and World War II, the education of language minorities suffered. Scholars and school officials often expressed the belief that BILINGUALISM interfered with intellectual functioning. Students were routinely punished for speaking their native languages at school, whether they were Mexican or Shoshone Indian.

After the Sputnik satellite was launched in the late 1950's by the Soviet Union, attention was turned to upgrading American educational practices. This new interest, combined with the CIVIL RIGHTS MOVEMENT of the 1960's, brought the problems of educating language minorities back to the forefront of educational concerns. The BILINGUAL EDUCATION ACT OF 1968 and the 1974 U.S. Supreme Court case of *LAU V. NICHOLS* highlighted the needs of limited English proficient (LEP) students. The courts mandated that school officials seek to develop educational programs to serve their needs. Since that time, both BILINGUAL EDUCATION and ESL programs have grown tremendously.

Second Language Proficiency. Effective ESL programs are based on an understanding of how people become proficient in a second language. In language learning, there is a very conscious, analytical approach to understanding the rules of grammar and their application. Language acquisition, by contrast, is a natural, almost subconscious process of picking up a language by living and operating in a natural speech environment and communicating real messages. Language learning focuses on form with an emphasis on error correction, while language acquisition focuses on content with an emphasis on communication. Young students are generally more efficient at using acquisition strategies while adults and teenagers can also benefit from direct instruction that focuses on form and structure.

Language acquisition evolves naturally in stages in a fairly predictable sequence, whether the learners are children or adults. Students move from simple to complex, from known to unknown. The first stage is called the silent period, in which students become accustomed to the rhythms and patterns of the new language. In this stage students respond nonverbally or with single-word responses. Students perform best when they are not forced to produce language beyond their level of comprehension. They will make fewer errors later if allowed time to move through these stages naturally at their own rate.

There are two kinds of language proficiency, and they develop at different rates. The first kind consists of basic interpersonal communication skills, stemming from conversation in a variety of social settings. Children may acquire these skills naturally through exposure to native speakers in one to two years and have near-native fluency. Older students may take longer and may never completely achieve near-native fluency, especially in regard to accent. The second type of proficiency is called cognitive academic language proficiency. This is the abstract language of academic instruction. Since children are less sophisticated cognitively, it may take them five to seven years to completely master grade-level proficiency in content areas. Adults, who are more cognitively sophisticated, are usually better able to handle this type of proficiency sooner.

Program Models. As school districts and communities work together to meet the needs of non-English-proficient students, they consider many factors in designing their programs. They must match their awareness and knowledge of the process of second language acquisition with a program model that best utilizes the school's resources. ESL programs can be part of a bilingual education program or stand alone as the school's response to LEP students.

If there are large populations of language minority students who speak the same language, the school may decide to establish a bilingual education program in which the native language of the students is used as the language of instruction for part of the time or for designated parts of the curriculum. Bilingual programs also have an ESL component in which students receive instruction in English.

Immersion programs are also used in districts with large concentrations of limited and non-English-speaking students. In this approach, instruction of all subject matter is conducted in English, but English is never taught as a subject per se. Students acquire English by being exposed to it as the medium of instruction rather than by studying it formally. In immersion programs, students are usually separated from English-speaking students for all or most of the day. They are not as likely to fall behind in their content area subject matter, and they are less likely to feel overwhelmed or pressured to perform in English before they are ready. Drawbacks to ESL immersion programs include lack of exposure to native English-speaking students who act as peer language models and stigmatization as a result of being separated from the English-speaking mainstream.

Afghan American man celebrates his graduation from an ESL program with fellow students. (Odette Lupis)

There are many variations of ESL pull-out programs in which LEP students are "pulled out" of mainstream classes for part of the day to receive instruction in English. This approach is often used when the school or district has a number of LEP students at different grade levels or scattered in different schools. In pull-out programs, students receive English instruction from an ESL specialist and content area instruction from regular classroom teachers in English. Regular teachers may consult with and have content area concepts reinforced by the ESL teacher, or the district may be able to provide native language tutoring in content areas. These pull-out programs are the most likely type of program to be found at the secondary level, although they are common at the elementary level as well. They have the advantage of serving schools that do not have high concentrations of non-English students or that have many different language groups present. Another advantage is the LEP students' exposure to native-English-speaking students. The main disadvantage is the potential for students to fall seriously behind in content area development. If the schools do not provide any other assistance, LEP students may find classroom instruction in English baffling, overwhelming, and possibly intimidating.

Another ESL model, known as high-intensity language teaching (HILT), is generally targeted at adults or teenagers. In this type of program, students are separated from other English-speaking students, as in immersion, but are provided with direct formal instruction in English, as in pull-out programs. All instruction is conducted in English for several hours, focusing on English grammar, vocabulary, and dialogues. There is a strong emphasis on speaking, listening, reading, and writing immediately and correctly. This type of intense, fast-paced program is typical of programs that help international students prepare for entrance into American universities. It is not appropriate for children because the nature of high-intensity instruction requires cognitive maturity and a long attention span.

These three main models of ESL programs take on different variations in different communities according to their need. Other factors that influence the way a program is implemented include variations in teaching philosophy, methodology, classroom management, and availability of trained personnel. There is as much diversity in ESL programs as there is in languages spoken in the United States.

SUGGESTED READINGS. For more information regarding some ESL considerations, see Alba Ambert and Sarah Melendez's *Bilingual Education: A Sourcebook* (1985) or the California State Department of Education's *Schooling and Language Minority Students: A Theoretical Framework* (1981). Another source of helpful information is the Ohio State Department of Education's guide *Strategies for Developing Language Programs for National Origin Minority Students* (1983). See also *ESL in America: Myths and Possibilities* (1991), edited by Sarah Benesch.—*April L. Haulman*

English Only movement: Movement seeking a constitutional amendment and other legislation declaring English the official language of the United States. Originating in 1980 with the passage of a citizen-initiated antibilingual ordinance in Dade County, Florida, the movement became national in 1981 when Senator S. I. HAYAKAWA introduced "Official English" legislation in the U.S. Congress. Such legislation is supported by a number of organizations, including the American Legion, Council on Inter-American Security, English First, and U.S. English. The most influential organization is U.S. English, which has more than 400,000 members and includes on its board of advisers prominent Americans such as Walter Annenberg, Alistair Cooke, and Arnold Schwarzenegger.

Although English language amendments (ELAs) were repeatedly introduced in Congress in the 1980's, none made any significant legislative progress. The movement met with some success on the state level; official English legislation was adopted in seventeen states by 1990. Attempts to pass ELAs in additional

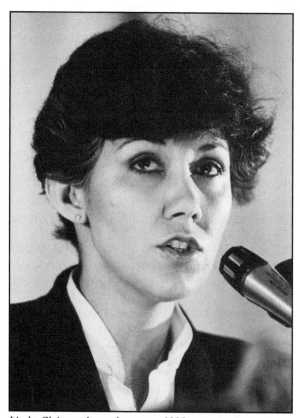

Linda Chávez, shown here at a 1985 press conference, was deeply involved in the English Only controversy during the 1980's. (AP/Wide World Photos)

states were rejected, however, and court decisions in several states diminished the effects of Official English laws that had already been passed.

Political Ideology. The major goal of the English Only movement is the adoption of a constitutional amendment to make English the official language of the United States. Consequently, many supporters regard the term "Official English" a more accurate descriptor of their movement; English Only, however, has remained the more commonly used term. English Only proponents say their basic motivation is a desire for national unity, a wish to assimilate immigrants into the American mainstream while upholding the concept of the society as a MELTING POT. They argue that the unity of United States historically has been tied to its near-uniformity in language and that this linguistic uniformity needs to be protected and bolstered in order to strengthen American culture and influence in the world.

English Only adherents fear that the United States might be torn apart by political battles over language such as have occurred in Canada, Belgium, and Sri Lanka. Consequently, they are particularly opposed to BILINGUAL EDUCATION, believing that it promotes the support of other languages to the detriment of English and erodes the unifying force of English. They maintain that immigrants will learn English faster, and therefore become better assimilated, if they are completely immersed in the English language as soon as possible.

English Only proponents also seek enforcement of the requirement that immigrants know the English language in order to be naturalized, and they want multilingual ballots and voting materials eliminated. In response to protests by opponents concerning possible inhumanitarian effects of Official English legislation, English Only adherents insist that such laws would not eliminate health and safety measures for non-English speakers or interfere with private businesses.

Historical Background. Although movements to establish English as the official language of the United States have appeared and disappeared cyclically since the beginning of the nation, the term "English Only movement" generally refers to the movement that began in 1980. The movement seemingly grew as a response to the IMMIGRATION AND NATIONALITY ACT OF 1965, which opened the way for massive immigration from Latin America and Asia, and subsequent official actions designed to assist minorities or to protect their rights, including their languages and cultures.

The 1968 Bilingual Education Act, for example, provided federal funds for educating children with limited English-speaking ability, and in *LAU v. NICHOLS* (1974) the Supreme Court ruled that non-English-speaking children thrown into English-only classrooms were being deprived of their right to equal educational opportunities. The 1975 Voting Rights Act extended voting rights protection to Latinos, American Indians, Alaska natives, and Asian Americans by providing support for bilingual balloting.

Opponents of English Only support expanding bilingual education, encouraging children to learn and read in more than one language. (Odette Lupis)

While minority activists, especially Latino leaders, hailed the bicultural/bilingual approach supported by the courts, newspaper surveys showed that most Americans favored rapid ASSIMILATION of non-English speakers. That attitude, coupled with widespread concern in the 1980's over the declining prestige and power of the United States internationally, led many Americans to view support for English and opposition to bilingual education as a matter of patriotism. To them being American meant being able to speak English. They were also concerned that bilingualism could lead to division along language or ethnic lines.

Public sentiment for an ELA spread following introduction of Hayakawa's bill in Congress and especially gained momentum in 1983 with the founding of U.S. English by Hayakawa and John Tanton, a

Michigan ophthalmologist. This group became the major lobbying force for the English Only movement, and it received support from other groups including English First, primarily a direct-mail fund-raising campaign. U.S. English grew rapidly in membership, and in 1987 Linda CHÁVEZ, a former staff director of the U.S. Civil Rights Commission under President Reagan, was named its president. Although heavy lobbying failed to produce any federal legislation during the 1980's, it did influence the passage of several state ELAs.

Cronkite, a member of the board of advisers, also submitted his resignation and directed the organization not to use his name in any fund-raising efforts. To avoid further controversy and lessen negative effects on Official English initiatives pending in Arizona, Colorado, and Florida, Tanton also resigned from the organization. Initiatives did subsequently succeed in those three states, and opinion polls showed that most Americans retained a positive attitude toward the concept of a federal ELA.

Opponents. Although various individuals and

Extremists in the English Only movement would have this sign read "Men" only. (James L. Shaffer)

In 1988 controversy struck U.S. English and, by association, the English Only movement, when an internal memo by cofounder Tanton was made public along with information about his involvement in a network of organizations seeking immigration restriction and population control. Tanton's memo expressed concern about the harmful effects of increased numbers of immigrants and the high fertility rates of Latin American immigrants. Chávez resigned in protest of what she deemed anti-Latino sentiments. Walter

groups criticized the English Only movement from its beginning in 1980, opponents did not begin organizing until several years later. In 1985, in reaction to former Secretary of State William Bennett's attack on BILINGUAL EDUCATION in the United States, the Spanish-American League Against Discrimination (SALAD), a civil rights and educational group in Miami, urged the substitution of an English Plus movement for the English Only movement. In 1987, a coalition of more than fifty educational and civil rights organizations opposed to the English Only movement established the English Plus Information Clearinghouse (EPIC) in Washington, D.C. Some of the major organizations that support English Plus are the American Civil Liberties Union, Modern Language Association, National Council of Teachers of English, and the National Education Association.

The major goal of English Plus is the defeat of all federal, state, and local initiatives designed to make English the official language of the United States or any state or city. The organization promotes proficiency in English for all members of society along with proficiency in additional languages for both non-English and native English speakers. English Plus supporters argue that the English Only movement expresses XENOPHOBIA, NATIVISM, isolationism, and RACISM; they believe English Only policies are divisive instead of cohesive because they are based on PREJUDICE toward other languages and cultures.

English Plus supporters also claim that passage of a federal ELA will deter rather than encourage the learning of English because it will isolate non-English speakers from the mainstream. Additional negative impacts they foresee on non-English speakers include elimination of basic rights such as freedom of speech, disfranchisement of voters not proficient in English, and hindrance of educational and economic advancement.

English Plus adherents reject concerns about the decline of English, citing studies that show non-English-speaking immigrants being assimilated as rapidly as ever. Non-English speakers are motivated to learn English not because of legislation but because of the need to know English to survive educationally and economically. What is needed then, according to English Plus, is not elimination but expansion of bilingual education and accessibility of language classes to all.

Legislation. Official English legislation was repeatedly introduced in Congress throughout the 1980's, but no ELA ever made it out of committee to a vote on the floor. Prior to 1980, only two states (Nebraska and Illinois) had Official English laws, but fifteen additional states passed some version of an ELA by 1990 (Virginia, 1981; Indiana, Kentucky, and Tennessee, 1984; California and Georgia, 1986; Arkansas, Mississippi, North Carolina, North Dakota, and South Carolina, 1987; Arizona, Colorado, and Florida, 1988; Alabama, 1990). The most highly publicized battle over Official English legislation occurred in 1986 in California with the passage of Proposition 63, an English language amendment to the state's constitution. The proposition not only declared English the official language of California but also instructed the legislature to enforce the law. Although most of the state's politicians, Roman Catholic bishops, and numerous interest groups opposed the measure, it received the support of 73 percent of the electorate statewide. Following the California model, Arizona, Colorado, and Florida Official English initiatives were also successful.

Soon after the passage of some of the state ELAs, reports of various discriminatory incidents spread widely. Examples included a Florida store clerk's being fired for using Spanish; a Colorado bus driver's requiring children to stop using Spanish on their way to school; and a Denver restaurant worker's being fired for translating a menu for a Latino customer. Generally, however, state ELAs appear to have had primarily a symbolic effect and attempts to enforce them have often been unsuccessful. In California, for example, attempts to reject bilingual education, stop the use of bilingual ballots, and dismiss workers who persist in speaking Spanish have all been defeated in the lower courts. In February, 1990, a federal district judge in Phoenix, Arizona, ruled that the Arizona ELA violated the right of free speech. By 1993, no clear ruling on the issue had been made by the U.S. Supreme Court.

A slowdown in the adoption of state ELAs began in the late 1980's. All but three states had considered an ELA by 1990, but most states had failed to pass such a measure. Furthermore, in some states, with the support of the English Plus movement, a backlash of legislation opposing English Only occurred. Three states (Hawaii, Louisiana, and New Mexico) already had policies in place supporting minority languages, and in 1989 New Mexico reiterated opposition to English Only by adopting a resolution supporting the concepts of English Plus. Washington and Oregon followed in 1989 with their own English Plus legislation, and a number of cities and counties elsewhere adopted resolutions supporting language pluralism. The English Plus movement also influenced the introduction of federal legislation in opposition to English Only. A bill introduced in 1990 by Senator Daniel INOUYE of Hawaii supporting preservation of native American languages—specifically the languages of American Indians, Alaska natives, native Hawaiians, and native Pacific Islanders—passed the Senate and the House by a voice vote and was subsequently signed by President George Bush.

In the early 1990's, despite strong opposition from English Plus groups, declining legislative success, and unfavorable court rulings, the English Only movement continued to push for implementation of its language policies through state and federal legislation and to attract significant public support.

SUGGESTED READINGS. For a presentation of the English Only ideology from the perspective of a major supporter, see S. I. Hayakawa's article "Make English Official: One Common Language Makes Our Nation Work," in *The Executive Educator* 9 (January 29, 1987), p. 36. An examination of the movement from the viewpoint of its opponents is available in *Not Only English; Affirming America's Multilingual Heritage* (1989), a collection of essays edited by Harvey A. Daniels. The most comprehensive work available on the movement is James Crawford's *Language Loyalties; A Source Book on the Official English Controversy* (1992).—*Verbie Lovorn Prevost*

Entertainment industry: The entertainment industry in the United States—theater, motion pictures, audio recordings, radio, and television—has long had great power over the shaping of popular images of the country's diverse peoples. There are two remarkably different aspects to the entertainment industry: the performance that the audience sees or hears and the backstage production work that makes the performance possible. Minorities have had greater success joining the ranks of performers than penetrating other areas of the entertainment industry such as the technical fields and, most important, the executive-level positions at which decisions are made. Jewish Americans have been the great exception to the rule. Control of these industries, and therefore of the images they present, has been almost exclusively in the hands of European Americans, nearly all of them male.

Gradually, during the last third of the twentieth century, individuals of diverse racial and cultural backgrounds began to win places in, and control a greater part of, the powerful entertainment industry. Change, which has come slowly and incompletely, can best be understood by examining the histories of specific types of entertainment.

Live Performance. Before the relatively recent technical innovations of motion pictures, audio recording, radio, and television, all entertainment consisted of "live" performances such as plays, musical perfor-

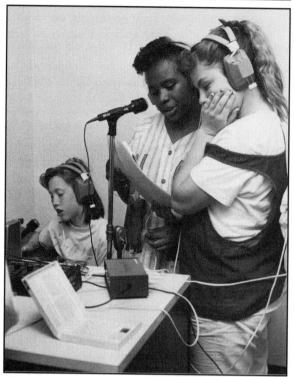

Children of all races dream of one day breaking into the entertainment industry. (James L. Shaffer)

mances, dramatic readings, and dance. One very popular mode of light entertainment was the vaudeville show, which came into its own in the late nineteenth century. Vaudeville consisted of variety shows that presented a number of unrelated acts—singers, dancers, jugglers, comedians—in an evening.

The business leaders of vaudeville followed the dominant trends and mores of the late nineteenth century, aiming their shows at a white audience. Vaudeville, for example, presented blackface "minstrel" acts. Minstrel shows, using simplified and caricatured versions of African American music and dance, had become popular in the nineteenth century. Although there were black minstrel performers, most were whites in blackface, and they promulgated stereotypical and racist images of black people. By the time of vaudeville, some of the most scurrilous and offensive racist aspects of minstrelsy had been toned down. The most successful blackface performer in vaudeville was Al Jolson, a Jewish American remembered for singing to his "mammy" with his face darkened by being rubbed with blackened cork.

Only rarely did vaudeville acts present performers of color or from minority cultures. Asian Americans, Latinos, and American Indians appeared only as they fit the existing stereotypes of the day, such as the "warrior Indians" in the famous traveling "Wild West" shows of Buffalo Bill. The popularity of elements of these shows continued as vaudeville attractions in the late nineteenth century, setting the stage for the Western film, which became possibly the most popular entertainment genre of the first half of the 1900's all around the world.

Live entertainment became more sophisticated as the twentieth century progressed, but it long continued to show a decided ignorance in its portrayal of any culture other than that considered to be mainstream America. The play *Show Boat*, which opened on Broadway in 1927, is often considered the prototype of the musical comedy, or "Broadway show." It was considered daring in its day for its portrayal of miscegenation, or racially mixed marriage. *Show Boat* presented an odd blend of racial images, containing a sympathetic portrayal of interracial love yet also presenting a blackface minstrel act and portrayals of stereotypical black characters. Although strides were made in American drama, such as *A Raisin in the Sun* (1959), with its fine portrayal of an African American family, musicals generally continued to portray nonwhite characters in stereotypical roles until the 1960's. One milestone was the all-black version of the hit show *Hello, Dolly!* (1967), with a cast headed by Pearl Bailey. Controversy continued to be generated by racial and ethnic issues in theater, however, as in all areas of the performing arts. In 1991, for example, the play *Miss Saigon* created heated debate because the role of a Eurasian was played by a white performer.

Motion Pictures. The motion picture industry, perhaps more than any other enterprise in the United States, was driven in its early years by European immigrants. Because the cinema became so popular so quickly, beginning at the end of the nineteenth century, motion picture production had no entrenched power structure; many ambitious people with a dream and a drive to succeed moved to Hollywood and managed to maneuver their way into powerful positions. A large number were Germans and Austrians, including directors Fritz Lang, Eric von Stroheim, and Josef von Sternberg. Adolph Zukor was a Hungarian immigrant. Many of the European immigrants and children of immigrants who created the motion picture industry were Jewish.

Among the legendary "movie moguls" who were Jews were Harry Cohn, Louis B. Mayer, the Warner brothers, David O. Selznick, and Samuel Goldwyn.

As films became more sophisticated in the 1930's and 1940's, the style of German expressionism, brought to Hollywood by German directors and writers, was pervasive in its influence on the Hollywood style of motion pictures.

First-generation Europeans, as well as American-born producers and directors, unabashedly created work that reflected their own views of other races and cultures—views that in retrospect appear stereotypical at best and blatantly racist at worst. Trends were set that would later be reflected in other popular media, particularly radio and television. African Americans, Asian Americans, Latinos, and American Indians were long kept on the sidelines, and their images were stereotypical. American Indians, for example, were portrayed as fiery warriors who spoke monosyllabic broken English. They were ever seeking to impede progress and prevent the Manifest Destiny of European settlers taking the West for themselves.

African Americans were particularly debased in portrayals in early motion pictures. Since the innovation of the medium in the 1890's, African Americans appeared in films, but in film's early years they were usually depicted as servants or slaves. They often pro-

Popular early Chinese American screen star Anna May Wong. (AP/Wide World Photos)

594 — Entertainment industry

vided a form of comic relief taken directly from racist minstrel shows or vaudeville acts. Moreover, in the silent film era prior to 1927, white actors in blackface often portrayed African American characters, as in the influential motion picture *Birth of a Nation* (1915). Black actors were seldom seen in major roles in silent films; James E. Lowe, featured as Uncle Tom in Universal's 1927 production of *Uncle Tom's Cabin*, was a notable exception.

The coming of "talkies" brought little improvement. In the 1930's there were a few African American stars, such as dancer Bill "Bojangles" Robinson, Hattie McDaniel, Stepin Fetchit, and Willie Best. McDaniel, in fact, won an Academy Award for her supporting role in *Gone with the Wind* (1939), but far more popular with white producers and audiences were Fetchit and Best playing variations on the demeaning role of the "shufflin' lackey coon," essentially recycled from nineteenth century minstrelsy.

Change commenced during World War II as the federal government pressured the film industry to include more realistic African American characters. Finally, in motion pictures of the 1950's such as *Carmen Jones* (1954), *Island in the Sun* (1957), and *Take a Giant Step* (1959), Americans saw black men and women as leading actors. Sidney POITIER became a star, winning an Academy Award for the film version of *A Raisin in the Sun* (1961). By the 1970's there was even a genre (sometimes called "BLAXPLOITATION" FILMS) featuring black action heroes such as Jim Brown and Richard Roundtree. There were also positive images of blacks in *Sounder* (1972), *Claudine* (1974), and *The Wiz* (1978).

Eventually, a few black filmmakers managed to enter the directorial ranks of Hollywood. In the 1980's, independent African American filmmakers began making powerful and widely distributed films. The most famous filmmaker to emerge was Spike Lee, with *Do the Right Thing* (1989) and *Malcolm X* (1992). Lee's epic film of the life of Malcolm X was distributed by Time Warner, the largest media conglomerate in the world.

This same historical cycle—negative stereotyping followed by slow transformation—has been played out in the images of other ethnic groups in film. The "Mexican greaser" was a minor character found in films of the 1920's and 1930's, principally Westerns. This only changed during World War II as the U.S. government, seeking better relations with neighbor nations to the south, pressured Hollywood to offer more

positive images. Momentarily, such films as *Juarez* (1939) offered a more realistic picture of Mexicans. After the war, however, this pressure abated, and it was only many years later that Latino subject matter and stars, in films such as *La Bamba* (1987) and *Stand and Deliver* (1987), entered mainstream Hollywood. Edward James OLMOS emerged as one of the most influential Latino actors and directors (*American Me*, 1992).

Through much of the twentieth century, Asians and Asian Americans were frequently portrayed in films by white actors in heavy makeup. They tended to depict Asians (most often Chinese) either as buffoons or as mysterious, exotic people. The famous film detective Charlie Chan was played by various white actors in some fifty motion pictures. From the silent 1917 film *War of the Tongs* to the 1985 *The Year of the Dragon*, the Chinatown milieu has served as a backdrop for violence and crime, often involving secret societies and opium rings. Nevertheless, Asian Americans have been active in the film industry since the earliest days, both in front of the camera (Sessue HAYAKAWA and Anna May WONG) and behind it (Leong But-jung and Moon Kwan). The best-known Asian American behind the scenes is Academy Award-winning Chinese American cinematographer James Wong HOWE.

Women filmmakers have always operated under severe constraints. While women stars have always been among the most popular of performers, very few have wielded power behind the camera or in Hollywood's boardrooms. Yet from the beginning there have been pioneers. Alice Guy began making films in 1907. A decade later, Mary Pickford assumed the rare mantle of studio chief as head of United Artists. Through the 1920's, it was more likely for women to be screenwriters (for example, Frances Marion, Anita Loos, and Bess Meredyth) or editors (Margaret Booth and Dorothy Arzner) than studio executives.

It was not until the 1980's that one could locate more than a single working female director of commercial Hollywood films. (Indeed, in 1980 the Directors Guild reported that during the previous thirty years only seven women had directed feature films in Hollywood.) Since 1980, Elaine May, Claudia Weill, Martha Coolidge, Joan Maklin Silver, Amy Heckerling, and Susan Seidelman have made some of Hollywood's best films.

Recorded Sound. This sector of the entertainment industry also became popular at the beginning of the twentieth century. White investors owned the major labels, from Columbia to Radio Corporation of America (RCA), and they dictated conservative, restrictive policies. It was therefore at the level of recorded performance that minorities could best make their way.

Recordings of JAZZ and BLUES MUSIC by African Americans in the early twentieth century became widely popular. Recording artists such as Louis ARMSTRONG and Bessie Smith found themselves in the odd position of being world-famous yet living as second-

white musicians, composers, and bandleaders of the big band era of the 1930's and 1940's. By this time, Latino music also began to have an influence on popular American music. At various times in the 1940's and 1950's, music of the Caribbean and South America (with varying degrees of Spanish and African influences) achieved popularity, although often in watered-down versions. Among the styles were calypso and Afro-Cuban music as well as music for dances such as the samba, mambo, and cha-cha.

Mexican American NBC-television executive David Ochoa. (Hazel Hankin)

class citizens in the segregated society of their homeland. (Playwright August Wilson effectively dramatized the situation of black musicians of the 1920's in his 1984 drama *Ma Rainey's Black Bottom*.) Jazz and blues had tremendous influence; the styles were incorporated into symphonic pieces by European and American composers. They were also adopted by the

In the 1940's and early 1950's, recordings of African American music based on the blues were known as "race records," and then as RHYTHM AND BLUES. In the mid-1950's, the genre that became known as ROCK AND ROLL—largely an outgrowth of rhythm and blues—became tremendously popular with both black and white American audiences. Rock and roll actually contained a merging of black and white influences, as another formative influence was white country ("hillbilly") music. It was not the black pioneers of the form such as Chuck BERRY or Little Richard who ultimately became the most successful. It was white performer Elvis Presley (formerly known as a hillbilly singer) who gained the greatest fame and fortune in rock and roll. Indeed rock and roll, though African American inspired, has always been primarily marketed by white companies to white consumers, with a few notable exceptions. Berry GORDY, Jr.'s MOTOWN INDUSTRIES, founded in the late 1950's, was a rare example of an African American-owned record company. The "Motown sound," which smoothly blended rhythm and blues, rock, and SOUL, crossed over to be popular with a huge multiracial audience. Groups such as the Supremes and Temptations made Motown famous and Gordy rich. With GOSPEL, rhythm and blues, soul, and RAP MUSIC, much of the popular music of the latter twentieth century is of African American origin.

During the 1980's and 1990's, a more diverse music industry came of age, on tape and compact disc as well as in live tours. Multinational influences began to enter the American mainstream as reggae music, African pop music, and greater numbers of Latino artists found places in recordings and (more tentatively) on the air. The "Latin pop" sound became popular. Latino artists who released popular recordings exploring traditional music of their cultures included Linda RONSTADT, Gloria ESTEFAN, and the rock band LOS LOBOS. Even country music, long a bastion of white entertainers (and sometimes exhibiting ugly strains of bigotry) had a major African American star, Charlie Pride, and a major Latino star, Johnny Rodriguez. Asian and Asian American musical artists were generally still unsuccessful in penetrating the mainstream United States commercial market, but Japanese pop culture made one notable inroad into the United States: the introduction of karaoke (in which audience members get to become performers by singing along with prerecorded background music) in thousands of bars and restaurant lounges in the late 1980's.

Radio. The National Broadcasting Company (NBC) and Columbia Broadcasting System (CBS) radio networks were created in the 1920's, ushering in the network era dominated by a handful of stations in each city. A young Russian immigrant named David Sarnoff was one of radio's pioneers, and he became immensely powerful as the president of RCA. Women and minorities made few inroads into the medium, except as performers, through the 1940's.

When television became popular in the 1950's, the era of network domination of radio ended. Radio stations turned to various formulas in order to compete with television and with one another, and new opportunities opened for minorities. Some stations in metropolitan areas concentrated exclusively on programming for African American or Latino audiences; others devoted part of their broadcasting hours to minority programming. One example was a weekday radio program hosted by Louis H. CHU in New York between 1951 and 1961 called "Chinese Festival." Chu's program enabled Cantonese-speaking CHINESE AMERICANS to remain in touch with their heritage by broadcasting news, interviews, and the music of traditional Chinese opera. Chinese who lived far from Chinatown could, Chu once said, be brought "back to China" by the show.

By far the most numerous foreign-language broadcasters in the United States are the Spanish-language stations; there are hundreds of Spanish stations serving various Latino communities. Many are low-power stations that serve only a small local area. An occasional criticism of Spanish-language stations has been that they provide few opportunities for local Latino artists, instead predominantly playing music of Mexican or South American musicians (this has gradually become less true). On the other hand, Spanish-language radio and television stations, in spite of the language difference, serve as instruments that help Spanish speakers adapt to American culture and society.

In the radio marketplace of the 1990's, a major metropolitan area may have more than a hundred stations playing many different types of music, aimed at all cultural groups in society. In a 1993 ratings survey in Los Angeles, Spanish-language KLAX was the city's top-rated station. Special programs or entire stations cater to various Latino and Asian national groups, African Americans, American Indians—indeed, a full range of ethnic groups from Poles to Iranians. In 1992 a twenty-four-hour gay and lesbian station began operation in Colorado. Radio programming is simply so much cheaper to produce than television (or motion pictures) that many groups can participate in the medium. Independent community and public stations offer a diversity of cultural viewpoints.

Television. Early television programming was rife with the stereotypes of early motion pictures. The title characters of *Amos 'n' Andy*, which made the transi-

Pop music star Linda Ronstadt honors her Mexican heritage on stage. (AP/Wide World Photos)

tion from radio to television in 1951, were stereotypical black characters (although the program did provide rare opportunities for African American actors). The series *Bonanza* (1959-1973) and *Bachelor Father* (1957-1962) both featured stereotypical Chinese characters in small roles; the former featured Hop

Video producers and founders of Downtown Community TV in Chinatown, N.Y., Keiko Tsuno and her husband, Jon Alpert. (Hazel Hankin)

Sing (the ranch cook), and the latter had Peter Tong, the "helpful but inscrutable" houseboy. In television, as in motion pictures and early radio, there were few minorities or women behind the scenes in either executive or technical positions. During the formative years between 1950 and 1980, for example, only twenty-three women were employed as directors of prime-time television.

It was not until the mid-1960's, with Bill COSBY in *I Spy* (1965-1968) and Diahann Carroll in *Julia* (1968-1971), that lead characters in major prime time series were portrayed by African Americans. The long-running series *All in the Family* (1971-1983) broke new ground by portraying the bigoted, ignorant Archie Bunker as a figure to be laughed at; it also featured

a black family that went on to a successful spin-off series called *The Jeffersons* (1975-1985). The 1970's saw many steps toward presenting new images on television. The comedy series *Chico and the Man* (1974-1978) starred Latino comedian Freddie Prinze; *Barney Miller* (1975-1982) depicted a multiethnic group of New York police officers. Women's roles were slowly changing as well; *The Mary Tyler Moore Show* (1970-1977) featured a single woman with a career in television news. (Moore also has been one of the few women performers who has managed to achieve a position of power behind the scenes in television; other notable examples are Oprah WINFREY and Roseanne Arnold.)

In 1977, the miniseries *Roots*, based on Alex HALEY's 1976 novel tracing the African ancestry of an American black family, set ratings records and marked the beginning of a new era. The 1980's saw a huge increase in shows—mostly situation comedies—featuring African Americans. Network programmers realized that African Americans represented a large and loyal audience and that if shows could appeal to them without losing white viewers, the ratings could be very strong. The longest-running of these series was *The Cosby Show* (1984-1992).

The same slow transformation was also happening in network news reporting. In 1955, for example, there was not a single African American in television or radio network newsrooms above the position of janitor. Pressure from the CIVIL RIGHTS MOVEMENT was among the factors leading to gradual changes. By the 1980's CBS had Ed Bradley, the Cable News Network (CNN) had Bernard Shaw, and the American Broadcasting Company (ABC) had Carol Simpson reporting the news to millions on a daily basis. In 1993 Chinese American Connie CHUNG was named coanchor of the CBS Evening News. Many more representatives of minorities were on the air as reporters on local stations throughout the country.

The television industry fundamentally changed during the late 1970's with the spread of cable television and inexpensive video technology. Channels multiplied and programming diversified. By the end of the 1980's, a multicultural array of cable networks and channels was in place. These included BLACK ENTERTAINMENT TELEVISION, an African American-owned network of sports, films, and original shows made by and offered to persons of color; the Spanish-language network Univision, offering Latinos around-the-clock programming from game shows to films to soap operas; and the Lifetime cable channel, with talk shows, films, and selected reruns aimed at women's interests. In addition, cable provided a way for local community access channels to go on the air at low cost, thereby providing another avenue for programming directed at specific national or ethnic groups.

While by the early 1990's cable television showed greater responsiveness than the networks to multicultural audiences, progress was still needed in the area of industry ownership by nonwhites. The reality of a negligible minority presence in executive positions was echoed in other areas of the entertainment industry. As gains have been made in reducing stereotypes—and slowly increasing the presence—of ethnic minorities in front of the cameras and microphones, much less progress has been made in the more difficult area of increasing the presence of persons of color in positions of power. This poses the greatest challenge for the future.

SUGGESTED READINGS. For excellent accounts of changes in images of African Americans in cinema prior to the 1980's, see Thomas Cripps's *Slow Fade to Black* (1972) and *Black Film as Genre* (1978). The more recent *Split Image: African Americans in the Mass Media* (1990), edited by Jannette L. Dates and William Barlow, covers not only film but also music, radio, and television. Women's issues are discussed in *Women and the Cinema* (1977), edited by Karyn Kay and Gerald Peary. On American Indian contributions to Hollywood, see *The Pretend Indians* (1980), edited by Gretchen M. Bataille and Charles L. P. Silet. General histories include Philip K. Eberly's *Music in the Air* (1982), Edward Jay Whetmore's *The Magic Medium: An Introduction to Radio in America* (1981), J. Fred McDonald's *One Nation Under Television* (1990), and Robert C. Toll's *The Entertainment Machine* (1982).—*Douglas Gomery*

Episcopalians: Tracing its roots to the Church of England, the Episcopal church was founded in the United States by necessity following the American Revolution, when ties to England were effectively severed. The two churches share essential points of doctrine, discipline, and worship, including use of the Book of Common Prayer as a source for services and acceptance of the apostolic succession of bishops. Although Episcopal church authorities have modified these and other aspects of organization and worship to suit the American experience, they have not departed substantially from their English originators. There are an estimated 2.4 million members of the Episcopal church in the United States and about 7,300 churches.

Anglican (Church of England) clergy visited the North American continent with English explorers, but the first Anglican services did not take place until 1607, in Jamestown, Virginia. Congregations grew from the middle colonies northward; Anglicanism flourished in New York but faced hostility from New England PURITANS. Adherents to the Anglican faith were persecuted in the North during the AMERICAN REVOLUTION as Loyalists to the crown, and the church suffered severe financial setbacks, even in the supportive southern colonies, when public funds were withdrawn. Also lost was the substantial financial support of the Society for the Propagation of the Gospel, an English missionary group.

Within a few years, despite these circumstances, remaining leaders of the clergy and laity drew together and formed the Episcopal church. Although the first four American bishops were sent to England to be legally consecrated, thereafter the American bishops consecrated their own. In 1789, church organization was set with the adoption of a constitution and a set of canons for church governance.

The Episcopal church grew in the early nineteenth century, sending missionaries to the western frontier as well as overseas to Liberia, China, and later, Japan. The Civil War did not affect the church much, as northern and southern Episcopalians did not split up over slavery issues. Although southern Episcopalians temporarily formed a new church when the Confederacy formed, they were reunited at the end of the Civil War.

Since the 1880's Episcopalian bishops have appealed for Christian unity. In the 1960's, the Episcopal church joined with the PRESBYTERIAN church, the METHODIST church, and the United Church of Christ in an attempt to find common ground for eventual union.

In the late 1960's, Episcopalians pledged $3 million to aid African Americans and other minority groups to achieve self-determination. In the mid-1970's, the first women were ordained as Episcopalian priests without the sanction of church leaders. This was rectified in 1976 with the first officially sanctioned ordination of a woman priest and the acceptance of the women ordained previously.

Equal Employment Opportunity Commission (EEOC): Government agency. The EEOC is charged with ensuring that the fundamental rights of all people, especially women and minorities, are upheld within the workplace. The EEOC was established as part of the CIVIL RIGHTS ACT OF 1964. It monitors and enforces various federal discrimination laws, such as the AMERICANS WITH DISABILITIES ACT OF 1990 and the Civil Rights Act of 1964. Originally, the agency could mediate but could not bring suit in court; in 1972, the Equal Employment Opportunity Act allowed it to file suits. In the 1980's, the EEOC began to emphasize individual cases over class-action suits; critics said that this was a less effective approach.

Equal Pay Act of 1963: First federal act that prohibited sex discrimination in wages for equivalent work. President John F. Kennedy's Commission on the Status of Women recommended that sexual inequality in the labor force could be limited if laws protected equal pay for equal work. Several barriers remained. Sex-segregated labor markets hired men and women for different categories of jobs, making it difficult to establish the equal characteristics of their work. When men and women worked in the same type of job, measuring their skills proved difficult. A shift to comparable worth or sex equity evaluations later improved the situation by finding ways to measure the value of the work performed.

Equal Rights Amendment (ERA): Proposed amendment to the U.S. CONSTITUTION, intended to outlaw discrimination based on gender. As proposed, the amendment states that "equality of rights under the law shall not be denied or abridged by the United States nor by any state on account of sex."

The ERA was originally introduced in the U.S. Congress in 1923. After its defeat at that time, the amendment faded from prominence as a national and constitutional issue. It was resurrected, however, in 1970 by a number of women's organizations, the most prominent of which was the NATIONAL ORGANIZATION FOR WOMEN (NOW). Further, the endorsement in 1970 of the ERA by a group appointed by President Nixon, the Citizen's Advisory Council on the Status of Women, focused renewed attention upon the amendment.

Historical Background. In 1923, the NATIONAL WOMAN'S PARTY (NWP) first proposed an Equal Rights Amendment to the U.S. Constitution. The NWP had been one of the leading groups in the fight for SUFFRAGE, which women had finally won in 1920 with passage of the Nineteenth Amendment. The NINE-

TEENTH AMENDMENT, having granted women the right to vote, was often invoked as having rendered sex discrimination virtually nonexistent. For example, the U.S. Supreme Court opinion that struck down a woman's minimum wage law referred to the Nineteenth Amendment as having corrected women's civic inferiority. Whereas another prominent women's rights organization, the National American Women's Suffrage Association, considered the attainment of the vote to have been the culmination of the struggle for equality, the NWP convened in 1921 to decide

Two attentive listeners at a pro-ERA rally in 1977. (AP/Wide World Photos)

whether to disband or to continue the fight on other frontiers.

The NWP decided to seek complete equality between men and women through an amendment to the Constitution, as well as through legislative efforts on state and local levels. Having described voting rights as only the first step toward equality, and having agitated for further legal equalities immediately after the suffrage victory, the NWP gained a reputation as a radical organization. Consisting entirely of white middle-class and upper-class women, the group expressed no special concern for women who belonged to ethnic minorities, or to women of the working classes.

Crucial to the defeat of the ERA during the 1920's was the opposition of most of organized labor. In some states, there existed at the time legal limitations upon the length of the working day for women, as well as limitations of the weights women could lift on the job. The threat of losing this protection was widely publicized by labor. This obstacle to the passage of the ERA persisted throughout subsequent decades and reemerged, as a major roadblock in the 1970's.

The Senate approved an Equal Rights Amendment resolution by a wide margin in 1950 and again in 1953. Both times, however, it was amended by a

ers of the women's movement of the 1960's did the amendment became potentially viable.

The Push for the ERA in the 1970's. In order to become law, the ERA needed to be passed by Congress and then ratified separately by the legislatures of thirty-eight states (roughly three-quarters of the states). Congresswoman Martha Griffiths of Michigan played an important role in sending the amendment to the floor of the U.S. House of Representatives in 1971. Widely considered a nonpartisan amendment with limited potential effects, the ERA passed in the House by an overwhelming majority. Some public

Unlike most labor unions from the 1920's to the 1980's, steelworkers Local 8880 supported the ERA. This 1980 Richmond, Va., rally drew more than 7,000 participants. (AP/Wide World Photos)

qualification providing that the ERA would not impede any benefits conferred by the law upon females. In the view of many legal analysts, this qualification emptied the amendment of meaning, since its purpose was to eradicate legal distinctions between the sexes. The amendment, supported by most presidents since World War II, was often given token support by legislators. Yet it languished for years in the crevices and back pages of a labyrinthine legislative system. Not until the ERA gained passionate advocates from lead-

opinion polls at the time suggested that a majority of Americans supported the amendment.

The amendment faced somewhat stronger opposition in the U.S. Senate, traditionally the more conservative body of Congress. Women's groups organized broad-based letter-writing campaigns, successfully pressuring senators to avoid the embarrassment of appearing to vote against equality. The Senate passed the ERA in 1972.

After their successes with the formidable U.S. Congress, many women's groups relaxed their lobbying efforts, assuming that the state ratifications would follow inevitably. A coalition consisting of representatives of more than twenty women's groups, the ERA Ratification Council, was indifferently managed during 1972 and 1973, and it eventually voted to disband. Only thirty states voted to ratify the amendment in 1973. ERA supporters had been taken by surprise by a quickly yet carefully organized opposition, which targeted the legislatures of southern and Rocky Moun-

were willing to pay lip service to the ERA but would not actually support it.

In 1978, Congress passed special legislation extending the deadline three more years. As some states voted to ratify the amendment, others would reverse earlier decisions to ratify; thus support remained at roughly the same inadequate level, year after year. From 1978 to 1982, supporters of the amendment attempted economic boycotts against states failing to ratify. On June 30, 1982, time ran out; the national

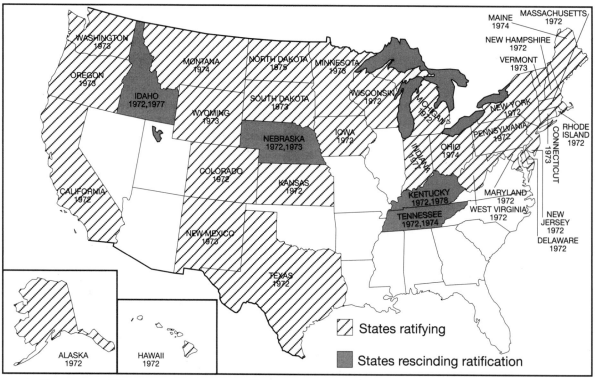

STATES RATIFYING AND RESCINDING THE ERA: 1972-1982

Source: Data are from Janet K. Boles, *The Politics of the Equal Rights Amendment*. Pp. 2-3. New York: Longman, 1979.

tain states for lobbying. In 1974, a mere three states ratified the amendment, followed by one in 1975 and one in 1977. Congress had set a seven-year period (1972-1979) within which ratification by all thirty-eight states was required.

In 1975, the ERA suffered another symbolic blow when voters in two states that had already ratified the national amendment—New Jersey and New York—rejected state versions of the ERA. The defeats came despite public opinion polls that indicated the proposed state laws were supported by a majority. Opponents of the national amendment argued that people

amendment was defeated after only thirty-five states had ratified it.

Significance of the ERA. There was, and is, widespread disagreement over the legal significance and potential effects of the ERA upon society and upon a broad range of employment and rights issues. The amendment was intended, in part, to supplement the FOURTEENTH AMENDMENT, which had been made law during the nineteenth century in order to protect the rights of former slaves. The Fourteenth Amendment, which prohibits any state from denying "to any person within its jurisdiction the equal protection of the laws," had come to be cited in sex discrimination cases. Supporters of the ERA argued that pursuing the protection of women's rights under the Fourteenth Amendment had proven laborious and inefficient, requiring constant efforts on a case-by-case basis. They also suggested that the Fourteenth Amendment is in-

the explicit designation of gender bias as illegal would prove enormously beneficial to women bringing discrimination cases.

Another view has held that the ERA would have proved to be a largely symbolic amendment. Because it would forbid the denial of equal rights only "by the

Gloria Steinem was a visible and vocal proponent of the ERA, seen here at a 1981 rally outside the White House. (AP/Wide World Photos)

adequate in relation to sexual inequalities and that the ERA would explicitly clarify women's rights in regard to issues such as employment, taxation, divorce, Social Security, credit, and insurance.

Some proponents of the ERA believed that the amendment would shift the burden of proof in individual discrimination cases from the party alleging discrimination to the accused. Gender, unmentioned in the Fourteenth Amendment, would be newly specified as a "suspect" classification, on the model of racial and religious classifications, as unlawful grounds for discrimination. According to some legal experts,

United States or by any state," the amendment would be applied only to the conduct of government entities and officers, according to this interpretation.

Opposition to the ERA. Proponents as well as opponents often exaggerated the potential effects of the ERA on American society. Opponents claimed that the ERA would render women susceptible to unsuspected penalties and strip them of numerous rights. The most vocal opposition to the ERA was expressed by an organization called STOP ERA, founded in 1972 by a conservative public figure with extensive grassroots political skills, Phyllis SCHLAFLY.

STOP ERA considered the Fourteenth Amendment adequate protection of women's rights, and further claimed that there exists a biologically constituted inequality between the sexes that cannot be legally renegotiated. Schlafly also argued that ERA would prove detrimental to the family, marriage, and the benefits accruing to women from a tradition of dependence upon men.

The members of STOP ERA were women; Schlafly recognized that a potent opposing argument must be articulated by women in order to be taken seriously. The opponents of the ERA succeeded in making the amendment controversial, especially on the state level. A formerly nonpartisan issue became increasingly associated with the Democratic Party. This trend allowed the amendment to become another in a series of issues bitterly contested by Democrats and Republicans, and opened the way for Republicans to oppose the amendment.

A significant bloc of states that opposed ERA was in the South. STOP ERA was active in that region, often portraying ERA as an attack upon holy Scriptures, marriage, family, and the privileges of traditional womanhood. Schlafly argued that women already enjoyed superior rights in many respects. Arguments against the ERA often depended upon a presumption of natural differences between men and women, which dictate distinct roles at home and at work.

The disagreement among legal scholars who advocated the ERA as to its effects left a space open for the opposition to characterize the effects in alarming terms. For example, STOP ERA argued that the ERA would by definition legalize homosexual marriages; that it would eliminate traditional biases in favor of women in divorce and child custody settlements by abolishing alimony and child support; and that it would require women to be drafted into the armed services and to serve in combat. STOP ERA also claimed that the amendment would enable men to force their wives to gain employment. Some extreme opponents also charged that the ERA would lead to the demise of laws against rape and of separate restrooms for men and women.

Opponents of the ERA succeeded in exploiting anxieties among men and women concerning the increased participation of women in the nation's businesses and industries. Because constitutional amendments tend to be worded in very broad phrases, the ERA was susceptible to very different charac-terizations. It became a confused issue for many Americans.

Multicultural Perspective. The women's movement of the 1960's and 1970's was led and dominated by white women of the middle and upper classes, such as members of NOW. Despite contributions to the movement by working women of all ethnic and educational backgrounds, feminist groups concerned with the ERA tended to focus on hiring practices in the privileged professions as opposed to blue collar work opportunities. Obsessed with the struggle for sexual equality, ERA supporters were sometimes susceptible to accusations of having developed a blind spot for race and class.

Yet the struggle for the ERA often found itself working on the model of the Civil Rights movement. The fight for racial equality and the pursuit of women's rights have more in common than has always been acknowledged. In particular, they share a wide range of common enemy tactics: presumptions of biological or natural inequalities between people; the assertion of state's rights over federal law as a means of obstructing justice; and insincere, obfuscating manipulations of the legal process.

Suggested Readings. For insightful explanations of the failure of the ERA, see Jane J. Mansbridge's *Why We Lost the ERA* (1986) and Mary Frances Berry's *Why ERA Failed* (1986). For a thorough account of the fate of the ERA in the state of North Carolina, see Donald Mathews and Jane De Hart's *Sex, Gender, and the Politics of ERA: A State and the Nation* (1990). Janet K. Boles's *The Politics of the ERA: Conflict in the Decision Process* (1979) provides a lucid account of both legislative and political issues relating to the amendment. Malvina Halberstam's *Women's Legal Rights* (1987) explores both the ERA and legal alternatives to it.—*James Knippling*

Erdrich, Louise (b. July 6, 1954, Little Falls, Minn.): American Indian novelist, short-story writer, and poet. Of Chippewa and German American descent, Erdrich was reared in Wahpeton, North Dakota, and had strong ties with her Chippewa relatives on the Turtle Mountain Reservation. A writer since her youth, she majored in creative writing at Dartmouth College and earned her bachelor's degree in 1976. After receiving her master's degree in creative writing from Johns Hopkins University in 1979, Erdrich dedicated herself full-time to writing. Erdrich and her husband, Michael Dorris (of Modoc descent), have collaborated on virtually all of their pub-

Chippewa-German American writer Louise Erdrich in her publicity photograph for the novel Tracks. *(Michael Dorris)*

lished works. Although known for her early short stories dealing with American Indian themes, Erdrich's first book-length publication was *Jacklight* (1984), a collection of poetry. The same year saw the publication of her first novel, *Love Medicine* (1984), based on her Chippewa family stories that had appeared in prestigious magazines such as *The Atlantic Monthly* and *The Kenyon Review*. The novel was a national best-seller and won several prizes, including the National Book Critics Circle Award for Fiction. Erdrich's subsequent novels—*The Beet Queen* (1986) and *Tracks* (1988)—continued the family saga. *Baptism of Desire*, her second volume of poetry, was published in 1989. In 1991, she and Dorris received joint credit as authors of *The Crown of Columbus*.

Escalante, Jaime (b. Dec. 31, 1930, La Paz, Bolivia): Latino educator. Although Escalante had a degree from San Andreas University in La Paz and had been a physics and mathematics teacher in Bolivia, he was not allowed to teach after he moved to the United States in the late 1960's because he did not have an American degree. He worked as a busboy, cook, and electronics technician while studying at Pasadena City College and California State University in Los Angeles, where he earned a B.S. in mathematics. Beginning in 1974, he was hired to teach at Garfield High School in EAST LOS ANGELES, where

he developed his own innovative mathematics program to motivate otherwise apathetic inner-city students. The 1987 film *Stand and Deliver* was based on Escalante's life and teaching, and he hosted *Futures*, a Public Broadcasting Service television series about mathematics in the real world. Escalante received the Jefferson Award from the American Institute for Public Service in 1990. In 1991, he began teaching math at Sacramento's Hiram High School, where he hoped to repeat the success he achieved with students at Garfield.

Eskimos. *See* **Inuits**

ESL programs. *See* **English as a second language (ESL) programs**

Estefan, Gloria (Gloria Maria Fajardo; b. Sept. 1, 1957, Havana, Cuba): Cuban American singer. Estefan's family took refuge in the United States in 1959 in the wake of the revolution, and she grew up in Miami. While still a teenager, Estefan joined the band Miami Latin Voice, which later became the Miami Sound Machine. The band enjoyed great popularity in Miami and Latin America before breaking into the U.S. pop music scene. Named *Billboard* magazine's Best New Pop Artist in

Controversial educator Jaime Escalante had spectacular success teaching in the Los Angeles schools. (AP/Wide World Photos)

Gloria Estefan with her 1989 American Music Award. (AP/ Wide World Photos)

1986, Estefan embarked on a solo career the following year. Her albums include *Primitive Love* (1986), *Let It Loose* (1987), and *Cuts Both Ways* (1989). Injuries from a bus accident in March of 1990 while on tour in Pennsylvania nearly ended Estefan's career. She rebounded, however, with *Into the Light* in January of 1991. In 1992 she received a Musica Latina Award for lifetime achievement. In 1992, Estefan released a Spanish-language album of Cuban music from the 1930's and 1940's entitled *Mi Tierra*.

Estonian Americans: In the last decade of the twentieth century, the Estonians numbered only a few more than one million (both in and outside Estonia). Estonians come from a land area northeast of the Baltic Sea which has been populated by the Estonians and their ancestors for at least five thousand years. Modern Estonia encompasses an area about the size of Vermont and New Hampshire combined, which borders the Gulf of Finland to the north, the Baltic Sea to the west, Russia to the east, and Latvia to the south.

The Estonian language belongs to the Finno-Ugric language group, which means that linguistically Esto-

nians are closely connected to Finns and more distantly to Hungarians. It also means that Estonians have no linguistic or ethnic kinship with the peoples who have ruled Estonia (Russians, Germans, Danes, and Swedes). Religiously, most Estonians are Lutheran. Culturally, Estonians are more similar to the Protestant Finns and Scandinavians than to Orthodox and Roman Catholic Slavs.

History. In the thirteenth century, the Estonians and Latvians, who lacked a centralized system of government, were conquered by Germans. A German ruling class established itself at the head of a feudal order of non-German serfs in the conquered land they called Livonia. These medieval social and ethnic distinctions persisted in Estonia until the latter part of the nineteenth century. With the collapse of medieval Livonia in the sixteenth century, Sweden gained control of Estonia. During the Great Northern War (1700-1721), Russian forces conquered the area and ruled until Estonia declared its independence in 1918.

During Swedish and most of the period of Russian rule, the Baltic German nobility continued its domination over the Estonian peasants; the oppression reached its height in the eighteenth century. It was not until the mid-nineteenth century that the institution of serfdom was effectively dismantled.

In the latter part of the nineteenth century, Estonians experienced a national awakening. The spread of education, the printing of books and newspapers in the Estonian language, urbanization, and the appearance of the first Estonian intellectuals all contributed to the development of an Estonian cultural identity and desire for self-determination. The Russian Revolution in 1905 fueled Estonian hopes for self-determination. The upheavals of World War I enabled Estonia to declare its independence from Russia in 1918; independence was achieved in 1920.

This first period of independence (1920-1939), though brief, is seen by most Estonian Americans as a period of great strides in Estonia's economy and culture. In 1939, the three Baltic states became pawns in the diplomatic negotiations of larger European powers. A secret agreement between Nazi Germany and the Soviet Union signed over Finland, Estonia, Latvia, and later Lithuania to the Soviet sphere of influence. In 1944, Estonia became a Soviet republic.

The chance for Estonia to reassert its right to self-determination began in March, 1985, when Mikhail Gorbachev began to institute his policies of *perestroika* (restructuring) and *glasnost* (openness) in the

Soviet Union. In 1988, Estonia went from a one-party system to a pluralistic system. On August 20, 1991, Estonia declared its independence from the Soviet Union.

Immigration. There are records of a few Estonians living in colonial America. The first major waves of Estonian immigration, however, came toward the end of the nineteenth and the beginning of the twentieth centuries. At this time, Estonia was part of the Russian empire. The pressures of Russification, adverse economic conditions, and political repression following the Revolution of 1905 all contributed to a substantial number of immigrants arriving in North America from Estonia and other parts of the Russian empire.

Until 1922, Estonian immigrants were classified as Russians, making the number of Estonians difficult to ascertain. Some scholars estimate that the number of Estonians living in the United States in 1920 was about 180,000.

During the period of Estonian independence (1920-1939), the level of emigration was very low. The next major wave of emigration took place during World War II. In response to the Soviet annexation of Estonia in 1940, German occupation from 1941 to 1944, and Soviet reentry in 1944, approximately 10 percent of Estonians (about 100,000) fled the country. After some years in refugee camps in Western Europe, the émigrés were settled in various countries, including the United States. The beginning of *glasnost* in the Soviet Union in 1985 resulted in an increased number of émigrés being able to obtain permission to leave Estonia.

Organizations and Publications. The earliest Estonian American organizations were Lutheran congregations in rural South Dakota and Wisconsin and in the cities of New York, Philadelphia, and Boston. They were founded by a Lutheran minister, Hans Rebane, who also published the first Estonian American newspaper, *Ameerika-Eesti Postimees* (the "Estonian American Courier"), from 1897 until his death in 1911. Because of the pietistic orientation of these Lutheran congregations, they did not play a significant role in the larger Estonian American community.

In the early 1900's, lay Estonian societies and beneficial organizations were established in various cities such as San Francisco, New York, Portland, and Philadelphia. Most of these organizations were designed to help new immigrants and to provide an opportunity for social and cultural activities with fellow Estonian Americans.

Between the Soviet annexation of Estonia in 1940 and 1965, about fourteen thousand new Estonian immigrants arrived in the United States. Because of their experiences with Soviet executions, deportations, and forced mobilization, most post-World War II Estonian immigrants were vehemently anti-Communist, determined to fight Soviet domination of their homeland, and marked by a strong sense of national and cultural identity.

In the 1950's and 1960's, old Estonian American organizations were revitalized and new ones proliferated. Most cities with Estonian communities established a Lutheran congregation, a chorus, FOLK DANCING and gymnastics groups, an Estonian language school to supplement the education of Estonian American children, veterans' organizations, BOY SCOUT and GIRL SCOUT troops, and women's clubs. Regional, national, and international umbrella organizations also developed, connecting Estonian Americans to a worldwide network of Estonians.

Many national organizations established headquarters in New York, including the Estonian-American National Council, the Estonian Schools Fund, the Estonian Music Center, and the Estonian Amateur Athletic Union. In 1949, a weekly newspaper, *Vaba Eesti Sõna* (Free Estonian Word), began publication in New York.

Estonian Americans also maintained close ties with Estonian Canadians. From the 1950's through the early 1990's, joint activities included international Estonian Festivals, scouting jamborees, song festivals with participating choruses from numerous cities, and Metsaülikool (Forest University), a yearly ten-day symposium led by academics and cultural leaders from both Estonian immigrant communities.

Although post-World War II Estonian émigrés maintained their ethnic identity and took steps to preserve their culture and language, they also achieved U.S. citizenship and economic viability quickly. By the 1960's most Estonian Americans had become part of the middle class. Politically, most post-World War II Estonian émigrés supported the foreign policies of the Republican Party because they perceived the Democratic Party as the party of Franklin D. Roosevelt, who signed the Yalta agreement that in effect gave Estonia to the Soviet Union.

Following the reestablishment of Estonian independence in 1991, Estonian Americans lobbied to allow persons who were citizens of Estonia in June, 1940, or their descendants to reclaim Estonian citizenship. According to established U.S. policy, Estonian

Americans who take advantage of this opportunity do not thereby revoke United States citizenship, but rather maintain dual citizenship. In September, 1992, Estonian Americans took part in the elections for the first democratically elected president and state assembly in the newly independent Estonia.

In the late 1980's and early 1990's, Estonian American organizations established cooperative links with corresponding organizations in Estonia. The 1992 Estonian Festival held in New York with about five thousand participants included participants from independent Estonia.

the United States in the second half of the twentieth century included Ants Oras, literary critic and professor of English at the University of Florida in Gainesville from 1949 to 1972; Aleksis Rannit, poet, critic, essayist, and curator of Slavic and East European studies at Yale University from 1961 to 1985; and Ivar Ivask, poet and literary critic, editor of *Books Abroad* and professor of comparative literature at the University of Oklahoma from 1967 to 1991.

Another notable Estonian American cultural figure is conductor Neeme Järvi, who emigrated to the United States in 1980. He has worked with leading

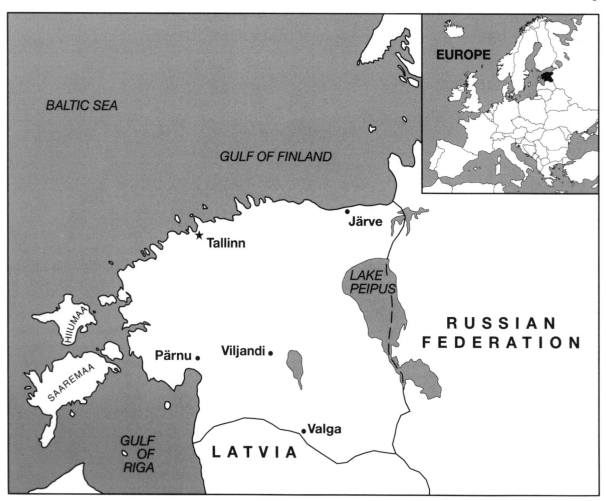

ESTONIA

Cultural Contributions. Estonian Americans have made contributions in their professions in high proportion to their small numbers. Estonian American writers and scholars who established institutional affiliations and had an influence on wide audiences in

orchestras and prominent opera houses in the West and has introduced to wide audiences the music of leading Estonian classical composers such as Eduard Tubin and Arvo Part.

SUGGESTED READINGS. A good history of Estonia in

English is Toivo U. Raun's *Estonia and the Estonians* (2d ed., 1991). For a history of developments in Estonia in the 1980's and early 1990's, see Rein Taagepera's *Estonia: The Road to Independence* (1993). *The Estonians in America, 1627-1975: A Chronology and Fact Book* (1975), compiled and edited by Jaan Pennar in association with Tõnu Parming and P. Peter Rebane, is a useful source on Estonian immigrants. See also Tõnu Parming's "Estonians" in the *Harvard Encyclopedia of American Ethnic Groups* (1980), edited by Stephan Thernstrom.—Tiina Allik